THE ZONDERVAN 2013

PASTOR'S ANNUAL

AN IDEA & RESOURCE BOOK

T. T. CRABTREE

ZONDERVAN

The Zondervan 2013 Pastor's Annual
Copyright © 1992, 2012 by Zondervan

Requests for information should be addressed to:

Zondervan, *Grand Rapids, Michigan* 49530

Much of the contents of this book was previously published in *Pastor's Annual 1993*.

ISBN 978-0-310-49394-5

12 13 14 15 16 17 18 /DCI/ 26 25 24 23 22 21 20 19 18 17 16 15 14 13 12 11 10 9 8 7 6 5 4 3 2 1

CONTENTS

MISCELLANEOUS HELPS

CONTRIBUTING AUTHORS

T. S. Brandon	A.M.:	September 1, 8, 15, 22, 29
H. T. Bryson	A.M.:	May 26
J. E. Carter	P.M.:	August 4, 11, 18, 25
H. C. Chiles	P.M.:	September 1, 8, 15, 22, 29
T. H. Epton	A.M.:	July 7, 14, 21, 28
		August 4, 11, 18, 25
	P.M.:	July 21
D. E. Evans		Messages for Children and Young People
W. T. Flynt	A.M.:	December 1, 8, 22, 29
J. G. Harris	A.M.:	March 24
		April 21
D. G. Hause	A.M.:	March 31
		April 7, 14
	Wed.:	October 2, 9, 16, 23, 30
		November 6, 13, 20
R. F. Kenny	P.M.:	May 5, 12, 19, 26
H. S. Kolb	P.M.:	March 31
		April 7, 14, 21
C. J. Lawrence	Wed.:	May 15, 22, 29
		June 5, 12
G. T. Lawyer		Funeral Meditations and Wedding
J. R. McBride	P.M.:	November 3, 10, 17, 24
		December 1, 8, 15, 22, 29
R. Moody	Wed.:	March 6, 13, 20, 27
W. J. Oldham	Wed.:	November 27
		December 4, 11, 18
R. T. Otey	A.M.:	November 3, 10, 17, 24
E. White	A.M.:	May 5, 19
		June 2, 9, 16
B. W. Woods	P.M.:	January 6, 13, 20, 27
		February 3, 10, 17, 24
		March 3, 10, 17, 24

PREFACE

Favorable comments from ministers who serve in many different types of churches suggest that the *Pastor's Annual* provides valuable assistance to many busy pastors as they seek to improve the quality, freshness, and variety of their pulpit ministry. To be of service to a fellow pastor in his continuing quest to obey our Lord's command to Peter, "Feed my sheep," is a calling to which I respond with gratitude.

I pray that this issue of the *Pastor's Annual* will be blessed by our Lord in helping each pastor to plan and produce a preaching program that will meet better the spiritual needs of the congregation to which he is called to minister.

This issue contains series of sermons by nineteen contributing authors who have been effective contemporary preachers and successful pastors. Each author is listed with his sermons in the section titled "Contributing Authors." I accept responsibility for those sermons not listed there.

This issue of the *Pastor's Annual* is dedicated to the Lord with a prayer that he will bless these efforts to let the Holy Spirit lead us in preparing a planned preaching program for the year.

January

- **Sunday Mornings**

    The gospel is "Good News about God." This is the suggested theme for the morning messages in January. In a time when there is so much bad news, we ought to preach the "Good News about God."

- **Sunday Evenings**

    As we face the new year, let us hear "The Ancient Prophet Speaks to the Present." These messages are based on texts from the prophecy of Isaiah.

- **Wednesday Evenings**

    The theme for the Wednesday evening messages is "How Does a Sinful Man Find Acceptance with the Holy God?" This is the question answered by the apostle Paul in his epistle to the Galatians. All of us need to rejoice in the peace that comes through justification by faith.

Wednesday Evening, January 2

Title: Christ the Great Liberator

Text: "Grace be to you and peace from God the Father, and from our Lord Jesus Christ, who gave himself for our sins, that he might deliver us from this present evil world, according to the will of God and our Father" **(Gal. 1:3–4).**

Scripture Reading: Galatians 3:1–9; 5:1

Introduction

Paul's epistle to the Galatians is a powerful polemic against the Judaizers who were trying to draw the churches of Galatia away from the evangelical gospel. These young churches were plagued with false teachers who were alleging that the death of Jesus Christ and his victorious resurrection from the dead were not an adequate basis on which to trust for a right standing before God. They were contending that faith in Christ must be supplemented by a keeping of the Mosaic law and the traditions of the Fathers.

The very existence of evangelical Christianity was at stake. If the position of these Judaizers were to be established, then Christianity would simply be a sect of Judaism rather than a revelation of the true purpose of God.

A study of the epistle to the Galatians reveals that these false teachers used three main arguments to promote their cause. First, they questioned Paul's apostleship and denied that he had the right to be an authoritative teacher.

Second, they glorified various aspects of Judaism with particular emphasis on keeping the ceremonial law. Third, they implied that Christian liberty led to a life of lawlessness and license that was contrary to God's will.

The epistle can be outlined in view of these three erroneous teachings. Chapters 1 and 2 are biographical in nature. The apostle Paul explains and defends his role as an apostle with full authority to preach and teach the gospel. Chapters 3 and 4 provide an explanation of Paul's basic doctrine of justification by faith. He affirms and illustrates from the Old Testament that people are given a right standing before God on the basis of their faith rather than by a keeping of the law. Chapters 5 and 6 declare that instead of trying to satisfy the claims of the law, the followers of Jesus Christ are to concentrate on living in a manner so as to meet the obligations of love. This is to be done in the power of the Holy Spirit who took up his residency in the heart of each believer in a conversion experience.

I. Paul, an apostle.

The apostle defends his apostleship on the grounds that he did not receive it as a gift from man but as an assignment from Jesus Christ and God the Father. He is bold to claim an equality with the apostles who had walked and talked with Jesus Christ.

II. Grace and peace.

These words are more than a salutation from the apostle to his children in the faith. They express the provisions of God for his children. God wants to deal with us on the basis of his grace rather than on the basis of law. He desires that we live in the harmony that produces inward peace and joy.

III. Christ gave himself for our sins.

Paul strongly proclaims that the death of Jesus Christ on the cross was intended to deal with our sin problem. That is the heart of the glad tidings of God's love and of God's provision of salvation for people. Paul later declares in this epistle that people are given a right standing before God on the basis of their faith in the death of Jesus Christ for their sins and his victorious resurrection from the dead. Our sins have been forgiven because Christ loved us enough to go to the cross on our behalf.

IV. Deliverance from this present evil world.

Christ Jesus died on the cross for more than the forgiveness of our sin. He died and rose again that he might deliver us from the power and practice of sin as well as from the penalty of sin—death. He came to do something more than deliver us from an eternity of exile from God. He came to bring the rule of heaven into our hearts in the present. It is his plan that we live a life triumphant over evil in this present evil world (Titus 2:11–14).

V. The will of God our Father.

The apostle asserts that grace, peace, forgiveness, and deliverance from the power of evil are a part of the will of our heavenly Father for each of us. Truly ours is a wonderful Savior. Our God is a great and a good God. We are indeed fortunate to know him who is the great Liberator from the penalty of sin in the past, from the power of sin in the present, and from the presence of sin in the future.

Conclusion

Our response should be to dedicate ourselves to our Lord and to the will of God so that we may bring glory to him both now and forever.

SUNDAY MORNING, JANUARY 6

Title: The God of Good News

Text: "Now after that John was put in prison, Jesus came into Galilee, preaching the gospel of the kingdom of God, and saying, The time is fulfilled, and the kingdom of God is at hand: repent ye, and believe the gospel" **(Mark 1:14–15)**.

Scripture Reading: Luke 15:11–24

Hymns: "To God Be the Glory," Crosby

"I Love to Tell the Story," Hankey

"O, for a Thousand Tongues to Sing," Wesley

Offertory Prayer: Heavenly Father, we thank you for the privilege of being alive in this new year. We thank you for your offering to us new opportunities, responsibilities, and joys as we face this new year. We come today with our tithes and the gifts of our love, offering ourselves to you afresh. Help us as we seek to give ourselves in ministries of mercy to others. Bless these gifts today to the advancement of your kingdom and to the accomplishment of your purpose in the hearts and lives of people. In Christ's name. Amen.

Introduction

We live in a world where people are accustomed to hearing bad news. The front pages of our newspapers are filled with the accounts of tragedies that produce suffering for individuals, families, and whole nations. Much of the time allotted to newscasts on radio and television is utilized to communicate bad news. One would get the impression that bad news is more important than good news.

On this first Sunday of the new year, let us focus our minds and hearts on the good news about God. God is the God of good news. To hear the good news about God can cause us to have kind feelings toward him and can create a deeper faith in him as we face the uncertainties of the road ahead. Some people associate nothing but bad news with God because the devil has been misrepresenting the nature and character of God from the dawn of human history. Some listen only to the suggestions of Satan concerning the nature and purpose of God.

Some people associate God only with their guilty conscience. Their dirty, evil past causes them to fear God and to dread the possibility of a confrontation with him. Their pride prevents them from asking forgiveness for their sins. Their misunderstanding of his nature and character makes it difficult for them to believe that God has purposes of love and mercy toward them. Today we will look into the Bible to discover some good news about God so that our hearts may be encouraged and that some may find it possible to put faith and trust in him.

The wise men and the prophets of the Old Testament recognized and responded to the good news about God: "You who bring good news to Zion, go up on a high mountain. You who bring good news to Jerusalem, lift up your voice with a shout, lift it up, do not be afraid; say to the towns of Judah, 'Here is your God!'" (Isa. 40:9 NIV). We hear Isaiah speaking in a similar tone of voice again and again. "How beautiful on the mountains are the feet of those who bring good news, who proclaim peace, who bring good tidings, who proclaim salvation, who say to Zion, 'Your God reigns!'" (Isa. 52:7 NIV).

The greatest good news about God is revealed in the coming of the Christ. While Zechariah was in the temple, a divine visitor announced to him the mighty work of God that was to happen in the immediate future. "And the angel answering said unto him, I am Gabriel, that stand in the presence of God; and am sent to speak unto thee, and to show thee these glad tidings" (Luke 1:19). On the night when Jesus was born in Bethlehem, an angel appeared to shepherds in a field and said, "Fear not: for, behold, I bring you good tidings of great joy, which shall be to all people" (Luke 2:10). The Bible is a record of the activity of the God of good news.

The English word *gospel* means "the good message." It denotes the good tidings of the kingdom of God and of salvation through faith in Christ Jesus on the basis of his substitutionary death, his burial, his victorious resurrection, and his ascension back to the throne of the Father. All of these events and the interpretation of them are wrapped up in this word *gospel*, which is the gospel of God.

I. The good news about God was spoken in the garden of Eden following Adam and Eve's sin.

We read of how God said to the serpent, "I will put enmity between thee and the woman, and between thy seed and her seed; it shall bruise thy head, and thou shalt bruise his heel" (Gen. 3:15). Here we read of the divine decree to defeat and destroy the evil that had come into the world to rob Eden of its beauty and humankind of their privilege of fellowship with God. At the very dawn of human history, God was announcing that there was hope and that a plan had been designed for forgiveness, redemption, and deliverance. The God of good news had spoken.

II. The good news of God was announced to Abraham (Gen. 12:1–3).

Paul affirmed that the gospel was preached during the days of Abraham: "Scripture foresaw that God would justify the Gentiles by faith, and announced the gospel in advance to Abraham: 'All nations will be blessed through you'" (Gal. 3:8 NIV). The God of good news was seeking to penetrate the minds and hearts of people during Abraham's day. From the beginning, God intended that his people be a missionary people. He desires that they be involved in communicating the good news of his love to those who are in spiritual darkness and despair.

III. God announced the good news to Moses.

A study of Exodus 3:6, 8, 10 indicates the redemptive program of the gracious God who was planning to deliver Israel from the tyranny and bondage of Egypt. This was wonderful news for people in slavery.

Moses, like many modern followers of Jesus Christ, offered a number of excuses as to why he should not be personally involved in communicating this good news about God to Israel.

A. *Moses offered the excuse of a lack of personal fitness: "Who am I, that I should go unto Pharaoh?" (Ex. 3:11).*

B. *Moses offered the excuse of inadequate knowledge of the nature and character of God (Ex. 3:13).*

C. *Moses offered the excuse of a lack of authority (Ex. 4:1).*

D. *Moses offered the excuse of a lack of speaking ability (Ex. 4:10).*

E. *Finally, Moses demonstrated his lack of faith as being his real reason for offering excuses (Ex. 4:13).*

   We read in the following verse that "the anger of the LORD was kindled against Moses" because of Moses' unwillingness to be a part of the effort to communicate the good news of deliverance and the promise of peace and victory to God's people. We can be safe in assuming that our neglect to cooperate with God in communicating the good news concerning his plans for humankind is displeasing to him.

IV. Jesus began and closed his ministry by emphasizing the good news about God.

A. *From the very beginning, Jesus concentrated on announcing the good news about God (Mark 1:14).* Throughout his entire earthly ministry, he concentrated on communicating the good news of God's love, grace, mercy, forgiveness, purpose, and power.

B. *Following Jesus' resurrection, he commanded his church to concern itself with the proclamation of the good news about God to all creatures and to take it to the ends of the earth (Mark 16:15).*

V. The early church was excited over the good news from God (Acts 8:4).

The gospel was not good advice. The gospel was good news from God and about God that concerned people. The gospel was the good news about what

15

God was doing in the life, death, resurrection, and ascension of Jesus Christ for the benefit of the human race. The early disciples were tremendously excited over their new understanding of the love of God that was so great that it brought Jesus Christ to die a humiliating death on a cross for them.

The early disciples were thrilled beyond words over the fact that in Jesus' resurrection he had revealed that death was not the end and that the grave was not the goal of this life. Immortality ceased to be a dream or a hope. It became a reality that was very real and wonderful.

Conclusion

The greatest news and the latest news from God is that he loves us. He has a wonderful plan for our lives. He wants to forgive us our sins. He wants to deliver us from the power of sin. He wants to grant us the gift of wisdom for renewed living. He wants to provide us with divine energy that will enable us to do the work that he would have us to do in the world today.

What have you done with the good news about God? Are you willing to respond to the Good News? God loves you. Accept this great truth with your mind. Put the confidence of your heart in it, and move forward with a new optimism and with a new spirit of faith, hope, and love as we march into another year for the glory of God.

SUNDAY EVENING, JANUARY 6

Title: Who Will Go?

Text: "Also I heard the voice of the Lord, saying, Whom shall I send, and who will go for us?" **(Isa. 6:8)**.

Scripture Reading: Isaiah 6:1–11

Introduction

The adventures of Robinson Crusoe have long captivated the hearts of readers. Perhaps it is because everyone has at one time or another dreamed of being stranded on some island paradise. Robinson Crusoe, a master of resourcefulness, set about to provide himself with food and shelter to sustain life. He trapped goats until he had his own herd. He built a lodging for warmth and protection. Every day he explored the island for food. His activities were determined by the fact that he was alone on an island. Suddenly one day he discovered a footprint in the sand. He was not alone after all. Now his whole concept had to change. His little island was not as solitary as he had assumed.

Isaiah 6 is the moving account of a statesman who, living in a secure circle of royalty, suddenly discovered the imprint of God's presence in his own life. In a moment, all was changed. His plans, his commitments, his whole future had to undergo drastic revisions.

Isaiah was made acutely aware of God—and of an embarrassing question:

"Who will go for us?" The Septuagint reads, "Who will go to this people?" One of the Jewish Targums translates, "Who will go teach?" Although this passage has been the basis of many missionary sermons, the immediate context reminds us that this is the call to witness right where we are. Isaiah was not even asked to move across the street. He would not even have to leave Jerusalem for a weekend. The call was to stand for God in the very same city where he had lived since birth.

For a number of reasons, God's question, "Who will go?" is an embarrassing question.

I. Because of past sin (Isa. 6:5).

You cannot see the holiness of God without also seeing your personal sinfulness. The person who claims a personal experience of faith but whose life continues in complacent self-righteousness is deceived. Isaiah's first thought was of his own unworthiness: "Then said I, Woe is me! for I am undone; because I am a man of unclean lips, and I dwell in the midst of a people of unclean lips: for mine eyes have seen the King, the LORD of hosts" (Isa. 6:5).

Suddenly Isaiah saw that his private life had not been private at all. Rather, it had been going on in the very midst of God's throne room. The angelic beings announced what was to Isaiah a new concept: "The whole earth is full of his glory" (Isa. 6:3).

Isaiah's lips had been given to secular and political causes but not to God's cause. Perhaps Isaiah was like some of our contemporary politicians who feel they must use enough vulgarity to appeal to the person in the street and enough Scripture to satisfy the people of God.

No doubt Isaiah had been involved with many people in whose eyes he had lost respect. Now he was asked to be a witness to them of God's righteousness. Perhaps he already was reminded of homes where he would not be welcome because of some business deal. Yet the excuse of being unfit was not acceptable, for God offered a way of cleansing. One of the angelic beings touched Isaiah's "unclean lips" with a live coal from the altar fire, signifying the cleansing power of God.

II. Because of past blindness (Isa. 6:1).

Another embarrassing aspect involves the sudden realization of past blindness. When Isaiah finally became aware of God's holy presence, he was overwhelmed by how blind he had been.

People often see clearly for the first time through tears. Telescopes may intensify our awareness of the distant heavens, but tears sometimes make us aware of the heaven that is all about us.

King Uzziah had died after a rule of more than fifty years. Uzziah and Isaiah probably were cousins. At any rate, Isaiah had lived and worked in the royal court and had no doubt depended greatly on the king. Uzziah had done much for his nation and perhaps was second only to David in this respect. Sadly, the records (2 Chron. 26) indicate that late in life Uzziah was filled with pride and assumed the role of a priest. Instead of confessing his trespass, he was angry with the priests who warned him of his action. In the heat of wrath, he was suddenly stricken with leprosy. His last years were spent in a leper colony. At last the king, so long a symbol of power, lay dead.

Suddenly Isaiah realized that no matter what man sits on the throne, the real King of Kings is the Lord. To trust in man is to find one's hopes buried in a coffin. Only God's power is everlasting.

Sometimes only death can show people that there is more to life than carefree pleasures and earthly riches. In our brightly lighted festivities, we would never see the stars unless from time to time God turned out the lights, took us by the hand, and led us to the window.

III. Because the task is undesirable (Isa. 6:10).

The call to stand for righteousness in the midst of one's hometown is a call to an undesirable task. Isaiah was a wealthy man of position accustomed to walking in the king's court and circulating with the upper class. No doubt, because of his royal rank, he had been a popular figure at all the gala festivities of the court. Now he was asked to become unpopular, to become a fly in the ointment. He was called to stand as a messenger of God and confront his lifelong friends with the reality of their ungodliness and call them to repentance.

Adding to the undesirability of the task was the promise that Isaiah's ministry would be a thankless one. He would often see his eloquence wasted on dull ears, blind eyes, and hard hearts: "Make the heart of this people fat, and make their ears heavy, and shut their eyes; lest they see with their eyes, and hear with their ears, and understand with their heart, and convert, and be healed" (Isa. 6:10). This was God's way of telling Isaiah that his witness would often merely result in the hardening of hearts as people rejected God's message. Isaiah's task was to be comparatively fruitless. Great crowds would not flock to respond to his message.

In light of God's warning about the difficulty to which Isaiah's call was a summons, we hear the prophet's natural response: "Then said I, Lord, how long?" Sooner or later, every faithful disciple asks this question. When faced with uncaring and unmoved audiences, when confronted by the frigid selfishness of the world that warms up only to earthly lusts, we ask, "How long, Lord, must we continue?"

The answer is always the same: "Until the cities be wasted without inhabitant, and the houses without man, and the land be utterly desolate, and the LORD have removed men far away, and there be a great forsaking in the midst of the land" (Isa. 6:11–12). In other words, God expects us to serve him as long as there is life, as long as there remains one solitary person on the earth. The only way to "graduate" from the role of disciple is to die.

Yet the task is necessary. Whether or not people listen, our responsibility is to see that they have the opportunity to decide. Jesus himself attracted only a meager minority, but this in no way branded him a failure. The few who do find life make all efforts worthwhile.

IV. Because of the personal aspect of the question (Isa. 6:8).

Regardless of how large the crowd we are in, when God speaks, it is always on an individual basis. Isaiah realized he was an audience of one. God was asking who would yield to his call, and Isaiah was the only one addressed. God was asking him to be a part of the working of an invisible kingdom. He was asking him to labor for unseen, though eternal, rewards.

Conclusion

Life is never rightly spent until seen as a divine errand for God. When one greater than Moses legislates and one wiser than Solomon speaks, we do well to listen.

WEDNESDAY EVENING, JANUARY 9

Title: The Authority of Personal Experience

Text: "Paul, an apostle—not from men nor through man, but through Jesus Christ and God the Father" **(Gal. 1:1 RSV)**.

Scripture Reading: Galatians 1:6–2:10

Introduction

The occasion for Paul's epistle to the Galatians is set forth in 1:6–9. Some of the members of the churches in Galatia had defected from Christian liberty. They had departed from their belief in a gospel of grace and were seeking to find acceptance in the sight of God by keeping the Mosaic law (Gal. 5:4). The false teachers, commonly called Judaizers, had convinced them that if they were to be right with God, they must keep the law of Moses and the traditions taught by the rabbis. This was a perversion of the gospel of grace, a departure from the truth that people find acceptance in the sight of God through faith and commitment to his promises.

Paul declares repeatedly in his letter to the Galatians that the promises of God to his people were made on the basis of their faith rather than on the basis of their keeping a law. The Jewish people seemingly completely ignored the fact that the covenant relationship between God and his people was established on the basis of God's promise and their faith. Abraham is the dramatic illustration of this truth throughout the epistle.

In seeking to discredit Paul and his teachings, his enemies apparently made an attack on his apostleship. If he could be discredited as an apostle, his authority as a preacher and teacher would be undermined. The first two chapters of the epistle are biographical in nature. In them the apostle explains and defends his apostleship. His authority grows out of his personal experience with Jesus Christ.

I. Paul's apostleship was based on a divine intervention in his life (Gal. 1:10–17).

Paul dogmatically declares that his gospel finds its origin in a personal revelation by Jesus Christ. He points out that his life had been completely transformed by this personal experience with Christ.

A. *Originally he was the arch persecutor of the church (v. 13).*
B. *Before his conversion, he was a fanatic who excelled all others in keeping the traditions of his faith (v. 14).*
C. *This career of pharisaic righteousness and fanatic persecution was interrupted by a divine intervention (v. 15).*
D. *Paul affirms that he was chosen by God for the purpose of revealing Jesus Christ (v. 18).*

II. Paul's apostleship was not dependent on the Jerusalem church (Gal. 1:18–24).

The Judaizers may have implied that authority must be received from the "mother church" in order for one to be an authoritative teacher. They would have declared that Paul had received no such authority.

Paul is bold to declare that his authority does not rest on any commission by the leaders in the church at Jerusalem.

A. *Instead of going to Jerusalem for authority to preach the gospel, he affirms that he remained in Damascus and/or Arabia for a period of three years before making a brief visit to Jerusalem.* During this visit of fifteen days, he saw only Peter and James (Acts 9:26–30).
B. *Paul made another visit to Jerusalem to distribute the relief funds that the brethren in Antioch had provided (Acts 11:29–30).*
C. *Paul made still another visit to Jerusalem for the great conference that was dealing with the same problem that was plaguing the churches of Galatia (Acts 15).* In none of these three visits did the church in Jerusalem ordain or commission Paul as an authoritative teacher. His authority was not dependent on any official action by the church in Jerusalem. His authority was direct and personal and grew out of his experience with Jesus Christ.

III. Paul's apostleship was confirmed by the Jerusalem church (Gal. 2:1–10).

In these verses, Paul gives us an inside view of what happened during the great conference in Jerusalem described in Acts 15. He affirms that James, Peter, and John recognized him and the authenticity of the gospel that he was preaching to the Gentiles. They extended to him and to Barnabas the right hand of fellowship and encouraged them to continue their ministry to the Gentiles (Gal.

2:9). By declaring that James, Peter, and John—leaders in the church at Jerusalem—had confirmed as the truth of God that which he had preached and that which the Galatian Christians had originally believed, Paul refutes the charges of those seeking to discredit him.

IV. Paul had exercised apostolic authority in the presence of Peter's defection from the truth (Gal. 2:11–21).

It is difficult for modern Christians to recognize the narrow exclusiveness of Judaism during the days of our Lord and the days in which the apostles lived. They followed the most rigid and minute regulations in order not to contaminate themselves by associating with non-Jews. Peter had already had some difficulty over the matter in his experience with Cornelius (Acts 11:1–18). Paul relates an experience in which Peter had made a visit to Antioch and associated freely with Gentile believers until some others arrived from Jerusalem who had not yet opened themselves up to the possibility that one could be saved apart from the observance of the ceremonial laws of Judaism. Upon their arrival, Peter withdrew from the Gentile converts and resumed his custom of eating only the foods that were kosher. Paul openly rebuked him for his inconsistency. It took Paul a great deal of courage to rebuke the leader of the original twelve apostles. Paul affirmed that even a Jew was not justified by the works of the law but by faith in Jesus Christ.

In the last part of chapter 2, Paul begins to affirm the great doctrine of justification by faith alone. He declares that if one could find a condition of acceptance in the sight of God by the keeping of the law, then the death of Christ would be in vain (Gal. 2:21).

Conclusion

Paul did not teach or preach or write on the basis of a secondary experience with God. His was a primary, personal experience with Jesus Christ that provided him with inward motivation for ministry.

If we want to serve Christ acceptably and minister to people effectively, we must do so out of a personal experience with the living Christ rather than out of a secondary relationship with God. Let each of us seek to follow a program of personal devotion and self-discipline that will lead us to know Jesus Christ experientially that we might have the proper motivation for ministry and service.

SUNDAY MORNING, JANUARY 13

Title: The Good News Concerning Forgiveness

Text: "Be generous to one another, tender-hearted, forgiving one another as God in Christ forgave you" (**Eph. 4:32 NEB**).

Scripture Reading: Isaiah 55:6–9

Hymns: "My Faith Looks Up to Thee," Palmer

"Christ Receiveth Sinful Men," Neumeister

"Though Your Sins Be as Scarlet," Crosby

Offertory Prayer: Heavenly Father, we rejoice today in the generosity of your gracious gifts to us. We thank you that you have adopted us as your children. We thank you for the gift of forgiveness. We thank you for the inward disposition that causes us to be attracted to you and to love you. Today we bring tokens of our love in the form of a tithe of our income and an offering to express our gratitude. Bless these gifts to the advancement of your kingdom's work and to the relief of suffering. May those who benefit as a result of these gifts worship you and love you. In Christ's name we pray. Amen.

Introduction

The sermon for today has your address on it, and it is marked "Personal." This is true because "all we like sheep have gone astray; we have turned every one to his own way; and the LORD hath laid on him the iniquity of us all" (Isa. 53:6). Paul stated it clearly: "For all have sinned, and come short of the glory of God" (Rom. 3:23).

Each of us is guilty of sins of commission. We have broken God's holy law and have done that which is contrary to God's will and to our own conscience. We are guilty of doing that which has been hurtful to others. All of us must admit that we are sinners.

Each of us is guilty of sins of omission. We have neglected to worship God and to pray. We have refused to serve. We have failed to behave as we should. We have neglected and refused to give of our time and of our substance to others. We have neglected to give our testimony concerning the goodness of God. We have refused at times to listen to the still, small voice within. We are probably guilty of more sins of omission than of commission.

Each of us is guilty of sins of disposition. We have had times when we have been motivated by false pride and by a self-righteousness that was hurtful to others and was actually hypocritical. We must confess that we are often motivated by unadulterated human selfishness. It is so easy to think of "I, me, and myself." Who is able to declare that he has never harbored a critical fault-finding spirit that looked for flaws and defects in the lives of others? Perhaps we have been unwilling to admit it even to ourselves, but at times we have harbored hate and hostility toward others.

Sin, in its variegated forms, always affects people in a destructive manner. Sin creates a sense of shame and guilt in the heart of the offender. Sin causes people to flee from the presence of God. Sin causes people to fear death and eternity. Sin creates despair within the heart and robs people of a meaningful purpose for life. Sin alienates people from God and from their better selves. Sin separates people from others and destroys all of those things that are most beautiful and satisfying in life.

The miracle of miracles is that a holy God offers forgiveness to sinful people.

This is such good news that it is difficult for people to believe it; it is almost too good to be true.

Through Isaiah, God declared that he forgives sin because of his own nature and for his own joy (Isa. 43:25). Through Ezekiel, the prophet to the exiles, God communicated his desire to forgive sin and to see people enter into eternal life (Ezek. 33:11). The psalmist rejoiced in the free, full forgiveness of God (Ps. 103:1–4). Forgiveness is described in many ways in the Bible. It is a "blotting out of transgressions." It includes a divine forgetfulness in which God chooses to remember our sins no more. He covers our sins so as to conceal them even from his own penetrating eyesight. Forgiveness is the removal of a charge against an offender, a restoration of kind feelings. Forgiveness is also defined as a decision to repudiate the right to retaliate and punish the offender.

God offers forgiveness to us through faith in Jesus Christ, who died for our sins (Acts 10:43).

I. Through forgiveness, God lets us get right with himself.

There is no way by which sinful people can atone for their own sin, can purchase redemption from punishment, or can be good enough to earn God's favor and title to an eternity of fellowship with God. People are totally helpless at the point of either purchasing or meriting the favor of God. Isaiah described the worth of human efforts to earn the favor of God as having no more value than filthy rags (Isa. 64:6).

God offers us forgiveness as a gift of his mercy. He offers us the privilege of being right with him as a free gift. Forgiveness will never come by purchase or by human achievement. It comes through the grace of the God who has loved us and manifested that love through Christ Jesus. David described the joy of being forgiven in Psalm 32:1: "Blessed is the one whose transgressions are forgiven, whose sins are covered" (NIV).

II. Through forgiveness, God leads us to get right with one another.

The words of our text tell us that because God has forgiven us, we should be forgiving toward others. Inevitably each of us will experience injury at the hands of others. Some of these injuries will be accidental; others will be deliberate. We can live by the law of retaliation and seek to punish those who mistreat us. But those who do so will discover that hostility within the heart brings more harm to the vessel that contains it than it does to the victim upon which it is poured.

The model prayer our Lord gave to his disciples reveals that if we would experience God's full forgiveness, we must practice forgiveness toward others (Matt. 6:12, 14–15).

III. Through forgiveness, God enables us to get right with ourselves.

Some people find it exceedingly difficult to forgive themselves for their own sins. They continually punish themselves for their past mistakes. To refuse to forgive ourselves is to refuse to do what God has willingly and graciously already

23

done for us. To refuse forgiveness for ourselves is to be guilty of painful self-destruction as time goes by. To forgive does not mean that we condone or permit something that is wrong. To forgive means that we renounce the right to retaliate and so restore kind feelings.

Every pastor could bear testimony concerning the agony that some of his members experience because of their refusal to forgive themselves for a mistake they made in the past. Perhaps their feeling of guilt is a part of the wrath of God upon them because of their sins. Perhaps the feeling of guilt is due to their personal refusal to forgive themselves and to accept God's forgiveness.

The apostle Paul could have spent his life in a mood of melancholy self-condemnation because of his mad career of persecution before he was converted. However, when God forgave him, Paul forgave himself. He recognized that there were some things in the past that must be forgotten if he was to face the future positively and constructively (Phil. 3:13).

We Christians do ourselves, God, and others no service by continuing to dwell on our own past failures and sins. We must forgive ourselves if we want to live in God's love and grace.

IV. Through forgiveness, God encourages us to worship with joy.

The heavenly Father wants us to approach his throne of grace in love, with gratitude, and with praise in our hearts and on our lips.

God wants the time of worship with his people to be a time of joy and victory. He wants us to lift our voices with joy and happiness. This we are able to do only when we have accepted his forgiveness and when we have forgiven ourselves.

A sense of guilt can be good only if it leads to confession and an experience of forgiveness and cleansing. When God causes us to feel guilty, it is in order that we may experience cleansing and the joy that follows.

V. Through forgiveness, God invites us to engage in service.

After Isaiah experienced cleansing from the filth of sin, he was able to hear the voice of God calling for those who would serve him (Isa. 6:8). After he had experienced this cleansing, gratitude within Isaiah's heart caused him to say, "Here am I; send me."

It is impossible for us to labor under a burden of guilt for unforgiven sin and to serve God and be the greatest possible blessing to others at the same time.

VI. Through forgiveness, God fills our hearts with hopes and dreams of heaven.

The heavenly Father does not want people to live in fear of missing the heavenly home at the end of the way. He wants us to live in the glad consciousness that we are to be a part of God's family and that we are to dwell in the Father's house forever. Our Lord sought to comfort his disciples with this precious promise as he informed them of his immediate departure from them (John 14:1–3).

To have the assurance that heaven is to be our eternal home encourages an indescribable love for God. It gives rise to gratitude within the heart. It makes possible a life of service and sacrifice based on thanksgiving.

Conclusion

Although God offers forgiveness that is full and free and forever, he does not bestow this gift indiscriminately. Forgiveness can be received only by those who are willing to seek the Lord with all their hearts as they inwardly turn from the attitudes and ways that are contrary to God's will (Isa. 55:6–7). Forgiveness comes when we are sincerely willing to turn from evil and trust God for the guidance and help that is necessary to turn from evil. Conversion is primarily a change in the basic inner attitude toward God, toward sin, toward self, and toward others. When this occurs within our hearts because we have heard the good news of God's love, divine forgiveness takes place (Acts 3:19; 10:43).

God is a forgiving God. He is interested not only in forgiving past sins, but is also interested in delivering us from the destructive practice of sin in the present and future. Repentance, a deep inward change of attitude that involves turning from sin to God, makes it possible for God to bless us with forgiveness that is full and free and forever. You can have forgiveness now.

SUNDAY EVENING, JANUARY 13

Title: Walking with God

Text: "O house of Jacob, come ye, and let us walk in the light of the LORD" **(Isa. 2:5).**

Scripture Reading: Isaiah 2:1–22

Introduction

Aaron Burr had the ability and the opportunity to rise high in the political life of his country. Historians say that his ambition, coupled with his inability to meet opposition, was his ruin. Following an illustrious career in the Continental army, he became one of the leading lawyers in New York State. At one time he was a candidate for the presidency of the United States, but he lost after a tie vote led to the House of Representatives electing Jefferson instead, leaving Burr as vice president. After killing Alexander Hamilton, his archenemy, in a duel, Burr's reputation plummeted. Ambition led him to the Southwest, where apparently he hoped to raise his own army and conquer the area of Texas, perhaps establishing a republic with himself at its head. For this venture, he was brought to trial. Though Burr was acquitted, his reputation was ruined, and he lived the rest of his life a lonely, defeated man.

The root of the selfish ambition that destroyed Aaron Burr can be traced to an event that occurred while he was a student at Princeton, where his father and his grandfather, the great Jonathan Edwards, had both been president. During this time, the entire college was shaken by great revival. Burr shut himself in his room, saying that before the night was over he would decide the matter of his relationship to God. Tradition says that late that night the students living near him heard him raise his windows and exclaim, "Good-bye, God!" This was indeed the turning point of his life. In our time, the words of Aaron Burr have grown into a sweeping chorus as the multitudes continue to bid farewell to God and his holiness. Those who walk with the Lord, however, have successful lives on earth and a bright future with Christ in eternity.

I. They are made joyous by the promises of the future (Isa. 2:1–4).

A. *The exaltation of the church.* Isaiah 2:1–4 presents the most beautiful and poetic descriptions of the future of the redeemed to be found anywhere in Scripture. "And it shall come to pass in the last days, that the mountain of the LORD's house shall be established in the top of the mountains, and shall be exalted above the hills; and all nations shall flow unto it" (v. 2). The temple was built on Mount Moriah, which was referred to as "the mountain of the LORD's house." This is a prophecy, in germinal form, of the future exaltation of the church of the redeemed. The church is destined to rise up like a veritable mountain so that all eyes will see it and none will be able to ignore it. The church may struggle amid trials during its earthly sojourn, and it may be at the point of despair because of loneliness experienced in a world filled with ungodliness, but it has a destined glory that no force will be able to deny. A time is coming when the church will be recognized by all as God's instrument in bringing in his kingdom and in keeping his gospel before a perishing world.

B. *Converts from all nations.* We often hear the expression, "It's a small world." Though it is a small world, it is far from being a unified world. However, the Scriptures affirm that the time is coming when multitudes will come from all nations and all walks of life to worship God: "And many people shall go and say, Come ye, and let us go up to the mountain of the LORD, to the house of the God of Jacob; and he will teach us of his ways, and we will walk in his paths: for out of Zion shall go forth the law, and the word of the LORD from Jerusalem" (Isa. 2:3). Jesus himself spoke along these lines as he said, "That many shall come down from the east and west, and shall sit down ... in the kingdom of heaven" (Matt. 8:11). He was describing a worldwide pilgrimage that includes people of all races in the kingdom of God.

C. *The peace of God's eternity.* People have always hungered for peace and yet have never been able to achieve it. The Bible makes this promise: "They shall beat their swords into plowshares, and their spears into pruning-hooks: nation shall not lift up sword against nation, neither shall they learn war any more" (Isa. 2:4). Something about this promise quickens the heart of every person who reads it. However, we need to realize that Jesus added a footnote to this promise that helps us know when we can expect its fulfillment: "And ye shall hear of wars and rumors of wars: see that ye be not troubled: for all these things must come to pass, but the end is not yet. For nation shall rise against nation and kingdom against kingdom: there shall be famines, and pestilences, and earthquakes, in divers places ... and this gospel of the kingdom shall be preached in all the world for a witness unto all nations; and then shall the end come" (Matt. 24:6–14). If I understand Jesus' footnote correctly, he was saying that this promise is never to be experienced until his second coming. In other words, we should not expect this kind of peace until the millennium.

II. They avoid the pitfalls of a barren prosperity (Isa. 2:6–9).

Isaiah 2:6–9 speaks of a barren prosperity. One might well call it a prosperous poverty. We are urged to walk in the light of God lest we stumble into the hidden pitfalls that a barren prosperity holds for us. The people of Isaiah's time, like people of our own, seem to have filled their lives with material things. Isaiah said that God had forsaken them because they were "replenished from the east." In other words, they were filled up with goods and philosophies from the East. When a motel is full, the "No Vacancy" sign is hung out. This means there is room for no one else. There are many people today who, if they were honest, would put "No Vacancy" signs around their necks because they have filled their lives with their own fancies and activities so that there is no room at all for God.

A. *The prosperity.* The people are pictured as being filled with what the East has to offer. Of course, the East was the direction from which the caravans and tradesmen came bringing goods, riches, and foreign ways of life. Isaiah described the land as being "full of silver and gold ... full of horses ... full of idols" (Isa. 2:7–8).

B. *The barrenness.* It seems strange that barrenness is often brought on by prosperity, but history records the proof of the sequence. Thus this barrenness was not brought on by drought or famine or financial depression, but rather by abundance.

The most fearful part of the barrenness comes from the fact that God has turned his back on the people: "Therefore thou hast forsaken thy people the house of Jacob, because they be replenished from the east" (Isa. 2:6). It is a costly prosperity that achieves the wealth of the world while losing the treasures of heaven. People are in great peril when they forsake God, but they are without hope when God forsakes them.

Another result of a prosperous poverty is that of living by superstition instead of by faith in the will of God. Part of what the people were full of were the "soothsayers like the Philistines" (Isa. 2:6). From the East had come the astrologers and the fortune-tellers who practiced the same superstitious magic known by the Philistines. Again and again the Old Testament warns the people of God that these kinds of people are to be looked upon as enemies. Deuteronomy 18:10–12 firmly states: "There shall not be found among you any one ... that useth divination, or an observer of times, or an enchanter, or a witch, or a charmer, or a consulter with familiar spirits, or a wizard, or a necromancer. For all that do these things are an abomination unto the LORD." There is only one who is able to guide our destinies, the heavenly Father himself. To attribute such force to anyone else is to depart from the faith. There is no more frightful way to live life than to live under superstition.

The barrenness was further evidenced in that the people lived without forgiveness: "And the mean [lowly] man boweth down, and the great man humbleth himself: therefore forgive them not" (Isa. 2:9). This describes a kind of universal apostasy wherein the lowly, as well as the rich, bow down before the trinkets of prosperity and worship them. Because of this, they live without a knowledge of God's forgiveness. Life can be full of many things, but it will always remain void of peace and genuine happiness as long as life is void of God's forgiveness. The solemn bell of history tolls, "In Adam all die," while the silver trumpets of the sky call us to the message of the gospel: "In Christ shall all be made alive."

III. They are delivered from certain judgment (Isa. 2:12–17).

A. *When the world dies.* Everywhere in the Bible we are reminded that the world is to perish. The Bible tells us this will be brought about by the instrumentality of God, and that in that moment we shall all be summoned to the final judgment. Thus when heaven is rolled up like a scroll and we see the perishing of all things, we will know in all fullness what is meant by the day of the Lord.

B. *When God shakes all things.* Scripture vividly tells us that the death of the world is to come about by God's shaking of a dying world until all earthly things be released from its deathly grasp. Isaiah said, "And they shall go … into the caves of the earth, for fear of the LORD, and for the glory of his majesty, when he ariseth to shake terribly the earth" (v. 19).

The author of Hebrews expressed this same theme, writing that God has promised, "Saying, Yet once more I shake not the earth only, but also heaven" (Heb. 12:26). The day of the Lord will be a time when people find themselves shaken loose from the material abundance for which they have sold their very souls.

C. *When people have waited too long.* God is pictured in the Scriptures as being patient and longsuffering, but he is also pictured as one who has a limit to his patience. There comes a time when a person takes one step too far and passes the point of no return. The tragic aspect of the day of the Lord is that it will find people who have waited too long to throw their idols away and to accept the living God: "In that day a man shall cast his idols of silver, and his idols of gold, which they made each one for himself to worship, to the moles and to the bats" (Isa. 2:20). In that day, it will be too late to throw away that which has brought about their downfall. This pictures people as being cursed by what they possess because they have been possessed by their possessions.

D. *When self-sufficiency perishes.* There is coming a time when all people will realize that humans are nothing apart from God: "Cease ye from man, whose breath is in his nostrils: for wherein is he to be accounted of?" (Isa. 2:22). Where is the bank account that is able to buy off the trumpet of heaven that will mark the end of time and the power of God that will bring every person to account? We try to prepare for every emergency of life, but there comes a final emergency for which there is no preparation other than faith in God. Humans, who are so prone to trust in themselves, need to be reminded that their lives are no more certain than the breath that is in their nostrils—it can cease at any moment.

Conclusion

Someday life's portrait will be given its last brush mark and will stand forever. In 1937 Evangeline Booth, the daughter of the founder of the Salvation Army, returned to the United States after three years of extensive travel. When asked by an interviewer, "What is amiss with the world?" she quickly answered, "There is just one thing wrong with the world, and it is this: The world is trying to get along without God—and it can't be done." Jesus Christ lived among us and died for us that by faith we might be born spiritually into his kingdom and walk in his presence. "Come ye and let us walk in the light of the Lord."

WEDNESDAY EVENING, JANUARY 16

Title: Acceptance through Faith

Text: "Justified by faith in Christ" **(Gal. 2:16 RSV).**

Scripture Reading: Galatians 2:15–21

Introduction

Throughout all of the ages, people have asked, "What must I do to be acceptable in the sight of God?" This is the question that is in the background of every verse in Paul's epistle to the Galatians.

Paul had preached that salvation—forgiveness, acceptance before God—was found through faith in Jesus Christ as Lord and Savior. Many had put their confidence in the Christ as the Son of God and as the Savior from sin. They had received the gift of the Holy Spirit. They had been blessed with many wonderful experiences. They were now being misled by false teachers who were insisting that in addition to faith in Jesus Christ, they must obey the law of Moses if they were to find acceptance before God. Paul refuted this error in the strongest possible terms.

I. Even Jews find acceptance with God through faith (Gal. 2:15–16).

Paul affirms that even those who are the physical descendants of Abraham can find acceptance before God only through faith in Jesus Christ. He is bold to declare repeatedly in verse 16 that people are not "justified by the works of the law ... for by the works of the law shall no flesh be justified." He comes to the very center of the controversy that is raging among the churches of Galatia. Some were affirming the only way to find acceptance in the sight of God was through obedience. Paul later affirmed that all people have broken the law and consequently are under the condemnation of a law that has been transgressed.

II. The law produces death instead of life.

The law was not given by God through Moses as a pathway to life. It was given to reveal the wrongness of sin (Gal. 3:19–24). The law produces an awareness of guilt because of transgression. This brings about spiritual death rather than spiritual life. An awareness of guilt leads to an awareness of our need for a redeemer or savior from the curse that follows the transgression of the law (Gal. 3:10–11).

III. The life of faith.

Paul had found a freedom and joy through faith in Jesus Christ that he was never able to experience by seeking acceptance before God through a keeping of the law (Gal. 2:20–21).

He speaks of the mystical union that he now knows through faith in Jesus Christ rather than through an attempt to keep the law of Moses.

Conclusion

Paul declares that if acceptance before God could come through a keeping of the law, then the death of Christ had been a waste. He encourages the Galatians to trust Jesus Christ implicitly for abundant and eternal life. Only through faith in Christ can we find acceptance in the presence of the holy heavenly Father.

SUNDAY MORNING, JANUARY 20

Title: The Good News Concerning the Judgment Day

Text: "Therefore being justified by faith, we have peace with God through our Lord Jesus Christ: by whom also we have access by faith into this grace wherein we stand, and rejoice in hope of the glory of God" **(Rom. 5:1–2)**.

Scripture Reading: Daniel 7:9–10

Hymns: "O Worship the King," Grant

"Grace Greater Than Our Sin," Johnston

"Blessed Assurance, Jesus Is Mine," Crosby

Offertory Prayer: Heavenly Father, we offer to you our thanks for your blessings on us. We come bringing gifts that are but indications of the generosity of your provisions for us. We remind ourselves that every beast of the forest and the cattle on a thousand hills are yours. We come bringing gifts that we might share in the work of your kingdom in proclaiming the gospel to the ends of the earth and in ministering to the needs of the unfortunate about us. Bless these gifts and multiply them to your honor and glory. In Jesus' name. Amen.

Introduction

Both the Old and the New Testaments tell us that there will come a time when each person will stand before God to give an account for the life that he or she lived.

If we believe in the truth of the Word of God, we must accept as fact that one day each of us must stand before our Creator to be judged. Many passages of Scripture speak concerning the certainty of judgment, the universality of judgment, and the basis on which people will be judged. We can rest assured that the decrees of this day of judgment will be final (Acts 17:30–31).

I. For two groups there can be no good news concerning the judgment.

A. *There is no good news for those who have refused or neglected to trust Jesus Christ as Lord and Savior.* We can search the Bible from beginning to end for a glimmer of hope for those who refuse or neglect to accept Jesus Christ as Lord, but we will find none. There is salvation in no other. In every instance in which the Bible speaks concerning the certainty of judgment and the basis of judgment, no hope is held out for those who have chosen to neglect or reject the Lord Jesus Christ as Lord and Savior (cf. Matt. 10:32–33; 25:31–46; Rev. 20:11–25).

B. *There can be no good news concerning the judgment for those who are seeking to obtain a righteousness that is acceptable to God through their own efforts.* Some people labor under the impression that in addition to trusting Jesus Christ as Lord and Savior, they must keep the Mosaic law or some other law to guarantee their salvation. Those who believe that at the end of the way their good deeds must outweigh their bad deeds cannot possibly have peace of mind as they face the judgment day unless they have lowered God's requirements to the point where they are easily reachable. The Word of God clearly states that people are not saved or justified by the keeping of the law (Rom. 3:20). We are not saved by our good works; we are saved by our faith in Jesus Christ, who has provided salvation for us by God's grace (Eph. 2:8–9).

II. There is good news concerning the judgment day for the saved.

Someone has said that in order to go to heaven, one must have a perfect record. Since all of us are sinners, this puts us in a bad position. However, God has provided for us a Savior in Jesus Christ. We are given the privilege of going to heaven on the record of his perfect obedience to the law of God and because of his sacrificial death on the cross for our sins. It is faith in this crucified but resurrected Lord that brings us into a position where God justifies us (Rom. 5:1; Gal. 2:16). Justification is something that God does for us. To be justified means to be given a position of acceptance in the presence of God. God treats justified sinners as if they had never sinned.

In this experience in which sinners who put their faith in Jesus Christ are justified in the sight of God, a spiritual birth takes place in which they receive the very nature and character of God. This means they have a new appetite and new ambitions. They want to live according to their new nature. They want to live so as to be pleasing to God. The good news of the gospel for believing sinners is that their sins have already been judged and they are no longer alienated from God. The good news is that they are now children of God and at peace with God, and condemnation has been removed (John 3:17–18). Furthermore, in this experience of the new birth, believers not only have condemnation removed, but they pass out of the realm of spiritual death into the realm of spiritual life. They enter into a relationship with God in which there is not even a possibility of being condemned and rejected by the Father (5:24).

This is good news that can cause the heart of the believer to rejoice with joy unspeakable.

III. The good news of possible rewards on the day of judgment.

The purpose of the day of judgment is not to determine whether we are saved or lost or whether we will go to heaven or to hell. That is determined by what we do with Jesus Christ before the judgment day ever arrives. As death finds us, so will the judgment day receive us, and so will eternity retain us. The Bible clearly teaches that there will be degrees of condemnation or judgment for the unsaved. It also clearly teaches the possibility of believers so serving as to receive a high commendation from the Lord.

   A. *For believers there is the possibility of receiving great rewards (Rev. 22:12).* Our Lord repeatedly promised to reward his followers according to their labors.
   B. *The apostle Paul speaks of the possibility of people living and serving in such a manner as to have no rewards following the judgment day.* He speaks of a time of testing when every person's works shall be tried by the fires of judgment. If people have built on the foundation of Jesus Christ and out of the materials that endure, they will have a reward. On the other hand, if people do not serve, give, minister, witness, and help, they will be saved without having the joy of receiving a reward (1 Cor. 4:11–15).

Conclusion

If you have put your faith and trust in Jesus Christ as the Lord of life and as the Lord of death, you need have no fear at all of the day when you will stand before God as far as your being accepted by him is concerned. The heavenly Father does not want us to live in an agony of anxiety about our eternal destiny. He desires that we serve him and others from a motivation of love and gratitude rather than from a fear of being rejected if we do not.

We should earnestly and sincerely labor and serve so as to hear the Master say, "Well done, thou good and faithful servant" (Matt. 25:21). Through Jesus Christ there is good news for believers as they contemplate the fact that one day they will stand before God. They need have no fear of being rejected. They can rejoice in the possibility of being commended and rewarded by the eternal God who has revealed himself in the person of Jesus Christ.

SUNDAY EVENING, JANUARY 20

Title: What Is There to Talk About?

Text: "Come now, and let us reason together, saith the LORD; though your sins be as scarlet, they shall be as white as snow; though they be red like crimson, they shall be as wool" **(Isa. 1:18)**.

Scripture Reading: Isaiah 1:1–18

Introduction

The first chapter of the prophecy of Isaiah calls our attention to a much needed discussion. That this is a high-level discussion is seen from the fact that it involves God himself. The Bible indicates that some people have been allowed to reason with God.

Every person has been subpoenaed to appear in court—God's court, the court of eternity. In it stands every person beset by personal sin and deserving the sentence of death. Isaiah sounds the first "hear ye" of a divine summons, the themes of which are to be found throughout the rest of his prophecy—themes of a great indictment.

I. The forfeiting of life (Isa. 1:2–6).

A. *By rebellion.* Isaiah pictures God as a loving Father who mourns the disobedience of his children: "I have nourished and brought up children, and they have rebelled against me" (v. 2). The story of the prodigal son is as old as the story of man. Here we see it reenacted on a nationwide scale. Shakespeare's King Lear, suffering the heartbreak of having his own children depose him, cries out, "How sharper than a serpent's tooth it is to have a thankless child." How pathetic it is to see children mistreat a father who has given them everything. How foolish to see children turn from a heavenly Father who offers them life itself.

B. *By ungratefulness.* Coupled with rebellion is the sin of being inconsiderate of the source of one's blessings. Isaiah sadly states, "The ox knoweth his owner, and the ass his master's crib: but Israel doth not know, my people doth not consider" (v. 3). It is useless for people who frivolously ignore God to pretend that he is in any of their thoughts.

C. *By being saddled with sin.* When Isaiah says, "Ah, sinful nation," he is literally saying, "Shame on you." He further says that they are "a people laden with iniquity" (v. 4). Here are people who are burdened down with the weight of their own sins, who have chosen to live life saddled with sin. This is the way it is for all who forsake God and try to live on their own.

33

D. *By ignoring the malignancy of the soul.* Periodically some national figure succumbs to the dreadful menace of cancer, and we are again reminded that it strikes both the rich and the poor. The Bible speaks of a more fearful malignancy that destroys the soul. Isaiah says, "Why should ye be stricken any more? ye will revolt more and more: the whole head is sick, and the whole heart faint. From the sole of the foot even unto the head there is no soundness in it; but wounds, and bruises, and putrefying sores: they have not been closed, neither bound up, neither mollified with ointment" (vv. 5–6). The malignancy described is the result of unforgiven sin. There is no medicine for such wounds.

II. Spiritual confusion (Isa. 1:11–14).

In describing the worship of the people, Isaiah quite frankly states that they remind him of the leaders of those ancient wicked cities Sodom and Gomorrah: "Hear the word of the LORD, ye rulers of Sodom; give ear unto the law of our God, ye people of Gomorrah" (1:10). These two cities, known for their gross wickedness, had a form of religion.

A. *Sacrifice without meaning.* Sacrifice, rightly understood, is basic to any genuine worship experience. In the Old Testament it involved the sacrifice of animals. In the light of the New Testament, sacrifice becomes personal, involving one's own life. Yet we hear Isaiah say, "To what purpose is the multitude of your sacrifices unto me? saith the LORD: I am full of the burnt offerings of rams, and the fat of fed beasts; and I delight not in the blood of bullocks, or of lambs, or of he goats" (v. 11). Real sacrifice must involve giving something that you will miss tremendously. For this reason, the Old Testament sacrifice was to be a perfect animal without blemish. The New Testament pictures the sacrifice of placing one's daily life on the altar in such a way that self is denied and Christ is honored (Rom. 12:1–2).

If what you are giving to God is something you will never miss, then you have no concept of real sacrifice. Also, sacrifice to God implies undivided allegiance. This was not true of the people to whom Isaiah spoke. During his reign as king, Ahaz went to Damascus seeking to pacify the king of Assyria. Out of this experience we are told that Ahaz sacrificed to the gods of Damascus (2 Chron. 28:23). Having succumbed to the might of Assyrian pressure, Ahaz then imposed idolatry and polytheism, Assyrian style, in his own land of Judah. Judah became like the other territories under Assyria and mingled the cult of the Assyrians into the temple worship at Jerusalem. It is this kind of religious compromise and meaningless sacrifice that Isaiah has in mind. It does not take a seer to recognize that our contemporary society has many gods and many altars on which people give life itself. We do well to remember that God accepts only the sacrifice of those who worship him alone.

B. *Monotonous worship.* When people come to God's house with a worldly attitude and a noncommittal way of sacrificing, they accomplish little more than getting dirt on the carpets. The Lord said through Isaiah, "When ye come to appear before me, who hath required this at your hand, to tread my courts?" (v. 12). Therefore, God says of all their observances: "Your new moons and your appointed feasts my soul hateth: they are a trouble unto me; I am weary to bear them" (v. 14). If worship services seem monotonous to you sometimes, just remember how they must seem to God when multitudes keep trampling down his courts without really meaning anything by it. Of course, the thing that makes worship monotonous to you is that too often you leave your heart outside the door. Bending the knee at God's altar means nothing unless one's will is bent as well. Monotonous worship comes when you refuse to make any new adventures in faith, refuse all new opportunities for commitment, and decide to scale no new heights for the Lord.

III. The demands of holiness (Isa. 1:16–17).

The admonition to stop sinning and to start living for God seems simple enough, and yet the simplicity of it leads many people to think it is something that they can do on their own anytime they desire. Few people have stopped to realize that there is difficulty involved in obeying this admonition. Evil has such a grip on people that they cannot free themselves from its clutches without outside help.

Isaiah admonishes the people to "learn to do well." Animals by instinct do things as well the first time they do them as the last. But people are different. Sin has blinded them, and they have everything to learn and little capacity for the learning of it until somehow they can be granted a new nature. How then does one live up to the demands of God's holiness? "We are no worse than others" would be a good excuse if the world were to judge us, but God is the Judge. This means that life has to be argued out with God. How then can we measure up?

IV. The offer of God (Isa. 1:18).

God reminds us that if we are willing to listen to him, there is a way out of our sin problem. God offers to help us meet his own demands of holiness. The only way this can be accomplished is by conversion. People have to become new creatures through faith in Jesus Christ. Being born spiritually, through faith, is spoken of as being born again. It is said that poets are born and not made. Whether this is so or not, I cannot say, but I do know that it is true where Christians are concerned. Christians have to be born spiritually from above. This is the essence of Jesus' message to Nicodemus as he said, "Except a man be born again, he cannot see the kingdom of God" (John 3:3). Isaiah vividly pictures our sins as the stain of blood that sinks into our very souls and cannot be bleached out with any human remedy. God's offer is that our sins can be made white — free from the stain of guilt. Only God can erase the stain of sin. To accept God's offer, we must confess our sins and the futility of our own way of life.

V. The crisis (Isa. 1:19–20).

The crisis comes as we contemplate our own decision in this matter. Isaiah sets forth the great "if": "If ye be willing and obedient, ye shall eat the good of the land: but if ye refuse and rebel, ye shall be devoured with the sword: for the mouth of the LORD hath spoken it" (Isa. 1:19–20). God is saying that everything depends on whether we are willing to consent to his terms and to hear his commands. Above the clamor of the marketplace where men and women are selling their souls for trinkets, comes this word of God calling us to the crisis of decision. Since God gave us life, it is for him to say how it can be lived and how it can be forfeited. God's invitation to reason with him is another way of urging us to reconsider our plans, to examine what we are about to do with our souls.

If somehow we would take the time to write out every planned decision and then follow through with only those we could conscientiously justify in the light of God's Word, we would drastically revise our itinerary. Isaiah reminds us that commitment to God is not made in wild emotion but must ever be the result of clear reasoning. We must always be on guard against confusing our opinions with the reasons given by God. We may say we do not like apple pie, but if we have never tasted it, we are being unreasonable. We may prefer to reason only on the way we treat our families, friends, or neighbors, but God says that our relationship to him is dependent on how we have treated Jesus Christ.

Conclusion

You must face God's invitation alone. No general has ever made a more crucial stand than that which God asks you to make. The offer is still yours, and while you wait, there is a time of crisis.

WEDNESDAY EVENING, JANUARY 23

Title: The Role of Faith

Text: "For by grace you have been saved through faith" **(Eph. 2:8 RSV)**.

Scripture Reading: Galatians 3:1–29

Introduction

The big question in the background throughout the entire epistle to the Galatians is "How can a person find a position of favor and acceptance in the sight of God?" The Judaizers were alleging that in addition to trusting Christ as Lord and Savior, people must also observe the law of Moses and give reverence to the tradition of the Fathers. They were saying that the death of Jesus Christ on the cross and his resurrection from the dead were not a proper basis on which to hope for justification in the sight of God.

The apostle Paul is trying to call the unstable believers back to a true faith in the gospel that sets people free from the condemnation of the law and permits them to live in the liberty of a Spirit-filled life. In Galatians 3 the apostle presents a number of different proofs or arguments in support of his great emphasis that justification in the sight of God is through faith in Jesus Christ—plus *nothing*.

I. The gift of the Holy Spirit is by faith (Gal. 3:1 – 3).

The Galatian Christians had experienced the indwelling of the Holy Spirit from the moment of their conversion to Jesus Christ. They had had no opportunity to obey the law or to observe the tradition of the rabbis so as to earn or merit this gift of the Spirit. Paul declared that the presence of the Spirit in their hearts was a proof that justification is by faith in Christ Jesus.

II. The gifts of the Spirit are by faith (Gal. 3:5).

Not only had the Galatian Christians received the gift of the Spirit in their conversion experience, but they had experienced his ministry and his power through various spiritual gifts and miracles. Paul inquires whether this working of the Spirit through them was the result of faith or of the works of the law. He affirms that these miraculous gifts from the Spirit prove that justification in the sight of God is through faith.

III. Abraham was justified by faith (Gal. 3:6 – 9).

Paul affirms that the promise was made to Abraham on condition of his faith. Furthermore, the promise of God to bless and to redeem the Gentiles through Abraham and his descendants was conditioned on a faith response. And those who put their faith in God become people of faith and the children of Abraham through faith in Christ Jesus (cf. Gen. 12:1 – 3).

IV. The law produces condemnation rather than justification (Gal. 3:10 – 14).

To be justified by the law, it would be necessary for us to keep the law perfectly in every minute detail. No one in the past or in the present has been able to do that. To break the law places us under the curse of condemnation rather than under the blessing of justification. Paul affirms that the blessing of Abraham comes through faith in Christ Jesus who suffered the curse of our sin on the cross, dying to redeem us from the curse of the law. The law was given not as a way of securing justification in the sight of God, but as an instrument to be used by God (Gal. 3:19). The giving of the law in no way annulled the covenant of promise through Abraham. The law was designed to reveal to us our need for the Savior who bore the penalty of our sin on the cross.

Conclusion

Paul affirms that we become children of God through faith in Christ rather than by keeping the law of Moses (Gal. 3:26). Baptism is declared to be the formal and public manner by which believers publicly identify themselves as believers and put on the uniform of a Christian. In this new fellowship, the old distinctions and differences that separate person from person and group from group have been erased, and we are to be one great family of equals as children and servants of God (Gal. 3:28–29).

SUNDAY MORNING, JANUARY 27

Title: The Good News Concerning Death

Text: "Our Saviour Jesus Christ, who hath abolished death, and hath brought life and immortality to light through the gospel" **(2 Tim. 1:10)**.

Scripture Reading: 1 Timothy 1:7–11

Hymns: "Great Redeemer, We Adore Thee," Harris

"Majestic Sweetness Sits Enthroned," Stennett

"I Know That My Redeemer Liveth," Pounds

Offertory Prayer: Heavenly Father, for the bounty of your blessings on us, we thank you. We thank you for the forgiveness of our sins, for the gift of eternal life, for your leadership and guidance, and for the generosity of your material blessings upon us. Bless the giving of our tithes and offerings to the continuing of your work in the world. We rejoice in this opportunity to participate in the proclamation of the Good News to the ends of the earth, through Jesus Christ our Lord. Amen.

Introduction

Death is a melancholy subject that we do not like to think about. We usually associate death with sorrow and grief. But through Jesus Christ, there is some good news concerning death. Some of the best news is to be had only from Jesus Christ.

The fear of death has filled the hearts of people since Cain murdered Abel. Because death invades the family circle to destroy the dearest and most precious of human relationships, it is only natural that the question recorded from the lips of Job should occur again and again: "If a man die, shall he live again?" (Job 14:14).

If there is some good news about death, then people should be eager to hear it. It would be most profitable and helpful if people could hear it and believe it. Henry Van Dyke said, "Some people are so afraid to die that they never begin to live." To have a proper attitude toward death contributes much toward our being able to live an abundant life. We are then able to major on life rather than live in fear of death.

A proper response to the good news concerning death enables us to rearrange our priorities. It enables us to generate more concern for the nonbelievers about us. It enables us to face this last enemy of humanity with steady eyes and an attitude of confidence.

John Milton said, "Death is the golden key that opens the palace of eternity." Only one who has heard and responded to the gospel can believe this.

I. Death has been the great enemy of humanity.

A. *Death has been a robber.*

B. *Death has been a despoiler of human hope and life.*

C. *Death has been a grim reaper.*

D. *Death has carried dear ones into "the undiscovered country from whose bourn no traveller returns" (Shakespeare,* Hamlet, *act 3, scene 1).*

E. *Death has conquered the great.*

F. *Death has conquered the strong.*

G. *Death has conquered the wise.*

H. *Death has conquered the wealthy.*

II. The experience of death is certain.

Only the time of our death is uncertain. Death may come in infancy, youth, the prime of life, or old age. Death should never surprise us; however, it is often a shock when it happens to someone else.

It has been said that death is life's final frontier. Each person must discover it for himself or herself. No one will escape it except those who remain alive when the Lord Jesus Christ returns triumphantly the second time.

III. The warnings of death are about us.

A. *There are vacant chairs in the family circle that speak to us concerning the reality of death.*

B. *Death is abroad in the land. We read about it in the newspapers; we hear about it on television; it confronts us every day on the Internet.*

C. *The decline of our health speaks concerning this experience.*

D. *The advance of age should call our attention to the fact of death.*

IV. What is the good news about death?

There is no more melancholy subject for us to consider than death. None of us will clap our hands and rejoice at the thought of it. Most likely this fear and dread of death is due to the fact that we are all sinners and the Bible teaches that there is an inseparable connection between sin and death. It was sin that brought death into the world. Because we are sinners, we must die (Gen. 2:17; Rom. 5:12).

A. *The good news concerning death is inseparably associated with the coming of Jesus Christ into the world.* Apart from him, there is absolutely no good news concerning death. The answer to Job's piercing, penetrating question, "If a man die, shall he live again?" will be heard only from the lips and life of Jesus Christ.

B. *Jesus Christ came to dwell among people "for the suffering of death" (Heb. 2:9).* His death was no accident in the divine plan. The death of Christ was not merely the result of the anger and the hostility of the Jewish authorities or the cruelty of the Roman soldiers. In a mysterious but wonderful way, because of the grace of God, Christ Jesus came that he might "taste death for everyone" (Heb. 2:9 NIV). In a way that defies human comprehension, Christ came to die for each of us that by his resurrection he might bring about the death of death.

C. *Christ entered the realm of death in order that he might destroy the power of the devil and death (Heb. 2:14–15).* When Christ arose from the dead on the first Easter, he did something more than just demonstrate divine power. He was revealing the victory over Satan and death. He was giving a demonstration of God's plan to deliver the believing ones from the realm of death and the grave.

D. *For individual believers, the complete conquest over death is in the future (1 Cor. 15:26, 51–54).* The resurrection of Jesus Christ is but the firstfruits of the resurrection of all the saints from the dead (1 Cor. 15:23).

Conclusion

With the ear of his soul, the apostle John heard a voice from heaven say, "Write this: Blessed are the dead who die in the Lord from now on. 'Yes,' says the Spirit, 'they will rest from their labor, for their deeds will follow them'" (Rev. 14:13 NIV). The word *blessed* has within it all that we include in our golden word *success.* It refers to happiness and joy and contentment and well-being. The inspired writer speaks concerning those who have died with faith in Jesus Christ as being happy and joyful in the presence of God.

Our Lord replaces death with life—eternal life in the here and now as well as in the hereafter. Our Lord replaces fear with faith—faith that gives confidence in the present and hope for the future.

Our Lord replaces grief with joy for those who are willing to trust both his love and his power. He demonstrated his love on the cross when he died for us. He demonstrated his power by conquering death and the grave.

Through faith in Jesus Christ, we can overcome the fear of death. Through faith in him, we can rearrange our priorities and live with the values of eternity in mind.

There is good news concerning death.

SUNDAY EVENING, JANUARY 27

Title: Bypassing God

Text: "But the word of the LORD was unto them precept upon precept, precept upon precept; line upon line, line upon line.... Wherefore hear the word of the LORD, ye scornful men, that rule this people which is in Jerusalem. Because ye have said, We have made a covenant with death, and with hell are we at agreement ... for we have made lies our refuge, and under falsehood have we hid ourselves: Therefore thus saith the Lord GOD, Behold, I lay in Zion for a foundation a stone, a tried stone, a precious corner stone, a sure foundation: he that believeth shall not make haste" **(Isa. 28:13–16)**.

Scripture Reading: Isaiah 28:1–17

Introduction

Along cross-country highways, we often see signs that say, "Truck Bypass" or "Business Bypass." The weary traveler anxious to miss congested downtown areas learns the importance of these signs. Although advantageous for cross-country traveling, the same procedure can be disastrous in one's spiritual pilgrimage, for some tempting bypasses bring tragic results. People are often tempted to bypass facing up to their relationship to the living God. Occasionally we find a person who is well versed in the Bible but who has spent hour upon hour reading it, not to find direction but to look for loopholes by which to justify himself and to provide grounds for argumentative activities.

The context of our Scripture passage is the first years of King Hezekiah's reign, prior to the fall of Samaria. While predicting the fall of Samaria as God's judgment on their sin, Isaiah at the same time addresses Judah, who is guilty of the same sin—that of bypassing the holy law of the Lord. Dark is the future when one turns off the road of life at the sign that says, "Exit Here to Bypass God."

I. Bypassing a crown of glory for a crown of pride (Isa. 28:1–5).

It is impossible to travel in two directions at the same time. Every crossroad involves a decision. To turn to the right means that one must give up that which lies to the left.

A. *A crown of glory.* God breathed into man the breath of life that he might someday wear a crown of glory. Isaiah, in referring to the faithful remnant, promises, "In that day shall the LORD of hosts be for a crown of glory, and for a diadem of beauty, unto the residue of his people" (v. 5). Nothing so crowns a life as the blessing and fellowship of God which shall, on that final day, be fully revealed for all eyes to behold.

Every person is traveling toward his day of coronation. He awaits a crown. As the death of winter quietly touches the leaf and bush on the mountainside, creating a radiant beauty, so the end of life can likewise be made into beauteous praise to the Lord. Even death can be a silent witness to the grace of God when faced in the quiet assurance of faith. But multitudes are turning off the road of life and bypassing the crown of glory.

B. *A crown of pride.* Using "Ephraim" to denote the northern kingdom of Israel, Isaiah sternly warns, "Woe to the crown of pride, to the drunkards of Ephraim, whose glorious beauty is a fading flower.... The crown of pride, the drunkards of Ephraim, shall be trodden under feet: and the glorious beauty ... shall be a fading flower" (vv. 1–4). Sitting on a hill surrounded by rolling green slopes, the city of Samaria, the capital of the northern kingdom, resembled a beautiful crown resting on soft velvet. Though as radiant as a flower in full bloom, its beauty was doomed to fade. To begin with, the people are drunken with pride and with the exhilaration of their own self-sufficiency. No doubt this had given way to literal drunkenness as human appetites were given full sway. In but a short time, Samaria would fall victim to the cruel Assyrians. Their luxurious

41

way of life would soon be given over to slavery. Their families would be ravished, and their nation would forever be scattered and lost. Isaiah tells them ahead of time the reason for it all: they have bypassed God.

II. Bypassing scriptural instruction for worldly instruction (Isa. 28:11–13).

There is a sense in which Scripture and the world both teach the same lessons. The difference is that Scripture seeks to prepare people ahead of time that they may know how to live, while the world makes people aware of their mistakes after it is too late to make a difference.

The Bible affirms that life is always empty when God is left out. Yet people prefer to learn from the world that life without God is empty. Once having lived life out, the knowledge that it has been empty is poor consolation when nothing but an eternity of emptiness lies ahead.

A. *The Scripture as an instructor.* For some strange reason, people resist the teaching of God's Word. Although Isaiah is speaking specifically concerning the sins of Samaria, he is speaking to the inhabitants of Jerusalem and trying to make them aware of their similar sins. Isaiah finds a very poor response. Those who refuse to hear Isaiah's message accuse him of treating them like babies, of lecturing them on petty morality: "But the word of the LORD was unto them precept upon precept, precept upon precept; line upon line, line upon line; here a little, and there a little" (v. 13). Isaiah's listeners are broad-minded people who have somehow managed to rise above the "simple" demands of holiness and have "seen" that these demands are rather unimportant. The taunts thrown at Isaiah can be rendered in terms of a mother's instruction to a young child: "Yes, yes; no, no." They feel themselves to be beyond commandments, to have come of age so that they are quite capable of doing what they want to do without having any religious instruction. They reason that a man's life is his own business and, after all, he has a right to do what he wants with it.

B. *The world as instructor.* To refuse God's teaching is to learn at the hands of the world. Of course, God is behind that lesson also. But when God uses the world as an instructor, he is present in wrath, not in mercy. Since people will not listen to God, they must suffer the consequences and learn from bitter experience. When people, drunken with pride, reject the teachings of Scripture, they then can expect severer instruction. Samaria, proud and self-sufficient, will learn her lesson from lips that speak foreign languages: "For with stammering lips and another tongue will he speak to his people" (v. 11). Isaiah refers to the wicked and cruel Assyrians. Though their speech is foreign, they will teach Samaria a sobering lesson. Samaria may well take lightly the message of God's prophet, but when the fierce invaders stand within the city walls and their language controls life in the streets, the people of Samaria will then have learned the hard way the lesson God sought to teach them gracefully. The Bible reminds readers that "the way of transgressors is hard" (Prov. 13:15).

III. Bypassing Christ for human alliances (Isa. 28:16 – 17).

Isaiah turns from the discussion of the sin of Samaria to the problem near at hand—the sin of the men of Jerusalem. "Wherefore hear the word of the Lord, ye scornful men, that rule this people which is in Jerusalem" (v. 14). They too are guilty of bypassing God.

A. *Christ the Foundation.* Isaiah, more than any other Old Testament prophet, looked ahead to God's promised redemption. We see in his words the promised Christ: "Behold, I lay in Zion for a foundation a stone, a tried stone, a precious corner stone, a sure foundation" (v. 16). Christ is not only a foundation stone for life that has withstood every test, but he is also a stone that in turn tests every character. Isaiah's hearers knew much about cornerstones. Those in Solomon's temple were as much as thirty-eight feet long and weighed over one hundred tons each. A life, like a temple, must have a firm foundation. People cannot refuse the gospel and be at peace. They cannot reject God and stand on firm ground.

Christ is the only safe guide. The Lord warns, "Judgment also will I lay to the line, and righteousness to the plummet" (v. 17). What God is saying is that his rule of measurement will be divine justice and that the plumb line by which he will judge every person will be that of his righteousness. People build their lives much like a brick mason builds a wall. The foundation, the method of building, and the plumb line are all important. When life is built apart from the law of God, it resembles a wall laid by an inexperienced craftsman. The bulge gets larger and larger until at last life comes tumbling down.

B. *Self the foundation.* People do not deny the presence and certainty of death, yet they seem to feel as though they have, by prior arrangement, made everything all right without having to become involved with God (v. 15).

Back of Jerusalem's self-sufficiency lies its secret weapon. The people of Jerusalem have quietly made an alliance with Egypt and therefore feel no need of prayerful supplication of God's deliverance (Isa. 30:2 speaks of this alliance specifically). Evil people always suppose they have an ace up their sleeve.

An old proverb reminds us that we must live with the results of poor bargains: "You have made your bed; now you must lie in it." Isaiah warned, "For the bed is shorter than a man can stretch himself on it: and the covering narrower than that he can wrap himself in it" (Isa. 28:20). When a man chooses to live without God, he is condemning himself to a future as cramped as a coffin. The bed he is making will provide neither rest nor protection from winter's night. The Jewish people as a whole, by rejecting Christ, made for themselves a bed in which they have never found rest.

Conclusion

God has many signposts in this world. The church stands as a visible testimony to God. The Bible points people to Jesus Christ. History proclaims day by day that sin brings judgment. Wise people read the road signs, but the foolish rush madly on, bypassing God.

WEDNESDAY EVENING, JANUARY 30

Title: The Heirs of God through Faith

Text: "So through God you are ... a son, and if a son, then an heir" **(Gal. 4:7 RSV)**.

Scripture Reading: Galatians 4:1 – 7

Introduction

Galatians 3 and 4 take the form of a powerful argument against those who were contending that one finds favor in the sight of God through the keeping of the law rather than through faith in the promises of God that were fulfilled in Jesus Christ.

These two chapters provide a clear illustration of how a knowledge of the historical situation in which the inspired writer lived and wrote helps us to understand and interpret the Word of God. This particular passage is exceedingly difficult to comprehend by casual readers of today who have no knowledge of the contrast between orthodox Judaism as it existed during the first century and the new faith that was seemingly threatening the very existence of what had been considered as the true faith. The apostle Paul is taking the position that Judaism as it existed then was a misunderstanding and a misinterpretation of the will and plan of God.

Paul is contending that people have always found acceptance in the sight of God through faith in the promises of a Savior. The law was never given as a way of salvation by which people could secure acceptance in the sight of God. The law was given, first, to reveal the sinfulness of sin and, second, to help restrain and place limitations on evil.

Paul affirms in the strongest possible way that we become the children of God and the heirs of the promises of God through faith in Christ Jesus. The death of Jesus Christ delivers us from the penalty of the law and makes possible a new relationship with God.

I. Christ died that the blessing of Abraham might come on the Gentiles through faith (Gal. 3:14).

The law as such contains no provisions for the blessings of God upon the Gentiles. The blessings of God are to come upon the Gentiles because of a promise to Abraham (Gen. 12:1 – 3). This promise preceded the giving of the law by at least 430 years. The blessings of God come through faith in the promises rather than through obedience to a moral code.

II. Christ died that we might receive the promise of the Spirit through faith (Gal. 3:14).

Paul had already declared that the Spirit came by the hearing of faith rather than by the keeping of the law (3:2). Here he says that the promise and the coming of the Spirit are a result of Jesus' redeeming us from the curse of the law by his death on the cross.

III. Christ died to redeem us from the curse of the law (Gal. 4:4–5).

No one ever kept the law perfectly; consequently, the law brought only condemnation and guilt. In the fullness of time, God sent forth his Son to enter into the slave market of sin where all of us were in bondage, that by his death he might redeem us from the curse of the law.

IV. Christ died that we might receive adoption as the children of God through faith.

In other passages of Scripture, believers are spoken of as having a spiritual relationship with God established in the new birth. In this instance, Paul is speaking of a legal relationship with God. Adoption is the definite act in which God assigns to believers in Christ the title, the position, and the privilege of being his children. We are the adopted children of God, not through our efforts to keep the law, but through faith in Christ Jesus.

Conclusion

Not only are we the children of God through faith, but we are the heirs of God. Paul has spoken of an inheritance that we receive through faith in the promise of God (Gal. 3:18).

As the children of God, we are indwelt by the Spirit of God. The Spirit assures of our adoptive relationship to God. The Spirit seeks to reproduce within us the character of Jesus Christ. We can rejoice in these precious privileges that come to us through faith in Jesus Christ.

SUGGESTED PREACHING PROGRAM FOR

FEBRUARY

■ **Sunday Mornings**

Continue with the theme "Good News about God." The Bible is filled with good news that can cheer the hearts of God's people.

■ **Sunday Evenings**

Using the book of Isaiah, continue with the theme "The Ancient Prophet Speaks to the Present."

■ **Wednesday Evenings**

Continue with the studies in Paul's epistle to the Galatians. "Life in the Power of the Holy Spirit" is the theme of these messages.

SUNDAY MORNING, FEBRUARY 3

Title: The Good News of God's Great Love

Text: "For God so loved the world, that he gave this only begotten Son, that whosoever believeth in him should not perish, but have everlasting life" (**John 3:16**).

Scripture Reading: Romans 8:35–39

Hymns: "Love Divine, All Loves Excelling," Wesley

"At Calvary," Newell

"Love Lifted Me," Rowe

Offertory Prayer: Our loving heavenly Father, we thank you for the warmth of the sunlight, for the refreshing breezes that blow, and for the beauty of the world in which we live. We thank you for life, health, and friends. We thank you for your grace and mercy toward us, which you have revealed to us and toward us in Jesus Christ. Today we bring tithes and offerings to you because we love you and because we want others to experience your love. Bless these gifts to the proclaiming of the Good News around the world. Bless these offerings for the coming of your kingdom in the hearts of people. In the name of our Lord, we pray. Amen.

Introduction

Today with the help of the Holy Spirit let us confront what some believe to be the greatest verse of Scripture in the Bible. Let each of us examine John 3:16, and let us relate our heart and life to the greatest news about God that the human ear can ever hear.

46

By confronting the good news of John 3:16, we may discover our personal worth. To the football coach, a member of the team may be worth five yards. To an employer, a clerk may be worth four hundred dollars per week. To your child, you may be worth the price of the toys you bring home from time to time. But, to God, we are worth everything.

By studying our text, we become informed concerning the high cost of our wonderful salvation from sin. Salvation from sin is the free gift of God to those who will receive Jesus Christ as Lord and Savior. We cannot purchase it with money, and we cannot merit it with a life of moral excellence. However, its freeness to us does not mean that it did not cost God something. It cost him heaven's best—the life of his precious Son.

Let us confront the good news in our text in order that we may discover that there is hope for us as we face tomorrow. Not only has God loved us in the past, but the Scriptures teach us that nothing in the past, present, or future can separate us from the love of God in Christ Jesus, our Lord (Rom. 8:35–39). God loves us because it is his nature to love. His love for us in the future will not be determined by how lovable we are. We can face the future without any fear of the possibility of the withdrawal of divine love.

In the good news of our text, we may find an explanation for some of the mysteries of life. The disciples of our Lord could not even begin to comprehend why he was going to die; they were incapable of comprehending the full extent of God's love for them. There are many things that cannot be understood at the moment. Some of these things happen because God's love is at work, and we will be able to understand these mysterious things only from the perspective of history.

The good news of John 3:16 reveals the reason for our being and the purpose of our lives. God has poured out his love on us in order that through us he might love others.

The good news about God contained in the text explains the reason for the existence of the church in the world today. God continues to love the world. God continues to seek sinful people that he might save them from sin. He is doing this through his church, because the church is the chosen instrument for the proclamation of this good news. It deserves our love and loyalty.

I. The measure of God's great concern for us.

    A. *God has shown his concern through speech.*

    B. *God has shown his concern through his actions in history.*

        1. God chose Israel as his instrument.

        2. God has been patient with Israel despite Israel's unfaithfulness.

        3. God's command to the prophet Jonah illustrates his concern for a lost world.

        4. God's discipline of Jonah reveals his determination to deal redemptively with a lost world.

    C. *God has shown his concern through the gift of his Son, Jesus Christ.*

D. *God has shown his concern through the sufferings of his Son on the cross.*

E. *God has shown the good news of his love for us through the sufferings of his fatherly heart.*

F. *God has shown his concern through his patient waiting for people to return from the far country.* The parable that is often called the parable of the prodigal son is actually the parable of the waiting father. The prominent person in the parable is not the son who went astray. It is the father who waited with a longing heart to welcome the wayward son home.

II. The measure of Christ's concern for us.

A. *His concern can be seen in his perfect self-forgetfulness.*

B. *His loving concern can be seen in his perfect humility as he went about his tasks.*

C. *Christ's loving concern can be seen in his attitude of forgiveness toward those who nailed him to the cross.*

D. *Christ revealed the measure of his concern by his persistent efforts to save the very worst of people.*

E. *Christ revealed the measure of his concern by his persistent habit of always seeing the best in others.*

Conclusion

God's great concern for us was greater than his concern for the comfort of the Christ. God was willing to suffer and sacrifice in order that he might save people from the ravages of sin. God's concern for a lost world should move his children today to engage in evangelistic and missionary activities.

John the apostle put it very forcefully: "Hereby perceive we the love of God, because he laid down his life for us: and we ought to lay down our lives for the brethren" (1 John 3:16). The only way by which we can be absolutely certain that we are the children of God is to discover within us a concern similar to that which God had for us. We can know that we have passed out of spiritual death into spiritual life and that we are indeed the children of God if we find love for others within our hearts (1 John 3:14)—if we can discover within our hearts a compassionate concern that expresses itself in ministries of loving helpfulness toward the unfortunate (1 John 3:17–19).

Will others discover the measure of God's great love for them through our love for those about us? It will be exceedingly difficult for us to give an effective witness to the love of God unless we let God's love express itself through us in ministries to those who are in need in the world today.

God so loved you that he gave his only begotten Son that if you believe in him, you will not perish. He has made it possible for you to have everlasting life. Put yourself right in the middle of the good news of this great verse from the Word of God. Respond with full faith in the Christ who came and lived and died for your sins. You can have eternal life through him today if you have not already received this precious gift from God.

SUNDAY EVENING, FEBRUARY 3

Title: The Way to Life

Text: "A highway will be there; it will be called the Way of Holiness; it will be for those who walk on that Way. The unclean will not journey on it; wicked fools will not go about on it" **(Isa. 35:8 NIV)**.

Scripture Reading: Isaiah 35:1 – 10

Introduction

We live in a time of highway projects and road building. Turnpikes and freeways are springing up across the land. Bridges are being built over rivers and tunnels underneath. Yet none compare in importance to the "Way of Holiness" described by Isaiah. People have hewn out footpaths in deep valleys and along high mountains, treading blindly among the crevices of life. In contrast to the circuitous maze of man-made roads—whether footpaths or freeways—stands a mighty project, a divine highway: "the Way of Holiness." It is the way of life.

Forgetting Sennacherib's siege of Jerusalem, Isaiah looks toward the city's destruction by Babylon and the ensuing exile. Using poetic imagery, Isaiah describes God's deliverance from Babylonian exile and the return of faithful Israel. "The desert shall rejoice, and blossom as the rose" (35:1). God ordered Isaiah to speak words of encouragement to those on whom a total eclipse is about to descend: "Say to them that are of a fearful heart, Be strong, fear not: behold, your God will come with vengeance, even God with a recompense; he will come and save you" (35:4).

As usual, Isaiah is not content to speak only in terms of an immediate context. His vision is lifted beyond the return from Babylonian exile to the final deliverance of God, inaugurated by the coming of the Messiah, Jesus Christ: "Then the eyes of the blind shall be opened, and the ears of the deaf shall be unstopped. Then shall the lame man leap as an hart, and the tongue of the dumb sing" (35:5 – 6). No doubt this is one of the passages to which Jesus referred as proof that he was the Messiah (Matt. 11:1 – 5). What Christ did in the healing of a few people shall be done for all the redeemed, in a fuller way, at the consummation of the ages. Christ did not come to build the highway to God. He stood at the crossroads of the temporary trails of humans, on a hill called Golgotha, and proclaimed himself "the way, the truth, and the life" (John 14:6).

I. A clearly marked way (Isa. 35:8).

God's highway cannot easily be ignored. Isaiah pictures life in terms of the surrounding desert with its barren, tractless wastes. Well-worn trails disappeared overnight because of the blowing, shifting sands. Every path was temporary. Into such life God has prepared a "way of holiness." It is described in terms of a mighty roadway built on a high embankment, like some mighty monarch's royal road. It stands out against the barren, shifting sands of the desert.

49

The Bible and the church stand as visible road signs. People have tried to pull down the signs and burn them, but all such efforts have failed. People have tried to discredit God's Word, and yet it remains. They have sought to find fault with the church and thus discredit God's offered salvation. Admittedly there are churches that are like poorly lettered, darkly faded signs, but they point to an untarnished and unblemished Savior. Men are not accountable to a church but to the Savior. Yet the church stands, often weak but always indestructible, because it is God's ordained instrument for directing people to salvation.

God's way of life is easy to find, hard to miss: "The wayfaring men, though fools, shall not err therein" (Isa. 35:8). It is not that people cannot find this way. Rather, it is that people hesitate to commit themselves to this way, for it has its price. The way is a person—Jesus Christ. He must be accepted as Lord. He demands everything of his disciples.

II. A demanding way (Isa. 35:8, 10).

A. *Demands commitment.* One cannot travel the way to life without a faith commitment. This is how the journey is inaugurated. *Ransomed* and *redeemed* are terms used to speak of those who have willingly yielded to God's gracious call. Having found their guilt erased by the crucified Christ, they have committed themselves to the living Christ.

B. *Demands dedication.* Salvation is not merely a past experience. It is a present reality. Discipleship is a daily experience. There must be no reservations. The Christian life is not like a cafeteria where each person picks out what suits him. There is no place for harboring certain "decent sins."

We worry about the growth of liberal theology because it cuts things out of the Bible. The Virgin Birth is not rational, so liberalism snips it out. Miracles are not rational; hence, they too must fall before the scissors. The same lot befalls the doctrine of the resurrection. How can mortal humans dare to become judges of God's revealed Word? The answer is simple. Liberals do their scissor work just like the staunch conservative who reads that the tithe belongs to the Lord (Mal. 3:10) yet snips it out of his Bible by ignoring it, who reads about compassion and snips it out by indifference (Luke 15), who reads about the necessity of assembling for public worship (Heb. 10:25) and snips it out by making every other weekend a holiday.

III. A joyous way (Isa. 35:10).

The human soul has an inner yearning for a utopia wherein joy abides. Materialism, with its view that life consists in an abundance of things, is only one of the many mirages pursued by people today. The lure of a morality where sex outside of marriage is commonplace and acceptable is another popular mirage. The problem with mirages is that they promise satisfaction but never deliver. The fulfillment always vanishes at the last moment, leaving only frustration, shame, or emptiness.

In contrast to the world's illusions, God keeps his promises: "The parched ground shall become a pool" (Isa. 35:7). A more literal reading would be: "The mirage shall become a pool." God's promises do not vanish as the morning mists. The fountain of life is a reality that satisfies. The greatest and most joyous moment awaiting Christians is that time when heaven and earth pass away and the heavenly Zion is manifest for all to behold.

In the meantime, God's faithful have a daily joy of deliverance expressed by the psalmist: "He brought me up also out of an horrible pit, out of the miry clay, and set my feet upon a rock, and established my goings. And he hath put a new song in my mouth" (Ps. 40:2–3).

IV. The only way out (Isa. 35).

The "way of holiness" found in Christ is the only road without a dead end. It is the spiritual route open to every sinner who desires freedom from guilt and ruin. Isaiah 35 cannot be appreciated fully apart from the preceding chapter. The two chapters are in reality a poem divided into two parts. Isaiah 34 pictures the storm of God's judgment on sin. Isaiah 35 is the offer of peace in the midst of the storm. In Isaiah 34, Edom personifies all that opposes God. The final judgment is described as a time when "all the host of heaven shall be dissolved, and the heavens shall be rolled together as a scroll" (v. 4). God's wrath is real: "For the indignation of the LORD is upon all nations" (v. 2). "For my sword shall be bathed in heaven: behold, it shall come down upon Idumea, and upon the people of my curse, to judgment" (v. 5).

Whereas the Promised Land was divided by lot that every man might have his rightful inheritance, so shall hell be divided among those who have chosen it: "And he hath cast the lot for them, and his hand hath divided it unto them by line: they shall possess it for ever" (Isa. 34:17).

This coming storm is no accident. It is a part of the divine time table. The Bible stands as a solemn warning against that moment: "Seek ye out of the book of the LORD, and read: no one of these shall fail ... for my mouth it hath commanded" (Isa. 34:16).

Yet there is an alternative: the "Way of Holiness." All the forces of evil seek to keep people from that way of life. Only the gospel of Christ, the "Way of Holiness" offers any solution, any way to face these certainties in calm assurance.

Conclusion

Through faith in Christ, life becomes a pilgrimage that will reach its final destination beyond death. Death becomes merely the last port of entry this side of glory. It is said that recorded on Dean Alford's grave underneath an old yew tree in St. Martin's churchyard are the words "The inn of a traveler on his way to Jerusalem."

WEDNESDAY EVENING, FEBRUARY 6

Title: The Fruit of the Spirit

Text: "The Spirit ... produces in human life fruits such as these: love, joy, peace, patience, kindness, generosity, fidelity, tolerance and self-control" (**Gal. 5:22 PHILLIPS**).

Scripture Reading: Galatians 5:16–25

Introduction

In Paul's epistle to the Galatians, he places great emphasis on the ministry of the Holy Spirit. He affirms that believers receive the gift of the Spirit through faith. The Spirit comes in the moment of conversion to dwell in the heart of the believer and to provide assurance of salvation (Gal. 4:6).

The Holy Spirit comes into hearts to deliver believers from living on the level of fleshly appetites. The Holy Spirit lifts people to live on the level of the Spirit and to invest their lives in the things of the Spirit.

Paul declares that believers are to follow the leadership and guidance of the Spirit who dwells within rather than following the external code of the law given through Moses (Gal. 5:18).

Paul deals with the struggle of the Spirit with the earthly, fleshly nature that remains even after the miracle of the new birth has taken place. Only as we respond with faith in the Holy Spirit and with faithfulness in following his leadership can we overcome the fleshly nature and manifest the higher nature of children of God.

Paul contrasts the works of the flesh with the fruit of the Spirit.

I. The fruit of the Spirit is love.

The Holy Spirit pours out the love of God within the heart of the believer (Rom. 5:5). Our Lord commanded us to love not only our friends but even our enemies. The love he commands is a persistent, unbreakable spirit of goodwill that will manifest itself in our relationships with others.

II. The fruit of the Spirit is joy.

A study of the book of Acts reveals that when the Holy Spirit was doing his greatest works, believers were experiencing their greatest joy. Joy is a result of gratitude toward God because of his goodness to us. The Holy Spirit makes it possible for us to recognize and experience God's goodness and grace.

III. The fruit of the Spirit is peace.

Through faith in Jesus Christ, we obtain peace with God. By cooperating with the Holy Spirit, we enjoy a peace that defies human comprehension. This peace is something more than an absence of turmoil. It is an inward harmony with the will of God that brings tranquillity and poise even in the midst of unfavorable circumstances.

IV. The fruit of the Spirit is patience.

Patience is that gracious trait of being able to keep on keeping on, bearing the load of responsibility and difficulty. Many of us are very impatient. We do not have the disposition to stay with the task until it is completed. The Holy Spirit enables us to endure until we have finished the work that we were put here to accomplish.

V. The fruit of the Spirit is kindness.

Kindness is love in action with velvet gloves on. Kindness involves time, energy, and interest spent on others. Kindness can be expensive. Kindness toward others may bring inconvenience for us. Kindness is an attitude of thoughtfulness and helpfulness that enables us to render gentle service to others in their time of need. The Holy Spirit will enable us to serve in this spirit if we will permit him.

VI. The fruit of the Spirit is generosity, or goodness.

The Holy Spirit will enrich us with the blessings of God and will lead us to give ourselves extravagantly in service to others. The Holy Spirit will lead us to give ourselves until we have a warm feeling on the inside concerning the ministry we have rendered. The Holy Spirit will lead us out of stingy, self-centered ways of thinking and acting. He will enlarge our concern for others and cause us to walk in ways that are pleasing to God and to others.

VII. The fruit of the Spirit is fidelity.

We need to have faith in faith as the way to please God. We need to have faith in faith as the way that leads to the abundant life in the here and now. Real faith is more than just belief about God. Genuine faith expresses itself in fidelity to God and his will for our lives. The Holy Spirit will lead us to be faithful to our God, to his precious Book, to his church, to our family, to our Christian calling, and to our highest possible destiny in life. Our rewards in heaven will be determined largely by our faithfulness to the opportunities we have had. The Holy Spirit works within us to produce the fruit of faithfulness.

VIII. The fruit of the Spirit is meekness, or tolerance.

Meekness is not weakness, and tolerance is not compromise. The meek person is one who is completely under the control of the Spirit of God. He is open and responsive to the suggestions of God. At the same time, he is considerate and tolerant of others. God loves us and accepts us as we are. He does not wait until we have brought ourselves up to a certain quality or condition before he begins to love us. The Holy Spirit will lead us to love and to accept people as they are, because that is the way God responds to people.

IX. The fruit of the Spirit is self-control.

The Holy Spirit comes into our hearts to help us exercise self-control over our impulses and ambitions. He dwells within that he might warn us in the presence of evil and in the time of danger. He dwells within to help us overcome the appetites of the flesh that would be destructive to ourselves and hurtful to others and to create within us new appetites and aspirations. He delivers us from living according to the moods of the moment and impulses that would lead us astray.

Conclusion

If we are to experience the full fruit of the Spirit, we must recognize that the Holy Spirit does dwell within and that all of his purposes are benevolent. We need to respond to the thrilling truth that God's greatest works arise from within us rather than from external stimuli. The Holy Spirit is eager to produce within us that attitude and disposition of heart and mind that will manifest itself in our conduct and cause others to see the beauty of Christ within us.

SUNDAY MORNING, FEBRUARY 10

Title: The Good News of Divine Sonship

Text: "Beloved, now are we the sons of God, and it doth not yet appear what we shall be: but we know that, when he shall appear, we shall be like him; for we shall see him as he is" (**1 John 3:2**).

Scripture Reading: John 3:1–15

Hymns: "God, Our Father, We Adore Thee," Frazer

"A Child of the King," Buell

"This Is My Father's World," Babcock

Offertory Prayer: Heavenly Father, we rejoice in the glad consciousness of being your children. Today we come into your throne room to bring expressions of our love and gratitude in the form of tithes and offerings. Accept these tithes and offerings as symbols of our desire to be completely dedicated to your purposes in the world today. Bless not only these tithes and offerings, but bless us in the proper use of the money we retain for our own use. Help us to use what we have wisely and in a manner that will bring good into the hearts and lives of all concerned. We offer our gratitude through Jesus Christ our Lord. Amen.

Introduction

John, the beloved apostle, rejoiced over the good news of God's love for people as revealed in their obtaining divine sonship as a present possession. He saw this assurance of divine sonship as one of the expressions of God's great love for sinners (1 John 3:1).

John rejoiced in a precious gift from God that is a present possession. He rejoiced in the glad assurance that eternal life had come to himself and to other believers through faith in Jesus Christ. This great joy of knowing that you are a child of God is made possible by the birth from above, the birth of the Spirit.

I. The must of the new birth.

When Nicodemus, the ruler of the Jews, came to Jesus, he discovered that to truly be a child of Abraham and a child of God, a person must experience a birth from above, a birth of the Spirit (John 3:1–7). Nicodemus had labored under the mistaken impression that to be a citizen of the Jewish nation automatically made one a child of Abraham and a child of God. Jesus shocked and disturbed him with the news that Jewish citizenship was not adequate for a person to enter into the kingdom of God as a child of God. Jesus informed this outstanding Jewish religious leader that obedience to the law and a life of excellent moral behavior did not equip one for citizenship in heaven. Jesus affirmed that a spiritual birth must take place within the heart if one is to receive spiritual life and become a participant in the work of God on earth.

 A. *People need a new birth from above because of their sinful nature.* Since the fall of humankind, each descendant of Adam has received a nature that makes it natural to live a life of sin rather than a life of righteousness. In the natural state, people are not fit for heaven. In the natural state, people would not be happy in heaven if they could go there at the end of their earthly lives.

 B. *God's holy nature requires that we experience a new birth.* God is holy, righteous, and pure. God is love. For humans to have fellowship with God, they must have a nature similar to God's. This new nature is received in embryonic form in the spiritual birth experience by which believing sinners put faith and trust in the Lord Jesus Christ as Savior.

  Apart from a spiritual birth, people do not enjoy divine sonship. Instead, they are the children of the evil one (John 8:44). This may be a shocking truth for some to discover. People need to recognize that they do not receive the divine nature in the physical birth. They are, however, made with a capacity to experience the divine birth and to receive the divine nature.

II. The marks of the new birth.

 As children bear physical features and characteristics similar to those of earthly parents and grandparents, even so children of God will receive a new nature that will make it possible for them to experience and manifest the nature and the characteristics of the Father God.

 A. *A new appetite for righteousness.* Until people have experienced the new birth, they have no intense hunger and thirst for the things of God. Once they have been born into the family of God, they have a hunger for the things of God (Matt. 5:6). As a newborn baby hungers for nourishment, even so the new child of God will hunger for the truth about God and for fellowship with God.

 B. *A new adoration for God (1 John 4:19).* Until they have experienced the new birth, people may fear God and resent him as they rebel against him. Once the Spirit of God has brought about the miracle of the new birth within, there comes with it a love for the Father.

 C. *A new attitude toward sin (1 John 3:8–10).* Sin has been recognized as that which is destructive. It is that which brings harm and hurt into one's life. It is that which grieves the heart of God. Newborn Christians have within

55

their hearts turned from the love of sin. They want to do the will of God. They want to avoid that which is displeasing to God.

D. *A new affection for the people of God (1 John 3:14).* Those who have experienced the new birth now have a love for the church, the people of God, that they did not have before. They recognize in their fellow believers their brothers and sisters in Christ Jesus. They discover that there is a tie that binds their hearts together in Christian love and fellowship.

E. *A new desire to do the will of God (1 John 2:17).* Instead of revolting against the will of God, newborn Christians discover that the will of God is the road map to the highest possible happiness and to the greatest possible achievement in life. Obedience to the revealed will of God becomes the normal pattern for their behavior once they have experienced the miracle of the new birth.

III. The means to the new birth.

Our sonship with God is a spiritual relationship. It is the result of the creative activity of God's Spirit.

Our sonship is divine. We become partakers of the divine nature (2 Peter 1:4). The very nature of God is planted in the life center of the soul when we become new creatures in Christ Jesus.

In this experience, God becomes our Father. He knows our needs and our problems. He responds to us in love and mercy. Thus Jesus Christ becomes our Elder Brother. He is not only our Savior, but he is our Leader and Guide.

Conclusion

We do not obtain this experience of the new birth as the result of strict obedience to the law of God. Jesus Christ is the only one who has ever kept the law of God perfectly.

We do not receive the new birth as a result of great benevolence and faithful service. The new birth is a divine spiritual change that is wrought in the heart and life of a person when he responds with faith to the Christ who was lifted up to die for the sins of us all. As the Israelites looked with faith to the brazen serpent and were healed of the malady that was bringing about death, we must look with faith to Christ who was crucified that we might receive forgiveness and obtain the gift of eternal life (John 3:14–15).

The new birth is the divine side of the experience of our conversion. The human side calls for us to turn from the life of self-righteousness and sin and turn to Jesus Christ, trusting him and him alone for the forgiveness of sin and the gift of new life. This response on our part to the good news about God makes it possible for God to bring about within us the miracle of the new birth. Once this has happened, we can join with the apostle John in saying, "Now are we the sons of God."

SUNDAY EVENING, FEBRUARY 10

Title: Everything Is Going to Be All Right

Text: "Comfort ye, comfort ye my people, saith your God. Speak ye comfortably to Jerusalem, and cry unto her, that her warfare is accomplished, that her iniquity is pardoned: for she hath received of the LORD's hand double for all her sins" (**Isa. 40:1–2**).

Scripture Reading: Isaiah 40:1–24

Introduction

A husband stands facing his wife. He remembers the day she broke his heart by running away with another man. He remembers the day he read of her indictment in the paper after she unwittingly allowed her lover to involve her in a life of crime. Now she faces her husband, broken and repentant. Ahead of her lies a prison term. He opens his heart to her, and with a spirit of forgiveness, he reaches out to take her hand and says tenderly, "Everything is going to be all right." He is saying that when she has paid the punishment decreed by law, he will take her back, and together they will pick up the pieces of their marriage.

The assurance he gives to her is not an easy one. Rather, it is akin to the assurance of the doctor as he says to the patient, "Everything is going to be all right," but as he says it, he stands with a mask on his face, a scalpel in his hand, anesthetic nearby, and a great surgical light glaring down on the operating table. What he means is that after the operation and the healing, everything will be all right.

Isaiah 40 has this kind of tone. "Comfort ye, comfort ye," translated into our daily conversation, might be, "Everything is going to be all right." Having delivered God's prophecy of chastisement through wicked Babylon, Isaiah is called upon now to speak words of comfort, looking beyond the Babylonian captivity to God's restoration of his people. In Isaiah 39:6 the prophet proclaims, "Behold, the days come, that all that is in thine house, and that which thy fathers have laid up in store until this day, shall be carried to Babylon: nothing shall be left, saith the LORD." The coming judgment at the hands of Babylon is God's way of judging his own people for their sins. God's judgment, however, is always for a purpose. Following the judgment in Babylon, God's people are to be restored to their land and forgiven their sins.

I. When sin is forgiven (Isa. 40:2).

A. *Assurance of forgiveness.* With eyes of prophetic vision, Isaiah looks beyond the coming punishment to God's promised restoration. The phrase "Speak ye comfortably" has the literal meaning of speaking to the heart in order to give comfort. Spiritual comfort can come only after sin has been forgiven, after chastening has renewed the child of God. As much as they would like to, the church can offer no comfort to people as long

57

as they remain wayward and evil. Yet when people repent, God assures them of forgiveness. The prophet is told to proclaim forgiveness for Israel, because in the coming exile, they will suffer double for all their sins. Here the Old Testament law of retribution with regard to money is applied to the matter of judgment because of sin.

  B. *The price of forgiveness.* The Bible never presents forgiveness as a frivolous or simple process. The cost of sin is always high. It was over six hundred miles from Jerusalem to Babylon — a trip of at least four months for prisoners walking in chains. Not only were the Babylonians to rob them of all riches, but they were to make them slaves as well. One can scarcely imagine the mistreatment of women and children that transpired. Families were separated and husbands were tortured by the mistreatment of their families. Having declared their freedom from the living God, they found themselves being led away in chains.

Just as the moon is eclipsed when the earth comes between it and the sun, so our lives lie in darkness when we allow the material world to come between us and God. The Lord gave to the Israelites a Promised Land, and they in turn devoted themselves to the land instead of to the God who gave it.

Although the chastening has not yet come, Isaiah is so sure that it is to be followed by pardon that he speaks in the past tense: "Her iniquity is pardoned." It is this assurance that enables him to speak of comfort. Though God's chastisement may lie between our sin and our pardon, we gain encouragement by knowing that pardon does lie ahead.

II. When life is adjusted to God (Isa. 40:4–5).

  A. *Spiritual adjustment.* When Middle-Eastern monarchs prepared for long journeys, officials were sent ahead to pick the best route and to see that all the roads were passable. Ravines were filled in and rocky places smoothed over. The prophet uses this figure to speak of the spiritual adjustments necessary to make the message of comfort a reality. Before God can come into our lives to bring forgiveness, a way into our hearts must be prepared — a way hewn out by repentance. Each of us lives in a wilderness of human sin, and God will not force his way in. There are a lot of crooked things in our lives that must be made straight. There are self-indulgences that we must be willing to forsake.

  B. *Practical adjustment.* If spiritual adjustment is real, practical adjustment will follow. Genuine repentance always finds its way into practical application. All of life must be adjusted to God's schedule — our work days as well as our worship days. God's holy demands know no limits. They are not restricted to the stained-glass arena. The man who schedules seven full days of work for each of the fifty-two weeks of the year need not deceive himself into thinking that everything is going to be all right. A woman may choose to spend every penny she makes on her own needs, giving nothing for the work of the Lord, but she need not deceive herself into thinking that everything is going to be all right. A man may choose to have a profane mouth and a wayward heart, but let him never think that he will see the glory of the Lord.

III. When life's perspective is true (Isa. 40:6–8).

Twenty-twenty vision is never more necessary than when applied to our spiritual perspective. Unless we learn to see things in the proper order of their importance, we shall stumble into one wrong path after another.

A. *Concerning man.* The prophet is ordered to pronounce a message of comfort for the hearts of the people. Yet beyond that he seems unsure as to what message should follow. Then he finds God's direction: "A voice says, 'Cry out.' And I said, 'What shall I cry?'" Then comes the answer: "All people are like grass, and all their faithfulness is like the flowers of the field. The grass withers and the flowers fall, because the breath of the LORD blows on them. Surely the people are grass. The grass withers and the flowers fall, but the word of our God endures forever" (vv. 6–8 NIV). People are frail and temporary. Unless they realize their predicament, they are in no frame of mind to listen to the words of comfort from God. No one disdains offers to help quite so much as people who suppose they need none. People are so busy building their own kingdoms that they often overlook God's kingdom.

B. *Concerning God.* When people see themselves properly, they are in a position to see God in proper perspective. God is omnipotent and eternal. Whereas humans are frail and temporary, "the Word of our God shall stand for ever" (v. 8).

IV. When God is trusted (Isa. 40:27–28, 31).

A. *The natural cry.* People, because of their finite nature, are anxious creatures. So often the people of God do not actually trust in God. On every hand, the prophet Isaiah hears natural cries of anxiety: "My way is hid from the LORD, and my judgment is passed over from my God" (v. 27). The word translated "way" is commonly used to speak of one's fortune or fate. The word translated "judgment" refers to a lawsuit or petition. The people are saying, "Our destiny has been forgotten by God, and our petition for help has been neglected."

B. *The supernatural help.* To the discouraged, defeated exiles, Isaiah speaks of the divine help promised by God: "They that wait upon the LORD shall renew their strength; they shall mount up with wings as eagles; they shall run, and not be weary; and they shall walk, and not faint" (v. 31). The great God who has created the earth and sustains it with his power (v. 28) has the power to sustain his people. God will put a new strength in the place of their present weakness. This renewal will take place when the people learn to "wait upon the LORD."

The concept of waiting upon the Lord means not only to trust in him for deliverance but also to serve him daily. This is not a passive idleness; it is an active commitment. To wait upon the Lord means to do his every bidding, trusting in his wisdom and purpose even when they remain obscured to human perception. Kings have those who wait upon them to carry out their every whim. The King of Kings expects his people to do his bidding as well. God promises, "They shall not be ashamed that wait for me" (Isa. 49:23).

Conclusion

The Word of God speaks a message of hope to all the prodigals, whether their waywardness is at the point of lustful passion (like the adulterous woman confronted by Jesus), or self-righteous pride (as Nicodemus), or dishonest manipulation (as in the case of Zacchaeus). To all he says: "Behold your God! He comes to take you home." The good news of the gospel is that everything can be all right with God's help. We too can affirm with Paul, "We know that in everything God works for good with those who love him, who are called according to his purpose" (Rom. 8:28 RSV). And from this vantage point we can take the next step: "For I am persuaded, that neither death, nor life, nor angels, nor principalities, nor powers, nor things present, nor things to come, nor height, nor depth, nor any other creature, shall be able to separate us from the love of God, which is in Christ Jesus our Lord" (Rom. 8:38–39).

WEDNESDAY EVENING, FEBRUARY 13

Title: The Ministry of Restoration

Text: "Brothers and sisters, if someone is caught in a sin, you who live by the Spirit should restore that person gently. But watch yourselves, or you also may be tempted" **(Gal. 6:1 NIV)**.

Introduction

It is interesting to note how the words of our text are translated in some of the modern translations of the New Testament.

Williams New Testament, In the Language of the People: "Brothers, if anybody is caught in the very act of doing wrong, you who are spiritual, in the spirit of gentleness, must set him right; each of you continuing to think of yourself, for you may be tempted too."

The New Testament in Modern English: "Even if a man should be detected in some sin, my brothers, the spiritual ones among you should quietly set him back on the right path, not with any feeling of superiority but being yourselves on guard against temptation."

The New English Bible: "If a man should do something wrong, my brothers, on a sudden impulse, you who are endowed with the Spirit must set him right again very gently. Look to yourself, each one of you: you may be tempted too."

New International Reader's Version: "Brothers and sisters, what if someone is caught in a sin? Then you who are guided by the Spirit should correct that person. Do it in a gentle way. But be careful. You could be tempted too."

Our text confronts us with a message from God. It reveals the will of God for the family of God. It reveals the danger to which each of us is exposed. It reveals the duty to which love requires a response. It reveals a need that is urgent and continuous.

I. Who are these erring brothers and sisters?

    A. *Those who have experienced the birth of the Spirit.*
    B. *Those who rejoice in the love of the heavenly Father.*
    C. *Those who have a faith relationship with Jesus Christ.*
    D. *Those who live in the hope of an eternity of fellowship with the family of God in heaven.*

II. The danger to which erring Christians are exposed.

People are mistake-makers, and sin is an aggressive force. No one is immune from temptation and from the assaults of evil.

God's concern for our welfare does not come to a conclusion at the time of our conversion. Genuine conversion does not automatically produce spiritual maturity. We must beware of the peril of accepting a part of God's plan and provision for us instead of searching for and reaching forth to obtain the whole.

    A. *Some yield to the constant increased pressure to participate in practices that are socially acceptable but are spiritually destructive, such as excessive drinking and gambling.*
    B. *Some drift into the use of filthy and profane language.*
    C. *Some assume an attitude of self-righteousness that produces a harsh and critical spirit toward others.*
    D. *Some lower themselves by living on the level of instinctual needs.* They devote their interests and energy to the securing of food, sexual pleasure, and security.
    E. *Some seek to escape from the difficulties of life through drugs, alcohol, gaming, Internet activities, entertainment, seclusion, or noninvolvement.*
    F. *Some become so preoccupied that they neglect the means of spiritual growth.*

III. Our Christian duty toward erring Christians.

    A. *Our attitude toward those who fall into sin is of tremendous importance, because it can powerfully impact their lives.*
      1. We must put love to work in their behalf.
      2. We must practice forgiveness toward them.
      3. We should lift them up before God's throne of grace in prayer.

4. We should encourage them to consider the claims of Christ on their lives.
5. We should provide appropriate compassionate help to them with their difficulties.

B. *Our actions on their behalf are also of tremendous importance.*
1. We need to restore them to church attendance and Christian fellowship.
2. We need to restore them to a process of spiritual growth and service.
3. We need to try to restore them to activity and usefulness.
4. We need to restore them to harmony and understanding within the church family.

Conclusion

Our text is directed to those who are spiritual. The apostle has spoken concerning those who are indwelt by the Spirit (Gal. 4:6). He has also mentioned those who are led by the Spirit (5:18). He has discussed those who are experiencing the fruit of the Spirit (5:22–23). He also has given attention to those who are walking in the Spirit (5:25).

Clearly our Lord would have the most faithful, devoted members of the church, members of his family, dedicate their time and efforts toward restoring the erring believers who have fallen behind and are following afar off. We need to face up to our duty toward the erring members of our church family.

SUNDAY MORNING, FEBRUARY 17

Title: The Good News about Heaven

Text: "And I John saw the holy city, new Jerusalem, coming down from God out of heaven, prepared as a bride adorned for her husband" **(Rev. 21:2)**.

Scripture Reading: Revelation 21:1–4

Hymns: "Guide Me, O Thou Great Jehovah," Williams

"Face to Face with Christ," Breck

"O They Tell Me of a Home," Alwood

Offertory Prayer: Holy, heavenly Father, we bring ourselves to you. We offer ourselves as a living sacrifice to be devoted to your service. Help us day by day to make ourselves available to the guidance of the Holy Spirit that we may be your servants in the world. Today we bring tithes and offerings. Bless them for the advancement of your kingdom in ministries of mercy to those who suffer, to those who are in need, and to those who need support in your work. In Christ's name. Amen.

Introduction

Most of us do not spend very much time giving consideration to life beyond this life on earth. Perhaps this is because all of our treasures are in this world and we are living as if we are creatures of one world.

Jesus warned his disciples against the peril of investing their time, talents, and treasure in values that are perishable (Matt. 6:19–21). He affirmed that "where your treasure is, there will your heart be also." It is possible that our refusal to think about the life beyond is due to the fact that we have invested everything in this present life.

A part of the good news of the gospel that Jesus brought to the minds and hearts of people concerns the life beyond. Although he did not say as much about heaven as some would like, there is much in the New Testament that can bring comfort and confidence to the hearts of those who believe in Jesus as Lord and Savior.

I. The nature of heaven.

   A. *Heaven is described as a place (John 14:1).* The Bible does not describe the geography of heaven, neither is it explicit concerning its location or address. However, our Lord described it as a place.

   B. *Heaven is a prepared place.* We can assume that it is beautiful, commodious, comfortable, and appropriate for every need for the existence we will enjoy with God.

   C. *Heaven is a place of perfect holiness.* We read that nothing will enter heaven that would defile it (Rev. 21:17). The followers of Christ will be like him, for we will see him as he is (1 John 3:2).

      The battle with sin will be over. This will be one of the most wonderful things about heaven.

   D. *Heaven is described as a place of rest (Rev. 14:13).* This does not mean that the saints will spend eternity in idleness. It does mean that they will not know the burdens and tensions and discomforts of grueling labor as some have known it on earth.

   E. *Heaven is a place of active service (Rev. 22:3).* The children of God will be able to worship God and serve him in a manner that will bring joy to their hearts for ages without end once this life is over.

   F. *Heaven is a place from which tears, death, and pain will be exiled forever.* Sorrow and death will never again touch the lives of those who go to be with God.

   G. *Heaven is described as the home of the heavenly Father (John 14:2).* There the children of God will enjoy the hospitality of God. They will rejoice in his love, grace, and mercy. Love will be the law of heaven.

II. A description of heaven.

We search in vain for a literal description of heaven in the Bible. We get into all kinds of difficulties when we take symbolic language and try to make it literal. The descriptive powers of human language were likely exhausted as the inspired writers attempted to describe that which the Holy Spirit was revealing to them. Let us look at some of these descriptions of heaven.

   A. *Heaven is described as a tabernacle (Rev. 21:1–4).* In this beautiful pavilion, God comes to dwell with his people. Never again will they feel separated from God. Never again will they feel separated from each other. Never again will they experience suffering, sorrow, and death. They will dwell with God, and God will dwell with them, and they will have indescribable joy.

B. *Heaven is described as a beautiful city (Rev. 21:19–27).* The inspired writer exhausts the descriptive power of language as he seeks to set before us a picture of the splendid pageantry of a Middle-Eastern city. It is described as a place where the citizens enjoy perfect protection in absolute spaciousness in the midst of indescribable beauty.

C. *Heaven is described as a beautiful garden (Rev. 22:1–5).* In this beautiful garden, the necessities for eternal life are provided. In the midst of the garden is located the throne of God and the throne of the Lamb of God who came to take away the sin of the world. The original curse that had been placed on the earth is no longer in effect. The Lamb of God himself is the light, and there is no darkness.

Humans began their existence in a garden, and the book of Revelation, which portrays a picture of God's plan for the future, locates God and redeemed humans back in a beautiful garden.

III. The way to heaven.

The Bible is a record of the activity of God in which he has been seeking to restore humans to the garden from which they were cast because of sin. It is the desire of the Father that death be eradicated and that humans enjoy eternal life and fellowship with their Creator and Redeemer.

Heaven is described in such wonderful terms that it is illogical to believe that one could ever purchase at any price the privilege of spending eternity in the heavenly Father's home. It is illogical to believe that one could live good enough to merit the favor of God and to earn the privilege of spending eternity in heaven. People must beware of attempting to earn the privilege of entering heaven by their own efforts.

It is the testimony of the Word of God from beginning to end that those who go to heaven go because of the mercy and grace of God. There is no other way to reach heaven except through God's mercy and grace. The way to heaven is found only through faith in Jesus Christ. It was he who declared, "I am the way, the truth, and the life: no man cometh unto the Father, but by me" (John 14:6).

Jesus Christ was God in human flesh. He was appointed to be our Savior from the penalty of sin and therefore came and died a substitutionary death on the cross for us. He conquered death and the grave and revealed the reality of immortality by his resurrection from the dead. Christ alone has authority over death and can offer hope of a life beyond this life.

Christ alone gives people the gift of eternal life in the present. That life is received as a present possession by those who receive him into their hearts as Lord and Master. It continues beyond the experience we call death. It reaches its fulfillment and consummation in the heavenly Father's home described so beautifully in many different ways in the Scriptures.

Conclusion

What are your plans for eternity? Do you have any hope for a home beyond this life? Do you have a desire to be prepared not only for living the full and abundant life here and now but also living with God throughout the endless ages of eternity? If so, your hope is through faith in Jesus Christ.

Respond to Jesus Christ with the faith that causes you to make him the Lord of your heart and the Leader of your life. Let him bring the rule of heaven into your heart now, and you will discover that heaven has moved into your heart in the present. Heaven is not only a place in the hereafter; it can be an experience in the heart of believers now. "When Christ, who is our life, shall appear, then shall ye also appear with him in glory" (Col. 3:4).

SUNDAY EVENING, FEBRUARY 17

Title: Belonging to God

Text: "But now thus saith the LORD that created thee, O Jacob, and he that formed thee, O Israel, Fear not: for I have redeemed thee, I have called thee by thy name; thou art mine" **(Isa. 43:1).**

Scripture Reading: Isaiah 43:1–24

Introduction

The loneliest people in the world are those who do not feel they belong to anyone or anything. This kind of solitary loneliness can be felt even in the midst of a great crowd. You can rub shoulders with people all day long and still feel alone unless you can feel you belong to someone. One of the great threats of our advanced technology is the shattering process of making our lives so impersonal.

I. Brings assurance (Isa. 43:2).

    A. *Companionship amid trials.* The Lord who begins by saying, "I have redeemed thee, I have called thee by thy name; thou art mine," elaborates on what it means to belong to him by continuing, "When thou passest through the waters, I will be with thee; and through the rivers, they shall not overflow thee: when thou walkest through the fire, thou shalt not be burned; neither shall the flame kindle upon thee" (v. 2). Dangerous waters on the rampage and fiery conflagrations are but metaphors to depict the trials that come to every person sooner or later in life. God does not promise they will bypass his children. Rather, he promises to face them with his children.

    B. *Courage amid fears.* Not only do we find ourselves beset by trials on every hand, but we find ourselves worrying about things that have not yet happened but which may well happen. In the face of such prospects, God says, "But now thus saith the LORD that created thee, O Jacob, and he that formed thee, O Israel, Fear not" (v. 1). Having affirmed his presence

65

in every trial, God continues by reiterating again his concern about our fears: "Fear not: for I am with thee" (v. 5). In the midst of our anxieties about tomorrow, God tells us we need not fear. In our mad scramble for earthly security, God tells us we need not fear.

II. Sets forth life's basic purpose (Isa. 43:10).

When people decide to belong to God, they at the same moment find growing out of their relationship with the heavenly Father their reason for existence. To be called by name (Isa. 43:1) is to be called to a purpose. Isaiah outlines this purpose for us: "Ye are my witnesses, saith the LORD, and my servant whom I have chosen" (v. 10). Every child of God takes on the role of a key witness. "I'd rather not be involved" is not an option. You either testify concerning the truths of God or you perjure yourself.

A. *The audience.* To whom are you to witness? To a very definite audience: "Bring forth the blind people that have eyes, and the deaf that have ears. Let all the nations be gathered together, and let the people be assembled: who among them can declare this, and show us former things? Let them bring forth their witnesses, that they may be justified: or let them hear, and say, It is truth" (Isa. 43:8–9). Isaiah vividly pictures a gigantic courtroom where all the unbelievers of the world are gathered to give account of their ungodliness. They must provide proof that they are justified in their unbelief, or they must accept the truth of God. They are the people who have eyes yet are blind to what is real. They have ears, yet they are deaf to the message of God. Once assembled, God's message is to be presented by his own witnesses—his children. The prophet is merely reminding us that not only is "all the world a stage," but in a very real sense, all the world is a courtroom.

B. *The message.* What shall we tell the unbelieving world? God does not leave this to our imagination. Instead, he outlines our message for us: " 'I, even I, am the LORD, and apart from me there is no savior. I have revealed and saved and proclaimed—I, and not some foreign god among you. You are my witnesses,' declares the LORD, 'that I am God. Yes, and from ancient days I am he. No one can deliver out of my hand. When I act, who can reverse it?' " (Isa. 43:11–13 NIV).

God's declaration (Isa. 43:12) has to do with his control of events. God is able to *predict* the future because he has the power to *determine* the future. The future will be as he desires it. History is under God. This means nations and people are under God. Two definite historical references are mentioned. God declared his intention to set the Israelites free from Egyptian bondage and then brought it to pass (vv. 16–17). The brilliance of Pharaoh's armed might became like a tiny candle that God easily blew out, leaving only darkness. The second reference is to God's destruction of Babylon in order to set Israel free of their captivity (v. 14). God predicted the Babylonian captivity as his personal chastening and predicted the return from exile as his personal promise. We must ever point the unbelieving world to the only God and remind them that he never abdicates his throne.

C. *The implied warnings.* God promises that those who belong to him will be his witnesses one way or another. We can be a witness of the victory that comes to the person of faith, or we can be a witness of the chastening love of God that sometimes comes because of disobedience. The Lord reminds us that up to the present time about all we have brought to him are our sins: "You have burdened me with your sins and wearied me with your offenses" (Isa. 43:24 NIV). Israel was sent into exile because they failed to be witnesses of God's grace. God explains it as follows: "Who gave Jacob for a spoil, and Israel to the robbers? did not the LORD, he against whom we have sinned? For they would not walk in his ways, neither were they obedient unto his law" (42:24). God seems to be saying that one way or another he intends to make something out of us.

III. Depends on conversion (Isa. 43:1).

Belonging to God brings a wonderful assurance and a meaningful existence to life. However, not everyone belongs to God in the sense the Bible here intends. Only through personal conversion does any person belong to God. Although God is the creator of all, and although he sent his Son to die for all people, only those who voluntarily choose to surrender to his grace and love can accurately be termed his children. It is to those who have experienced conversion that God speaks: "I have redeemed thee, I have called thee by thy name; thou art mine" (v. 1). The significant word here is "redeemed." It has in it the idea of the payment of price. A man could redeem a slave by paying the owner the price on his head. After that, if the new owner desired, he could set the slave free. There is a sense in which every man finds himself on the auction block of life. Yet unlike the slave of Isaiah's day, or even of pre–Civil War days, every person has the privilege of crying, "No sale!" God offers to redeem us, but we can refuse his offer. We can choose to reject the privilege of belonging to God.

Because of sin and unbelief, people find themselves scattered amid the perishing dust like a priceless gem lost and overlooked. God graciously reaches down and offers to lift us out of our helpless plight and restore us to a place in his spiritual family. Literature is full of stories centering around the theme of a lost heir or a lost prince, living in obscurity, who suddenly is discovered and restored to his rightful place of inheritance. This, in effect, is the good news of the gospel.

A. *Conversion is expensive.* We must never let God's gracious offer to bail us out cause us to forget the great cost involved. Through Isaiah, God reminded the Israelites that their deliverance had come at great expense: "I am the LORD your God ... I give Egypt for your ransom, Cush and Seba in your stead" (43:3 NIV). He continued, "For your sake I will send to Babylon and bring down as fugitives all the Babylonians, in the ships in which they took pride" (v. 14 NIV). He said, "Since you are precious and honored in my sight, and because I love you, I will give people in exchange for you, nations in exchange for your life" (v. 4 NIV).

B. *Conversion is undeserved.* God reminds us that about all we have brought to him are our liabilities—our sins (Isa. 43:24). He does not offer us deliverance because of all that we have done for him or because of the sacrifices we have brought him. Rather, it is out of his grace: "I, even I, am he who blots out your transgressions, for my own sake, and remembers your sins no more" (v. 25 NIV). In our own strength, we can never overcome our sin and stand on bargaining ground with God.

C. *Conversion is a necessity.* Most of life's needs can be substituted, but the need for personal salvation is irreplaceable. Whatever else a person may have, unless he or she has God's salvation, that person is on a journey to despair. Kierkegaard warned of the danger of losing one's own self without being aware of it. If a man loses an arm or a leg, he knows it. If he loses a fortune, he is aware of it. If he loses his family, he lives in grief because of it. Yet a person can lose his own soul and allow the loss to go unnoticed.

Conclusion

When a man and woman decide to marry, they come together in a public ceremony and pledge the commitment of their hearts. This is an outward sign of their inner commitment. When men or women join the armed forces, they are asked to raise their right hands and repeat a pledge. This is an outward sign of an inner commitment to duty. Therefore it is not out of place for God to expect us to publicly commit our lives to him in faith. Belonging to God is our greatest opportunity. Let us claim it!

WEDNESDAY EVENING, FEBRUARY 20

Title: A Cross or a Burden?

Text: "For every man shall bear his own burden" **(Gal. 6:5)**.

Scripture Reading: Galatians 6:2–5

Introduction

As Paul writes concerning the outward expression of our inward experience with Christ, he talks in terms of burdens and crosses. He glories in the cross of the Lord Jesus rather than in his obedience to the law of Moses.

He also speaks concerning the manner in which we are to deal with the burdens of life. Some people consider every burden as a cross. This is not necessarily a true concept. While a cross may be a burden, not every burden is necessarily a cross. The Christian's cross is something that he or she voluntarily assumes and bears for the glory of God. Burdens may come on us without our choosing to accept them. Burdens are inevitable in life. To recognize the burden of a fellow believer will cause us to be slow to criticize and eager to sympathize.

I. "Every man shall bear his own burden" (Gal. 6:5).

A. *Every individual has a work or responsibility.*

B. *Each individual must assume his or her own work or responsibility.* We cannot transfer the individual burden that we should be bearing to the shoulders of someone else.

C. *Each individual must bear the burden of responsibility for his or her own decision for or against Jesus Christ.*

II. "Bear ye one another's burdens" (Gal. 6:2).

A. *Some burdens must be shared.*

1. The members of a family share certain burdens.
2. Community burdens must be shared by generous people.
3. The church is a fellowship of those who are banded together to share burdens for God, for each other, and for those in need.

B. *We are to be of service to those who labor under a crushing burden of guilt (Gal. 6:1).* We are instructed to be compassionate toward them and to put forth the efforts that are necessary to effect their restoration.

C. *We are to live for others in terms of the compassionate concern that our Lord commanded (John 13:34).* The poet put it in the following words:

Lord, help me live from day to day
In such a self-forgetful way
That even when I kneel to pray
My prayer shall be for others.

—C. D. Meigs

Conclusion

Our Lord assumed the burden of our guilt and sin (John 1:29). He lifted the burden of condemnation from our hearts. Because our greatest burdens have been lifted, we are to help others with the burdens that life brings to them.

The psalmist had a word for all of us at this point. He said, "Cast your cares on the LORD and he will sustain you" (Ps. 55:22 NIV).

SUNDAY MORNING, FEBRUARY 24

Title: The Good News Concerning God's Present Activity

Text: "For it is God which worketh in you both to will and to do of his good pleasure" (**Phil. 2:13**).

Scripture Reading: Philippians 2:12–16

Hymns: "Come, Thou Almighty King," Anonymous

"He Leadeth Me! O Blessed Tho't!" Gilmore

"Have Thine Own Way, Lord," Pollard

Offertory Prayer: Holy Father, it is impossible for us to express our thanks adequately for the abundance of your blessings upon us. You are gracious to grant to us the privilege of being your children. We thank you for the gift of eternal life. We also thank you for lesser gifts that are present in the world about us. We make our gratitude tangible by bringing tithes and offerings to your altar. Bless the use of these gifts in communicating the wonders of your love and the measure of your mercy. Bless these gifts to the relief of human suffering and to the enrichment of the human spirit, and may your name be honored and glorified in it all. Amen.

Introduction

When Paul wrote to the Christians in Corinth, he gave them a statement of the good news about God in capsule form. He described this good news as being centered in the death of Jesus Christ for our sins according to the Scriptures, and he explained that Jesus was buried and then arose on the third day according to the Scriptures (1 Cor. 15:1–4).

Many of us have never entered into our heritage and legacy as children of God and followers of the Lord Jesus because we have thought of the gospel as being good news about something that happened almost two thousand years ago. If we would fully respond to the Good News, we must see it in its present significance. We must recognize and respond to the present good tidings of the activity of God.

There is a vital and inseparable relationship between the good news about God as it was expressed historically in the life, death, and resurrection of Jesus Christ and his activity in the present. We do injury to the gospel if we do not recognize its relevance for the hour in which we live.

Our text deals with the good news concerning God's activity today. This is the gospel that must be preached and proclaimed throughout the whole world. This is the good news that we need to discover and rejoice in and get excited over. We must not leave the activity of God in the distant past or think of it only in terms of something that is going to happen in the future. God is at work in the world today within and for his children.

I. God is within you.

It is one thing to talk about the majesty and the glory of the Creator God who spoke and caused the sun to start shining. It is another thing to recognize that the eternal God who sits on the circle of the earth has come to dwell within the heart of each believer.

He is the God of love, grace, mercy, and power. He is the creator, sustainer, and consummator of history.

The God who gave his Son to die on the cross for our sins has chosen to come and dwell within us by his Spirit. He is a God near at hand rather than a God afar off. He is the God who has promised never to leave us nor forsake us. He suffers for us in our sufferings and rejoices for us in our times of victory.

II. God is at work within you.

A. *God is no absentee God.* He did not create the world, wind it up like a clock, and then abandon it. Our God is at work in his world. The good news of our text is that God is at work in our hearts. He works within us to deliver us from evil and lead us toward the good.

God is at work within our homes. He wants to help husbands and wives to be at their very best toward each other. He wants to assist us as we face the complexities of the task of rearing our children during these frustrating and dangerous days.

B. *God often works within us by giving us a holy dissatisfaction with ourselves as we are (Matt. 5:3–5).* He convicts us of our sins and brings about grief within us over our faults and failures.

C. *God works within us by giving us a holy ambition and desire for the things of God (Matt. 5:6).* God intensifies the hunger and thirst of our soul for the things that are spiritually enriching and morally uplifting.

D. *God works within to assure us of the possibility of our achieving those things that are good in life (Phil. 4:13).* Through Christ Jesus we are able to adjust ourselves to whatever the circumstances of life may bring.

III. God's work within us is always good.

Our text declares that God works within us both to will and to do that which is in harmony with his perfect character and with his good pleasure for us.

God never works to accomplish evil in the lives of those who trust him. Behind his every purpose for us, there is benevolence, love, mercy, and grace.

A. *God helps us to arrive at the right decisions concerning the issues of life.* God works internally. He helps us to have an enlightened intellect; a sensitive, warm, responsible heart; and a will that wants to do his will.

B. *God is at work within us to help us have the mind of his Son, Jesus Christ.* Concerning Jesus, the Father said, "This is my beloved Son, in whom I am well pleased." God works within us so that he may be able to say concerning us at the end of the way, "Well done, thou good and faithful servant."

Conclusion

There is good news concerning God's present work for believers. God is at work within us that we may experience and achieve his wonderful purpose for us. We are not alone in our quest to live in the realm of the Spirit and by the law of the kingdom of heaven. God will continue his good work within us.

There is good news about God for nonbelievers. Perhaps you have delayed your decision to trust Jesus Christ because you have the fear that you would disappoint both God and yourself by your failure to live as you believe a Christian ought to live. You are to be commended for recognizing that Christ within the heart should make a difference. However, you should be aware of the fact that no one can live a Christian life in human strength and in the power of human resolution alone.

The Christian life is not that of straining to do the best that we can in the strength of the flesh alone. The Christian life is a cooperative venture in which we invite Jesus Christ to come in. We grant to God the place that belongs to him in our hearts. In the conversion experience, we decide and pledge to cooperate with God as he works his good work within us.

This is the good news about God's work in the present.

SUNDAY EVENING, FEBRUARY 24

Title: The Empty Man

Text: "Such a person feeds on ashes; a deluded heart misleads him; he cannot save himself, or say, 'Is not this thing in my right hand a lie?'" **(Isa. 44:20 NIV)**.

Scripture Reading: Isaiah 44:1–20

Introduction

Despite the economic downturn in recent years, our society remains relatively affluent. We have more of everything, and everything we have is bigger and better. Yet amid the fullness of prosperity walk multitudes of empty people. We have learned to live behind a glossy, successful veneer in order to hide the gnawing inner hollowness of our lives.

Many of the extremes of our age are merely efforts to find some meaning for life. The pain of emptiness is not easily sedated. Among the most prominent of the attempted cures are alcohol, drugs, and sex. Yet this is not true of every empty person. Some have high morals that will not permit such means of escape. They are the people whose only other avenue of escape seems to be the addition of activity after activity to an already busy life in an attempt to drown out the pain of emptiness and meaninglessness. Isaiah says of the empty person, "Such a person feeds on ashes."

I. Committed to a superficial view of life (Isa. 44:6–20).

A. *The distortion.* The phrase "Such a person feeds on ashes" is a proverbial saying used to refer to that which has no purpose. The man who feeds on ashes took a wrong turn somewhere back down the path and finds himself following a very superficial view of life: "A deluded heart misleads him." There are times when poor eyesight is the result of improper diet. In much the same fashion, the empty man's distorted view of life is because of his daily consumption. He has been filling his life with the temporary. He is concerned only with the physical.

B. *The confusion.* Any view of life that does not include God presents a tragic distortion. The fruits are utter confusion. The world is so busy demanding that the Christian come up with answers for every injustice or tragedy that it fails to examine its own destitute worldview. The Christian has an assurance of purpose because of his trust in the heavenly Father: "Thus saith the LORD the King of Israel, and his redeemer the LORD of hosts; I am the first, and I am the last; and beside me there is no God" (v. 6). The Christian looks around and realizes that God is the originator of all he sees.

The empty man, with his bankrupt philosophy, fails to see that science is merely a human attempt to discover the mechanics of God's working. Instead, he makes of the study a god. He fails to see that certain basic laws of morality have been set in operation and cannot be violated without harm. He feels free to write his own moral code and then wonders why he is left empty. He views the church as merely another civic club and fails to see that in spite of its human weaknesses, it is indeed the divine instrument of God to bring about God's kingdom. In such a state of bewilderment, the empty man supposes that one religion is as good as another, since none could be very important. He fails to see that he has made many and sundry gods of his own. To present this truth, Isaiah vividly depicts the situation of a man who chops down a tree (which grew because of God's sun and rain) in order to build a fire and cook his meal. Unaware of how ludicrous his actions are, he takes what is left of the tree and fashions from it an idol for himself and then prays to it for deliverance, saying, "Save me! You are my god!" (vv. 9–17 NIV).

II. Committed to a temporary hope (Isa. 44:20).

The empty man's basic fault is not a lack of commitment. Rather, it is that his commitment is a short-range one. The lamp of earthly hope casts at best a dim shadow, and its feeble gleams stop short at the grave. The final resting place of all his hopes is a crude hole in the damp earth. The boundary of his hopes is the mere dimensions of a coffin.

Such a man has chosen only an earthly itinerary. He has planned no other journey. Having eluded God's stamp, he has at one and the same time eclipsed God's promises. While others know the joy of crying, "I am the LORD's" (v. 5), he feels the loneliness of belonging only to himself.

In the Middle Ages, people often took pilgrimages to holy places, including the Holy Land itself. However, the greatest pilgrimage of all is that of the soul, which has nothing to do with geography or transportation. Rather, it is a pilgrimage of faith whereby one comes out of the shell of self-righteousness and into the warmth of God's grace. It is just this experience that sets a person on the eternal journey and its heavenly destination.

Commitment to a temporary hope circumscribed by the grave is to come at last to face the end of life alone—without God! I have read many testimonies of faithful Christians who have approached death, and in the moment of its grip, given their greatest testimony of assurance. I have read of atheists coming to the end of life and crying out in pathetic tones their futile feelings. I have never read any account of such people facing death with a glowing testimony endorsing their way of life.

From the great historical array of people who have sought to stand alone,

one can pick out men like Ahab, king of Israel. One glance at him lying in a pool of his own blood with an arrow piercing the tiny chink in his kingly armor has a way of obscuring his past years of lustful pleasure. His was the horror of dying alone. Or look at the wicked Herod (Acts 12) strutting about as a god and displaying himself as one who could live without God. Then see him stricken and dying alone. History is full of such examples of people whose hope was terribly temporary and pitifully limited. They are the empty people — people all dressed up with everything the world has to offer but with no place to go but to the cemetery and the lake of fire. The empty person has an empty hope because "he cannot save himself" (v. 20 NIV).

III. Committed to a lie (Isa. 44:20).

Not only is the empty man unable to deliver his soul, but he is also unable to admit that his greatest defense is nothing more than a lie. He does not seem able to say, "Is not this thing in my right hand a lie?" (v. 20 NIV). David faced Goliath with only a slingshot in his hand. However, he himself was in God's hand. The empty man faces the struggles and trials of life as well as the tentacles of death with nothing more than a lie in his hand. The lie to which he is committed is that somehow everything will work out all right. Satan assured Adam and Eve that the transgression of God's commandment would not matter greatly one way or another. His propaganda has changed little since that time. The Bible is bad news as well as good news. The bad news is that nothing works out all right apart from God. Only to those who "love the Lord" do "all things work together for good" (Rom. 8:28).

Life without God is like a long row of ciphers. It adds up to nothing. Put a digit in front of the ciphers and suddenly it means millions. Try taking God away, and life becomes an empty mausoleum. This is the testimony of the writer of Ecclesiastes. He tried all the pleasures and pursuits offered by life and concluded that they were all "vanity of vanities." It was not until he discovered God that other pursuits took on meaning. When God is ignored, some form of idolatry is all that is left, and the Bible reminds us that an idol is nothing — it is a lie.

Conclusion

In our nuclear age when there is much concern about survival should a bomb get into the wrong hands, we need to recognize that failure to survive is not the greatest danger. Rather, we should shun the possibility of survival without meaning or purpose. In a dog-eat-dog world, the empty man has learned to survive. What he has not learned is how to live. Novelist James Barrie writes, "The life of every man is a diary in which he means to write one story and writes another; and his humblest hour is when he compares the volume as it is with what he vowed to make it." Yet it is just such an inventory that is needed. The empty man sees life as an end in itself. But it is not so. Life is a battle to determine who is to serve in God's eternal kingdom. The empty man seeks only to dodge danger and stay alive. The wise man commits himself to the army of the eternal God and loses himself in service. It is in this very experience that emptiness fades away and fullness becomes a reality.

WEDNESDAY EVENING, FEBRUARY 27

Title: The Marks of the Lord Jesus

Text: "From henceforth let no man trouble me: for I bear in my body the marks of the Lord Jesus" **(Gal. 6:17)**.

Scripture Reading: Galatians 6:11–18

Introduction

Paul has delivered his message to the followers of Christ in the churches of Galatia. He has insisted that they put their faith in the Lord Jesus Christ rather than depend on keeping the law and observing the Mosaic traditions. He brings this epistle to a conclusion by declaring that he bears in his own body the marks of the Lord Jesus. Perhaps he is drawing a contrast between the distinguishing characteristics of a Christian and that which set the Jewish people apart from the pagan world. They placed great emphasis on the rite of circumcision being one of the distinctive marks of a son of Abraham.

Paul has emphasized the fruit of the Spirit in contrast to the works of the flesh (Gal. 5:19–26). It is highly possible that the apostle is talking about the literal scars that he bears on his body, suffered because of his faith in and his faithfulness to the Lord Jesus Christ (2 Cor. 11:24–27). It is not very likely that modern-day followers of Jesus Christ will be beaten and stoned as was the apostle; however, it is possible for us to bear in our bodies the marks of the Lord Jesus. It is possible for us to have distinctive features or distinguishing characteristics that will indicate to the world that we have been with Jesus Christ.

What were some of the distinctive features of Jesus Christ that can be reproduced in the life of his followers today?

I. Christ was full of the Holy Spirit (Luke 4:1, 14).

Our Lord was full of the Spirit and was led by the Spirit. It was by the power of the Spirit that he preached the good news of the kingdom, cast out demons, and rendered the ministries of the kingdom (Luke 4:14–19).

Our Lord commanded his apostles to wait in the city of Jerusalem until they were endued with the power of the Spirit so they could carry forward his redemptive program in the world (Luke 24:49). The Holy Spirit came on the day of Pentecost to abide within the hearts of Jesus' disciples and to enable them to do his work. His is to be an abiding ministry (John 14:16–18).

As the followers of Jesus Christ, we are commanded to "be filled with the Spirit" (Eph. 5:18). There is no way by which modern followers of Jesus Christ can reflect the presence of Jesus Christ unless they make a positive response to the

75

indwelling Spirit. We must depend on him for assistance in studying the Word of God, for praying, and for giving our Christian testimony.

One of the distinctive marks of the Lord Jesus was that of being filled with the Spirit. If we are to bear in our body the marks of the Lord Jesus, we must cooperate fully with the Holy Spirit.

II. Christ was fully surrendered to the will of God (John 4:34; Luke 22:42).

To Christ the will of God was not something that fate put upon him. The will of God was not something to resist or to revolt against. The will of God was the good plan of God by which he was to bring honor and glory to God and to render the greatest possible service to humankind. The will of God was also the pathway by which he would achieve his highest personal destiny in life. He lived and labored to do the will of God at all times. Jesus was able to say to his Father at the end of his earthly life, "I have brought you glory on earth by finishing the work you gave me to do" (John 17:4 NIV).

If we want to bear in our body the marks of the Lord Jesus, we will commit our lives fully and joyfully to the will of God as we understand it. To pray, "Thy will be done" is not merely to resign oneself to the difficulties and disappointments of life. It should be a pledge of confidence and cooperation with the loving Creator whose purposes for us are always purposes of love.

III. Christ lived in order to serve (Mark 10:45).

Our Lord did not define his purpose for being in terms of securing the service and the ministries of others. He lived and labored that he might minister to the deepest needs of others. He was the servant of God, and he was the servant of people. Someone has said that the best biography of Jesus is found in the statement that he "went about doing good" (Acts 10:38). Our Lord lived by the principle of love. He deliberately went about doing good. He was full of grace and truth.

If we would bear in our body the marks of the Lord Jesus, we must see ourselves as channels through which the blessings of God flow toward others. We must not become a reservoir into which the blessings of God enter without finding an outlet.

Our Lord pictures the judgment scene as being a time in which his servants will be highly commended because of their ministries of service to the least, the weakest, and the neediest (Matt. 25:31–40). Unless we define life in terms of an opportunity to serve, there is no way by which we can consider ourselves genuine followers of the Lord Jesus Christ.

IV. Christ came to seek and to save the lost (Luke 19:10).

A. *Christ came to earth that he might save people from the awful penalty and from the tragic waste of sin (Matt. 1:21).*

B. *Our Lord lived and labored, suffered and died that he might be the Savior of humankind.*

C. *Our Lord lives forever and intercedes in the interest of those who come to him that he may save them completely (Heb. 7:25).* Since our Lord lived to be the Savior, it would follow that we must live to help people come to know the Savior. Our Lord's Great Commission must involve every disciple of the Lord Jesus in helping others become disciples. Our Lord indicated that as we go about from place to place, we are to be involved in the task of making disciples (Matt. 28:19). The imperative in this verse is not at the point of going; the imperative is in the word that is translated "teach." We are to make disciples in our going about from place to place.

If we are true followers of the Lord Jesus, and if we bear in our body his marks, we will be involved in ministries that point toward the salvation of those about us.

Conclusion

The desperate need of our day is for Christians to bear in their bodies the marks of the Lord Jesus. We need to think as he thought. We need to love as he loved. We need to serve as he served. We need to forgive as he forgave. We need to be reflectors of his love.

The notorious agnostic Robert Ingersoll had a godly aunt. He once sent her a copy of one of his books in which he attacked the Bible. On the flyleaf, over his signature, he wrote, "If all Christians lived like Aunt Sarah, perhaps this book would never have been written!"

If we will bear in our body the marks of the Lord Jesus consistently and cheerfully, many will come to know the Lord Jesus Christ because of our influence.

SUGGESTED PREACHING PROGRAM FOR
MARCH

■ **Sunday Mornings**

The gospel is the glad tidings of all that God did and continues to do through Jesus Christ. Complete the series "The Good News about God." Appropriate sermons are provided for Palm Sunday and Easter, the last two Sundays of the month.

■ **Sunday Evenings**

Complete the series "The Ancient Prophet Speaks to the Present." On the last Sunday evening of the month, begin the series "Important People You Should Know." These messages are based on the lives of Old Testament characters.

■ **Wednesday Evenings**

The theme for Wednesday evenings this month is "Timeless Truths for Modern Times."

SUNDAY MORNING, MARCH 3

Title: The Good News in God's Final Invitation

Text: "The Spirit and the bride say, Come. And let him that heareth say, Come. And let him that is athirst come. And whosoever will, let him take the water of life freely" **(Rev. 22:17)**.

Scripture Reading: Matthew 11:28–30

Hymns: "O Worship the King," Grant

"Glory to His Name," Hoffman

"I Am Coming, Lord," Hartsough

Offertory Prayer: Holy, heavenly Father, we lift our hearts to you in reverent worship and praise. We thank you for your mercy and grace toward us in all areas of life. You have been gracious to us beyond our hopes and expectations. We never could deserve your generosity and kindness to us.

Today we bring a portion of the fruits of our labors and offer them up as a loving expression of our gratitude. Help us to be the channel through which your blessings continue to reach the hearts and lives of others. Bless these offerings to relieve suffering and to lead men and women, boys and girls to trust Christ so that they may avoid the consequences of a life of no faith and a life of sin. In the Savior's name we pray. Amen.

Introduction

The Bible is great partly because of the warnings that it contains. Were it not for these great stoplights on the road to destruction, many of us would fall into an abyss of despair because of the foolishness of our own decisions and the error of our ways.

The Bible is great also because of the gracious invitations that it extends to us. Some of the best news for the lives of people can be found in the invitations the Bible contains.

The Bible would be a great book even if it contained only one gracious invitation from God to humans. However, from beginning to end it contains a series of invitations. The God who made man and placed him in a beautiful garden with beloved companionship and with a pleasant occupation has been seeking to create within humans a condition that would make possible the restoration of that precious fellowship that they no longer enjoy by nature.

As we come to the last chapter of the Bible and almost to the very last verse, it is evident that the Holy Spirit of God led the inspired writer to repeat God's great invitation once more.

There is something very dramatic about God's final recorded invitation. If you study it closely, you will find that all of the persuasive powers of divine love are wrapped up in this verse. The Holy Spirit extends the invitation. The bride is a reference to the church, and the church is in the world to extend God's invitation to people. Individual believers are encouraged to extend this invitation. The text encourages people to recognize the hunger for God in their hearts and to respond to the divine invitation to find life in its fullness.

There is something very touching about God's final recorded invitation. Why should the great God extend more than one invitation for people to come to the banquet table prepared by divine grace that they may feast on the bread that satisfies their deepest hunger?

It is interesting to note in studying the life and ministry of our Lord how often words of invitation fell from his lips. Let us look at some of these gracious invitations.

I. The invitation to come for life.

On one occasion, our Lord, with deep pathos, expressed regret that people were refusing to come to him to receive life (John 5:39–40). On another occasion, he said, "I am come that they might have life, and that they might have it more abundantly" (John 10:10).

One of Jesus' parables deals with this gracious invitation to come to the great banquet table that God has prepared for those who are willing to come (Luke 14:16–23).

Jesus came to offer forgiveness to those who have sinned against God. He invited people to come to him for forgiveness. Christ came to give life to those who are in spiritual death. He invites people to come to him that they might have life (John 10:28).

II. The invitation to come for fruitfulness (Mark 1:17).

Perhaps the fishermen to whom our Lord spoke had been the disciples of John the Baptist. We are safe in assuming that they had already been following Jesus and listening to him and trusting in him. He called them, then, to a life of discipleship that would produce great fruitfulness if they would forsake their nets and follow him.

Our Lord is eager to do something more than just give us a ticket to heaven. He wants to lead us to true fulfillment in life. In order to do this, we must forsake our self-centeredness and give ourselves unreservedly to the service of our Lord and to ministries of mercy to others (Luke 9:23–24). We must, with the help of the Holy Spirit, put the selfish self to death. We must let the living Christ live within us. As we do so, we will find life in its fullness. We will open ourselves to the possibility of ministering to others in the area of their greatest possible need.

III. The invitation to come for relief and rest (Matt. 11:28–30).

Our Lord extends a gracious invitation to those who labor and struggle under the burdens and responsibilities of life. He speaks words of invitation to those who labor under a heavy burden of guilt, frustration, and failure.

He extends a gracious invitation to those who find the burdens and responsibilities of life to be crushing and difficult to bear. He promises, not to remove the burdens and the responsibilities completely, but to give us the assistance we need—that which can bring peace and encouragement to our hearts.

Because of Jesus' divine adequacy, he is able to extend this all-inclusive invitation. We rob him of the privilege of blessing us when we neglect to respond to his invitation. We rob ourselves of the rest and of the help that we need for the bearing of life's responsibilities.

IV. The invitation to come for insight and understanding (John 1:39).

The disciples of John the Baptist came to Jesus because of their curiosity, their deep hunger for insight into the meaning of his ministry, and their desire for a better grasp of the purposes of God. The Lord was gracious to them. He invited them to spend the day with him. Our Lord continues to extend this invitation to us: "Come and see."

We have the guidance of the Holy Spirit as we study and pray and enter into an understanding of the meaning and purpose of life. Our Lord is eager to give us light for the road ahead. He will provide us with the wisdom we need for living in these days. We need to hear his invitation to "come and see" and to respond, not only on the Lord's Day, but every day.

Enoch walked with God, and children of God can walk and talk with the living Christ today if they will trust and obey him.

V. The invitation to enter the heavenly Father's home (Matt. 25:34–40).

As our Lord approached the end of his public ministry, he spoke of preparing a place for those who loved him and followed him. He spoke of the mansion of the heavenly Father (John 14:1–3).

In the parable of the Great Judgment, Jesus implies that those who have given themselves in ministries of mercy will have the privilege of entering not only into the Father's house, but also into a divine, eternal inheritance. We do not earn our way into the Father's house. This privilege is granted to us by God's grace through faith in his Son. However, in order to have a rich and wonderful spiritual inheritance in the home of the heavenly Father, we must give ourselves in ministry to the Christ here among people. One simple and outstanding way in which we can minister to the Christ is in a ministry to the helpless, unfortunate, and needy. Our Lord said, "Inasmuch as ye have done it unto one of the least of these my brethren, ye have done it unto me" (Matt. 25:40).

Conclusion

The invitation in our text is the most gracious invitation ever extended. It is given by God the Father, God the Son, and God the Holy Spirit. It is given also by the church and by the individual Christian. It is understood by the man who has in his heart a yearning for the Bread of Life and Water of Life.

This gracious invitation offers salvation and security, forgiveness and cleansing—eternal life as the gift of God.

It is the will of God that people respond to his invitation in order to receive the blessing he offers. If you have not yet come to Jesus Christ for life and forgiveness, you would be exceedingly wise to do so now. Spend the rest of your life recognizing and responding to the gracious invitations of the Lord.

Sunday Evening, March 3

Title: While Men Were Busy

Text: "All we like sheep have gone astray; we have turned every one to his own way; and the LORD hath laid on him the iniquity of us all" **(Isa. 53:6).**

Scripture Reading: Isaiah 52:14–53:12

Introduction

What are the one hundred most important historical events? More than a half century ago, Grosset and Dunlap, in order to publicize a new history book, asked a group of twenty-eight journalists, educators, and historians to list what they considered to be the one hundred most crucial events in history. In first place was Columbus's discovery of America. Gutenberg's development of movable type rated second. Some eleven events tied for third place. These events tied for fourth place: "Ether makes surgery painless; the discovery of X-ray; the invention of the airplane by the Wright brothers; the U.S. Constitution taking effect; Jesus Christ is crucified" (Halford E. Luccock, *More Preaching Values in the Epistles of Paul* [New York: Harper & Bros., 1961], 2:223). Of course, in this day and age—with computers and so much digital media—we wouldn't be surprised to see Jesus' crucifixion much farther down on the list. The passage before us

81

indicates that had Isaiah been asked to make such a list, the Savior would have been at the very top. But such a rating requires spiritual awareness, and we live in a world that has little time for such thought. We are far too busy.

In his picture *Despised and Rejected,* Sigismund Goetze graphically illustrates people's indifference to Christ. The center of the picture is consumed with the suffering Christ surrounded by people of all kinds. In spite of his tremendous sufferings, Christ seems to be unnoticed by those about him. The workman has his glass of beer in hand, and the political agitator has his motley crowd. The scientist is aware only of his test tubes. The newsboy is busy selling his paper with the latest scandals. The social set are obsessed with their vain frivolities, and the military leaders have no interest in a suffering Prince. Even the religious leaders, instead of giving attention to the suffering Christ, consume themselves with disputes about the text of Scripture. Only a nurse, accustomed to seeing pain and anguish, turns an eye toward the suffering Savior. In the midst of busy people, Christ is "despised and rejected of men."

The problem still remains the same: "We have turned every one to his own way." Oblivious to God's world, people have tried to build their own worlds. Isaiah lifts his voice to those who are too busy and calls them to see what they have overlooked. He reminds us of all that God has done while people were busy with themselves.

I. The Savior came (Isa. 52:14; 53:2).

Inspired of God, Isaiah speaks of the coming of Christ: "His appearance was so disfigured beyond that of any human being and his form marred beyond human likeness.... He grew up before him like a tender shoot, and like a root out of dry ground. He had no beauty or majesty to attract us to him, nothing in his appearance that we should desire him" (52:14; 53:2 NIV). The ancient rabbis saw in this Scripture the promise of the Messiah. The Targum of Jonathan and the Talmud of Babylon interpret Isaiah as speaking of the coming Messiah. Only since the Jewish rejection of Christ have Jewish authors refused to see the Messiah in this passage.

At first reading, Isaiah's description of Christ differs greatly with that of the artist Warner Sallman. It is said that Sallman, struggling in an effort to paint the head of Christ, was inspired either in dream or vision and in a moment saw the head of Christ, which he then painted. Since that time, it has become world famous. Isaiah is making no effort to interpret the physical features of Christ. Rather, he pictures the inner anguish and suffering that people disdain to see.

With great accuracy, Isaiah predicts the blindness of people. We see in his words a tone of discouragement: "Who has believed our message and to whom has the arm of the Lord been revealed?" (Isa. 53:1 NIV). The "message" of which Isaiah speaks is explained in his following statement in terms of the "arm of the Lord." Isaiah is reporting the Lord's arm at work in human affairs. He is saying that God's hand is being revealed to those who will see. Yet he is discouraged because so very few desire to see. It seems that people have always preferred to shun the truth.

II. The Savior suffered and died (Isa. 53:3–5, 8–9).

Listen to Isaiah's condensed biography: "He was despised and rejected by mankind, a man of suffering, and familiar with pain…. Surely he took up our pain and bore our suffering, yet we considered him punished by God, stricken by him, and afflicted. But he was pierced for our transgressions, he was crushed for our iniquities; the punishment that brought us peace was on him, and by his wounds we are healed" (vv. 3–5 NIV). Isaiah uses words that indicate that it is the men of high places who reject this Christ, and the hatred they feel for him is akin to Esau's attitude in despising his own birthright, of seeing no lasting value in it.

When Christians question their plight and their griefs, they do well to remember that their Savior was well acquainted with grief. He suffered even the ordinary deprivations of life: "Foxes have dens and birds have nests, but the Son of Man has no place to lay his head" (Matt. 8:20 NIV). Yet he was not concerned with the luxuries of life that consume most of our planning. Rather, he was concerned with his sole purpose for having come into the world: "I have a baptism to undergo, and what constraint I am under until it is completed!" (Luke 12:50 NIV).

While people were busy with the wheels of business and the revelries of pleasure, "by oppression and judgment he was taken away. Yet who of his generation protested? For he was cut off from the land of the living; for the transgression of my people he was punished. He was assigned a grave with the wicked, and with the rich in his death, though he had done no violence, nor was any deceit in his mouth" (vv. 8–9 NIV). There is no way to explain the preciseness of Isaiah's prophecy apart from the inspiration of God. Jesus was taken from Pilate's judgment and forced to bear his cross to the place of execution. No one stood up for him.

The meaning and purpose of Jesus' death are simply stated: "He was pierced for our transgressions, he was crushed for our iniquities; the punishment that brought us peace was on him, and by his wounds we are healed" (v. 5 NIV). His chastisement was the price by which our peace was secured. The healing of our bodies and our sin-torn lives is made possible because of Jesus' stripes.

Dickens, in his *Tale of Two Cities*, tells the story of a young nobleman, Charles Darnay, imprisoned during the violence of the French Revolution. Condemned to the guillotine, he faced certain death. However, a man named Carton, because he admired Darnay's wife, visited the cell, drugged Darnay, exchanged clothing with him, and went to the guillotine in his place. This is an illustration of the purpose of Christ's death. He paid our death penalty, which we deserve because we have sinned. And when he did it, there were no trumpets, no fanfare, no newspaper headlines to glorify his action. The only attention drawn to his death was that which came from above as the sun was darkened and the earth made to tremble. People had more important things to think about. They were busy.

III. The Savior triumphed (Isa. 53:10–11).

Isaiah sees beyond the death of the Messiah to behold his victory: "He will see his offspring and prolong his days, and the will of the LORD will prosper in his hand.... By his knowledge my righteous servant will justify many, and he will bear their iniquities" (vv. 10–11 NIV). Though the crucifixion would seem to have snuffed out any lineage, Isaiah sees the Savior looking after his offspring. Through his death he made possible our adoption as children of God. Isaiah sees that, although death is certain for the Savior, beyond death he shall prolong his days. Although the cross was the greatest tragedy in the human story, it was also the greatest triumph, for it gave way to the resurrection.

Isaiah pictures the triumph of the Savior in terms of a conquering general leading back his procession of the spoils of victory and the captives of his conquest: "He will divide the spoils with the strong" (53:12 NIV). Christ defeated sin, death, and Satan. The forces that destroy people became his captives. He calls all people now to share in his victory. How tragic that people are too busy to hear.

IV. The Savior offered healing (Isa. 53:12).

People are at once aware of physical malady because it affects them outwardly. Sin is a hideous, incurable disease that may often go unnoticed because it affects a person inwardly. It distorts one's reason and perverts one's values. Yet people are guilty for having this disease because it is a willful one. Aware of salvation, people choose to ignore it. Told about the Savior, people tend to shrug off their need of him. Living in unbelief, people find themselves in all sorts of perversions and anxieties. Yet because Christ died for our sins, he can offer us healing for our souls. What we fail to realize is that Christ's offer of healing remains today, but it is for today only. We may not have tomorrow. Because we are busy today, we are tempted to put off all thought of our spiritual sickness until tomorrow, taking a chance that tomorrow will come.

Conclusion

Years ago, David Lockard, a missionary in Southern Rhodesia, wrote of the death of a little girl name Gela. Though she had been converted, her father was an unbeliever. Not knowing how the father would take the death of his daughter, Lockard waited until after the funeral and then spoke tenderly to him about God. Gela's father, with tears in his dark eyes, said, "My little girl used to run errands for me; she was always bringing me things. But today she brought me the greatest gift of all—God!"

Don't be too busy for this!

WEDNESDAY EVENING, MARCH 6

Title: The Hurt of Sin

Text: "The eyes of them both were opened, and they knew that they were naked; and they sewed fig leaves together, and made themselves aprons" (**Gen. 3:7**).

Scripture Reading: Genesis 3:1–24

Introduction

The fact of sin may be laughed at, but it can never be ignored. In every area of life the effects of it are revealed. As John R. W. Stott wrote, "Sin is not a convenient invention of parsons to keep them in their job; it is a universal fact." The Bible is quite clear about this truth. Paul wrote, "All have sinned, and come short of the glory of God" (Rom. 3:23). John declared, "If we say that we have no sin, we deceive ourselves, and the truth is not in us" (1 John 1:8).

The experiences of Adam and Eve in the garden of Eden are divine revelations of the hurt of sin. They discovered the painful truth that a person cannot transgress a command of God, deny God's right to command, or fail to attain God's standard without feeling the results of the choice. Like them, people today choose to yield to the natural impulse to sin. The severity of sin's hurt depends on many factors, but no one can escape it.

I. Sin hurts because it brings separation.

A. *Sin separates humans from God.* Satan promised Adam and Eve that they would be as gods, knowing good and evil, if they would only disobey God's command. He failed to tell them that their disobedience would cause them to be separated from the holy God whom they knew and talked with each day. Never again would their lives be the same.

As Adam and Eve were separated from all of God's fellowship and blessings, our sin brings the same results. W. T. Conner wrote, "This is the most serious thing about sin. All the woe of sin grows out of the fact that it cuts man off from God, 'from whom all blessings flow.'"

B. *Sin separates person from person.* Adam and Eve were the first to realize that sin separates person from person. This painful reality became personal for them when Cain killed his brother Abel. Since that time, people have been against other people. This should not come as a surprise to us, for the apostle Paul wrote years ago concerning the works of the flesh (sin): "Now the works of the flesh are manifest, which are these: adultery, fornication, uncleanness, lasciviousness, idolatry, witchcraft, hatred, variance, emulations, wrath, strife, seditions, heresies, envyings, murders, drunkenness, revellings, and such like" (Gal. 5:19–21). As long as people sin, there will be some type of separation among people, and the hurt of sin will be felt.

II. Sin hurts because it brings suffering.

We know from the experience of Adam and Eve that much of human suffering is directly related to human sin. Both the person who sins and others suffer because of the sins committed.

A. *Suffering as shame.* The fact that Adam and Eve tried to hid themselves from God's presence is a graphic demonstration of their sense of shame. Years later Ezra expressed his shame for sin with these words: "O my God, I am ashamed and blush to lift up my face to thee, my God: for our iniquities

85

are increased over our head, and our trespass is grown up into the heavens" (Ezra 9:6).

B. *Suffering as guilt.* For the rest of their lives Adam and Eve lived with the sense of guilt that became theirs because they had sinned. Since that time, all of humankind has suffered the pains of guilt due to sin. Many cry like David, "My guilt has overwhelmed me like a burden too heavy to bear" (Ps. 38:4 NIV).

C. *Suffering as pain.* Adam and Eve did suffer some physical pain because of their sin, but perhaps their greatest pain was mental, because they soon realized that their sin, while giving them the knowledge of good and evil, had robbed them of life.

It is not hard to see the physical pain suffered by many because of their sin, but we have no way to measure effectively the mental pain suffered because of it. In this light, we should remember Paul's words, "Be not deceived; God is not mocked: for whatsoever a man soweth, that shall he also reap" (Gal. 6:7).

III. Sin hurts because it brings death.

In Genesis 2:17 God said to Adam and Eve, "You must not eat from the tree of the knowledge of good and evil, for when you eat from it you will certainly die" (NIV).

A. *It brings physical death.* Although it would be foolish to claim that every physical death is caused by some particular act of sin, it is likewise foolish to overlook the fact that physical death is a part of the human experience. As a result of Adam and Eve's sin, Paul said, "death passed upon all men" (Rom. 5:12).

B. *It brings spiritual death.* Spiritual death is the chief penalty of sin. It means that because of sin every person is by nature destined to a final and complete separation from God. This is not a pleasant prospect, but sin is not pleasant. It hurts.

Conclusion

Only as people accept Jesus Christ as Lord and Savior do they overcome the hurt of sin.

SUNDAY MORNING, MARCH 10

Title: The Good News about Prayer

Text: "Ask, and it shall be given you; seek, and ye shall find; knock, and it shall be opened unto you" (**Matt. 7:7**).

Scripture Reading: Matthew 7:7–11

Hymns: "Brethren, We Have Met to Worship," Atkins

"Teach Me to Pray," Reitz

"Take Time to Be Holy," Longstaff

Offertory Prayer: Holy, heavenly Father, help us this day to give to you the things that we have to give. We come to bring a tithe of our income. Accept it and bless it. Help us to give the full trust of our hearts to you. Help us to give an unselfish love to you. Help us to recognize that all of the time that we have is your gift to us. Help us to give ourselves to you and your purposes during all of the time that we have. Help us to give a glad expression to the faith that we have and to tell others of your great love and of the measureless nature of your mercy, through Jesus Christ. Amen.

Introduction

Some of the best news that ever fell from the lips of the Savior concerns the privilege that we have of entering into communion and dialogue with the heavenly Father. Jesus taught repeatedly that it is possible for people to communicate with the eternal God in prayer. He encouraged his disciples to believe that the heavenly Father was eager for them to come into his throne room. He pictured God the Father as both generous and wise in the bestowal of good gifts upon those who come into his presence in prayer.

In the words of our text, our Lord encourages us to be persistent in our efforts to come into God's presence seeking and searching not only for the gifts of God but for his guidance and assistance as we face the mysteries and problems of life.

I. Our Lord himself had the habit of prayer (Mark 1:35; Luke 5:16; 6:12; 9:28; 22:41–45).

Jesus began his ministry in fasting and prayer. Prayer permeated his life and ministry. He faced the close of his ministry in prayer. While on the cross, he communed with the heavenly Father. The present ministry of the living Lord is described in terms of a ministry of intercessory prayer (Heb. 7:25).

II. Our Lord encouraged his followers to pray.

A. *Our Lord assumed that his disciples would pray (Matt. 6:6).* Perhaps Jesus made this assumption because he knew of the generosity of the heavenly Father and of the spiritual poverty of his disciples. Perhaps he made this assumption because he knew of their great enemy, the devil, or because of the enormity of the task they were to attempt.

B. *Our Lord instructed his disciples in the proper manner for effective praying (Matt. 6:9–13).* He reminded them that when they prayed, they should address their prayers to God as their heavenly Father rather than as the Creator of the universe. He thus reminded them of the Parent-child relationship that exists between the Father God and the believer.

87

Our Lord urged his disciples to avoid some erroneous ideas concerning prayer (Matt. 6:5, 7–8). He taught his disciples to pray by his example, by his parables, and by his specific suggestions and instructions. He declared that the Father God is a prayer-hearing and prayer-answering God. He affirmed that the heart of each person has the capacity to communicate with God and to hear from God. He declared that it is possible to receive rich blessings as a result of prayer.

III. The rich rewards that come through prayer (Matt. 6:6).

A. *A sense of the nearness of the Father God (James 4:8).* The heart of the child of God hungers for an awareness of the presence of God and for an assurance of the love of God. Scripture and experience testify that the more we seek to draw near to God in prayer, the nearer he draws to us. We become aware of his precious abiding presence when we seek him in the closet of prayer.

B. *An assurance of help is another of the great rewards that comes to the one who prays (Heb. 4:14–16).* All of us have certain basic needs that only God can meet. Each of us has individual needs that we at times consider to be uniquely our own. Each of us has tendencies toward evil or weaknesses that would threaten us with either despair or destruction. The writer of the book of Hebrews encourages us to give ourselves to prayer on the basis that we have a sympathetic Lord who has been tempted in all points like as we are. He encourages us to come boldly to God's throne of grace that we may obtain mercy and find grace to help in time of need. It is encouraging to know that we approach the throne of *grace* rather than a throne of *justice*. The writer of Hebrews encourages us to expect mercy, that which we do not deserve but which God is eager to give. There we can find grace to help in our time of need, as those who have developed the habit of praying have discovered.

C. *The blessing of divine cleansing and forgiveness is one of the rich rewards of the prayer of confession (1 John 1:9).* Our Lord held up before his disciples a pattern of perfection. At the same time, he encouraged them to confess their sins day by day and to forgive those who had sinned against them. An awareness of unconfessed sin causes believers to lose the joy of their salvation. The absence of this joy deprives believers of a winsome testimony for Christ.

Forgiveness and a full restoration of fellowship that expresses itself in the assurance of a divine cleansing comes to believers when they humbly confess their sin to God and sincerely forsake the way of evil.

D. *The gift of the fullness of the Holy Spirit is one of the great gifts of God to those who have the habit of prayer (Luke 11:13).* While we pray and release ourselves to God, we become intensely aware of the abiding presence of the Holy Spirit and of his benevolent purpose for us in the plan and work of our Lord.

The Holy Spirit provides guidance for the road of life and energy for doing God's work. He gives us wisdom as we face the complexities of life. He comes in his fullness to those who through faith ask him to take over and lead and guide and empower.

Those who neglect the privilege and habit of prayer grieve the divine Spirit. They rob themselves of the rich blessings of God and deprive others of the blessing they could be.

Conclusion

We enter into a saving relationship with the Lord Jesus Christ in prayer. We express our faith by confessing our sins and inviting him to come into our hearts as Lord and Master.

We experience guidance and help along the road of life only as we develop this habit and capacity for dialogue with the Father God. If we neglect to pray, we deprive ourselves of a divine understanding of the problems, opportunities, and circumstances that we confront along the way.

Much of what we will be doing in heaven when this life is over can be described in terms of prayer—communicating with God and enjoying communion with him. Our communion will be perfect and without the limitations and hindrances we know now.

If you have not yet accepted Jesus Christ as your Lord and Savior, now is a good time to do so. God has taken the initiative and is eager to be in communication with you this day and every day.

SUNDAY EVENING, MARCH 10

Title: When God Turns His Back

Text: "Behold, the LORD's hand is not shortened, that it cannot save; neither his ear heavy, that it cannot hear: but your iniquities have separated between you and your God, and your sins have hid his face from you, that he will not hear" (**Isa. 59:1–2**).

Scripture Reading: Isaiah 59:1–20

Introduction

All of us are prone to complain and quick to feel mistreated. There are times when even God does not act to suit us. Sometimes we get the idea that if we have led average, respectable lives, God is indebted to see that all goes well with us. When clouds come on our horizon, we suddenly feel the heavens have turned to brass and our prayers have been misplaced or ignored. God seems to be looking the other way.

Israel suffered from the same affliction. They supposed God had not been sufficiently appreciative of their merits. Observe their complaint: "Wherefore have we fasted, say they, and thou seest not? Wherefore have we afflicted our soul, and thou takest no knowledge?" (Isa. 58:3). They seemed to feel that time spent in religious performances did not pay, because every time they needed help, the Lord was looking the other way.

Usually the people who feel this way are those who have never given anything more than lip service to God. Dedicated disciples understand that a part of their calling involves giving a faithful witness in the midst of the same difficulties that beset all people.

But if in your life God has indeed turned his back, then a careful look at Isaiah's message is in order.

I. Sin is the reason (Isa. 59:1 – 2).

Sin separates a person from God. The problem is not lack of divine love; it is the foolishness of fleshly priorities. As long as people prefer their sin to God's grace, the gulf remains. God calls people from their sins but does not drag them screaming and kicking to the altar of sacrifice.

Isaiah mentions the sins of lying, dishonesty, and deceit (59:3 – 4). Every dishonest dollar, every moral perversion, every infringement on the purpose of the Sabbath — although done in secret — cries out the reason that God's back is turned. Personal sin is the problem! Like a stool pigeon, it rises at the most embarrassing times to testify against us: "For our transgressions are multiplied before thee, and our sins testify against us" (59:12).

Isaiah's words are very relevant: "Truth is fallen in the street" (59:14). Truth has been reported missing in action, a casualty amid the struggle of greedy people. Truth can be fully seen only as it is revealed in Jesus Christ (John 8:32). Dishonesty is as much a perversion of the true life as is adultery. Moral depravity is the source of both.

The great astronomer David Rittenhouse said that the stars are so far away that a silk thread laid on the lens of his telescope would completely cover a star. Even small sins shut God out of our view.

II. Despair is the result (Isa. 59:4).

People living apart from God produce a deadly harvest; they "bring forth iniquity" (v. 4). James pictures sin in terms of an abortive birth. Lust conceives and gives birth to sin, and when sin is of age, an evil pregnancy is observed. The offspring: spiritual death (James 1:15). Paul says it another way: "The wages of sin is death" (Rom. 6:23).

Before Pasteur's discovery of microbes, the medical profession was ignorant of the infection produced by germs. Few people survived surgery in the early nineteenth century. In a book on medical history, a Dr. Park tells of his own experience in a hospital in 1876. Though one of the largest in the country and though staffed by the leading surgeons of the time, the hospital record showed that with only one or two exceptions, every surgical patient operated on that winter died of blood poisoning (S. I. McMillen, *None of These Diseases* [Westwood, N.J.: Revell, 1967], 15 – 16).

Sin is even deadlier and more contagious. Parents worry about the sanitation provided their children but often allow their children to grow up in an atmosphere of spiritual contamination, which, like deadly radiation, silently destroys life.

A. *Plans fail.* Human schemes have a way of backfiring when God is omitted. Supposing themselves to be wise in the world's ways, "they hatch cockatrice's eggs, and weave the spider's web" (Isa. 59:5). Isaiah goes on to say that to eat the eggs of the cockatrice (a deadly serpent) — the fruit of human schemes — is to die.

Self-devised schemes either shrivel on the vine or grow into uncontrollable monstrosities. People living apart from God come at last to the predicament of the one who, having swallowed an egg, was afraid to move for fear it would break and afraid to sit still for fear it would hatch.

B. *Peace perishes.* Self-sufficient people build a kind of peace for themselves that sooner or later grows brittle and shatters: "The way of peace they know not ... they have made them crooked paths: whosoever goeth therein shall not know peace" (Isa. 59:8). Having spent their efforts weaving their own webs, plotting their own course, following their empty philosophies, they learn of their utter failure: "Their webs shall not become garments, neither shall they cover themselves with their works" (59:6). Suddenly the bank account is not able to solve every problem. No longer does it bring the great assurance it was once thought to possess.

C. *Misdirection prevails.* Isaiah pictures people as lost in the desert of sin: "We wait for light, but behold obscurity ... we walk in darkness. We grope for the wall like the blind, and we grope as if we had no eyes ... we are in desolate places as dead men ... we look for ... salvation, but it is far off from us" (59:9–11). People who prefer darkness to the light of God (John 3:19) grow so accustomed to darkness that when tragedy snatches aside their thick veil, they find themselves spiritually blind. Those who have long worn the smirk of ridicule, who have preferred to "stand amused" instead of "standing amazed," walk about as dead persons. They have totally missed life.

III. Repentance is the solution (Isa. 59:20).

Instead of wondering why God allows things to become chaotic, people do well to blame themselves and their own sin. Deliverance can come from God but only when people repent: "The Redeemer shall come to Zion, and unto them that turn from transgression ... saith the LORD" (v. 20). Sin obscures God and voids prayer, but God will turn and deliver all who repent. It is strange that our enlightened world remains as blind to this truth as when Isaiah voiced his cry. The Dutch Mennonites have a saying that is particularly applicable to the spiritual realm: "We are too soon old and too late smart."

Actually, God has not turned his back. Rather, we have turned from God. There is still hope for those who will seek him in repentance. Amos asks, "Can two walk together, except they be agreed?" (3:3). The implied answer is no!

What is the mark of repentance? It is the act of giving up, of turning oneself in, of confessing guilt. Repentance knows nothing of the bargaining table. It is an unconditional confession. Repentance and faith are two sides of the same coin. The act of turning to God involves both.

In rabbinical literature there is the story of a little boy who came running home tearfully because he had been playing hide-and-seek with his friends, and when it was his turn to hide, no one came to look for him. The father used the opportunity to point out how God must feel when people do not seek him. However, the fact of the matter is that God calls out to those seeking him. He does not desire to remain hidden (*Pulpit Digest*, December 1966, 19).

Conclusion

Several years ago, some noted historians wrote a book titled *If, or History Rewritten*. They elaborated on what might have happened if the Dutch had not sold New Amsterdam, if Lincoln had lived, if Lee had won the Battle of Gettysburg. Such speculations are interesting but useless. What might have been is beside the point.

What actually happens is all that counts. Your sin is your biggest problem. It separates you from God. Settle this matter before you tackle any other problem.

WEDNESDAY EVENING, MARCH 13

Title: The God We Worship

Text: "For the LORD is a great God, and a great King above all gods" (**Ps. 95:3**).

Scripture Reading: Psalm 95:1–11

Introduction

A small girl once asked her understanding father, "Daddy, who made God?" With her simple question, was she not expressing the burning desire of most of us in wanting to know more about the God we worship? It seems that every time we try to explain God to another person, we discover the painful and humiliating truth that nearly all of our explanations are inadequate. Even though we will never be able correctly and totally to explain to someone else the God we worship, there is much we can know and share about him.

Any explanation of the nature of God must consider his greatness. It is impossible to know and understand him without recognizing this truth. The writer of Psalm 95:3 said, "For the LORD is a great God, and a great King above all gods." The psalmist had made a comparison between his God, the God of the Bible, and the false gods known and worshiped by many of his contemporaries, and he concluded that his God was much, much greater. Still in our time, the outcome of a similar test would reveal that the God we know and worship as Christians is greater than all.

I. God is great in his holiness.

Through the revelation of the Bible we are able to see that God is perfectly holy. This fact causes him to be distinguished from things finite and sinful. The sudden realization of this fact caused Isaiah to cry, "Woe is me! For I am undone; because I am a man of unclean lips, and I dwell in the midst of a people of unclean lips: for mine eyes have seen the King, the LORD of hosts" (6:5). Likewise, when Moses had recognized God's holiness, he had fallen on his face before God. The realization of God's character causes us to be disturbed about our own sinfulness but thankful that the God we worship stands apart because of his great holiness.

II. God is great in his knowledge.

There are many people who have not awakened to the teaching of the Scriptures that God has perfect knowledge and knows all things. They fail to understand that his knowledge, being great and perfect, is not limited by time, space, or distance.

A. W. Tozer wrote, "Because God knows all things perfectly, he knows no thing better than any other thing, but all things equally well. He never discovers anything, he is never surprised, never amazed. He never wonders about anything, nor (except when drawing men out for their own good) does he seek information or ask questions."

III. God is great in his power.

God possesses what no creature has: absolute power. We know this from the psalmist's words, "Power belongeth unto God" (Ps. 62:11). But God will not use this unlimited power in a way that is inconsistent with his nature.

Perhaps the vastness and order of the physical universe stands as one of the greatest testimonies to the greatness of God's power. Of course, the ultimate testimony of his power is found in his ability to change people.

IV. God is great in his presence.

God is here, everywhere, close to everything, next to everyone. In every time and in every moment, God is present. David, king of Israel, wrote in Psalm 139:7–10: "Whither shall I go from thy spirit? Or whither shall I flee from thy presence? If I ascend up into heaven, thou art there: if I make my bed in hell, behold, thou art there. If I take the wings of the morning, and dwell in the uttermost parts of the sea; even there shall thy hand lead me, and thy right hand shall hold me."

V. God is great in his love.

The apostle John declares in 1 John 4:16, "God is love." With these three small words, he reveals the essential nature of God. Because of this nature, we are allowed to know and love through the forgiveness of sins given to us in the redemptive work of Jesus Christ.

Concerning the greatness of God's love, F. W. Robertson said, "To me this is the profoundest of all truths—that the whole of the life of God is the sacrifice of self. God is love: love involves sacrifice—to give rather than to receive. All the life of God is a flow of this divine self-giving love."

Conclusion

This great God can be personally known by you. He has revealed himself to all people through his Son, Jesus Christ. If you will receive Jesus Christ as Savior, you can and will know God.

SUNDAY MORNING, MARCH 17

Title: The Good News Concerning God's Promises

Text: "There shall not any man be able to stand before thee all the days of thy life: as I was with Moses, so I will be with thee: I will not fail thee, nor forsake thee" (**Josh. 1:5**).

Scripture Reading: Joshua 1:1–9

Hymns: "O God, Our Help in Ages Past," Watts

"'Tis So Sweet to Trust in Jesus," Stead

"Faith Is the Victory," Yates

Offertory Prayer: Holy Father, from your hand we receive the gift of life. It is by your grace that we have air to breathe, water to drink, food to eat, and clothes to wear. It is by your generosity that we have the power to get wealth. We do not forget that you are the source of every good and perfect gift. Today we come offering expressions of our gratitude and love. Accept these gifts and bless them that your kingdom may come in the hearts of men and women, boys and girls. Bless the missionary activities that these offerings make possible. Bless the ministries of mercy that these gifts support. Again, we thank you for your generosity to us, through Jesus Christ our Lord. Amen.

Introduction

How do you study the Bible? Do you study it merely as a historical narrative of what happened in the ancient past? Do you study it merely to receive devotional inspiration for the moment? Do you survey its pages to come to a deeper appreciation of the literary value of the world's greatest volume? Do you consider the Bible to be some kind of a secret disclosure of coming events, and are you concerned only to find out what will happen at the consummation of the age? Do you study the Bible to use it for the presentation of your arguments on theological subjects? Do you study the Bible to find fragments of truth that confirm and strengthen your prejudices?

Basically, and essentially, the Bible contains a message of good news concerning God that should be of great interest to every human being. Some have never been able to decipher the real good news that the Bible has for the hearts and lives of people. Perhaps this is because of the perspective from which they approach the Word of God. Many see only dark, harsh things in the Bible. Consequently, it provides no uplift or encouragement for them.

One of the most profitable goals in studying the Bible is the discovery of the exceedingly great and precious promises of our Lord to us (2 Peter 1:4).

The Bible is indeed a book of promises. The first great "promise" is the announcement of judgment found in Genesis 3:15. This is an indirect promise to sinful humans of a deliverer and redeemer. The Bible closes in the last chapter and almost the last verse with a promise of our living Lord to return for the redeemed (Rev. 22:20). In the hundreds of pages between these two biblical references, there are literally thousands of promises from God to his people.

Every great spiritual giant in every significant spiritual movement moved because of faith in the precious promises of God. We would do well to put ourselves in the circumstances of the biblical characters as they touch and relate to our lives and claim the precious promises of God. Without being specific, as far as some of the details are concerned, we can be absolutely certain that there is a principle we can claim as our own in every promise of God to his people. Because of this truth, many people have found the Bible to be a living book from its very beginning to its tremendous conclusion.

I. God's promises are for the present.

We must not make the fatal mistake of studying the Bible as a mere historical depository of the activities of God in the ancient past. It is that, but it is far more than that. It is a living revelation of what God did in the ancient past and what God wants to continue to do in the hearts and lives of those who will trust and obey him.

God's promise to bless Abraham as he gave himself in obedience to his redemptive purpose is a promise that is applicable to the heart and life of every person who is seeking earnestly to do the will of God in the present (Gen. 12:1–3). When we discover what God's will for our life is, we should do as Abraham did. We should arise and depart for our responsibility and our place of opportunity. We can be absolutely certain that the living Lord will accompany us, for he has promised to do so (Matt. 28:20).

Discover this promise; make it your very own. Move forward in obedience, trusting the Lord to bless you and to help you as time goes by. You will discover that he has never broken any promise spoken; he will keep his promise to you.

II. God's promises concerning the past.

The Old Testament prophets testify that God is eager to forgive the sins of those who put their faith in the Messiah who came to bear our iniquities and our sins on the cross (Acts 10:43).

All of us are sinners and have come short of the glory of God (Rom. 3:23). It is probably not an overstatement to say that all of us have pages in the story of

95

our lives of which we are terribly ashamed. The heavenly Father is not eager to remember our sins. He receives no delight in punishing sin. God forgives our sins and removes the record of our transgressions from us (Isa. 43:25). When God forgives our sins, he also forgets them, and his forgiveness is free. It cannot be merited with a good moral life. When God forgives, he forgives completely and forever. He will not dig up an old charge and hold it against us. He forgives all our iniquities and removes them from us as far as the east is from the west (Ps. 103:12).

III. God's promises are for the future.

As God promised Joshua that he would go before him and be with him, even so our Lord promised his disciples that he would be with them to provide light for the road ahead (John 8:12). At the beginning of his ministry, our Lord spoke to his disciples who were to become his apostles and said, "Follow me." Toward the very close of his earthly ministry, our Lord spoke to the apostle Peter and repeated this invitation and command: "Follow me." He had promised repeatedly that he would provide light for the road ahead as his disciples journeyed through life in obedience to his call.

In a world that is threatened with forces over which we as individuals have absolutely no control, we desperately need a living faith in the promises of God that he will be with us in the future. God has promised to be with us as long as life lasts. He has promised to be with us for eternity. Heaven itself is pictured as a home where God is, where sickness and sorrow and suffering never come to bring trouble and tragedy into the lives of God's people.

IV. God's promises are for his children.

God reveals himself through Jesus Christ as a loving Father who provides for his own.

    A. *God promises to hear the prayers of his children and to answer them according to his wisdom and power (Matt. 6:7–8).*

    B. *Our Lord promises rest for the weary (Matt. 11:28–30).*

    C. *We can rejoice in the promise of an eternal love from God (Rom. 8:35–39).*

    D. *We have the promise of our Lord of his abiding presence with those who meet together in his name (Matt. 18:20).*

    E. *We have our Lord's promise of an eternal home at the end of the way (John 14:2).*

Conclusion

God has made some exceedingly great and precious promises to the unbelievers, to those who are unsaved. If you have never yet opened your heart, inviting Jesus Christ to come in as Lord and Master, you should be encouraged to know that God has promised to forgive you if you will confess your sin. Forsake in your heart the desire to follow wicked ways and come to him for mercy and pardon (Isa. 55:6–7).

Our Lord has promised to accept everyone who will come to him in faith for salvation (John 6:37). He has promised to enter the heart of every person who responds by opening the door when he comes requesting entrance (Rev. 3:20). That which has been called the greatest verse of Scripture—John 3:16—offers the promise of everlasting life to each person who will put faith and trust in Jesus Christ as Lord and Savior. Put your faith in him today and let him become the Lord and leader and friend of your heart and life.

SUNDAY EVENING, MARCH 17

Title: When People Listen to God

Text: "The Spirit of the Lord God is upon me; because the LORD hath anointed me to preach good tidings unto the meek; he hath sent me to bind up the brokenhearted, to proclaim liberty to the captives, and the opening of the prison to them that are bound; to proclaim the acceptable year of the LORD, and the day of vengeance of our God; to comfort all that mourn; to appoint unto them that mourn in Zion, to give unto them beauty for ashes" **(Isa. 61:1–3)**.

Scripture Reading: Isaiah 61:1–11

Introduction

The prophetic word found in the Bible was given by the Lord for one purpose—that people might listen. The preaching of "good tidings" is of no avail apart from the people who will hear.

Dorothy L. Sayers, in her play *The Man Born to Be King*, warns against treating God's drama of redemption as though it were a dull, ordinary nursery tale. By and large, her warning goes unheeded.

At best our world is willing only to tolerate the preaching of the gospel. Like a domineering conversationalist who occasionally, with an air of polite indifference, pauses to allow someone else to speak but uses the pause to contemplate the next verbal onslaught, our enlightened age has little interest in hearing from God. Yet the hope of the world hinges on the few who do listen to the divine message.

I. They have freedom (Isa. 61:1–2).

People who hear God's Word are set free. The immediate audience of Isaiah 61 is exiled Israel. The good tidings from God are that they are to be allowed to return to their homeland of Palestine (Isa. 40:1–2). The good news amounts to a proclamation of emancipation. God's message comes "to bind up the brokenhearted, to proclaim liberty to the captives, and the opening of the prison to them that are bound; to proclaim the acceptable year of the LORD" (61:1–2).

To identify with the exiled captives is not difficult. Return from captivity is an experience needed by every person. The word *captives* literally refers to booty carried away by conquerors. What person is not enslaved by Satan's devious allurements, by selfish pride, and by barren habits and empty activities? Such persons need to escape the kingdom of darkness but are unable to do so. If only they will stop toying with the chains that bind them and listen to the good tidings that set people free.

"The acceptable year of the LORD" alludes to the Year of Jubilee described in Leviticus 25. It occurred every fiftieth year and was a type of messianic era. Commencing at the end of the Day of Atonement, it was heralded by the shrill blasts of the silver trumpets as priests in every hamlet from Dan to Beersheba announced the good news. In effect, the message was "You are free; all debts are canceled." Those who had been forced to sell themselves as slaves to their creditors were set free. Family property was restored. God's law decreed that an Israelite's inheritance could remain "sold" only until the next Year of Jubilee. This was God's way of periodically granting a new start for those defeated by circumstances of life.

Sadly enough, there is little evidence to show that Israel adhered to the requirements of the Year of Jubilee. For this reason, it became a shadow of the promised messianic era. The heart yearns to be set free, for all things to be made right. Jesus spoke to this yearning as he stood to read in the synagogue at Nazareth and selected Isaiah 61 (Luke 4:16–21). In that moment, he set himself before the world as the ultimate fulfillment of God's promise of freedom. The eternal Year of Jubilee became possible in Christ. All of sin's bonds are broken. People are set free.

II. They have peace (Isa. 61:1).

Those who listen to God have peace as well as freedom. Isaiah appeals particularly to the "brokenhearted." Literally the word means "that which is shattered." A broken arm can be set, and in time it will heal, but a broken heart is another matter. Only the grace of God can heal hurts.

But what kind of blow breaks a heart? Alas, there are many answers. Circumstances can pile one on another until the heart despairs. Anxieties can leave the heart empty. To feel oneself an outcast from the inner circle of things can break a heart. I remember reading somewhere about a preacher who said that as a young man, he worried about what the world thought of him. Later in life he came to the place where he did not care what the world thought of him. Then, toward the sunset of life, he discovered the world never had been thinking of him.

You diagnose a broken heart by looking for inner peace. As long as the heart has peace, it is not utterly broken. That which deprives the heart of peace is sin and the damning guilt that accompanies sin.

God's offered peace is not a ticket to security away from all life's raging storms. Rather, it is a calling to purpose. Nothing is quite so haunting as the fear that life is slipping away without anything being accomplished. Those set free in Christ are called to a purposeful labor that carries with it a certain inner peace that cannot be crushed by outward circumstances.

The rampant revolt and conflict sweeping today's world has come in the absence of inner peace. Paul Tournier ably depicted our civilization in terms of a neurosis (Paul Tournier, *The Whole Person in a Broken World* [New York: Harper & Row, 1964], 2–11). Like a rebellious child, our world is asserting itself in a purely negative form. We are suddenly against all the past, all authority, and all values, without offering anything to replace what we would wreck. Tournier defined a neurosis as an inner conflict. Quoting Jung, he said that the neurotic suffers because he is unaware of his problems. Having thrown Christ and the gospel out the back door, our world now wonders why it is sick, never dreaming what the real problem is. Tournier wrote that when God is dethroned, fear rules us. He attributed much of the emphasis on scientific research to humankind's desire to escape fear by banishing all mystery. Yet Harold Urey, one of the scientists who contributed to the development of the atomic bomb, said, "I write to make you afraid. I myself am a man who is afraid. All the wise men I know are afraid" (ibid., p. 25).

Only the gospel offers peace. Only God can garrison the human heart and ward off Satan's advances: "The peace of God, which passeth all understanding, shall keep your hearts and minds through Christ Jesus" (Phil. 4:7).

III. They have a crown (Isa. 61:3).

The promise of a crown is crouched in a poetic figure: "To appoint unto them that mourn in Zion, to give unto them beauty for ashes." By divine decree, those who listen to God are promised "beauty for ashes." To understand the promise, one must remember the customs for mourning among the Israelites. Ashes were put on the head as a grim crown. By God's grace, the ashes shall be replaced by a royal diadem denoting the heritage of God's people. "Beauty for ashes" is equivalent to "joy for mourning," hope for sorrow, life for death, and heaven for hell.

Apart from God, every person's life and works come at last to ashes. Ashes are but a useless form of what once was of value. Sin, like a gluttonous fire, consumes a person's kingdom and dreams, leaving only ashes. Eternal mourning is one of the most frightening aspects of hell.

In Egyptian mythology a bird called the phoenix brought about its own destruction by fire every five hundred years and then rose anew from its own ashes. The phoenix was a symbol of the ancient desire for immortality. People have always feared coming to the end of life without any hope. Only God's message offers anything beyond the ashes of human strength.

People who listen to God with a sincere desire to claim his promises have made a choice. The gospel presents both the glorious and the fearful. The prophet dares not speak of the "acceptable year of the Lord" (the day of God's grace) without also warning of the alternative, "the day of vengeance of our God" (61:2). To offer good is to concede the presence of evil; to offer reward is to imply the reality of punishment; to present heaven is to acknowledge the alternative of hell.

Conclusion

Jesus Christ promises to visit us in an hour we know not. This visit will be glorious for those prepared, ruinous for all others.

How strange, in the light of this, that people throw up every conceivable argument against making preparation to meet God. A few years ago the newspapers carried the story of a condemned killer living on death row. When news reached him that a pardon was being considered, he pled fervently against it. His action brought on additional psychiatric study, for no rational person would reject a pardon. So it is with God's offer of salvation. It would seem that no rational person would reject it. The fact that multitudes argue against it is a monument to the power of Satan to blind people to their greatest need. There is hope only when people listen to God.

WEDNESDAY EVENING, MARCH 20

Title: Our Great Salvation

Text: "Blessed be the God and Father of our Lord Jesus Christ, which according to his abundant mercy hath begotten us again unto a lively hope by the resurrection of Jesus Christ from the dead, to an inheritance incorruptible, and undefiled, and that fadeth not away, reserved in heaven for you, who are kept by the power of God through faith unto salvation ready to be revealed in the last time" (**1 Peter 1:3–5**).

Scripture Reading: 1 Peter 1:1–5

Introduction

Have you ever tried to explain the meaning of salvation to someone who had not experienced it? It was not easy, was it? There are at least two reasons for this difficulty. First, it is hard to translate an experience normally described in biblical language into twenty-first-century nonbiblical expressions. Second, salvation includes many individual truths that must first be understood in order to comprehend the whole.

Much of the New Testament was written to help us better understand our faith. This was one of the primary purposes of Peter's first epistle. To him, salvation was the greatest experience any person could have, even if he did not completely understand it.

I. Great because it comes from God.

James wrote, "Do not err, my beloved brethren. Every good gift and every perfect gift is from above, and cometh down from the Father of lights, with whom is no variableness, neither shadow of turning" (James 1:16–17). This is especially true of salvation; it comes only from God.

A. *God planned it.* It is not surprising that Peter praised the Lord, for he knew that God alone had planned salvation. This planning took place even before the creation of the world. In Revelation 13:8 John called Jesus "the Lamb slain from the foundation of the world." We often see people seeking to find God. In salvation we see God's plan for finding people.

B. *God provided it.* God's plan to bring people out of their lost condition was made possible because he sent Christ to be the Redeemer of all humankind (John 3:16).

C. *God shares it.* In Jesus Christ we are able to recognize not only God's planning and provision, but also his willingness and desire to share this salvation with everyone. As Peter said, "The Lord is ... longsuffering to us-ward, not willing that any should perish, but that all should come to repentance" (2 Peter 3:9).

II. Great because it changes us.

When Peter said, "hath begotten us again," he meant being born again, or as Paul wrote in 2 Corinthians 5:17, "Therefore if any man be in Christ, he is a new creature: old things are passed away; behold, all things are become new." In salvation God does not just fix people, he changes them.

A. *Salvation changes our relationship with God.* Before salvation people are without a vital relationship with God. But after salvation they become "no more strangers and foreigners, but fellowcitizens with the saints, and of the household of God" (Eph. 2:19). This change in relationship with God causes one to become interested in living a life pleasing to God.

B. *Salvation changes our relationship to sin.* No longer does sin need to have control over us. Its penalty has been removed in the redemptive work of Christ. We now find that it does not bring the joy and pleasure that we once thought it did. We can now face its tempting power because, as Paul wrote, "God is faithful, who will not suffer you to be tempted above that ye are able; but will with the temptation also make a way to escape, that ye may be able to bear it" (1 Cor. 10:13).

C. *Salvation changes our relationship to life.* Never again will our lives be the same. There is no more a lack of purpose, a fearful uncertainty about the future, nor meaninglessness, because God has changed our relationship to life. It is as Jesus said, "I am the resurrection, and the life: he that believeth in me, though he were dead, yet shall he live" (John 11:25).

III. Great because it is secure.

The Bible indicates that salvation is a secure and permanent relationship. Paul wrote, "And if children, then heirs; heirs of God, and joint-heirs with Christ" (Rom. 8:17). Jesus said concerning those that have responded and accepted his salvation, "I give unto them eternal life; and they shall never perish, neither shall any man pluck them out of my hand" (John 10:28).

A. *Secure because it is an unchanging gift from God.* Peter uses the word *inheritance*, which means that salvation is a gift that is a settled and secure possession. Paul Rees said of the words Peter used to describe this inheritance, "It is 'imperishable': no termites, no moulding, no decaying! It is 'undefiled': its beauty will be forever undiminished, its charm forever enchanting!"

B. *Secure because it is protected by God.* Peter used two words to make clear God's protection of salvation. The first word is *reserved*, which means "to watch, to observe, to guard, to protect, to reserve, to set aside." The second word is *kept*, which is a military term meaning "to guard and protect." God has reserved salvation in heaven and keeps a constant guard over it until we safely arrive there.

Conclusion

This great salvation is available to anyone who accepts Christ as Savior. Even you!

SUNDAY MORNING, MARCH 24

Title: The Lord Needs You

Text: "The Lord hath need of them" (**Matt. 21:3**).

Scripture Reading: Matthew 21:1–11

Hymns: "God of Grace and God of Glory," Fosdick

"Rise Up, O Men of God," Merrill

"Wherever He Leads I'll Go," McKinney

Offertory Prayer: Our Father, we bring our gifts to you, knowing that these are but a token of all that you have given to us. We pray that you will take not only our tithes and offerings, but that you will take our lives and make them more completely yours. May we ever strive to be more like our Lord who gave himself for us; and may we learn to give as he gave—with love and compassion for humankind. Amen.

Introduction

The last several decades have witnessed a steady succession of public demonstrations for special causes. A nonviolent demonstration in Montgomery, Alabama, in the mid-1950s began the civil rights movement and started Martin Luther King Jr., on a spectacular career as the movement's leader. In more recent times, protests associated with the Occupy movement have sprung up in cities all across the United States to protest corporate greed and corruption. And throughout the years, protestors have held peace marches to call to end our participation in war.

Demonstrations are not a new means of expression of public opinion. The triumphal entry of Jesus into Jerusalem on the last week of his earthly life was an emotional demonstration. Jerusalem was crowded with those who had gathered to observe the Passover, the most important feast of the year. The crowds were keyed up with national expectations that God would raise up a king to deliver them from the power of Rome. Shouts of "Hosanna!" filled the air as the crowd acclaimed Jesus as King. The King came riding, not as an earthly king on a white horse, but as the Prince of Peace on a lowly donkey.

I. We marvel at Jesus' courage.

Jesus publicly entered the hostile city. He could have skipped this dramatic entrance and slipped into Jerusalem after dark through the back streets. But his hour of coronation had arrived, and he willingly occupied the center of the stage. Every eye was on him, including the envious and vengeful eyes of his enemies.

II. We marvel at Jesus' open claim for himself.

Jesus allowed the multitude to recognize him as God's Messiah. Had he been satisfied to be just another prophet, he would likely have escaped death at the hands of his adversaries. But he could not deny himself. To be Lord of all and, surely, to be the Savior of humankind, he consciously and confidently traveled a road that would lead irrevocably to the cross.

III. We marvel at Jesus' tears.

A strong man weeping is always a moving scene. But there come times and experiences when words are powerless and when the only release from an overwhelming sorrow is the flow of tears. At such a time, tears are the good gift of God.

Jesus stood above the beloved city of Jerusalem and saw its poverty, its materialism, its empty religious forms and practices, and its unbelief. He saw the hate and bitterness of those who plotted his death. He saw the calloused rejection of his spiritual claims by the multitude. He saw the impending doom that hung over the city. He saw people, teeming multitudes of people, as sheep without a shepherd. And he wept in his overwhelming sorrow as they faced the judgment of God.

IV. We marvel at Jesus' gracious lowliness.

Jesus appeared riding on a donkey. The unsympathetic witnesses were probably amused and perplexed and scornful at this ludicrous demonstration. They were too blind to see that he was teaching them a vital lesson. His kingdom is not of this world. His victory comes not through war but through peace. Those who would follow him are not the proud but the humble, not the self-sufficient rich but the poor in spirit.

Why did Jesus choose a donkey, so awkward, so stubborn, so lowly? If he could not do any better, why didn't he walk? (This is the only time the Bible records that Jesus rode.) He was to teach us that whatever he touched, he dignified. He was to impress upon us that no matter how despised the object, Christ had use for him.

V. God uses average, ordinary people.

There was not a highly educated man among the original disciples. Not one was a scholar. Not one had wealth or fame. Four had been fishermen. One had been a noted tax gatherer. They were men with weaknesses and flaws like the rest of us. Some had a fiery nature. They stumbled and fell. Yet Jesus took these obscure men and through them turned the world upside down.

Christ will work with anyone who will give him a consecrated heart. He is not impressed with our pious, false humility when we say, "He cannot use me because I'm not clever, I'm not talented, I'm not articulate." He could use a lowly donkey. He can use you. Praise him as you surrender yourself to him.

VI. God uses dedicated people.

Among the greatest Christian people of history, there are many who had obscure beginnings. John Bunyan was not a polished writer. He was limited in his education. Scholars sneered at his writings. But the response of the multitudes established his allegory *Pilgrim's Progress* as the greatest in the English language.

When William Booth founded the Salvation Army, the press ridiculed him. The *London Times* always put his rank of "General" in quotes. But he led and inspired an army for Christ that has spread around the world.

Dwight L. Moody was an unlettered man. He never went to college. His manner was crude, and his grammar was atrocious. Someone said he was the only man he ever heard who could say "Mesopotamia" in one syllable. English teachers came to hear him in order to condemn his grammar. But they left praising the Christ whom Moody proclaimed. He was the greatest evangelistic influence of the nineteenth century. He gave God everything he had, and God used him far beyond other more talented but less dedicated preachers.

At Carisbrooke Castle in England, a donkey works in a little roundhouse. His job is to go around and around and around in a circle. That is all he does. There is no starting place and no stopping place. "Is there any purpose in this endless circle?" we ask. Then we observe that he is drawing water from a very deep well in the heart of the castle. He is not walking in circles for nothing. On a hot day, he can give you a cool drink. A spirited horse would not submit himself to such drudgery and monotony. But even the most obscure and humble among us can draw water from the wells of the Spirit of God and give a drink to the thirsty.

Conclusion

An impressive recruiting poster during World War II pictured Uncle Sam looking straight at you, pointing his index finger in your face. Beneath his picture were the words "I NEED YOU." The poster dramatically expressed urgency. America was fighting for its life.

Not only do we need Christ, but Christ needs us. He has no hands but our hands to do his deeds of kindness and mercy. He has no feet but our feet to do his errands of world mission. He has no tongue but our tongues to proclaim the good news of his gospel. You may feel that you do not have much to offer.

All he asks is the best of what you have. He does not even require success. All he requires is faithfulness. The Lord has need of you! He wants all of you right now and forever.

SUNDAY EVENING, MARCH 24

Title: The Church in Travail

Text: "For as soon as Zion travailed, she brought forth her children" **(Isa. 66:8)**.

Scripture Reading: Isaiah 66:1–24

Introduction

Birth comes only after travail. Just as physical birth must be preceded by labor pains, so also must spiritual birth. The travail need not be long, only genuine. False labor pains are agonizingly unfruitful. Isaiah stresses the need for real, spiritual travail by saying that spiritual birth follows so quickly that it is as though the birth came first: "Before she travailed, she brought forth" (66:7). Yet he goes on to explain, "For as soon as Zion travailed, she brought forth her children." The travail is necessary but not lengthy.

But what does Isaiah mean? We must look first at Zion. Zion is the famous hill on which the Jerusalem temple was built, the place of David's original fortress. Later Zion came to include the whole city as the people of God and ultimately came to include the church as the people of God.

The immediate birth to which Isaiah refers concerns the restoration of the exiles from Babylon, the return of a nation to the Land of Promise. But Isaiah always points ahead to a greater fulfillment, and such is the case here. Within his statement lies the birth of the church in the days of our Lord's ministry and the great ingathering on the day of Pentecost—three thousand born in a day!

Isaiah sets forth a great principle that remains relevant today: spiritual victories are not given by chance; they require a personal, agonizing search and sacrifice. If the church today is truly to be the church, it must be in travail. Because we are often guilty of activity without unction, we must give careful attention to what genuine travail involves on the part of a church lest we be deceived by false pains.

I. Genuine travail makes worship personal (Isa. 66:1–2).

Isaiah refers to those who have taken such pride in the glorious temple of Solomon that they have forgotten the God to be worshiped: "Thus saith the LORD, The heaven is my throne, and the earth is my footstool: where is the house that ye build unto me.... For all those things hath mine hand made ... but to this man will I look, even to him that is poor and of a contrite spirit, and trembleth at my word." God is not impressed with beautiful buildings, since his hand created all the materials anyway. What God really desires is a repentant and reverent heart. It is rather tragic that during the earthly ministry of our Lord the Jews were engaged in rebuilding the temple. The project was begun by Herod the

Great before the birth of Jesus as a means of gaining the goodwill of the Jews. The lengthy process was still in progress when Jesus was crucified. Busy building a temple, the Jewish leaders plotted the crucifixion of the Son of God, the Savior of the world.

Group worship is a failure unless each person also engages in personal worship. Unless worship comes from a yielded heart, it is blasphemy. God will not accept a gift unless the giver's heart is repentant. Therefore Isaiah declares that God looks on the man who, in cold formality, brings his ox as a sacrifice as though he had slain a fellow man: "He that killeth an ox is as if he slew a man" (66:3).

Real sacrifice comes as an outgrowth of a surrendered heart. Isaiah's prophecy began with God's question, "To what purpose is the multitude of your sacrifices unto me? saith the LORD" (Isa. 1:11).

Nothing is more irreverent than the formal offering accompanied by a rebellious and wayward heart. When David wanted to worship God, he bought the oxen and threshing floor of Araunah, refusing to accept it as a gift, saying, "Neither will I offer burnt offerings unto the LORD my God of that which doth cost me nothing" (2 Sam. 24:24). To be content with anything else is to divorce worship from all feeling and spiritual travail.

II. Genuine travail is serious about choices (Isa. 66:3–4).

Spiritual travail is marked by serious decision making. Life itself is the sum of an individual's choices. The making of wise decisions requires an accurate sense of values as well as the vision of the long haul.

I can well remember how we, as youngsters at school, chose up sides for a ball game. First one side got a choice and then the other. In life God gives you first choice. Your decision then determines his choice for you. This becomes a continuous procedure throughout the life of an individual as well as of a church: "Yea, they have chosen their own ways, and their soul delighteth in their abominations. I also will choose their delusions, and will bring their fears upon them; because when I called, none did answer; when I spake, they did not hear: but they did evil before mine eyes, and chose that in which I delighted not" (vv. 3–4).

God offers us direction. Sometimes he impresses us toward certain decisions while we are in private devotion, sometimes in public worship, sometimes amid our daily labors. The danger is not that God's direction may not come, but that we may pay it no heed. When such is the case, God chooses to grant us delusions, to let our fears boomerang on us.

As a result, we often revel piously in our own blessed delusions. We assume that if we scrupulously do what past generations have done, we are defenders of the faith. We assume that if we draw out every decision over a long period of time, we are sure to be doing God's will carefully. Imagine a church service suddenly interrupted by the shout of "Fire!" Wouldn't it be ridiculous for someone to ask, "Shall we call the fire department?" And what if the response came, "Let's appoint a committee to study the matter and to see if other churches have ever called fire departments, and if so, what the results were." If the discussion lasted long, the final decision would come too late to matter. It has been said that while the Bolshevik Revolution was raging in the streets of Moscow, the leaders of the state church held a three-day meeting to decide what color the clerical hat should be — red or black.

Jesus was not marked by a conservative outlook. He stepped over most of the fences built up by human tradition. He cast the money changers from the temple. He exposed the current religionists as hypocrites and whited sepulchres. He proposed to confront the pagan world and the Roman Empire with twelve unarmed men. He proposed to set men free of sins by allowing himself to be crucified, declaring that he would be resurrected on the third day.

Most of our hesitancy to follow Christ comes not because we are uncertain of his will but because we are uncertain of the price. We are afraid discipleship will make misfits of us. We fear that if we witness we will lose popularity. We fear that godliness will be too dull.

III. Genuine travail lives out of the life of Christ (Isa. 66:8–10).

Isaiah, more than any other Old Testament prophet, looked ahead to Christ. The travail of which he spoke is akin to that which marked our Savior's earthly ministry and which he bequeathed to his disciples.

John Foster in *Then and Now* tells about a Hindu inquirer who came seeking Christian baptism. Somehow a New Testament had fallen into his hands, and its message had captivated him. He determined to make Jesus his Master, but he had no intention of joining a church until his reading brought him through the Gospels and into the book of Acts. There he found that the ministry of Jesus' life was taken up and carried out by the church and that where Jesus had left off, the church continued. Said the Hindu, "I must belong to the church that carries on the life of Christ" (William Barclay, *Fishers of Men* [Philadelphia: Westminster, 1966], 6).

The church has never grown when separated from the travail of Christ. God did not deliver Israel from Pharaoh until their cry went up to him. Pentecost did not come until 120 disciples gathered for ten days in expectant prayer at the danger of life itself. The price of travail has often been the blood of the martyrs.

Savonarola, the great preacher of Florence, was excommunicated because he preached against the sins of the pope. Nevertheless, the citizens of Florence protected him at first because they recognized him as a prophet of God. Then the pope applied such economic pressure that all the businessmen faced ruin. At that point, Savonarola's own friends felt forced to arrest him. He was then strangled and burned at the stake. Shortly before his execution, he said, "If you ask me in general as to the issue of this trouble, I reply, Victory. If you ask me in a particular sense, I reply, Death.... But Rome will not put out this fire; and if this be put out, God will light another" (Clarence Macartney, *Macartney's Illustrations* [New York: Abingdon, 1946], 60). That was in 1498. Just nineteen years later, Martin Luther nailed his theses to the church door at Wittenberg, and the resultant flames ignited the Reformation.

WEDNESDAY EVENING, MARCH 27

Title: Our Christian Ministry

Text: "Therefore, seeing we have this ministry, as we have received mercy, we faint not" **(2 Cor. 4:1)**.

Scripture Reading: 2 Corinthians 4:1–18

Introduction

Do you consider yourself to be a minister of Christ's gospel? Probably not, because most people have been conditioned to think of ministers as being only pastors or some other full-time vocational Christian servants. Many find it hard to believe that the New Testament doctrine of the priesthood of believers taught that every Christian is in the gospel ministry and has a ministry to perform.

The effectiveness of each church's work would be greatly improved if all of the members were to view the gospel ministry as an "our" (pastor's and people's) ministry rather than a "his" or "hers" (pastor's) ministry. This viewpoint would then correspond with the writings of Paul concerning the Christian ministry.

I. Our ministry is a demanding ministry.

Through the testimony of his own personal life, Paul revealed to the Christians at Corinth and to us the demands of the gospel ministry.

A. *It demands our faithfulness.* Our text for the day says, "Therefore seeing we have this ministry, as we have received mercy, we faint not." In the use of the words "faint not," Paul showed that one in the ministry is not to lack courage, lose heart, or be fainthearted.

Faithfulness is most difficult because it is much easier to lose courage and become timid when faced with the responsibilities of the ministry. To be faithful, we must put into practice the truth of Paul's words, "I can do all things in him who strengthens me" (Phil. 4:13 RSV).

B. *It demands our truthfulness.* There is no place in our ministry for any dishonesty, unscrupulous conduct, or corrupting of the Word of God. Our truthfulness should please and honor God. The apostle Paul wrote, "I therefore, the prisoner of the Lord, beseech you that ye walk worthy of the vocation wherewith ye are called" (Eph. 4:1).

II. Our ministry is a proclaiming ministry.

Even though proclamation is an inherent part in the Christian faith, it must not be limited to the pulpit. All Christians are to proclaim the gospel of Christ with their words and actions wherever they go.

A. *It proclaims the truth about Satan.* Paul said, "But if our gospel be hid, it is hid to them that are lost: in whom the god of this world hath blinded the minds of them which believe not, lest the light of the glorious gospel of Christ, who is the image of God, should shine unto them" (2 Cor. 4:3–4).

If we are to proclaim the truth about Satan, as Paul did, we will speak of him as being the enemy of the Christian, of the lost, and of God. But he can be defeated through Christ.

B. *It proclaims the truth about Jesus Christ.* "For we preach not ourselves, but Christ Jesus the Lord" (2 Cor. 4:5). The Bible teaches that Jesus Christ is the eternal, virgin-born Son of God. He is the only Savior of humankind, who died on the cross but rose from the grave and lives today.

III. Our ministry is a powerful ministry.

Only the God-empowered ministry can be called successful. No one is capable of being a success in the ministry in his or her own power. There can be no self-sufficiency, because the pressures and demands of the ministry are too great. It is as the prophet Zechariah wrote, "Not by might nor by power, but by my Spirit, says the LORD Almighty" (Zech. 4:6 NIV).

A. *Powerful even though we are weak.* The gospel has been entrusted to frail people who are trying to do the work of the ministry. Every person has some type of weakness that could destroy the effectiveness of the gospel ministry if it were not for the power of God. The Lord speaks to us as he did to Paul: "My grace is sufficient for thee: for my strength is made perfect in weakness" (2 Cor. 12:9).

B. *Powerful even though we suffer.* No one in the ministry is exempted from the possibility of having to suffer for the gospel's sake. Some suffer more than others, but even with suffering, the ministry can be powerful. For we can say with the psalmist, "Though he fall, he shall not be utterly cast down: for the LORD upholdeth him with his hand" (Ps. 37:24).

IV. Our ministry is a victorious ministry.

There is a promised victory to every minister of the gospel. It is found in the words of the apostle John, "Everyone born of God overcomes the world. This is the victory that has overcome the world, even our faith" (1 John 5:4 NIV).

A. *Victorious over the failures of the flesh.* The same power of God that raised up Jesus Christ from the dead is able to be victorious over the failures of the flesh. As Paul said, "In all these things we are more than conquerors through him that loved us" (Rom. 8:37).

B. *Victorious over death.* Paul was aware that death does not stop the work of the ministry. "Death is swallowed up in victory. O death, where is thy sting? O grave, where is thy victory? The sting of death is sin; and the strength of sin is the law. But thanks be to God, which giveth us the victory through our Lord Jesus Christ. Therefore, my beloved brethren, be ye stedfast, unmoveable, always abounding in the work of the Lord, forasmuch as ye know that your labour is not in vain in the Lord" (1 Cor. 15:54–58).

Conclusion

Every Christian is in the ministry! This is both a privilege and a responsibility. Let us do our best to make "our ministry" what God wants it to be.

SUNDAY MORNING, MARCH 31

Title: If There Were No Easter

Text: "Now if Christ be preached that he rose from the dead, how say some among you that there is no resurrection of the dead? But if there be no resurrection of the dead, then is Christ not risen: And if Christ be not risen, then is our preaching vain, and your faith is also vain. Yea, and we are found false witnesses of God; because we have testified of God that he raised up Christ: whom he raised not up, if so be that the dead rise not. For if the dead rise not, then is not Christ raised: And if Christ be not raised, your faith is vain; ye are yet in your sins. Then they also which are fallen asleep in Christ are perished. If in this life only we have hope of Christ, we are of all men most miserable. But now is Christ risen from the dead, and become the firstfruits of them that slept" **(1 Cor. 15:12–20).**

Scripture Reading: Matthew 28:1–8

Hymns: "Christ the Lord is Risen Today," Wesley

"Great Redeemer, We Adore Thee," Harris

"Jesus Shall Reign Where'er the Sun," Watts

Offertory Prayer: On this day of joy and gladness, make our hearts thankful for every measure of your grace, Father. Through our tithes and offerings brought to you, we dedicate ourselves to the service of the living Lord. In Jesus' name. Amen.

Introduction

Verse 14 of our Scripture text begins with the phrase, "And if Christ be not risen." What a terribly oppressive assumption this is! There are many times in life when "if" would have made all the difference in the world. There is an accident on the highway, and the driver says, "*If* only we had taken the other road!" There is a house fire, and the owner says, "*If* only we had gone back to check!" There is a death in the family, and a loved one says, "*If* we could have gotten him to the doctor a little sooner!" These are terrible "ifs," but the most oppressive of all is that of our Easter text: "If Christ be not risen...." What if Easter is *not* true? What if Christ is *not* risen from the dead? Thinking of this terrible assumption, the apostle Paul draws some equally oppressive conclusions.

I. If there is no Easter.

A. *Our preaching is vain (1 Cor. 15:14).* "*Then* is our preaching vain." I purposely emphasize "then." I want you to feel the ironic force of this terrible "if." Paul begins this chapter by reminding the Corinthians that he has given his labor and life to declare the gospel. He says, "I preached it. You received it. You are saved by it. I was persecuted because of it. I labored abundantly for it. Now if Christ be not risen, if there is no Easter, all this was in vain." The logic could not be otherwise. Without an Easter, all preaching is empty and void. It is a pathetic fiasco; it is petty prattle. If there is no Easter, all preachers are guilty of giving stones for bread and serpents for fish.

Our world has known some great preachers. Through the Christian centuries their voices have been trumpets of the Lord to people.

Come with me to the hill of Monte Morello where the people of Florence, Italy, gather. They have come in the lingering light of late afternoon to hear a preacher. There he stands silhouetted against the sky. That preacher's name is Girolamo Savonarola. The pope's legate has offered him a cardinal's hat in exchange for his silence. Savonarola replies, "No hat will I have but that of a martyr reddened by my own blood." And martyred he was! But it was all vanity if there is no Easter.

In Boston Commons more than two and a half centuries ago, thousands stood through a chilling morning rain to listen to a preacher. And as Jonathan Edwards preached of the judgment of God on sins, the people cried out for mercy. But what he said was all a lie if there is no Easter.

And what shall we say of the preaching of Spurgeon, Moody, Sunday, and Graham? They are all voices of vanity if Christ is not risen.

B. *Your faith is in vain (1 Cor. 15:14).* I wonder what this little company of believers thought when they read those words: "Your faith is vain." What a price they had paid for their faith! They were despised, outcast, and tortured; others had died for their faith. But if there is no Easter, it is less than a tawdry trinket; it is all a burst bubble.

Hebrews 11 is a roll call of those who lived by faith. Noah believed what God said and obeyed him. For 120 years he preached God's judgment, and all the while he built the ark. But if there is no Easter, Noah was just a stubborn fanatic. Abraham, at God's command, left home, business, and friends to go to a place he did not even know about yet—some place God called the "Promised Land." He believed God and started walking. But Abraham was nothing more than the world's biggest tramp if there is no Easter. Moses believed God had a purpose for Israel, and he chose to suffer oppression with the children of God rather than to enjoy the pleasures of Egypt. What a fool he was if Easter is not true! And if Christ is not risen, *your* faith is vain, too. Tell this to the dear believer who has trusted God for half a century. Tell him his every prayer, his hopes, his longings are nothing—vanity—that there is no Easter.

C. *We are found false witnesses of God (1 Cor. 15:15).* We are not mistaken witnesses, but false witnesses; not deluded, but liars; not victims of our excited and overwrought senses, but deceivers. How this thought must have stung the apostle Paul! He was proud of his apostleship and calling. He was an ambassador for Christ. But if there is no Easter, he is rather a false witness. See what Paul endured to be a liar: his life was threatened at Damascus; he was stoned at Lystra, assaulted at Iconium, beaten at Philippi, and mobbed

111

at Thessalonica; and he was in peril of robbers, rivers, fever, hunger—all this—only at last to be proved a liar, if Christ is not risen.

D. *The believing dead are perished (1 Cor. 15:18).* These who died in faith thought they were going to their rest and reward. They thought they would be delivered from him who has the power of death. They thought that one day the trumpet of God would call them from their sleep. But they were wrong if there is no Easter. There is something more than hope lost here. The deepest instinct of the human heart is involved. Our hope of immortality is involved. Is this all a cheat? Is the grave the victor? It is—if there is no Easter.

> *Asleep in Jesus! Blessed sleep,*
> *   from which none ever wakes to weep,*
> *A calm and undisturbed repose,*
> *   unbroken by the last of foes;*
> *Asleep in Jesus! O how sweet,*
> *   to be for such a slumber meet.*
> *With holy confidence to sing,*
> *   that death has lost her venomed sting.*
> — Margaret Mackay

But if Christ is not risen from the dead, then death's sting is real and the grave is the victor.

II. But Easter is true.

The apostle Paul could not leave us at the grave without hope. He hastened to write verse 20: "But now is Christ risen from the dead." Glory! Hallelujah! From that terrible assumption "if," he moved to the glorious fact "is"! Christ *is* risen!

> *Up from the grave He arose,*
> *With a mighty triumph o'er His foes,*
> *He arose a victor from the dark domain,*
> *And He lives forever with His saints to reign.*
> *He arose, He arose, Hallelujah, Christ arose.*
> — Robert Lowry

Jesus lives today to quicken our mortal bodies to immortality, to bring forth incorruption from decay and death, to remove the dusty sandals and give us resurrection shoes, to lift us from this miry clay and set us in "the heavenlies."

Because there *is* an Easter, our preaching is not vanity; it is the power of God to salvation for all who believe. Your faith is not vain, for God is not ashamed to be called our God, and he has prepared for us a city whose foundation is in heaven.

We are not found to be false witnesses, but rather we declare the truth of the gospel—that which our eyes have seen and our hands have handled of the Word of Life. Those who are asleep in Jesus are not perished; rather, they await the resurrection call to a life immortal and eternal.

Because Easter is true and Jesus lives, we refuse to be pitiable people. We have marched through more than nineteen centuries with the banner of the cross. Wherever our feet have trod, we have put a song in the heart, we have lifted up the brokenhearted, we have set the captives free, we have declared the acceptable year of the Lord. Today, during another Easter, we declare this gospel hope and salvation. Believe it! Easter is true: Christ arose and has become the firstfruits of eternal life.

If Easter Be Not True

If Easter be not true,
Then all the lilies low must lie;
The Flanders poppies fade and die;
The spring must lose her fairest bloom,
For Christ were still within the tomb —
If Easter be not true.

If Easter be not true,
Then faith must mount on broken wing;
Then hope no more immortal spring;
Then love must lose her mighty urge;
Life prove a phantom, death a dirge —
If Easter be not true.

If Easter be not true,
'Twere foolishness the cross to bear;
He died in vain who suffered there;
What matter though we laugh or cry,
Be good or evil, live or die,
If Easter be not true?

If Easter be not true —
But it is true, and Christ is risen!
And mortal spirit from its prison
Of sin and death with Him may rise!
Worthwhile the struggle, sure the prize,
Since Easter, aye, is true!

—Henry H. Barstow

SUNDAY EVENING, MARCH 31

Title: The Person God Uses

Text: "After the death of Moses the servant of the LORD, the LORD [said] to Joshua son of Nun, Moses' aide" **(Josh. 1:1 NIV).**

Scripture Reading: Joshua 1:1–9

Introduction

It takes an unusual man to follow a great man. God's man to succeed Moses was Joshua. What do we know about Joshua? Joshua was an Ephraimite, son of Nun (1 Chron. 7:22–27). His name means "salvation." Two months after the exodus, he was made Israel's leader and successfully led the children of Israel into the Promised Land. His life might be divided into two sections: (1) as the aide of Moses and (2) as the new leader of Israel after the death of Moses.

Joshua never thought that he would one day be the leader of the Israelite host. He was content "to play second fiddle" and be Moses' aide. However, God was preparing him to be Israel's leader in the land of promise. Some people are too self-important for God to use. Some are too full of their own schemes for God to use. Some have to have their own way all the time, and God cannot use them.

In the Scripture passage under consideration some suggestions are made as to the kind of person God can use in his work. All of us need to search our hearts and see if we are the kind of people God can use. Let us consider some of the characteristics of Joshua and note in him the characteristics of people God uses.

I. The person God uses has a distinct call from the Lord (Josh. 1:1, 5; Num. 27:15–23).

A person assured of a divine call is ready for spiritual leadership. In fact, the source of strength for Christian leadership is a distinct call from the Lord. A person who is called of the Lord can cross broad rivers, conquer walled cities, and overcome the enemy of God's people. Knowing his own deficiencies, knowing the criticism that comes to those who dare to stand for God, Joshua looked away from these to the God who called him and was the source of his strength.

The great question for all of God's workers is not "Am I qualified?" but "Am I called to do this work?" God's workers need to be assured of God's call. God's workers need to know they are where God wants them to serve. In Joshua's call, God's command is given, God's presence is assured, and God's task is assigned. Joshua knew God had called him, and he was serving where God wanted him to serve.

Like Jesus, we must say, "My meat is to do the will of him that sent me, and to finish his work." Like the psalmist, we must say, "I delight to do thy will, O my God" (Ps. 40:8). His call must come first in our lives if he is to use us. There can be no rival calls.

II. The person God uses is faithful (Josh. 1:1).

Joshua was Moses' faithful minister. The word *minister* means "one who serves." Joshua served as Moses' minister for God's sake.

The historian Josephus pointed out that Joshua lived forty years in Egypt and forty years in the wilderness. He had endured hardship and privation, fought God's enemies, and faced a false report in the wilderness. He had seen the giants. After Joshua had served faithfully for eighty years, God spoke to him and placed him in a place of great leadership. A faithful person is one God can use.

Who can tell what God is preparing us for? We murmur and complain about our unimportant place of service. We feel we are worthy of far more than we have. However, let us be aware that God may be testing us as to our faithfulness. In Jesus' parable of the ten minas recorded in Luke 19, the master says to the faithful servant, "Well done, my good servant! Because you have been trustworthy in a very small matter, take charge of ten cities" (v. 17 NIV).

Faithfulness is a part of our task, and it is a required quality if we are to please the Lord and be used by him.

III. The person God uses is filled with the Word of God (Josh. 1:8).

God said to Joshua, "This book of the law shall not depart out of thy mouth; but thou shalt meditate therein day and night, that thou mayest observe to do according to all that is written therein: for then thou shalt make thy way prosperous, and then thou shalt have good success" (Josh. 1:8). If we are to be used of the Lord, we must meditate on God's Word. Reading God's Word will assure us of God's presence and power, and when we are filled with God's Word, we are ready to be used by God as was Joshua.

IV. The person God uses is courageous (Josh. 1:2).

Joshua was a man of courage. His first appearance on the stage of Israel's history was when he commanded the battle against the Amalekites at Rephidim. Of all the men in Israel, Joshua was chosen by Moses to lead the battle against the Amalekites.

The next appearance of Joshua was when he went up with the twelve spies to spy out the land of Canaan. All of them agreed that it was a fruitful land and one "flowing with milk and honey." However, ten of the spies said there were giants in the land and that the Israelites by comparison were as grasshoppers. Only Joshua and Caleb gave a courageous report: Israel could conquer the land.

Whenever a great work is to be done for the Lord, it calls for courage. At the beginning of Joshua's leadership of Israel, God said to Joshua, "Be strong and of good courage.... Only be strong and very courageous.... Have not I commanded thee? Be strong and of good courage" (Josh. 1:6, 7, 9).

Too many people have the grasshopper complex. Too many are timid and afraid of the enemy. If God is to use us, we must have courage that is born of unfaltering faith in the Lord God!

V. The person God uses is decisive (Josh. 24:14–15).

Joshua was a man of decision. He had decided to follow God, and the deeds of his daily life rang with that decision. He was a man who did not waver, did not falter, did not hesitate, did not delay. When God's will was clear to him, he did it immediately.

Joshua was not only decisive himself, but he called upon others to be decisive.

He said, "Now, therefore fear the LORD, and serve him in sincerity and in truth: and put away the gods which your fathers served on the other side of the flood, and in Egypt, and serve ye the LORD" (Josh. 24:14).

Conclusion

Whom will you serve? Joshua told the people there were many gods they could serve. And there are many gods to be served today: business, society, money, power, fame, appetite, pleasure, and sex. But what are these gods compared to the Lord Jesus Christ? Serve him! Let him use you for his glory!

APRIL

- **Sunday Mornings**

    The truth of the resurrection permeates the morning messages between Easter and Mother's Day.

- **Sunday Evenings**

    Continue the series "Important People You Should Know."

- **Wednesday Evenings**

    The theme for the Wednesday evening messages is "Thanks Be to God." We hear this refrain repeated time and time again in the New Testament.

WEDNESDAY EVENING, APRIL 3

Title: God's Unspeakable Gift

Text: "Thanks be unto God for his unspeakable gift" (**2 Cor. 9:15**).

Scripture Reading: 1 Timothy 1:12–16

Introduction

The apostle Paul was continually amazed at the greatness of God's grace to him through Christ Jesus. He found it beyond his power to comprehend why God should love the chief of sinners. Paul would have been very much at home with the songwriter who said:

> *I stand amazed in the presence*
> *Of Jesus the Nazarene,*
> *And wonder how He could love me,*
> *A sinner, condemned, unclean.*
>
> *How marvelous! how wonderful!*
> *And my song shall ever be;*
> *How marvelous! how wonderful!*
> *Is my Saviour's love for me!*
>
> —Charles H. Gabriel

The apostle Paul did not have words to describe the gratitude of his heart as he considered God's indescribably wonderful gift to him through Jesus Christ.

I. God's gift is indescribably wonderful because of the love that thought it.

Our salvation was born in the heart of a loving God. God loves us not because we are lovely but because God is love.

Love caused God to determine to rescue people from the waste of sin. Love caused God to call Abraham to be his redemptive servant. Love caused God to rescue the Israelites out of Egypt. Love caused God to call the prophets as his spokesmen. Love caused God to inspire the psalmists to sing.

II. God's gift is indescribably wonderful because of the love that brought it.

Love in the heart of God conceived the idea of the only begotten Son becoming a man. Love selected a maiden to be the mother of the Christ. Love brought the Savior to the lives of humans. Love motivated Jesus' life from the very beginning. Love caused him to perform miracles of healing and deliverance and to speak words of encouragement as well as words of warning.

III. God's gift is indescribably wonderful because of the love that wrought it upon the cross.

The death of Jesus Christ can be viewed from many different perspectives.

The apostles of our Lord saw it as the greatest personal tragedy that had ever happened to them. It was a cruel, inhuman murder of their dearest and most precious friend. It was the defeat of all of their plans and hopes for the future.

Christ's death on the cross was a horrible, indescribable shock to his mother and to the women who stood near the cross. Neither words nor emotions can begin to fathom the agony that these women must have experienced.

To the scribes, Pharisees, and the high priests, Jesus' death was a great personal victory. They had succeeded in the accomplishment of their plans to put to death the man who threatened their authority and their status. From the viewpoint of the Roman soldiers, it was just another routine execution. To the idle passersby, it was a horrible experience to hurry past.

Something mysterious was happening that day. One of the thieves who was crucified with Jesus radically changed his attitude while on the cross. He recognized something unique about the Man on the center cross and requested consideration when he entered into his kingdom. Following Jesus' death, the centurion in charge of the crucifixion said, "Truly this man was the Son of God" (Mark 15:39).

Conclusion

It was only after the resurrection that the apostles and disciples of our Lord were able to begin to understand the greatness of the love of God that permitted Jesus Christ to die on the cross. It was only under the guidance of the Holy Spirit who came on the day of Pentecost that they were able to see that the crucifixion was not a tragedy but a triumph. They perceived that while the crucifixion was a revelation of the vile depravity of the human heart, it was at the same time a revelation of the indescribable love of God for his creatures.

These early followers of our Lord were moved to love with all of their hearts him who had labored for the rest of their lives to be channels through which that love might reach the hearts and lives of the people of the world.

Today we are the recipients of this great gift through faith in Jesus Christ. We should join with the apostle Paul who said, "Thanks be unto God for his unspeakable gift." Our lives should demonstrate our thanksgiving and gratitude for God's goodness to us.

SUNDAY MORNING, APRIL 7

Title: The Sunday after Easter

Text: "And after eight days again his disciples were within, and Thomas with them: then came Jesus, the doors being shut, and stood in the midst, and said Peace be unto you. Then saith he to Thomas, Reach hither thy finger, and behold my hands; and reach hither thy hand, and thrust it into my side: and be not faithless, but believing. And Thomas answered and said unto him, My LORD and my God" (**John 20:26–28**).

Scripture Reading: John 20:19–29

Hymns: "Rejoice, the Lord Is King," Wesley

"Come, Thou Fount of Every Blessing," Robinson

"Where He Leads Me," Blandly

Offertory Prayer: Dear risen Lord, on the Sunday after Easter, may our love for you be no less strong than last week. In the gifts we bring to your altar, may we show to a waiting world the strength of faith we have in the saving gospel. In Jesus' name. Amen.

Introduction

A minister once suggested to his music director that they sing "Christ the Lord Is Risen Today." The director protested, "But this is the Sunday *after* Easter." The minister replied, "I know, but every Sunday is an Easter." The good pastor had not misread the calendar. He was quite right in saying that every Sunday is an Easter.

The music director was right too. This is the Sunday after Easter. Anyone can see that! Last Sunday the churches were crowded, chairs were placed in the aisles, and to accommodate the throngs at worship, many churches had to have multiple services. That was last Sunday. Last Sunday the minister read the resurrection story and the choir sang "Christ the Lord Is Risen Today." Then most of us went home to the same old kind of living. We became occupied again with the "cares of this world." We were beset by frustration, fear, and fatigue. Did Easter really make any difference? So what that Christ the Lord is risen today?

It must have been a little like that the first Easter. The women had come back from the empty tomb with the wonderful news that Christ had risen, but that seemed like an idle tale. Peter and John, the investigating committee sent to check out the women's story, returned with the disappointing news that the tomb was indeed empty, but they could not find the Lord. Officially, the report was that the disciples had stolen the body away. It is no wonder their hearts were filled with fear and doubt. What should they do now? It seemed best to call for a church meeting that night to hear all the stories and try to get at the truth. Many questions needed answering. Where is he now? Would he show himself again? Would we recognize him? What would he look like? It was a group of anxious disciples that met that Easter Sunday night in the Upper Room.

I. Easter Sunday night.

A. *The risen Lord.*

> *Then the same day at evening, being the first day of the week, when the doors were shut where the disciples were assembled for fear of the Jews, came Jesus and stood in the midst, and saith unto them, Peace be unto you. And when he had so said, he showed them his hands and his side. Then were the disciples glad, when they saw the Lord. Then said Jesus to them again, Peace be unto you: as my Father hath sent me, even so send I you. And when he had said this, he breathed on them, and saith unto them, Receive ye the Holy Ghost. (John 20:19–22)*

Glory! Hallelujah! It is the Lord. He is risen indeed! What an unexpected blessing it was to experience the living presence of the Lord himself. He gave his blessing of "peace" and breathed on his disciples the Holy Spirit. You never know what may happen at church on Sunday night!

B. *The absent Thomas.* "But Thomas, one of the twelve, called Didymus, was not with them when Jesus came" (John 20:24). I wonder why Thomas was not at church that Sunday night. Maybe he was sick, or maybe company came and he forgot about the meeting. Maybe he got tied up in some business matter, or maybe he stayed home to watch a movie. Whatever the reason for his absence, he missed a great blessing.

C. *The witnessing disciples.* "The other disciples therefore said unto him, We have seen the Lord. But he said unto them, Except I shall see in his hands the print of the nails, and put my finger into the print of the nails, and thrust my hand into his side, I will not believe" (John 20:25).

That whole week after Easter, Thomas was on the prayer and visitation list of the church. On Monday Peter and John visited Brother Thomas and shared their story of running to the tomb at the report of the women, of finding the tomb empty, and then of seeing the risen Lord in person. Thomas said, "I don't doubt what you saw, but unless I see it too, don't expect me to believe." On Tuesday he was visited by Mary Magdalene. Mary related her story of the early morning visit to the garden, of seeing the empty tomb, and through tears and weeping for sorrow, of seeing the risen Lord also. Thomas said, "You've had a great emotional experience,

Mary. I've just been reading *The Motivational Psychology of Apparitional Experiences*. You know, doctors claim that sometimes in the midst of a great emotional experience, you can see and hear just what you want to—real or not."

Poor Thomas, see what doubts he had by missing church last Sunday night! But the story of "doubting Thomas" does not end here.

II. The Sunday after Easter.

A. *The risen Lord appeared again (John 20:26–29).* Oh the blessed patience and grace of our Lord! He did not write Thomas off. He would not let him go on in doubting faith. How tenderly the Lord stooped to Thomas's demands. Jesus allowed Thomas the very proof he had been demanding. He allowed Thomas the double proof of sight and touch. Jesus said, "Be not faithless but believing." "Faithless" here means a state of contentment with disbelief—a settled condition of doubt. This is the danger of missing church! Your faith cools off. The joy you once knew in Christian service and fellowship is lost. You begin to deny and doubt and grumble. Do not let this happen to you.

B. *Thomas's confession of faith (John 20:28).* This is the cry of personal faith. Thomas is not quoting someone else. It is his own conviction: "My Lord and my God." Being in church the Sunday after Easter had done something to Thomas. He had a fresh vision of the risen Lord. He made a rededication of his life. His faith was revived. What Thomas said became the pattern of confession for all believers. Others had called Jesus the Christ, good teacher, miracle worker, and the Son of God, but Thomas called him "Lord and God"—"Adonai and Elohim." Condensed here in one utterance is the meaning of the person and work of Jesus. He is Lord; that means Sovereign, the Master of life. All is committed to him. He is God; that means he is divine, Messiah, Savior.

> *Jesus thou art my Lord and God.*
> *I joy to call thee mine;*
> *For on thy head, though pierced with thorns,*
> *I see a crown divine.*

Conclusion

Jesus spoke a beatitude in John 20:29. He said, "Thomas, because thou hast seen me, thou hast believed: blessed are they that have not seen, and yet have believed." It is what we do not see that is the strength of our hearts. The apostle Paul said, "We look not at the things which are seen, but at the things which are not seen: for the things which are seen are temporal; but the things which are not seen are eternal" (2 Cor. 4:18). There is a danger in seeing—in making sight the satisfaction of curiosity—and then being content. Seeing and touching may *help* faith, but they can never *produce* it.

Years later the apostle Peter remembered that Sunday after Easter and wrote: "Whom having not seen, ye love; in whom, though now ye see him not, yet believing, ye rejoice with joy unspeakable and full of glory" (1 Peter 1:8). I call you to such a faith and joy today—this Sunday after Easter.

SUNDAY EVENING, APRIL 7

Title: The Man Who Was Not for Sale

Text: "And Naboth said to Ahab, the LORD forbid ... that I should give the inheritance of my fathers unto thee" (**1 Kings 21:3**).

Scripture Reading: 1 Samuel 21:1–29

Introduction

The story of Naboth, the man who was not for sale, is one of the strangest dramas in the entire Bible. The drama speaks of love, courage, and fear of God. By contrast, the drama speaks of covetousness, hatred, immaturity, false witness, death, and the judgment of God.

The drama introduces us to seven characters: (1) Naboth, a humble, God-fearing man owned a vineyard in Jezreel. He would not sell his vineyard, was not flattered by an interview with the king, and was not impressed by the king's invitation to the royal palace. (2) Ahab was the son of Omri and was the seventh king of the northern kingdom. His capitol was at Samaria, but he lived in Jezreel in an ivory palace surrounded by all the pleasures and luxuries of royalty. The writer of 1 Kings summarized his character when he wrote: "But there was none like unto Ahab, who did sell himself to work wickedness in the sight of the LORD, whom Jezebel his wife stirred up" (1 Kings 21:25). (3) Jezebel was the daughter of Ethbaal, king of the Zidonians, and she was also Ahab's queen and a zealous worshiper of Baal. She supported 450 prophets of Baal (1 Kings 18:19) and killed all the prophets of God on whom she could lay her hands (vv. 4–13). (4) The false witnesses, the men of Belial, were instruments in the hands of others. They were guilty of false witness and murder. (5) The corrupt elders and nobles were men who feared Jezebel more than they feared God. They were men of the law who, in the name of the law, violated all the laws of God and man. (6) Elijah the Tishbite was the prophet of God. He was a man of righteous power who listened to God and proclaimed his Word. (7) God is portrayed in the drama as the God who is watching. He is the God of anger, judgment, and punishment. Also, he is the God who delights in mercy.

Naboth had a vineyard the king wanted, but Naboth felt he could neither sell the vineyard nor give it away. Ahab and Jezebel were determined to have the vineyard at any cost. Naboth could not be bought; he was not for sale.

I. The man who is not for sale loves God supremely.

Naboth loved God first. He was a man who sought first the kingdom of God and his righteousness (Matt. 6:33). Naboth loved the Lord his God with all his heart, with all his soul, and with all his mind (Matt. 22:37). Therefore Naboth could not sell out to the wicked king. The man who loves God supremely will not sell out to the devil.

II. The man who is not for sale loves God's laws.

Three things stood in Naboth's way of selling his vineyard to Ahab.

A. *Naboth's duty to God (Lev. 25:23; Num. 36:7–9; 1 Kings 21:3).* Naboth knew about the laws of God, and Ahab knew about them too. To Naboth the law of God was a living reality; to Ahab the law of God was a dead letter. To Naboth no one's will was to be compared with God's will. To Ahab God's will was nothing.

B. *Naboth's duty to his forefathers and to his posterity.* Ever since the vineyard had been allotted to his first ancestor, that vineyard had been in his family. It had been transmitted through a long line to him. It was his duty to transmit it intact to those who came after him.

C. *Naboth's vineyard had always been his home.* For generations the vineyard had been in his family. He had played in it as a boy. By right, when life was over, his sons should inherit the vineyard.

III. The man who is not for sale loves his loved ones.

Naboth loved those who went before him. He loved those who would follow him. He wanted his heirs to have the vineyard. Everything about the drama convinces us that Naboth had a wonderful family that he loved, and he would not rob them of the beautiful vineyard that one day should be theirs.

IV. The man who is not for sale is not greedy for gain.

Ahab said to Naboth, "Give me thy vineyard, that I may have it for a garden of herbs, because it is near unto my house: and I will give thee for it a better vineyard than it; or, if it seem good to thee, I will give thee the worth of it in money" (1 Kings 21:2). Ahab was the owner of vast territories; he lived in an ivory palace, but he was not satisfied. He wanted more, more, and more. When Ahab did not get the vineyard, he felt his wishes were thwarted, his royalty insulted, his dignity compromised, and his will opposed.

One bold sign hangs over this drama for all to read: "Beware of Covetousness." Naboth could have used his vineyard for greed, but he was not for sale and would not sell his soul for silver.

V. The man who is not for sale does not give in to the whims of the wicked.

One is foolish to give himself to wickedness or to the ravenous desires of the wicked. The wicked are never satisfied. Ahab was not satisfied even though he owned vast territories.

The drug dealers, the gamblers, the criminals, the perverts, the abortionists, are never satisfied. They will buy our vineyard unless we stand against their wicked whims. Like Naboth we must say no!

VI. The man who is not for sale is a person of high principles.

Principle meant more to Naboth than worldly honor, more than money, and more than an invitation to the royal palace. Naboth could have asked a good price for his vineyard, and the covetous Ahab would have paid it. Cynics have said that every person has a price. However, let it be said that a person with godly principles is not for sale.

VII. The man who is not for sale is faithful unto death.

The great English scholar Alexander Maclaren pointed out that all forms of wicked character are portrayed in this drama. Ahab was wicked and weak. Jezebel was wicked and strong. The elders of Israel and the two witnesses were wicked and subservient. In Naboth we see the strength of spiritual character. We see a man dedicated to his Lord. We see a man who is faithful unto death (Rev. 2:10).

Conclusion

The conclusion of this drama reminds us of the proverb: "Though hand join in hand, the wicked shall not be unpunished" (Prov. 11:21). Ignoring the warning given to him by Micaiah, Ahab went to battle with Jehoshaphat against Syria to recover Ramoth-Gilead. Trying to escape death, he put off his royal robes and went to battle disguised as a private soldier. But no disguise can hide the sinner from God and his judgment. A random arrow mortally wounded Ahab. The unknown soldier who wounded him was the bowman of divine retribution.

Ahaziah and Joram, Ahab's sons, met violent deaths. What about the queen Jezebel? Eleven years after the death of Ahab, King Jehu had her thrown down from her tower in Jezreel and drove over her body with his chariot; her blood spattered the horses and the wall. Later Jehu gave instruction that she be buried, but it was found that the dogs had left nothing of her but the skull, the feet, and the palms of her hands (2 Kings 9:7, 30–37).

Do not sell yourself to evil. Naboth was a man who was not for sale. Where do you stand?

WEDNESDAY EVENING, APRIL 10

Title: Triumph through Jesus Christ

Text: "Thanks be to God, who always leads us as captives in Christ's triumphal procession and uses us to spread the aroma of the knowledge of him everywhere" (**2 Cor. 2:14 NIV**).

Scripture Reading: 2 Corinthians 2:14–17

Introduction

Through Jesus Christ, God is at work in all things to bring out every possible good for those who love him and are seeking to please him in life (Rom. 8:28).

The apostle Paul was exceedingly grateful to the Lord for victory after victory that he experienced as he gave himself in faith and faithfulness to God's purpose for his life. We find Paul always pointing to God as the source of all that was good and beautiful and significant.

I. Christ wants to cause us to triumph in our days of decision.

Life is made up of decisions. Some of these decisions involve the free choice of alternatives that are open to us. Other decisions confront us with no alternative except to do or not do what must be done.

The decisions we make from day to day determine our destiny. Where we are today has been determined largely by the choices we made yesterday. We are confronted with many doors of opportunity. Some of these lead to success and happiness; others lead to defeat and despair. It is of tremendous importance that we look to the Christ who stands at every fork of the road seeking to give us guidance.

Through the truths of God's Word and the guidance of his Holy Spirit, our Lord will help us to make the decisions that will lead to triumph in life.

II. Christ wants to cause us to triumph in our days of difficulty.

Some people have the naive and mistaken idea that if they trust Jesus Christ and try to do what is right, they will never have any great difficulty in life. It does not take long for this illusion to be shattered. There is nothing in the Bible to give us the impression that all will be rosy and peaceful if we will simply have faith in God and do the best we can. Perhaps no one has ever suffered as much because of his faithfulness to God as did the apostle Paul (2 Cor. 11:24–27).

When Paul wrote to the church at Philippi, he expressed joy over the fact that all of the things that had happened to him had served to advance the cause of Christ and to enlarge the kingdom of God (Phil. 1:12–14). He also wrote that through Jesus Christ he had found strength to adjust himself to all circumstances of life (Phil. 4:13). This statement, interpreted by its context, reveals that Paul was not writing about some tremendous achievement of a spectacular nature. Instead, he was writing in terms of finding strength through Christ to adjust himself to the most deprived of circumstances. He would affirm that Jesus Christ has caused us to triumph even in our time of greatest difficulty.

III. Christ wants to cause us to triumph in our days of defeat.

The Bible contains the record of many who triumphed over their defeats and disappointments.

A. *Joseph is an example of one who experienced some serious defeats in life, yet God was at work to help him experience victory.* Joseph had a firm faith in God, along with integrity and a desire for personal purity. Instead of remaining throughout all of his life as a slave or prisoner, he became the prime minister of Egypt when Egypt was at its greatest glory.

B. *Ezekiel was trained to be a priest in Jerusalem.* Nebuchadnezzar invaded the country, and Ezekiel was one of the captives who went into the land of

Babylon. While he was there, he had a vision of God and responded with faith and commitment. God used him to be a great prophet to the exiles. Instead of being destroyed by defeat, he experienced triumph.

C. *In the same general period, Daniel was taken as a captive into the land of Babylon.* Instead of giving way to despair, he determined to be faithful to his God (Dan. 1:8). God used this young man, and he eventually became second only to the king in the country.

D. *God wants to cause us to triumph over temptation even when we have been defeated in the past by the evil one.* God offers forgiveness and cleansing.

E. *Perhaps the greatest defeat that the natural human faces is death.* Death is said to be the last enemy of humans. Even over this enemy, God will cause his children to triumph through faith in Christ Jesus.

Conclusion

Can you not join with the apostle Paul in saying, "Now thanks be unto God, which always causes us to triumph in Christ"? Express this gratitude today. We should not wait until tomorrow to express our thanksgiving and our gratitude. To express our thanksgiving for the triumphs of the past and the present will strengthen our faith as we face the future. The greater our faith, the greater will be our triumphs through Christ Jesus.

SUNDAY MORNING, APRIL 14

Title: The Ultimate Question

Text: "So when they had dined, Jesus saith to Simon Peter, Simon, son of Jonas, lovest thou me more than these? He saith unto him, Yea, Lord; thou knowest that I love thee. He saith unto him, Feed my lambs. He saith to him again the second time, Simon, son of Jonas, lovest thou me? He saith unto him, Yea, Lord; thou knowest that I love thee. He saith unto him, Feed my sheep. He saith unto him the third time, Simon, son of Jonas, Lovest thou me? Peter was grieved because he said unto him the third time, Lovest thou me? And he said unto him, Lord, thou knowest all things; thou knowest that I love thee. Jesus saith unto him, Feed my sheep" **(John 21:15–17)**.

Scripture Reading: John 21:1–17

Hymns: "I Will Sing the Wondrous Story," Rowley

"Give of Your Best to the Master," Grose

"Have Thine Own Way, Lord," Pollard

Offertory Prayer: Father in heaven, we are twice made yours—by creation and by redemption. For such works of your love, we give thanks to you. In a spirit of dedication, we bring our tithes and offerings to you. Let this measure of our love be used to advance your kingdom. For Jesus' sake. Amen.

Introduction

The text we have just read is an "after Easter" story. It tells what happened during one of the resurrection appearances of our Lord. It is not like the dramatic announcement of the women that the tomb was empty. It is the simple story of the meeting of a Man and his friends early one morning. There are two main characters in the story: Peter and Jesus. Let us look first at Peter.

I. A backsliding disciple.

    A. *In Galilee (John 21:1–2).* Peter was in trouble. That was nothing new for him. It seems he was always opening his mouth and putting his foot in it. That is what he had done that terrible night of his Lord's arrest. At supper Peter had said that although all should forsake Jesus, he would not. Jesus replied that before the next morning, Peter would deny his Lord three times. When they had come to arrest Jesus in the garden, Peter tried to play "Prince Valiant" with his sword and save Jesus from his captors. All he got for his effort was the rebuke of the Lord. Peter could not understand it. He was sick in his heart. Then in a weak moment like that, the test came. While standing in Pilate's courtyard, a servant girl asked, "Are you not one of his disciples?" With an oath, Peter denied he ever knew the Lord. What a night of bitter weeping that was! How his heart was filled with remorse! After that dreadful night, Peter must have wished he could talk with Jesus and ask his forgiveness. Later he had indeed seen the risen Lord on two occasions, but both times the room was crowded with other disciples and there was no chance to talk to Jesus alone. Then Peter remembered what the angels had told the women at the empty tomb on the morning of Jesus' resurrection: "Go your way, tell his disciples *and Peter* that he goeth before you into Galilee: there shall ye see him" (Mark 16:7, italics added). That settled it; he would go to Galilee.

    B. *Fishing (John 21:3).* "I go a-fishing." Any fisherman can see the sense in that! When you have a troubled heart, go fishing. When you don't know which way to turn, go fishing. When your world has fallen in, go fishing. This seemed the only sensible thing to do. You see, Peter was all mixed up. His heart was still right; he still loved his Lord. But he could not forget that awful night of betrayal and denial. Maybe once too often he had lost his head. Maybe Jesus could no longer use him. Maybe he had no plans for Peter. When you are "down" like Peter was, the best activity for you is fishing.

    C. *Failure (John 21:3).* "That night they caught nothing." I wonder what Peter was thinking. "Failure" was written all over him. Possibly he was thinking, "I can't even succeed at my old job." Until Peter got right with Jesus, nothing would succeed.

        Many of us are like Peter. We have sinned against our Lord. By word or deed, we have denied we ever knew him. Nothing is going to be right again until we "have a little talk with Jesus."

II. The risen Lord.

A. *A voice in the morning (John 21:4–6).* Peter and his friends fished all night. In the morning, the boat still rode high on the water. They had caught nothing. They were more than heartsore now: they were weary, cold, and hungry. Suddenly, from the shore a voice called out, "Have you caught anything?" "No." Then that voice again: "Cast your nets on the right side." Who was that telling Peter how to fish? "Why, I've been pulling oars through these waters my entire life. I've caught more fish with a willow stick, a piece of string, and a bent pin than that fellow probably can with a throw net. Who's telling me how to fish?"

Like Peter, we all are touchy about our failures. When someone tries to help at a sensitive time like that, we thank them to mind their own business.

B. *A miraculous catch of fish (John 21:6).* I suppose Peter's friends persuaded him to give it a try on the right side. And when the nets were drawn in, behold, they caught a multitude of fish so great that the nets began to break!

C. *A marvelous discovery (John 21:7).* About then, John made a discovery. "That voice—I knew there was something familiar about that voice. And now, all these fish. It must be … it *has* to be … the Lord!" That was just like Jesus: there to help! When Peter needed him most—when he had backslidden and lost the joy and assurance of Jesus' presence—Jesus was there.

Just when I need Him, Jesus is near;
Just when I falter, just when I fear;
Ready to help me, ready to cheer,
Just when I need Him most.

—William C. Poole

III. The ultimate question (John 21:15–17).

A. *Jesus and Peter alone.* As soon as the fish were brought to shore, the disciples found Jesus standing beside a fire he had prepared. They ate breakfast together. When they had finished eating, Jesus went to Peter and quietly said, "Come with me, I want to talk to you." For a while, they walked in silence. Then Jesus asked the question Peter had been expecting.

B. *Lovest thou me?* "Simon, son of Jonas, lovest thou me more than these?" Jesus had gone back to Peter's old name—the name he had before he made his great confession. That must have stung Peter's heart a bit. But a contrite heart is a necessary part of confession and forgiveness. And what is this "more than these"? Did not Jesus mean, "Peter, *now* do you dare say that you love me more than these other disciples do?"

Another important thing is the play on the two New Testament words for love. They are the words *agape* and *philia*. Both words are translated in the English Bible as "love." However, there is a difference in their meaning. *Agape* love is self-sacrificing, self-giving, godly love. *Philia* is a fondness, a love of friends, a respect. Jesus kept asking Peter, "Do you love me with a self-sacrificing love, the kind of love one has for God, a deep and intimate spiritual devotion?" Peter kept replying, "I love you as a friend; I have an affection for you; I respect you." This kind of love simply is not enough. It is not the right kind. After asking his question the third time, I think Jesus must have slipped his hand into Peter's hand. And there was that scar—the rough scar left by the nail of the cross.

> *Lord, it is my chief complaint,*
> *That my love is weak and faint,*
> *Yet I love thee and adore,*
> *O for grace to love thee more.*

How do you answer this ultimate question?
Jesus then gave Peter the ultimate command.

IV. The ultimate command (John 21:22).

"Follow thou me." That is how it had all started for Peter—that same command by these same waters. Three years before, while he was fishing, Peter had heard Jesus say, "Follow me, and I will make you to become fishers of men." Now at the end, Jesus gave Peter the ultimate command again: "Follow me." This is the proper commission that comes from the Lord when one says, "My Jesus I love thee, I know thou art mine."

Conclusion

In a short while, Peter was to enter into a whole new ministry. He would be of no use to God if he was still a man of divided devotions. If he was to be a "shepherd of sheep," he had in truth to love the Lord with all his heart. Jesus had to be first and last and everything between.

SUNDAY EVENING, APRIL 14

Title: The Man Who Loses the Battle of Life

Text: "And Achan answered Joshua, and said, Indeed I have sinned against the LORD God of Israel, and thus and thus have I done: when I saw among the spoils a goodly Babylonish garment, and two hundred shekels of silver, and a wedge of gold of fifty shekels weight, then I coveted them, and took them; and, behold, they are hid in the earth in the midst of my tent, and the silver under it" (**Josh. 7:20–21**).

Scripture Reading: Joshua 7:1–26

Introduction

The arrival of Israel in the Promised Land was a success story. The Israelites had crossed the Jordan victoriously, had met God at Gilgal, and had conquered Jericho. When we come to Joshua 7 we find Israel in retreat and in defeat and

Joshua on his face before God, filled with dismay and crying out to God for an answer:

> Alas, O Lord God, wherefore hast thou at all brought this people over Jordan, to deliver us into the hand of the Amorites, to destroy us? Would to God we had been content, and dwelt on the other side of the Jordan! O Lord, what shall I say, when Israel turneth their backs before their enemies! For the Canaanites and all the inhabitants of the land shall hear of it, and shall environ us round, and cut off our name from the earth: and what wilt thou do unto thy great name? (vv. 7–9)

God answered Joshua's prayer:

> And the Lord said unto Joshua, Get thee up; wherefore liest thou thus upon thy face? Israel hath sinned, and they have also transgressed my covenant which I commanded them: for they have even taken of the accursed thing, and have also stolen, and dissembled also, and they have put it even among their own stuff. Therefore the children of Israel could not stand before their enemies, but turned their backs before their enemies, because they were accursed: neither will I be with you any more, except ye destroy the accursed from among you. (vv. 10–12)

Achan was the man who caused Israel to lose the battle of Ai. He is mentioned three times in the Bible and always with reference to the defeat at Ai (Josh. 7; 22:20; 1 Chron. 2:7). He not only caused Israel to lose their battle in the conquest of Canaan, but he lost his own battle with life.

God does not want his children to lose the battle of life. He wants us to be victorious. Why did Achan lose?

I. The man who is covetous loses the battle of life.

Achan said: "I coveted them" (Josh. 7:21). The tenth commandment is a prohibition of covetousness. Paul pointed out that covetousness is idolatry (Col. 3:5). Covetous persons give themselves to wrong appetites, wrong desires, and wrong intentions.

Achan gave himself to covetousness, to gaining this world's goods. He sought that which it was not right for him to have. He was a covetous man, and his covetousness is one of the reasons he lost the battle of life.

II. The man who disobeys God's commands loses the battle of life.

Joshua had given to Israel God's commands concerning Jericho (Josh. 6:17–19; 7:11). Jericho and all that was in it were to be devoted to the Lord. The people were to be put to death with the exception of Rahab and her family. The Israelites must have faced great temptation in having to destroy so many valuable things instead of taking them for themselves, but God had given his commands, and they were to be obeyed.

Achan disobeyed God and took of the spoils of Ai that were set apart by the Lord.

III. The man who transgresses God's covenant loses the battle of life.

God had made a covenant with Joshua and Israel for the seizure and capture of Jericho. The covenant must be kept. Everything in Jericho was to be devoted to the Lord. All living beings were to be slain. The destructible materials were to be burned, and the indestructible materials were to be consecrated to the service of God. The sin was more than an act of disobedience; it was a violation of the divine covenant.

The sin of Achan was a sacrilege, a robbery of God, an impious seizure. The secrecy with which the sin was committed was a defiance of the omniscience of God. Achan violated God's covenant with Israel.

IV. The man who steals from God loses the battle of life.

Achan took that which belonged to God: "Israel hath sinned, and they have also transgressed my covenant which I have commanded them: for they have even taken of the accursed thing, and have also stolen" (Josh. 7:11). The fact that God had condemned the property and consecrated the metals should have kept Achan from stealing the property.

Sin deprives God not only of silver and gold, but of honor, love, service, and talents.

What are you taking from God? Are you taking the tithe? Are you taking time set aside for the worship of him?

V. The man who is untruthful loses the battle of life.

The King James Version says Achan "dissembled." The New International Version translates the word as "lied." The word means "to act deceitfully, to play the part of a hypocrite." Achan acted untruthfully; he acted a lie.

Victories in life are won by people who are truthful before God.

VI. The man who serves self rather than God loses the battle of life.

The trouble with Achan was that he wanted to serve self rather than God. He was more interested in his own desires than the desires of God. What *he* wanted was more important than what *God* wanted. He was not fully committed to God and God's way.

You will not win the battle in life as long as you serve self. God's desires must be considered. The accursed thing must be taken away. Everything done must please God and must be done for God's glory.

VII. The man who dishonors God's name loses the battle of life.

Joshua felt that what Achan had done would dishonor God's great and precious name. "And what wilt thou do unto thy great name?" (Josh. 7:9).

No person can sin and glorify God's name. No person can sin without affecting others. No person can grow cold spiritually without lowering the temperature of those around. That person will either honor or dishonor the name of God.

Conclusion

Are you winning the battle of life? Are you following God's will for you and yours? Be an overcoming Christian and win life's battle.

WEDNESDAY EVENING, APRIL 17

Title: Victory through Our Lord Jesus Christ

Text: "But thanks be to God, which giveth us the victory through our Lord Jesus Christ" **(1 Cor. 15:57).**

Scripture Reading: 1 Corinthians 15:51–58

Introduction

In our Scripture text today the apostle Paul gives expression to the gratitude of his heart for a unique victory that is assured to those who exercise a firm faith in Jesus Christ as Lord and Savior. He is shouting with joy because of the confidence he has in the ultimate victory that will be ours through faith in Christ Jesus.

Paul has concluded his classic statement on the resurrection of Christ. He has expressed his confidence and conviction that those who trust Jesus Christ will likewise experience victory over death and the grave. His heart sings with joy and thanksgiving.

I. We can be thankful for victory over sin.

A. *Through Jesus Christ we have victory over the penalty of sin, which is death (Rom. 6:23).*

B. *Through Jesus Christ we can have victory over the power of sin (Phil. 2:13).*

C. *Through Jesus Christ we will one day have victory over the very presence of sin (Heb. 9:28).*

II. We can be thankful for victory over suffering (2 Cor. 12:7–10).

Sooner or later suffering becomes the lot of almost every person who lives. For some, suffering is a crushing blow that shatters them beyond repair.

How can one face suffering, disappointment, or defeat in a victorious manner?

Paul discovered that being a follower of Jesus Christ did not immunize one from hardship and suffering. There is no promise of exemption from suffering merely because one has faith and lives a life of faithfulness.

Paul found in the grace of God the strength and the wisdom to be victorious even in the midst of human suffering. We can do likewise if we will keep our hearts open and if we will let Jesus Christ have possession of our minds and spirits. Through Christ we can turn tragedy into triumph.

III. We can be thankful for victory over death.

Paul declared that the last enemy of humans is death (1 Cor. 15:26). Seemingly, death wins the victory over everyone. But our Lord came to demonstrate

132

that life is more powerful than death. He came to taste death for every person (Heb. 2:9). He came to put death to death and to destroy its power (Heb. 2:14). He came to deliver people from the fear of the power of death (Heb. 2:15).

Our Lord came to die for us that we might not have to die. He affirmed that his victory over death should be taken as a proof that we would also be rescued from death and that we would live as he lived.

First Corinthians 15 is the classic New Testament passage that affirms that through Jesus Christ we will experience victory over Satan, sin, death, and the grave. In view of this, it is understandable that this great chapter should close with an anthem of praise and with a challenge to faithfulness in working for the Lord Jesus Christ.

Conclusion

Victory is a beautiful word to those who are the victors. Through Jesus Christ we are assured of victory in the game of life in which everything is at stake.

Daily we should express our thanks to God for the joy and the assurance of this victory. To contemplate the full significance of the victory that is ours through Christ will fill our hearts with joy. Hearts that are filled with joy will find a way to communicate that joy to others. Our expressions of thanksgiving and joy will cause others to want to know our Savior.

The words of our text should be in our minds every day: "But thanks be to God, which giveth us the victory through our Lord Jesus Christ" (1 Cor. 15:57).

SUNDAY MORNING, APRIL 21

Title: Why I Preach the Cross

Text: "We preach Christ crucified" **(1 Cor. 1:23)**.

Scripture Reading: 1 Corinthians 1:17–23; 2:1–5

Hymns: "In the Cross of Christ I Glory," Bowring

"'Man of Sorrows,' What a Name," Bliss

"When I Survey the Wondrous Cross," Watts

Offertory Prayer: We thank you Father, for your goodness to us. We thank you for material blessings and for spiritual blessings. But most of all we thank you for a loving Savior who gave himself for us—who suffered a cruel death that we might have everlasting life. We thank you that we can serve our risen Savior today. Take our offerings, Father, and bless them for your service. Take us, Father, and make us a blessing in your world. In Jesus' name we pray. Amen.

Introduction

There are so-called experts today in the field of religious authority who believe that the day of preaching is gone. The sermon is looked upon as an uninterrupted

133

and unchallenged monologue, and this is the day of the dialogue, we are told. To live and prosper in this day, some say we must swing our emphasis from preaching to ministry.

I say we must have both, for preaching and ministry are two arms of the same body. Jesus was insistent that he came to be a minister (servant), and he went about doing good. The Bible also says, "Jesus came preaching." These are two sides of the same coin. I am pleased to observe that both of these roles are experiencing a resurgence of interest and response in our day.

Not only is there a renewed interest in preaching, but there has never been a greater response to the preaching of the cross. The apostle Paul could well have centered his preaching in philosophy, in the Old Testament Law, in the Prophets, in Jewish traditions and practices, or in a social gospel as an answer to the social problems of his society. Paul was a learned man, a scholar, but he chose to preach Christ crucified, and God blessed his preaching.

There are those who say, "Just preach Jesus." But that is not enough. Satan is content with the preacher who proclaims Jesus as a good man, or even as the best man who ever lived. If the preacher leaves out the cross—the blood—his message is incomplete and impotent.

As we remember the death and resurrection of our Lord, I would like for this sermon to be a personal testimony to my own ministry of the cross.

I. I preach the cross out of gratitude.

A preacher named H. S. Kolb tells this story:

> When I was a student pastor, a man in the church went to a physician who removed a skin cancer from his face. Few times in life have I seen a man so grateful. He told everyone who would listen how this surgeon had delicately removed the malignant growth from his face and he was freed from its terror. He would say to a person, "Do you have a cancer? Do you know anyone who has a cancer? I know a surgeon who can make that person well." What would you think of a person cured of cancer who would withhold information and hope from another who was gripped with the same dread disease?

Christ, through his death on the cross, has provided a remedy for a disease far worse than cancer. No surgeon can remove this malignancy, and it is humanly incurable. It is called *sin*. The outcome of this disease, if not cured, is death, not only of the body, but of the soul. Out of gratitude to the Great Physician, I want everyone I meet to know about him. When I think of so many others still in the throes of this enslaving disease, I must not rest until they have all been warned of its consequences and informed of its cure. And that remedy is proclaimed in the preaching of the cross.

II. I preach the cross because it never grows old.

I want to preach a fresh gospel, and the story of the cross is always fresh news. You may read the account of the cross in any of the Gospels in just a few minutes, you may memorize parts of Scripture, and you may become familiar with the contents of the Bible; yet each time you read Scripture with your heart open to the illumination of the Holy Spirit, new truth will leap out of the inspired pages and new applications will be revealed for your life. If you wish to preach a gospel ever new, then preach the story of Christ crucified.

III. I preach the cross because of its adequate comfort to the human heart.

Pastor Kolb also told this story:

During the dark days of World War II, I was called to a home where grief-stricken parents had just received a telegram telling them that their oldest son had died in combat. As I sat with those parents, seeking to bring them comfort, I did not say, "We'll get even with the enemy that killed your boy." This would not have brought comfort. I told them that God understood, for he, too, had experienced the loss of his Son in the war against evil. I assured them that someday the war would be over and we could carry the message of the Prince of Peace to all the world with the hope that wars would cease.

One day a number of years ago, a young Korean exchange student at the University of Pennsylvania and a leader in Christian affairs on the campus left his room to stroll down to the corner to mail a letter to his parents. Eleven leather-jacketed teenagers came upon him, and without a word, they attacked him with their fists, blackjacks, and lead pipes. Then they fled, leaving him dead in the street.

The city where this heinous crime took place was shocked and incensed. An international incident seemed imminent as the story of this tragic, senseless murder was announced throughout the world. Then a letter was sent from Korea, signed by the parents and twenty other relatives of the student. It was addressed to the law enforcement authorities where the crime had taken place. It read as follows:

Our family has met together and decided to petition that the most generous treatment possible within the laws of your government be given those guilty of this crime. In order to give evidence of our sincere hope contained in this petition, we have decided to save money to start a fund to be used for the religious, educational, vocational, and social guidance of the boys when they are released. We have dared to express our hope with a spirit received from the gospel of our Savior, Jesus Christ, who died for our sins.

IV. I preach the cross because it is the only means of salvation from our sins.

The night before Jesus died on the cross, he prayed, "O my Father, if it be possible let this cup pass from me." In other words, he said, "If there be any other possible means by which people may be saved from their sins, then let this bitter cup of crucifixion pass from me." God answered that prayer the next day when he allowed his Son to die on the cross. Forevermore it was declared, "There is none other name under heaven given among men whereby we must be saved." The way is Jesus Christ and him crucified.

Conclusion

In the center of downtown London is a famous landmark called Charing Cross. It is often called "The Cross." The story is told of a little boy lost in the London fog. A policeman sought to assist him. "Is there any building or monument that is familiar to you that is near your home?" he asked. A light came over the boy's face as he said, "If you will take me to the cross, I think I can find my way home from there." And this is our message—the preaching of the cross that has guided multitudes through the ages into the safety of the Father's house.

SUNDAY EVENING, APRIL 21

Title: The Man Who Plays the Fool

Text: "Behold, I have played the fool, and have erred exceedingly" **(1 Sam. 26:21).**

Scripture Reading: 1 Samuel 26:21–25

Introduction

"Saul took a sword, and fell upon it" (1 Sam. 31:4), and that was the end of Saul. Who is able to survey the life of Saul and size it up accurately and adequately? Possibly Saul did the best job of evaluating his own life when he said of himself, "I have played the fool, and have erred exceedingly" (1 Sam. 26:21). Clarence Macartney called Saul "the greatest shipwreck in the Old Testament."

When Saul became king of Israel, it looked as if he would be the greatest and mightiest leader in the Old Testament. From the outside, he appeared to have everything. But time revealed that he had some serious character flaws: impatience, rashness, disobedience to God, envy, disloyalty to God, and suicide.

In what ways did Saul play the fool?

I. A man plays the fool when he disobeys God's commands.

Saul began his reign under the favor of God and with the help of Samuel. In the third year of Saul's reign, he committed his first great sin against God. On the eve of a battle, Samuel was delayed in arriving, so Saul took over Samuel's job as priest and offered burnt offerings and peace offerings. Saul had no right to do this. Samuel came and rebuked Saul for his hasty action: "But now thy kingdom shall not continue: the LORD hath sought him a man after his own heart, and the LORD hath commanded him to be captain over his people, because thou hast not kept that which the LORD commanded thee" (1 Sam. 13:14).

At another time, God told Saul to take his army and utterly destroy the Amalekites (1 Sam. 15:3) with all their possessions. Saul won the battle, but he kept King Agag alive and kept the spoils of all the best of the cattle (1 Sam. 15:7–9). Again, Samuel confronted Saul and told of his disobedience. After first denying his sin, Saul admitted his wrong, making an excuse that the people wanted to make sacrifices. Then Samuel reminded Saul that God wanted obedience: "Because thou hast rejected the word of the LORD, he hath also rejected thee from being king" (1 Sam. 15:23).

To obey God is better than sacrifice and to hearken to him is better than the fat of rams (1 Sam. 15:22). To disobey God is a serious offense.

II. A man loses his best friends when he plays the fool.

After Saul's failure to destroy King Agag, the Bible says, "And Samuel came no more to see Saul until the day of his death" (1 Sam. 15:35).

Not only did Saul lose the friendship of Samuel, but he also lost the friendship of David. When David killed Goliath and gained popularity, the women sang, "Saul hath slain his thousands, and David his ten thousands" (1 Sam. 18:7). Saul could not stand David being more popular than himself, and the Bible says, "Saul eyed David from that day and forward" (1 Sam. 18:9).

Saul lost three great friends because of his actions: God, Samuel, and David. A man is a fool when he lets his sins cut him off from his best friends.

III. A man plays the fool when he seeks from the devil what he fails to find out from God.

There are some things we shall never know on this earth, "for now we see through a glass darkly, but then, face to face: now I know in part; but then shall I know even as also I am known" (1 Cor. 13:12).

Why do we insist on learning what God may not wish us to know? Why do we insist on resorting to fortune-tellers (1 Sam. 28:7–25)? It is foolish and fatal to seek from Satan and his imps what only God can tell us. Saul's sin cost him his throne (1 Chron. 10:13–14).

IV. A man fails some of the major tests of life when he plays the fool.

Saul lost the battle on Mount Gilboa, and there he lost his life (1 Sam. 31:1–6). Saul lost many battles, or tests, in life.

A. *A man fails the test of contact with God when he plays the fool.* Saul lived thirty years or more with the heavy responsibilities of kingship but without the Spirit of God. How tragic it is to live without God!

B. *A man fails the test of love when he plays the fool.* Saul became jealous, and his jealousy led to envy and hatred. To hate and to live without love in your heart is to fail one great test in life.

C. *A man fails the test of bigness when he plays the fool.* Instead of becoming a big man, Saul became a little man. Life is too short to live as a little person. We need to pray that God will make us giants for his sake.

Conclusion

One can live as a fool or as a faithful follower of the Lord. How will you live your life? Will you play the part of a fool? Will you be faithful to God's will for your life?

WEDNESDAY EVENING, APRIL 24

Title: Gratitude for God's Servants

Text: "But thanks be to God, which put the same earnest care into the heart of Titus for you" **(2 Cor. 8:16)**.

Scripture Reading: 2 Corinthians 8:16–24

Introduction

Paul was deeply indebted to God for divine blessings that came to him through the ministry and the assistance of others.

Barnabas rendered Paul a great service by putting confidence in him and introducing him to the leaders of the church in Jerusalem (Acts 9:27). Later it was Barnabas who invited Paul to come to Antioch where his services were needed both as a preacher and as a teacher (11:25–26). Paul was grateful for the assistance that others provided him and for the blessings of God that came to him through them. Timothy, Silas, and many others were not only his colaborers, but they were a channel for the blessings of God into the life of the great apostle.

In our text, the apostle Paul thanks and praises God for the life and ministry of Titus. Titus is mentioned several times in this epistle to the Corinthians (2 Cor. 2:13; 7:6, 13).

Paul's expression of gratitude to God for fellow laborers and helpers in kingdom service provides us with a pattern to follow.

I. We should be thankful to God for parents who have served as spiritual guardians and guides.

Some of us are fortunate indeed to have been born into a home that had been formed by Christian parents. God blessed us richly by letting us grow up in an environment that was conducive to our being converted and developing Christian character.

We should give expression to our gratitude to God for his blessing to us in our Christian parents. We bring joy to the hearts of our parents when we give expression to this praise and gratitude for their permitting God to use them as ministers to us.

II. We should be thankful to God for teachers who have stimulated us to spiritual growth.

Some of us have been very fortunate to have good teachers provided for us by the church where we hold membership. God uses laypeople as the communicators of his message of love, grace, and power, even as he uses pastors and missionaries.

A. *We have had teachers who have taught us in the context of the classroom.* They have explained to us the meaning of the Word of God. Our lives have been enriched by their hours of study.

B. *Perhaps our most effective teachers are those who have lived their lessons before us.* They have provided us a stimulus to faith and faithfulness and sacrificial self-giving. They have encouraged us to live a life of purity that leads to power and fruitfulness.

Our lives would be impoverished were it not for the fact that God has sent many blessings to us through teachers. It would do our hearts good, and it would do others good if we would give verbal expression to our praise and thanksgiving for God's blessings to us through others. How long has it been since you have written a letter to express gratitude for the contribution made to you through a teacher or through your pastor?

III. We should be thankful to God for Christian friends who have led us closer to God.

Someone has said, "Behind every great man, there is a great woman." There is truth in this statement. It may be the man's wife; it may be the man's mother; or it may be both of them.

It could also be said, "Behind the life of every great person, there is a group of good friends." Some of God's finest blessings to us have come through the channel of friendship.

A. *Some friends bless us by setting a challenging example.*

B. *Some friends are God's blessing to us because of the encouragement they give us.*

C. *Some friends are God's blessing to us because of the correction they give us.* There are times when we would go astray if it were not for a word of warning or counsel from a friend who loves us.

Conclusion

How long has it been since you thanked God for someone who was the channel through which his blessing came to you? It is rather difficult for you to experience a blessing that does not come through some human instrumentality.

As Paul was thankful for Titus who was God's minister to the Corinthians, even so let us take a spiritual inventory and express the deep gratitude of our hearts for those whom God has used to bless us.

SUNDAY MORNING, APRIL 28

Title: Jesus Sends the Holy Spirit

Text: "What? know ye not that your body is the temple of the Holy Ghost which is in you, which ye have of God, and ye are not your own?" (**1 Cor. 6:19**).

Scripture Reading: 1 Corinthians 6:12–20

Hymns: "Holy, Holy, Holy," Heber

"Holy Spirit, Faithful Guide," Wells

"Take My Life and Let It Be," Havergal

Offertory Prayer: Holy, heavenly Father, today we are grateful for the privilege of being alive and being able to be present with your people in your house for worship and praise and proclamation. We offer to you the worship of our heart and the praise of our lips. We come to offer some of the fruit of our labors for the extending of your kingdom's ministries of mercy and help. Accept these gifts and bless them to the glory of your holy name and to the blessing of needy people. In Jesus' name we pray. Amen.

Introduction

When Jesus left the earth forty days after his Easter morning resurrection, he did not leave his followers alone. He told them to wait in Jerusalem, and their days of prayer and fasting there were rewarded on the day of Pentecost when the Holy Spirit, promised by Jesus, descended on them in power. The best gift the human heart can ever receive is that gift promised by the Lord to his followers — the presence of the Holy Spirit.

Unfortunately, an overwhelming majority of Christians never enter into the fullness of the abiding presence of the Holy Spirit. Consequently, they grieve the Holy Spirit (Eph. 4:30); they quench the Spirit (1 Thess. 5:19); they deprive themselves of their spiritual heritage; they live their lives in barren unfruitfulness; they miss the joy that characterized the early Christians; and their lives are weak and feeble because they labor in the energy of the flesh alone.

We cannot do the work of God without the power of God. We cannot experience the fullness of God's power if we are unaware of the presence and purpose of the Holy Spirit within our hearts.

I. We need to recognize the presence of the Holy Spirit.

It is impossible for the Holy Spirit to render his greatest ministry or to produce his greatest benefits if his presence goes unrecognized and the believer doesn't respond to him.

A. *The promise of our Lord (John 14:16–18).* As our Lord approached the end of his ministry, he began to inform his disciples of the necessity of his substitutionary death on the cross. They found this news to be both disturbing and unacceptable. He sought to encourage them with a revelation of his plans to bestow on them the gift of the Holy Spirit.

1. "Another comforter." Both of these words are significant. When Jesus referred to a Comforter, he was using a word that literally means "one called to walk by the side of." Jesus had been by his disciples' sides for more than three years. They had formed an inseparable relationship.

The Greek word translated "another" (*allos*) means "another of the same kind." Jesus, when talking about the Comforter, was declaring that the Holy Spirit would be to them what he had been.

2. "That he may abide with you forever." Jesus had spent a brief three years with his disciples. Soon they were to be separated by his departure. In contrast, the promised Spirit was to dwell within them in a lifelong relationship.

B. *"This is that" (Acts 2:16).* The apostle Peter explained the mysterious and miraculous happenings that took place on the day of Pentecost as being a fulfillment of the promise of both the Father God through Joel the prophet and the promise of the Lord Jesus Christ. Something new was happening in the economy of God. The Holy Spirit, who had come only upon unique individuals during Old Testament days, had come to dwell within the church and to abide within the heart of each believer.

The living presence of the Holy Spirit is to be a vital part of the life of Jesus' followers. Without a positive response to the divine Spirit, our lives cannot even begin to be what our Lord meant for them to be.

II. We need to rejoice in what the Holy Spirit has done for us.

A. *It was the Holy Spirit who convicted us of sin, righteousness, and of judgment to come (John 16:8–13).* Jesus described the function of the Holy Spirit in terms of his opening the eyes of the soul so that all people might see their own sinful condition and their desperate need of salvation. This is true concerning every believer. Had it not been for the convicting presence and power of the Holy Spirit, we would have continued in the darkness and death of unbelief. Surely we should be praising Jesus Christ who died for us that we might be saved, but we should also rejoice in the work of the Holy Spirit who caused us to see our need for salvation.

B. *The Holy Spirit presented Jesus as the Savior we needed (John 16:13–14).* It is not the function of the Holy Spirit to call attention to himself. Instead, it is the function of the Holy Spirit to lift up and magnify Jesus Christ. He blesses every effort that is put forth to exalt Jesus Christ. The Holy Spirit is the one who made Jesus Christ real to us.

C. *The Holy Spirit effected the new birth (John 3:5; Titus 3:5).* The new birth is the creation of a new spirit. It is a divine work wrought in the hearts of believers when they receive Jesus Christ as the Lord of their lives.

D. *The Holy Spirit communicated to us the assurance of divine sonship (Rom. 8:16).* In terms of affection, the divine Spirit bears testimony to the believing heart that something mysterious and miraculous has taken place. As a father would gently speak in loving terms to a newborn child, affirming the paternal relationship and a sense of possessiveness, even so the precious Holy Spirit bears testimony concerning a new relationship that has been established with God.

III. We need to release ourselves to the Holy Spirit (Acts 5:32).

The Holy Spirit works in hearts that are obedient and cooperative with the will of God. We cannot be in revolt against the will of God and experience the blessings that he wants to bestow on us.

A. *The Holy Spirit wants to be our divine Teacher (John 14:26).* He will lead us as we study the Word of God. He will open up to us the truth about God. He will also open up our minds to understand the truths of God.

B. *The Holy Spirit will create inward conflict with the evil that dwells within our fleshly nature (Gal. 5:16–17).* This conflict of the Holy Spirit with our fleshly nature is benevolent, but at the same time, radically serious. The Holy Spirit wants to deliver us from every destructive passion and from every attitude or action that would be harmful to others.

C. *The Holy Spirit will produce within us the fruit that can come only as a result of his activity (Gal. 5:22–23).* Christian character is the outward expression of an inward experience. A Christian spirit can be present only when we are Christlike within. This is a part of the purpose of the indwelling Spirit.

Conclusion

Barren indeed are the lives of some who never recognize the presence of the Holy Spirit within. Tragic indeed is it for one to hear the good news about the indwelling Spirit and then, through fear or selfishness or some other reason, neglect to respond to his abiding presence.

If we want to experience the benefits of this good news, we need to recognize the person of the Holy Spirit as dwelling within our hearts. We need to respond to him with faith and joy and eagerness to cooperate with him as he seeks to work in us and through us for the glory of God.

The Holy Spirit will help us to overcome the evil that is within us and to resist the evil that is about us. The Holy Spirit will endue us with the spiritual energy that we need to do God's work in the world today if we will but recognize him and respond to him. Not to do so is to grieve him, to rob ourselves, and to deprive the Father God of the privilege of using us for his glory.

Recognize and respond to the good news concerning the Holy Spirit today.

SUNDAY EVENING, APRIL 28

Title: The Man Who Feels Sorry for Himself

Text: "But he himself went a day's journey into the wilderness, and came and sat down under a juniper tree: and he requested for himself that he might die; and said, It is enough; now, O Lord, take away my life; for I am not better than my fathers" (**1 Kings 19:4**).

Scripture Reading: 1 Kings 19:1–18

Introduction

Elijah comes upon the stage of Israel's history with the shout of a prophet and disappears from it in a whirlwind. When Jesus came on the earth, people thought he was much like Elijah, so much so that some said that he was Elijah come back to earth again. The prophet Malachi had said, "Behold, I will send you Elijah the prophet before the coming of the great and dreadful day of the LORD: And he shall turn the heart of the fathers to the children, and the heart of the children to their fathers, lest I come and smite the earth with a curse" (Mal. 4:5–6).

Jesus said that John and Baptist was that Elijah (Matt. 17:10–13). John the Baptist and Elijah had remarkable similarities: they wore the same kind of clothes, they were sons of the desert, they were called upon to preach messages of judgment, they displayed superb courage, they were hated by a woman, they were immortal in their faith, they stood with the Lord, and they suffered a temporary eclipse of faith.

F. B. Meyer said, "It is noteworthy that the Bible saints often fail just where we should have expected them to stand." Elijah showed human weakness when he was under the juniper tree. Sitting there under the juniper tree, he said, "It is enough." He felt he was through. He was a man who felt sorry for himself.

I. The man who feels sorry for himself must understand that God's people will experience opposition from Satan and the world.

Ahab and Jezebel were Satan's agents at work in Elijah's day. Ahab had said that Elijah was the one who was troubling Israel (1 Kings 18:17). Ahab also called Elijah his enemy (21:20). Ahab adopted this viewpoint because he was unrighteous, while Elijah was righteous.

The person who dares to stand for the right and live for the Lord can expect opposition from Satan and the world. Paul said, "All that will live godly in Christ Jesus shall suffer persecution" (2 Tim. 3:12). Elijah was feeling sorry for himself because he was now experiencing opposition.

II. The man who feels sorry for himself must remember that the most powerful forces are not vocal.

Elijah stood at the entrance of a cave on Mount Horeb. The sky blackened. The wind tossed boulders down the mountainside and broke them in pieces. Elijah said, "This is God." But God was not in the wind. Then an earthquake convulsed the land. Elijah said, "This is God." But God was not in the earthquake. After the earthquake there was a fire. Elijah said, "This is God." But God was not in the fire. After the fire there was a small voice—the sound of gentle stillness; God spoke (1 Kings 19:8–18).

The most powerful forces in the world are not always those that make the most noise. Often we confuse noise with influence, prominence with eminence, glaring light with sunshine. Too often we fail to distinguish between shadow and substance.

God speaks to us when we feel sorry for ourselves.

III. The man who feels sorry for himself puts himself at the center of the universe and God at the circumference.

When Elijah lay down under the juniper tree, he put himself at the center of the universe and God at the circumference. Jezebel got after him, and she became central in his thoughts. He started feeling sorry for himself.

The moment God is not central, life becomes complex, filled with frustration and futility, and we feel sorry for ourselves.

Have we put God at the circumference and humanity at the center of our universe today? Do many not believe that science is the ultimate source of knowledge? Do many not look to the government for their needs? Humanity has accomplished much, and many feel that ingenuity is sufficient for any and all situations. Do many not believe that the absence of faith is a sign of intellectual acumen?

Well, we should know better. Our world has not turned out so well. The moment God is not central, life becomes confused and we feel sorry for ourselves.

IV. The man who feels sorry for himself underestimates the power of God.

Elijah became too sure of himself and too unsure of God. He said, "I have been very jealous for the Lord God of hosts: for the children of Israel have forsaken thy covenant, thrown down thine altars, and slain thy prophets with the sword; and I, even I only, am left; and they seek my life, to take it away" (1 Kings 19:10). God answered Elijah by saying, "Yet I have left me seven thousand in Israel, all the knees which have not bowed unto Baal, and every mouth which hath not kissed him" (v. 18).

Because our plans fail is no reason to conclude that all other people have failed or that God is dead and his cause defeated. When our purposes turn sour, God's cause is not doomed. When we feel sorry for ourselves, God does not become weak, and his work does not stop. God is not indifferent. He always cares, and he is always at work.

Conclusion

Look to the Lord in the hour of discouragement. Look to the Lord in the hour of defeat. Look to the Lord, and he will show you the way. He will speak to you and lead you out of your despondency.

MAY

■ **All Messages**

The preaching program for the month of May centers on the needs of, the threats to, and the potential of wholesome family life. Each individual has a vital stake in the institution of the home. The forces that affect the family have an effect on the community and ultimately on the whole country. The church should be concerned with, and involved in, ministering to family needs.

Beginning on Mother's Day and concluding on Father's Day, we have a time period of six weeks in which we can very profitably focus on the needs of both individuals and groups within the family. The needs of the family provide the theme for all of the messages suggested for this period.

WEDNESDAY EVENING, MAY 1

Title: The Joy of Jesus

Text: "These things have I spoken unto you, that my joy might remain in you, and that your joy might be full" (**John 15:11**).

Scripture Reading: John 15:1–11

Introduction

Jesus spoke of a fullness of joy that he was eager to impart to his disciples. He declared that his desire that they experience this fullness of joy was the controlling motive behind the things he taught them.

What was the joy of which Jesus spoke? It certainly was not the joy of ownership in our normal definition of that term. Jesus knew the pinch of poverty rather than the comfort of affluence.

The joy of which Jesus spoke was not the joy of popularity in the usual definition of that term. Although he was the center of attention in every group, he was not seeking the applause that comes to those who obtain a position of fame.

The joy of Jesus was not the joy of security, for he was opposed on all sides by the established authorities.

When the Lord spoke of a fullness of joy, he referred to a joy that grows out of something other than the joy of ownership, the joy of popularity, or the joy of security.

I. Jesus experienced the joy of knowing God.

A.   *At the age of twelve, our Lord gave expression to an insight into the business of his Father God (Luke 2:49).*

145

B. *Our Lord's favorite title for the eternal God is wrapped up in his loving name "Father."* In every instance, with only one exception, when our Lord was engaging in prayer, he addressed the eternal God as *Father.* He taught his disciples to approach the throne of grace in prayer with thoughts of the parent-child relationship uppermost in their minds (Luke 11:2).

C. *Just before his death on the cross, Jesus cried out, "Father, into thy hands I commend my spirit" (Luke 23:46).*

To our Lord, the eternal God was more than a vague blur. He was more than just the principle behind the universe. To Christ, God was his loving Father. He was eager that his disciples experience and appreciate this joy of knowing God.

II. Jesus experienced the joy of glorifying God (John 17:4).

Christ Jesus came into the world to reveal the nature of God to the hearts of humans. He came as a demonstration of God's wonderful plan for the human race. He came to reveal the greatness of God's love for people and to give them abundant life. He came that people might understand the love, grace, and power of the creator of the universe.

As Jesus communicated this insight into the nature and purpose of God, he was glorifying God and making God known by every means at his command. He was seeking to introduce people to the Father God. He rejoiced that God was revealing himself to babes (Luke 10:21), and he continued to rejoice as people came to an understanding of who God really was.

Our Lord was exceedingly eager that his disciples experience this great joy of glorifying God.

III. Jesus experienced the joy of perfect harmony with God's will.

The will of God for Jesus Christ was the road map for his life. There was no discord between Jesus' will and the will of the Father. In his mind, there was no rebellion or revolt against the work God had for him to do. He was in perfect harmony with the Creator and with the universe in which he lived.

Jesus leads us to accept the will of God as the guiding principle of our lives. He gives us the great inward peace of being in tune with the eternal God and his loving purpose for the world.

IV. Jesus experienced the joy of giving himself for others.

A. *Jesus' life and teaching proclaim that there is joy, happiness, and fulfillment in a life dedicated to ministering to the needs of others, in contrast to a life dedicated to selfish interests.* Jesus' words in Acts 20:35 — "It is more blessed to give than to receive" — are no primer for an offering; rather, they express his fundamental philosophy of life.

B. *We receive only as we give (Luke 6:38).* There is only one word of command from our Lord in this verse: "give." Our Lord is talking in terms of a principle and a philosophy. The rest of the verse is an observation and a promise. Jesus observed that those who live to give receive an abundance beyond what they hoped for.

Our Lord knew this joy that comes only as a result of a life of dedicated giving. He was eager that his disciples know this joy. Do you know this joy? This joy cannot be experienced by merely reading a book or hearing a sermon. You must become a giver in order to experience this joy.

V. Jesus anticipated the joy of returning to the Father God.

Our Lord spoke repeatedly of the fact that he would return to the Father. He told of the many rooms in his Father's house. In Jesus' prayer in John 17, we can sense the joy that filled his heart as he anticipated the completion of his earthly ministry and his return to the Father.

On at least one occasion, Jesus urged his disciples to rejoice greatly because their names were written in heaven (Luke 10:20). He was eager for them to rejoice in the glad consciousness that heaven was to be their eternal home. He did not want them to live in anxiety concerning the joy that was before them.

Conclusion

Our Lord lived a life of joy. He is eager that we know the great joys available to us through faith and faithfulness.

SUNDAY MORNING, MAY 5

Title: Can the Church Help Your Family?

Text: "Zacchaeus, make haste, and come down; for today I must abide at thy house" **(Luke 19:5)**.

Scripture Reading: Luke 19:5–10

Hymns: "Love Divine," Wesley

          "Tell Me the Story of Jesus," Crosby

          "Lead Me Gently Home, Father," Thompson

Offertory Prayer: Our heavenly Father, we thank you for your blessings given to us through the home. May our tithes and offerings be used to bless this most sacred of institutions. Help our church to strengthen the home life of its members. Bless these tithes and offerings to the proclamation of the gospel so that others may become followers of Christ. In Jesus' name we pray. Amen.

Introduction

A certain woman bought an exercise plan. When the time for the use of the plan had expired, she went to the company complaining that she had not been helped at all. In fact, she said that she weighed more than she did before purchasing the plan. When the company checked its records on her attendance at the exercise classes, they discovered that she had attended only two of them.

For many families, the church is as ineffective as this woman's exercise plan,

147

and for the same reasons. Christ can do much for our homes if we will allow him to work through his church. However, the church can be only as effective as a family will allow.

Zacchaeus discovered the difference Christ makes when he enters a life and thereby enters a home. Zacchaeus had a problem seeing Jesus because of the crowd Jesus attracted, and he solved it by rising above the crowd in a sycamore tree. He did not go unnoticed, for Jesus spotted him as we heard in the verses of our Scripture reading for this morning.

Jesus declared that Zacchaeus's home was saved by Jesus' presence. When Christ comes into our homes, they are saved. However, for Christ to help your family, he must do it through his body, the church. It is the church that helps bring the presence of Christ into your home. Three conditions are necessary if Christ is to help your home through the church.

I. Christ can help your family through the church if your habits allow it.

There is a style of life that makes the resources of the church available to the family. In this style of life, Christ can function. When there is a pattern of worship and Bible study, things like ideals, forgiveness, and purpose are made available for families to use in the Spirit of Christ.

Families that develop the habit of service for Christ create for themselves an atmosphere of unselfishness and giving. The members of a family that learns the joy of service will be able to function with each other in service.

Zacchaeus's household evidently came to have this atmosphere. Zacchaeus could readily tell our Lord that he was concerned about others and would thenceforth be honest in his relationships with others. Christ's coming had made the difference, and his presence would continue in a home where so wholehearted a response had been made and new habits of life established.

By contrast, a family that excludes the church from its activities cannot expect Christ to have much impact on the home. All or most of the interests many families have run contrary to the interests the church cultivates. What a family places in its schedule is what it decides is important. The absence of the Spirit of Christ in the home is usually due to the failure of the family members to give him opportunity. Zacchaeus's new habits made it possible for Christ to feel at home in his house.

II. Christ can help your family through the church if your attitudes encourage it.

Attitudes are the roots of habits. Attitudes can destroy Christ's effectiveness through his church for a family. Listen to the children of a family for a while, and you will discover what the attitude of a family is toward the church. Many families see the church as an enemy and treat it with suspicion. They have the attitude that the family needs to protect itself against the church.

Some negative attitudes come from families' feelings toward money. Because many families are more committed to money and material things than to anything else, the church is charged with being interested only in their money. Sometimes families charge the church with having other bad motives. This causes families to develop further resistance to the church's influence. In this way, a family can justify its criticism of the church and feel excused from participation in it.

When attitudes in a home cultivate personal animosities, petty jealousies, and lack of appreciation, these form in children a mind-set that is difficult for the church to overcome.

In an experiment, a speaker was introduced to two different audiences in different ways. To the first audience he was introduced as a criminal, and the audience showed a very negative response to his speech. To the second audience he was introduced as a scientist, and he was applauded warmly for the same speech. How the man was introduced determined the kind of reception he received. How Christ is introduced and how church is viewed in our homes determines the kind of reception he can be expected to receive in them. The church is hurt when it is introduced negatively to the home, but the family is the bigger loser.

On the other hand, encouraging attitudes allow the church to redeem the family. The church can teach our families what is valuable and lasting. Society, with its many loud voices, teaches our families pagan lessons every day. If our families never hear anything else, they will believe the only lessons they are taught. The church is one of the few places where eternal things can be learned. It is the church that teaches that we "cannot live by bread alone."

The family is built up when it takes part in the church's wholesome atmosphere and fellowship. Just as plants must have a favorable climate in which to grow, the Christian family must also have a nurturing climate in which to grow. Christian families working together in a church fellowship inspire each other for meaningful personal and spiritual growth.

Children and young people need guidance and inspiration. Adults need strength and determination. The church is uniquely equipped to provide for these needs if the attitudes of families will allow themselves to participate in the church.

Never has there been a time when more options were open to people. These options include vocational opportunities, moral choices, and value decisions. Never before have persons had so much responsibility to make wise choices among so many different appealing values. Where it is given an opportunity, the church can provide a framework of judgment in which Christian people can make Christian decisions.

Young people especially need to be given criteria by which to make wise and godly choices. The church can help families by providing this framework of judgment about life's important issues. Zacchaeus was seeking a framework of life by which to make his choices. When Christ came into his home, Zacchaeus discovered the one upon whose judgment he could rely.

III. The church can help your family if your heart responds to Christ.

Zacchaeus looked for Christ out of curiosity, but he responded to him out of interest. Christ spoke to Zacchaeus's heart, and Zacchaeus responded with his home and life.

There are many who have never learned to respond to Christ. In fact, many cannot respond to anyone else besides their own needs and concerns. Our culture teaches us, "Look out for yourself." When this lesson has been thoroughly learned, Christ can mean little to a person. Neither spiritual life nor the growth of others in the family is very important to the person who is concerned only with self.

Only when Christ is allowed to touch lives can he redeem a family. A father came to ask me to be his son's parole adviser. Since I was unacquainted with the family, I inquired about their background. I learned that the teenage boy had held up a gas station. I asked what church the family had attended. Very brusquely the father shot back, "I've had 240 acres of land to pay for, and I haven't had much time for church." I replied, "Then you taught your son to get what you want materially, and he simply took the shortcut to get it." The man now wanted the church to undo for his son what he had spent the last twenty years teaching him. He had kept Christ from touching the life of his family until now, but finally he needed the church.

Christ calls us out of the little circle of our selfishness and into a growing relationship with him when he comes into our homes. He also calls us into a growing relationship with others. When Christ comes into our homes, he changes our goals and helps us to find the important things in life. Jesus gave Zacchaeus a relationship with himself that would allow Zacchaeus's life to be totally changed.

The treasurer of a church was surprised one day to find a check for $2,500 and a note from a new member in the offering plate. The new Christian explained that the check was in gratitude for what the church had done to save his family. He said he knew that if he had not been introduced to Christ, he would have lost both his family and his house. He said the check was only a token of his gratitude for what Christ had meant to his life and family. Here was one man who allowed the church to help his family by responding to Christ.

The church is Christ's redeeming fellowship for the family. Christ can change our homes only when we are willing to pay the price of making a place for him in the family where we live.

SUNDAY EVENING, MAY 5

Title: In Times Like These

Text: "And [they] said to the mountains and rocks, Fall on us, and hide us from the face of him that sitteth on the throne, and from the wrath of the Lamb: For the great day of his wrath is come; and who shall be able to stand?" **(Rev. 6:16–17).**

Scripture Reading: Revelation 6:12–17

Introduction

The author of Revelation paints a very dark picture as he describes for us what he beheld in his vision at the opening of the sixth seal by the Lamb. In staccato fashion, there flashes across his vision an earthquake, a blackened sun, a bloody sun, a bloody moon, falling stars, the heavens rolling up like a scroll, mountains and islands moving from their places, and the people of the earth—kings and slaves alike—hiding in caves and crevices of mountains, crying out for the mountains to fall on them and to hide them from the wrath of the avenging Lamb. Then the author cries out in dismay, "Who is able to stand before the Lamb in the day of his wrath?" As we look at the day in which we live, are we not made to wonder how long we will be able to stand before the Lamb? In times like these, many fear what the end will be for our country. The breakdown in family life is the wintry slope on which society's present toboggan ride to destruction is taking place.

Let us look at the present condition of our society and see if in times like these we ought not fear the wrath of the Lamb.

I. It is a stressed-out age.

A. *We live in a continuous rush—busy, busy, busy.* Our technological age has robbed humankind of one of the greatest blessings of past years: the ability to live more graciously, leisurely, and contemplatively.

B. *We live in an age when people depend on painkillers to cope.* One authority recently estimated that nearly half of those occupying hospital beds are victims of stress. The use of painkillers by adults often leads to their dependency on drugs and may influence the younger generation in the home to seek solutions to life's problems by using drugs.

II. It is an immoral age.

A. *Divorce rate.* About half of all first marriages in the United States end in divorce, and even fewer second marriages survive. Many cohabiting couples are opting not to get married at all. The husband-wife relationship created by God himself is a sacred trust between two contracting parties that must not be entered into lightly. Too many young couples enter into marriage with the attitude that everything must be perfect between themselves. A marriage counselor once reminded a couple that the only perfect mates were to be found in pairs of gloves and pairs of shoes.

B. *Sex offenses.* Sex offenses in this generation are unparalleled by those of any other era and are steadily climbing. In fact, because there are so many cases of criminal sexual conduct, crimes that used to be first-page news in daily papers are now on the inside pages or are not even reported. The most widespread offense is the loose attitude of our present youthful generation toward sex. The sexual revolution has led to a very casual attitude toward that which God designed to be wholly sacred.

C. *Immorality in government circles.* The attitude of much of bureaucracy today is that one "wheels and deals" to the best advantage of one's voting constituency, regardless of the ultimate effect on our nation.

III. It is an age of crime.

A. *Crime is running rampant.* Parental laxity and lack of discipline in the home tend to create an attitude of demanding one's own way when away from home. Gang warfare, drug dealing, and prostitution are killing America's children.

B. *Alcoholism is on the increase.* Lives are being destroyed daily, and the influence for Christ is being greatly diminished by this "disease." People are being slaughtered on our highways by drunken drivers. Murder is being committed in homes by drunken spouses.

C. *Drug addiction has swept across our nation, affecting the lives of people from all walks of life.* The frantic desire to keep up with their extremely expensive habit causes these people to commit crimes of shoplifting, breaking and entering, robbery, prostitution, and even white-collar crimes.

IV. It is an age of war.

The wars in Iraq and Afghanistan are fresh in the minds of many Americans. Those in the military have firsthand familiarity with them, and the rest of us replay television war scenes in our heads. Daily we continue to follow conflicts in the Middle East. On all sides we are surrounded by wars and uprisings.

V. It is an age of insipid Christianity.

The cause of Christ is no longer the aim and goal of life for the majority of our nation's people. The rate of growth of Christianity is in no way keeping pace with the rate of growth of the population. Those within "the fold" are either sitting on the fence between the world's way and the cause of Christ or have slipped into spiritual indifference. The things of this world are fast becoming the thorns that are choking out the seed of Christianity in our hearts.

VI. These characteristics point to a need for a great revival.

A familiar hymn says, "In times like these you need a Saviour; in times like these you need an anchor."

A. *The decay within our society indicates:*

1. A need for a great spiritual awakening within the lives of individual Christians. We as Christians need to take a long look at ourselves and cry out, "Lord, have mercy; Lord, be patient; Lord, bring us to our knees before you." We need to realize that Paul was speaking of us and to us as well as to non-Christians when he said, "For all have sinned, and come short of the glory of God," and, "There is none righteous, no, not one" (Rom. 3:23, 10).

2. A need for a return to godly training in our family life. As children are trained in the home, so will they develop into maturity. It is said that the habit patterns one develops in the first five or six years of life are those that will shape one's later mode of living. It is, therefore, highly important that every God-fearing parent do all in their power to nur-

ture their children with Christ's teachings so that they may be able in later life to withstand the onslaught of the evil one.

B. *This decay in family living and in society in general indicates not only a need for an awakening but also a need for repentance.* Repentance has the following five traits:

1. A recognition of our sins. "It's not my brother, it's not my sister, but it's me, O Lord, standing in the need of prayer." We all must come to the point of seeing ourselves as sinners before almighty God and beg for mercy.

2. A sense of sorrow for our sins. When we see ourselves as the Lord sees us, as sinners steeped in unrighteousness, we need to come to our knees in shame and sorrow.

3. A turning away from sin. We sinners must make a great U-turn in lifestyle, especially in our attitudes toward sin and in our attitudes toward the Lord.

4. Faith in the Lord. It is of no value to sweep our spiritual house unless we fill it with the one who is holy and righteous. "Come into my heart, Lord Jesus," should be the prayer of all who come through this great experience of rebirth.

5. Committal. When we come to our spiritual senses through this experience of rebirth, we must take on the new way of life by committing ourselves unashamedly to Christ, openly, publicly, for all to know.

Conclusion

In times like these, we need to awaken as families and as individuals to our opportunities and responsibilities in the Lord. We need to turn away from sin to salvation in the Lord. Turn to the Lord in faith, believing that he is the answer to your soul's needs.

WEDNESDAY EVENING, MAY 8

Title: Christ in the Home

Text: "Jesus was called ... to the marriage" (**John 2:2**).

Scripture Reading: John 2:1–11

Introduction

Because of the strategic importance of the home for everything that makes life worth living, we can assume that our Lord is vitally interested in everything that affects home life.

I. Christ and the beginning of a home.

A. *Christ was invited to a wedding in Cana.* Many are involved in a marriage: parents, community, church, schools. Christ should not be left out.

B. *Christ attended the wedding in Cana.* In a day when the family is threatened by so many destructive forces, we can be assured that Christ wants to be present to help.

C. *Christ rendered a valuable service while at the wedding.*

D. *Christ revealed his glory in connection with the wedding.*

II. A suggestion of permanent significance.

Jesus' mother told the servants, "Do whatever he tells you."

A. *An attitude of faith and expectancy was present.*

B. *Faith and obedience are of supreme importance.*

It was while the ten lepers were in the process of obeying the command of the Master that they were healed (Luke 17:14).

The Sermon on the Mount emphasizes that we should not only hear but do all that our Lord commands.

III. Suggestions from the Savior for your home.

A. *"Have faith in God" (Mark 11:22).*

B. *Have the habit of prayer and do not break it (Luke 18:1).*

C. *Be a giver (Matt. 10:8; Luke 6:38).*

D. *Forgive each other until seventy times seven (Matt. 18:22)—that is, with a complete spirit of acceptance.*

E. *Practice the Golden Rule (Matt. 7:12).* A practice of the Golden Rule will bring the rule of heaven into your home.

Conclusion

Invite Christ to enter your home to improve the situation between husband and wife. Invite Christ into your home to improve parent-child relationships. Let Christ reveal his glory in what can be accomplished in your home. Christ comes to every heart and home and desires entrance (Rev. 3:20).

SUNDAY MORNING, MAY 12

Title: Can the Family Be Saved?

Text: "What therefore God hath joined together, let not man put asunder" **(Mark 10:9).**

Scripture Reading: Mark 10:6–9

Hymns: "Have Faith in God," McKinney

"O Blessed Day of Motherhood," McGregor

"Faith of Our Mothers," Patten

Offertory Prayer: Our Father, on this special day, we pause to thank you for your wonderful gifts to us through Christian mothers. Help us to be mindful that every good and perfect gift is from you. You have been most generous to us.

Today we bring our tithes and offerings as an expression of our gratitude for your great love to us. Bless these offerings to the end that others may come to know Jesus Christ as Lord and Savior. Amen.

Introduction

Sharp and loud voices are predicting and promoting the end of the family as we have known it. Articles such as "Is This the Last Married Generation?" proclaim the death of the family. More than half of all couples living together are not married, several states permit same-sex marriages, spouses "swap" partners, groups of married couples "swing," and "families" are often made up of any combination of people who choose to cohabitate.

What is the Christian response to the news that the nuclear family is rapidly losing ground? We must begin by purposefully working toward our Christian ideals without demanding of each other, or of everyone, absolute perfection. Ideals are goals toward which to work; they are not the absolute performance standards everyone must meet every day. Jesus gave us his ideal for family life as he described the intention of God for human existence in Mark 10:6–9.

Here is God's intention: He created us male and female for the purpose of fulfilling each other's lives. This arrangement leads to the establishment of a family in which two people commit themselves to each other for life. Their commitment to each other is a sacred covenant. It is entered into to accomplish the purposes of God for their lives.

With this ideal clearly in front of us with the dire pronouncements on current family life, what can we do? Three transfusions are necessary for the survival of the family in our time. Not every family will receive these transfusions, but those who care can receive them.

I. First, there must be a strong spirit of commitment in the family.

Many are denying and decrying the need for commitment. They are saying that commitment is totally out of place in any marriage arrangement. In fact, people do not need to consider marriage at all. They are saying commitment only leads to problems and denies freedom.

In much current thought, the only criterion for continuing marriage or family is whether it is a "presently satisfactory relationship." This moment-to-moment approach to marriage and the family gives it no permanence or stability. The attitude created by this lack of commitment is that if marriage gets uncomfortable, one should get out immediately.

This lack of commitment is most clearly seen in the norm of couples living together before marriage. Another way it is seen is in the recent development of marriage contracts by which a couple may opt out of marriage with no penalties after a set length of time. "Till death do us part" is passé. These trends assume that couples have no responsibility for maintaining or continuing the family. The family is to be continued only so long as both parties are pleased by the arrangement.

What is happening in marriage and the family is not too different from what is happening in other areas of our society. The same sickness plagues other segments of society as well. We have moved to the "no-frustration era," in which almost no one tolerates frustration. The factors creating frustration are multiplying, but our "instant" age wants immediate results and guaranteed happiness in everything.

In this society that encourages its people to commit themselves to nothing, meaningful marriage will be extremely difficult. We are taught to be ready to run if any difficulty develops. Thus we must learn again the meaning of commitment. We must teach young people what it means to commit oneself to another in love and to help that person and oneself grow together toward God.

Because society says, "Don't do it," it will take the courage of individuality for Christians to begin learning what it is to make marriage and family commitment a meaningful experience. Jesus was talking about the ideal of commitment when he quoted the words of Genesis that we find in today's text: "For this reason a man will leave his father and mother and be united to his wife, and the two will become one flesh" (Mark 10:7 NIV; see Genesis 2:24).

II. Second, if the family is to be saved, we must inhale the atmosphere of the church for the family.

We can say with indisputable evidence on our side, "Every family that is serious about its survival and health will find its place in the church." Families need survival kits for marriage in the jungle of American society. Those kits must include instructions on how to get into and be a part of a growing Christian fellowship. Families need to breathe the air of spiritual worship every week if they are going to be strong.

Families are constantly exposed to forces from the outside that will destroy them. These forces include such things as affluence, personal success, moral decay, and vocational pressures. A mass of lifestyle options from which one can choose also helps to deteriorate the family.

On the other hand, there are fewer strengths within the family. A husband's income is often no longer sufficient to support a family. Thus women often work outside the home while the children are cared for by a non–family member.

A few years ago, I attended a conference in New York City. One evening I walked down the street to a restaurant to eat my dinner. The bar was visible from the restaurant area where I was eating. It was early in the evening, and many people were just getting off work. As I watched the people coming off the street and into the bar, I saw them finding the same kind of satisfaction in the bar that we would expect people to find in their homes. Young and middle-aged men and women were greeting each other with handshakes and kisses. They inquired of each other how the business day had gone and who was giving them trouble. They joked and laughed with each other as they relaxed together. That bar had all the atmosphere of a family clan gathering for a holiday. These people had found what they hoped would be substitutes for marriage and the family in their lonely existences.

The church is one of the few remaining strengthening groups for family life. The bar substitute and all of the other substitute institutions and agencies deteriorate the family rather than strengthen it. The church does something for a family that no other ally can do for it.

If families would make time for church participation as they do for other things, the church could be far more effective for families. Church membership alone will not do it. Occasional church attendance will not do it. Critical attitudes toward the church will not do it. Blaming the church for every failure will not do it. Only wholesome, positive participation in Christian fellowship will allow your family to breathe the atmosphere of the church.

We are always pleased when there is money enough to add a room to the house. Sometimes families add a room even when they do not have enough money to do it. Isn't it amazing that many people will spend all kinds of time and money improving their *houses* but will not give the church any time to improve their *homes*? The church is the one fellowship that keeps the ideals of our text before people and families.

III. The third necessity for saving the family is the infusion of Christ into every functioning part of the family.

Every part that moves must have the strength of Christ flowing into it. The creator of family life is also the keeper of family life.

Social scientists today are looking for a new arrangement to replace family life. Many experimenters think they have found it in a variety of arrangements. We do not need a new arrangement; we need new persons. Social scientists for the most part are treating the symptoms instead of the cause of the failure of marriage and the family. Christ changes persons. He puts new blood in the veins of a marriage. He helps us find the purposes of God in marriage.

Every day that a family lives together, it needs the presence of Christ. It needs the presence of Christ to learn how to forgive, to learn how to share meaningfully with others, and to learn how to accept others by being accepted themselves. It needs the presence of Christ to learn how to love, not selfishly but self-givingly, and to learn how to trust others so that they will be built up.

Jesus' parable of the houses on the rock and on the sand was never more appropriate than for the homes of today. A home falls, not because homes will not stand anymore, but because it is built on the wrong foundation. Christ is needed in your home if you want your home to last and especially if you want your home to be meaningful.

The good of our homes is one of the most compelling reasons for responding to Christ. He gives us something that we can build on if we will let him guide us. The real question for you this morning is "Do you care enough about your home to let Christ change your life for his purposes?"

SUNDAY EVENING, MAY 12

Title: Don't Be a Sophomore

Text: "The fool says in his heart, 'There is no God' " **(Ps. 14:1 NIV).**

Scripture Reading: Psalm 14:1–4

Introduction

In one thing at least, times have not changed since the days of David, Solomon, and the other authors of the Psalms. In the days of these authors, there were abroad in the land those who were saying, "There is no God" (Ps. 14:1 NIV). Today we are having the same thought expressed in slightly different words: "God is dead!" This idea comes from people who obviously have so engrossed themselves in the study of theology that they have lost any relationship they may once have had with almighty God. These pronouncements must not be considered to be a new mode of thought, however, for a century and a half ago, the German theologian-philosopher Nietzsche had developed such a preachment. People of such thought may be classed as "sophomores," for this word is derived from two Greek words: *sophos*, "wise," and *moros*, "moron" or "fool." Truly "the fool says in his heart, 'There is no God' " (Ps. 14:1 NIV). These theological sophomores are practicing their philosophy in the following manner:

I. Denying God in order to deify humanity.

A. *Foolish people have always sought to build themselves up by assassinating the character of others.* The psalmist realized this when he said that the fool has declared that there is no God. Our generation has seen preachers and leading educators attempt to nullify the presence and power of almighty God by liberalizing their theology to the extent that it has become very, very broad and thus very, very shallow. The end result is that many unwary people have become practical atheists without realizing it. Their god is so small that he can be set aside on a small dark shelf of their lives while self is paraded in the forefront of life's living.

B. *Foolish people in our generation have exalted the human mind almost to the point of deifying the human scientific brain.* Now it is quite popular to worship at the shrine of human *sophos*, or wisdom. Science has become king, commanding the admiration and obedience of our generation. We have turned from the fine art of living in a Christ-centered culture to a culture dominated by the worship of science (human wisdom)—science bent on providing for pleasure and ease (Baalism). Elijah needs to appear once again and address us in the great Mount Carmel amphitheater of our lives, crying out as of old, "How long halt ye between two opinions? If the LORD be God, follow him: but if Baal, then follow him" (1 Kings 18:21).

II. Deifying the personification of humanity's best efforts—government.

Substitution of government for God goes on apace. Government has taken over one function of the Christian church after another:

A. *Education.* Until the nineteenth century, education was a sacred function of the church. The youth of the land had been taught, in addition to the "three Rs" a fourth R—religion. Even under the best of circumstances, today's churches have only some 130 hours of prime teaching time in the course of a year for religious instruction of our young people. Many of today's Christian universities are more concerned with keeping up with the standards of other colleges than with providing true religious training for their students.

B. *Charity.* The early church cared for the unfortunate to the extent that the members held all things in common so that no one would go hungry. In the early days of our Christian churches here in America, charitable works were emphasized to the point that there was little necessity of a welfare department in the government. With the passing of time, our churches lost their compassionate concern for the less fortunate, and finally this function passed on to the state.

C. *Foreign missions.* Every evangelical denomination has long since emphasized the Great Commission, "Go and make disciples of all nations, baptizing them in the name of the Father and of the Son and of the Holy Spirit" (Matt. 28:19 NIV). In this decade, many of the same type of young people who formerly answered the call to foreign mission service now feel that a secular or government-sponsored program is preferable. As fine as the Peace Corps is, it was never intended to replace our great world mission endeavor of winning the lost to Christ.

D. *Trust in the providence of God, once central in the faith of human hearts, now seems to be replaced by trust in the Social Security and welfare departments of our government.* These secular programs were never intended to replace a deep faith in the providence of God. We can see the real purpose of socialism coming to fruition in our society—that is, the reduction of life to pure materialism. When this has completely taken place in society, can we not say that government has taken over the role of "providential God" in the faith of humans?

III. In the final analysis, foolish humanity is really mocking at sin.

A. *The very idea of sin.* Fools reason thus: "Sin is just a little mistake; anyone can make a mistake." Money can "cover up" most "mistakes," a fool reasons. Further, he reasons, "It is just a *little* sin." Yet "little" sin can interrupt the spiritual life of a person even as a speck of dust in some delicate mechanism in a space shuttle could prevent a proper performance on its trip into space.

B. *The practice of sin.* As man is tempted to sin, he reasons with himself in his approach to the temptation:

1. "Just this once can't possibly hurt me." Just one experience of sexual sin, and a girl's life can be ruined. Just one hit of cocaine, and a young person's life can be changed or even snuffed out.

2. "I won't let this sin drown out the good in my life," says the sinner. With the passing of time, an onlooker observes that the sinner has gradually

"tilted" in the direction of sin so that the good in his heart and life has been crowded out. For example, the social drinker starts with just a drink now and then to keep up with his social set. Years later he comes to the end of life's journey as an alcoholic, having lost home, job, and family.

C. *The denial that one is a sinner.* Some people ignore the fact that sin is hereditary and a characteristic of all humans: "For all have sinned, and come short of the glory of God" (Rom. 3:23). All of the education and culture in the world will not change the nature of humans.

D. *Blindness to the effects of sin.*

1. Sin blights people. Sin blights and blackens people's spiritual lives to the point of ruining their influence. Once a group of young people wanted to go down into a mining shaft and thence into the area where the coal was being cut from the depths of the earth. One young lady had a dainty white dress, and the other members of the group remonstrated with her about wearing such a dress into the coal mine. "Can't I wear a white dress down into the mine?" she asked petulantly. "Yes, ma'am," replied the old miner who was to act as guide for the party. "There is nothing to keep you from wearing a white dress down there, but there will be considerable to keep you from wearing one back."

2. Sin destroys. Yes, sin destroys even while one is in the process of denying that he is a sinner. In 1941 there were ambassadors in our country giving the impression that all was well between their country and ours while all the time that country was in the process of planning a massive attack against our country at Pearl Harbor. In their blindness to the effects of sin, some fail to notice that sin is destroying them.

3. Sin is unpardonable—unless. People are without excuse if they contract a communicable disease simply because they refused to be vaccinated. Sin is unpardonable in the sight of a righteous God, because pardon is available in Christ Jesus.

Conclusion

Don't be a sophomore—a wise fool! Let us not be so self-sufficient and so spiritually dead that we begin to think that God is dead or that he just doesn't act anymore. Let us in these moments realize how foolish people are to deny the loving call of Christ Jesus to come to them in faith. And let us come, believing that he can and will save us.

WEDNESDAY EVENING, MAY 15

Title: The Family Yesterday, Today, and Tomorrow

Text: "Praise be to the LORD, who this day has not left you without a guardian-redeemer" **(Ruth 4:14 NIV)**.

Scripture Reading: Ruth 4:1–15

Introduction

Naomi and Ruth faced hard times after losing their husbands, but God did not forsake them. He provided them with a guardian who would care for them. Likewise, in the hard times the family faces today, God promises not to leave us alone. He sends us one who will redeem us in the time of trouble. Our focus this evening is on the family as it faces the problems of change.

I. The family yesterday.
   A. *Life within the family.*
      1. The goals of life were family goals: early settlers in America risked the unknown dangers of the new land to seek freedom and a better life for their families.
      2. The role of the individual was clearly defined, and each contributed to the needs of the family as a whole.
      3. Family ties were strong and intimate. Members were secure in mutual support and concern.
   B. *The family in the community.*
      1. The community was to the family what the family was to the individual members. The fortunes and misfortunes of life were shared.
      2. The church was central in the community life as spiritual activities were central in the family.
      3. The sanctity of marriage and the preservation of the home were protected by common commitment to Christian values and biblical principles.
      4. The care and nurture of children was the common responsibility of the church, the school, and the home.

II. The family today.
   A. *Changes within the family.* There is a different attitude toward the marriage relationship today. Marriage is a "deal" instead of a spiritual union. When one fails to give what the other expects, it is a "dirty deal," and divorce follows.
      Also, there is a lack of relationship and intimacy between family members. Each does his or her own thing. Home is just a base of operations. Real communication is minimal. In the office of the marriage counselor, one hears one spouse say to the other, "But you never told me you felt that way."
   B. *Changes within the community.* Families live in isolation from neighbors and seem to prefer it this way. What happens to others is not their concern.
      There is also public unconcern over forces that are destructive to family life and the welfare of children.

Who knows the ultimate consequences of these trends and changes? We have the uneasy feeling that we are losing something that we cannot do without. The church today is like "the voice of one crying in the wilderness." Few hear and few heed.

III. The family tomorrow.

A. *We must see the problems of the day as spiritual problems calling for spiritual solutions.* We need to identify these destructive forces for what they are: "We wrestle not against flesh and blood" (Eph. 6:12).

B. *Christ is the answer still.* The Christian faith is a "family affair," but the family itself must be saved. Joshua said, "As for me and my house, we will serve the LORD" (Josh. 24:15).

C. *The hope of America is the Christian home.* The home more than the church is the primary influence. The church must move to restore the family to its spiritual responsibility under God.

D. *God's instructions to families.* In his farewell address to Israel, Moses reminded the people to love God and to teach his commandments to their children. "These commandments that I give you today are to be on your hearts. Impress them on your children. Talk about them when you sit at home and when you walk along the road, when you lie down and when you get up" (Deut. 6:6–7 NIV). Paul was referring to the teaching tradition of the home when he reminded Timothy, "From infancy you have known the Holy Scriptures" (2 Tim. 3:15 NIV).

Someone has said, "Religion is more caught than taught" in the home. Once again Paul was writing to Timothy when he said, "I am reminded of your sincere faith, which first lived in your grandmother Lois and in your mother Eunice and, I am persuaded, now lives in you also" (2 Tim. 1:5 NIV).

Conclusion

What can the church do "in such a time as this"? In the midst of change, the divine purpose of God in establishing the home must be proclaimed. Christian homes within the church community must shine as "lighthouses" for the people lost in the sea of change. In a dry and thirsty land bereft of the Spirit of life, we must be as an oasis for those who are perishing.

"You are the salt of the earth" (Matt. 5:13 NIV). We offer Christ to a changing world. He is "the same yesterday and today and forever" (Heb. 13:8 NIV).

SUNDAY MORNING, MAY 19

Title: You Have to Have Hope

Text: "Whatever you do, whether in word or deed, do it all in the name of the Lord Jesus, giving thanks to God the Father through him" **(Col. 3:17 NIV)**.

Scripture Reading: Colossians 3:18–21

Hymns: "This Is the Day the Lord Hath Made," Watts

        "Guide Me, O Thou Great Jehovah," Williams

        "Just When I Need Him Most," Poole

Offertory Prayer: Holy, heavenly Father, you are our Creator and the sustainer of life. Today we thank you for giving us an inward disposition that causes us to hunger for the privilege of worship. Help us to receive all that you want to bestow upon us today. With our tithes and offerings, we come to give to you a portion of our time and talents, energy and effort. Bless this portion of ourselves to your glory and to the good of those who are in need. Through Jesus Christ. Amen.

Introduction

Twelve days ago, Mrs. Helen E. Hopke lay in her bed fighting to stay alive to see her daughter's wedding. Incurably ill for the past five years, Mrs. Hopke had been indirectly responsible for the meeting about a year ago of her daughter Rose Marie, twenty, and the girl's intended husband, Arthur Woodrow Hudson, twenty-six.

Rose Marie had acted as nurse and housekeeper to her bedfast mother. While buying medicine, she met Hudson, a pharmacist in a local drugstore. Friends said it was the girl's first romance.

They also said all that kept Mrs. Hopke alive in recent months was the thought of the impending marriage.

The fifty-six-year-old mother heard the couple enter the house laughing and talking about the April 4 wedding. She heard them enter the next room. Their chatter ended in three blasts from a shotgun.

Police said [Mr.] Hopke, opposed to the marriage, wanted his daughter to care for her mother. He became enraged at reading the wedding notice in the paper, shot the couple, then turned the gun on himself.

Rose Marie was taken to one hospital where she is recovering. Her mother was taken to another. Tuesday night, Mrs. Hopke died (Simon Doniger, ed., *The Nature of Man in Theological and Psychological Perspective* [New York: Harper & Brothers, 1963], 191).

Helen Hopke had been living on the hope in her family. When it was gone, she could no longer live. Neither individuals nor families can live without hope.

Hope hovers about the very heart of the Christian faith. Listen to the note of hope for which Paul pleads in family relationships in Colossians 3:18–21: "Wives, be subject to your husbands, as is fitting in the Lord. Husbands, love your wives, and do not be harsh with them. Children, obey your parents in everything, for this pleases the Lord. Fathers, do not provoke your children, lest they become discouraged" (RSV). In each of the four verses relating to each of the four relationships in this passage, the theme of hope is present. If wives, husbands, children, and fathers try to do what Paul is saying here, they will be building hope in their families. A sociology professor asked a minister one day what the minister could do for couples who came to him for help in their marriages. The minister replied, "We can give them hope." How important is hope in marriage and the family?

I. Hope is the life of a marriage.

Couples must believe in their marriage if a marriage is to live. The outstanding feature of most couples who come to marriage counselors and all couples who go to the divorce court is that they have lost hope. When hope is lacking, families are not able to function.

Disillusionment is common in many marriages. Couples get married expecting certain things to happen, and when they don't happen, disillusionment sets in. The lament of many a young wife to a friend, "You don't know what it is like," is the expression of disillusionment. Another expression of disillusionment is, "You weren't like that before we were married."

Every couple finds problems that can lead to despair. They find problems with each other, or they find despair in the problems they face together. Realizing how easy disillusionment and despair come, if a couple is to have hope, they will have to work for it. In Paul's prescription for family life, he tells family members how to work for hope in the family. Each of his instructions is a hope project for building better family relations.

Hope can be built in families if each member will look at the positive efforts of the other person. We are always more conscious of the failures of others than we are their efforts to do right. If we will look for it, we can usually find something good that a person is doing or trying to do. Noticing the good helps to build hope.

Another way of building hope is to accept others for who they are. The basic need of every one of us is to be accepted and loved. We know that God is revealed in Christ because Christ accepts us and loves us just as we are.

Accepting our partners in marriage means accepting them for what they are instead of rejecting them or trying to remake them into what we want them to be. Some families can never have peace because one member has decided what everyone else must be like if they are going to be accepted. This person takes on the project of trying to remake everyone else in the family, and no one can be very comfortable.

Accepting another person means accepting the bad as well as the good. It does not mean we will not try to change and grow but that change and growth must come from within, not from pressure of another person. In fact, it is amazing how much more family members will fit the expectations of the other family members if they are accepted than if they are rejected or pressured to be what someone else thinks they ought to be.

When Paul said, "Wives, be subject to your husbands, as is fitting in the Lord," he used a special kind of verb. This verb means "decide for yourselves that you can be under the leadership of (your husbands)." He did not say, "Be subjected." It is an attitude the wife must develop for herself, not one that the husband demands.

Hope, then, is the very life of a marriage. Couples must believe in each other and communicate the hope they have for each other.

II. Hope is the growth of a family.

Parents can help their children to grow with hope. If parents can see themselves as teachers, they will take a more patient and longer look at the lessons they want to teach their children. A good teacher knows that a student will not always learn something the first time he or she is shown. A good teacher uses reinforcement techniques. It is difficult for parents, especially for some fathers, to realize that they are their children's teachers.

We teach in many ways. We teach our children by the things we tell them. However, we teach them much more by the things we show them in the way we live. Many times what we tell our children and what we show our children are conflicting messages. They will usually believe what we show them more than what we tell them.

It is easy to discourage children from trying without realizing what we are doing. If parents cannot accept imperfection or failure in their children, the children will learn not to try anything at which they think they cannot succeed. If children's obeying their parents pleases the Lord, the best way for the children to know this is to know that it also pleases their parents. Children know quickly enough when their parents are displeased but not often enough when their parents are pleased.

One of the beautiful things about Jesus' parable of the prodigal son is what it teaches about parenthood. When the young man had left home defiantly thinking that he was going to be an immediate success but failed instead, his father received him back. Jesus knew that a good father is one who can accept failure and build something out of the person in spite of failure.

It is tempting to impose our adult expectations on our children and take away hope. In the second set of Paul's family instructions to the Colossians, he says to the fathers, "Fathers, do not provoke your children, lest they become discouraged" (3:21). He is saying that they should not vent their emotions on their children in such a way that they become discouraged from trying. If all our expectations of our children are the same as we expect of ourselves (in spite of our own failures), our children will very soon learn that they are in an impossible contest and give up.

Even the discipline we give our children, if it is Christian discipline, is given in hope of their growth and their learning, not in delight in their punishment and destruction. By the tone of our voices, by the manner of our discipline, or by the refusal to let them do anything for us when we are disgusted, we can give them the message: "You're through." That is a hard message to erase if it is reinforced very often when a child is growing up.

Hope is conducive to the growth of a family, not only because children grow with hope, but also because hope also allows families to have goals. Every family needs goals if it is to grow together in a real fellowship of hope.

The kind of goal Paul was talking about for a family is that of relationships with each other—such goals as growing in appreciation for each other, learning to listen to each other, learning to disagree with each other without disliking each

165

other, and other such goals of relationships. Spiritual goals are the ones we often miss placing in front of our families. Spiritual goals are a necessity for the Christian family. Spiritual goals include warm and growing relationships with each other, but they also include a growing relationship with God for each member of the family. Goals of worship, Bible study, and new life in Christ for each person in the family are some of the goals that make a family distinctively Christian.

In the Christian family, the source of hope is Jesus Christ. Paul could talk about hope in the relationships with each other in the Christian family because he always related these relationships to Christ. It is "in the Lord" that hope comes to the Christian family.

Christ is our hope because he accepts us as we are. Because he accepts us as we are, we can accept others just as they are without demanding perfection. When we accept each other, we can believe that there is something in each member of the family that Christ will cause to grow if we genuinely love each other.

Christ is also the hope of the family because he gives the family a common purpose. Many families go in different directions without any sense of shared purpose. When a family lets Christ come into the home, the family members share a close bond that helps keep them on the same track.

Christ is also the source of hope because he holds out before us the possibility of a new start. Everyone will make mistakes. Every family will make mistakes. When we make mistakes, we have to do something with them. Christ allows us to be able to start over. When a person has a chance for a new start, he then has a chance for hope. Christ continually says to us as persons and as families, "Behold, I make all things new."

We can realize that without Christ there is no real hope. Without hope there can be no life and no growing family. To be a Christian, then, is to have access to the greatest Hope, who allows us to have hope in life and hope in our families. How much hope do you have in your family? To have hope in your family, you must first of all have the source of hope in your heart.

SUNDAY EVENING, MAY 19

Title: Stronghold of Hope

Text: "As for thee also, by the blood of thy covenant I have sent forth thy prisoners out of the pit wherein is no water. Turn you to the strong hold, ye prisoners of hope: even today do I declare that I will render double unto thee" (**Zech. 9:11–12**).

Scripture Reading: Zechariah 9:9–14

Introduction

The prophet Zechariah was speaking to many of Zion who were yet held as prisoners in distant lands such as Babylon and Egypt. The word *pit* is used to denote the prisons of the day. The prophet indicated that they must rely on their great stronghold, which was the hope that one day they would again be in the beloved Jerusalem and that Zion would again be established. People without hope are unhappy. Today the Christian home is the last bastion of hope in a society that seems headed for moral and spiritual bankruptcy. It must be thoroughly Christian in an un-Christian world. It must realize that humanity is imprisoned by sin, that it is helpless and hopeless. Some years ago, there was a disastrous explosion in a West Virginia coal mine, trapping many men below ground. Those trapped below were "hopeless" and those above ground were "helpless," a physical situation so like the spiritual situation of humanity today. The Christian home must be a lighthouse shining in spiritual darkness, pointing the way through faith and love.

I. Faith.

A. *In the Christ of the cross.* The hardest human heart softens when it is brought face-to-face with the Christ of Calvary's cross. That person sees the Son of God hanging in physical and spiritual anguish on the cruel cross as he has heaped on him the sins of us all. And he hears Jesus' loving voice crying out, "Father, forgive them; for they know not what they do" (Luke 23:34) and "My God, my God, why hast thou forsaken me?" (Matt. 27:46). This compassionate and atoning Savior should be introduced to children in the home by their parents so that they don't grow up to be adults with hardened hearts. Introducing children to Christ is the greatest privilege parents have.

B. *In the God of creation.* The Lord God of creation is responsible for the creation of this great cosmic universe and for every detail of nature. He created the human body, a most finely wrought mechanism of clay that lasts surprisingly well for a period of some seventy, eighty, or even ninety years. The God of creation deserves the great song of praise "How Great Thou Art!"

C. *In the God of providence.* The family altar instills in the lives of children while yet in the family nest the faith to believe in the providential care of God through life's journey. When the going is rough, when health is uncertain, when one stands beside the open grave of a loved one, and even when all of life seems to "fall in" upon us, a firm faith will cause each one to have a forward look. The late Peter Marshall's last words to his wife, "I'll see you in the morning," should be the kind of faith every Christian who is rooted and grounded in the faith may have.

D. *In the Holy Spirit—the living, reigning God who is at work in the world today in the hearts of people.* In the family life of today, it is important that parents properly teach the youngsters about the omnipresence of God's Holy Spirit and his work in the hearts of people.

II. Love.

A. *Love of the Lord God with one's whole heart.* The teaching of the Ten Commandments in the family circle is of utmost importance. The commandment to love God above all must be taught to the younger generation not just by precept but also by example on the part of the parents. Children will sense the attitude of their parents toward God more than they will listen to their words.

B. *Love of one's fellow humans.* To love others as ourselves is the second great commandment, according to our Master. Love for fellow humans works wonders. It can melt the hardest of hearts and cause people to come out of spiritual darkness into spiritual light and life. Most people of our generation have heard the story of Jim Elliot and his fellow missionaries who attempted to take the gospel to the Waodani Indians of Ecuador because of their compassionate love for the lost. The natives responded by slaying the missionaries. But Elliot's wife, Elisabeth, and some other missionaries returned to witness to this benighted group and were able to win them. These missionaries may not have been the best trained for this specific task, but they had the most relevant of all ingredients for the task of missions—love for the lost. One great side effect of such love is that it boomerangs and comes right back to the ones showing it.

Conclusion

The stronghold of hope for tomorrow is the Christian home and its great influence for Christ on future generations. May God bless our homes with the presence of his Holy Spirit to guide us in bringing up tomorrow's citizens to be God-fearing and righteous people!

WEDNESDAY EVENING, MAY 22

Title: When Love Chastens

Text: "He restrained them not" (**1 Sam. 3:13**).

Scripture Reading: 1 Samuel 2:12–17; 3:11–14

Introduction

"It's ten o'clock! Do you know where your children are?" This question comes by way of television into countless homes. Imagine the different thoughts and the range of emotions experienced by parents whose teens are out for the evening. *Where* are the children? *Who* are they with? *What* are they doing?

Is it necessary that we be reminded of our responsibility for our children? We have reached the point of crisis.

I. How have we come to this failure in discipline?

A. *When the family fails to exercise authority.*

1. Discipline begins at home, the same as love. Eli was a good man who served God and people. But he neglected the discipline of his own

children. The Bible says that he knew that his sons were doing evil and "he restrained them not."

The failure of one father in Israel to restrain his children is a fore-warning to all generations. Judgment and doom came to Eli the priest, to his family, and to the nation of Israel (1 Sam. 3:12–13; 4:22). God is concerned with the discipline of children.

2. The primary responsibility for discipline must begin at home. It must include the willingness of parents to restrain their children when necessary.

B. *When the home has lost its authority over children — problems to consider.*
1. Conditions outside the home. *The pressure of the peer group* is often too much for youth to resist. Acceptance by the group means conformity to its values and loyalty to its demands. *The fascination of sin.* Youth are constantly bombarded by temptations and vices that society allows and law enforcement cannot reach. *Lack of common standards in other homes.* Some families are more *permissive*; others are just indifferent regarding limits and allowances. But even those who try to be consistent and responsible often face the rebellion of their own household.
2. Conditions within the home. Long business hours, both parents working outside the home, single parenthood, and social activities regarded as essential to "success" make parents less available, less aware of children's activities; hence, there is little guidance when it is most needed. The character of young people is undermined by fewer responsibilities. Too much is given and too little required, and this situation causes young people to feel the world owes them all that they take. The importance of the father role has changed so that the father feels and acts with little authority at home. Inadequate fathers and domineering mothers confuse and anger children.

II. What is the answer for families today?

A. *Return to biblical methods and principles of discipline.*
1. Time-tested wisdom from the past as shown in the proverb "Spare the rod and spoil the child" is unsophisticated wisdom, to be sure. This may be the only effective restraint when a child is not yet able to reason or be aware of danger. Discipline also includes guidance and training. "He who does not teach his child a trade teaches him to steal." This is a saying of the rabbis. Training for life is a part of discipline. Discipline was never intended to mean punishment alone. The word comes from the same root meaning as *disciple*, which means "learner."
2. The Christian view of human nature. Christian understanding of human nature is based on God's revelation (e.g., Isa. 53:6), which implies the need for discipline. People are sinners. From infancy we are self-centered and unhappy with restraints. Disobedience toward parents will become disobedience toward God. Sinners will assert their

will in opposition to that of their Creator and Lawgiver. Until sinners are reconciled to God, they live in a state of rebellion and guilt.

3. Christian guidance for the family. A primary responsibility of the home is to teach obedience through the discipline of the disobedient. The rights of others have equal claim. We have laws to ensure these equalities. The antisocial ways and lawlessness rampant among many of today's youth are a rejection of authority—an outright attitude of disobedience to all forms of order and restraint.

The modern aversion to the word *obedience* betrays the sin of pride and self-sufficiency. Christ, it is said, learned obedience through the things he suffered (Heb. 5:8). He "became obedient unto death, even the death of the cross" (Phil. 2:8).

4. The motive of Christian discipline is love. "'The Lord disciplines the one he loves, and he chastens everyone he accepts as his son.' ... If you are not disciplined—and everyone undergoes discipline—then you are not legitimate, not true sons and daughters at all" (Heb. 12:6–8 NIV).

There is no love that does not include discipline (Prov. 13:24). Those who say they love their children too much to punish them do not love enough to be responsible for the welfare and happiness of their children. It is the relationship that is most vital to effective discipline. Children know when they are loved. They know that the need for discipline and the certainty of it do not mean the end of the parents' love. In later years, they recognize that discipline was one expression of love. "Love never fails." Discipline is *love* when love chastens.

SUNDAY MORNING, MAY 26

Title: What Do You Give a Child Who Has Nothing?

Text: "Train up a child in the way he should go: and when he is old, he will not depart from it" (**Prov. 22:6**).

Scripture Reading: Deuteronomy 6:4–9; Proverbs 23:13

Hymns: "How Firm a Foundation," Rippon

"My Faith Has Found a Resting Place," Edmunds

"Be Thou My Vision," Byrne

Offertory Prayer: Our heavenly Father, we adore you. In this experience of worship we have sung your praises, heard your Word read, and sat in silence to hear you. We come to the part of our worship where we give to you. Help us to give with the right motive. Teach us to distribute what we receive in the offering for your kingdom's business. In Jesus' name. Amen.

Introduction

Two men were talking about what to give their children for Christmas. One commented that his son had a closet full of clothes, boxes full of toys, a storage room full of sporting equipment, and a go-cart in the garage. In his frustration of trying to think of a gift for his son, he asked, "What do you give a child who has everything?"

Think about this matter of parenting. Then turn the question around: "What do you give a child who has nothing?" Children come into the world with nothing. They come as pliable persons with enormous potential for good or for bad.

When God made a nation and called it Israel, he spoke frequently about the responsibilities of being a parent. Throughout the Scripture, God instructed Israel on what to give children. Our task this morning is to ask, "What do you give a child who has nothing?" and to answer the question from God's Word.

I. Parents need to give instructions to their children.

Think about the numerous instructions parents have to give a child. They give directions for hair combing, dressing, bed making, shoe tying, teeth brushing, bike riding, and a thousand other things.

    A. *Instructions constitute a necessary part of a child's life.* Children come into the world without instruction. They need parents to help them learn many skills required in life. Training cannot be left to chance. The Bible teaches the necessity of a parent training a child.

    B. *Instructions need to be given with a sense of urgency.* "Train up a child in the way he should go" (Prov. 22:6). Once T. DeWitt Talmadge preached a sermon titled "Things We Never Get Over." Among the things he mentioned was parental neglect. Training a child is one chance in a lifetime. A parent must have a sense of urgency in training a child, because a child becomes an adult all too quickly.

    C. *Instructions need to be specific.* The biblical writer said to train a child in the way "he should go." The writer did not say, "Train the child in the way he or she wants to go." The word *train* in Proverbs 22:6 can be translated in one of two ways. It can mean to imitate or to dedicate. Training a child means the parent has experienced the Lord and says, "This is the way; walk in it."

II. Parents need to give children the privilege of personhood.

Unfortunately, some parents depersonalize their children. They treat them as objects to be adored. Sometimes parents seek to live their lives over again through their children. Many examples of depersonalizing a child could be cited. Let us see what is involved in treating a child as a person.

    A. *Treating children as people means that parents must seek to instill a good self-image in them.* Dr. James Dobson emphasizes that parents can so depreciate their children that they will develop negative feelings toward themselves. He encourages parents to help their children have a realistic self-image.

    B. *Treating children as people means that parents must regard the children's autonomy.* Children are not robots to be programmed or puppets to be manipulated. Parents must allow their children to be people. Parental tension comes at the point of granting freedom. Parents need to gradually allow their children to get away from their dominance and become persons with the right to choose.

Think for a moment about the father Jesus spoke about in Luke 15. The boy wanted freedom, and the father granted the boy freedom, knowing the freedom could lead to either good or evil. Yet the father was a good parent because he treated his son as a human being.

III. Parents need to discipline their children.

Though the subject is touchy, parents need to discipline their children. Listen to the wisdom of the writer of Proverbs: "Do not withhold discipline from a child; if you punish them with the rod, they will not die" (23:13 NIV). Supervision and nurture are the positive sides of discipline. Punishment is the necessary negative side of discipline.

A. *Parents can misinterpret the real meaning of discipline.* Perhaps one of the most misunderstood aspects of parenting comes at the point of punishment or discipline. Let us think together of some abuses.

Discipline is distorted when parents respond out of anger to a child. Usually when this type of behavior happens, a parent has been inconvenienced. Also, discipline is distorted with tyrannical, strict punishment.

B. *Parents can use discipline in a beneficial way.* Discipline helps train a child. It is an evidence of love. "Whoever spares the rod hates their children, but the one who loves their children is careful to discipline them" (Prov. 13:24 NIV).

IV. Parents need to give a godly example to their children.

Religion is not as much taught as it is caught. The best fit a parent can give to a child is to live a godly life. Children imitate parents either for good or for bad.

A. *Parents can provide a godly atmosphere for children.* The best thing a child can observe is a mother or father deeply committed and in love with each other. Children get a sense of security and peace from such an environment.

Think about the influence of a child living in a home where prayers are offered, where the Bible is read, where church is attended. Genuine expressions of God's love are powerful.

B. *Parents can live godly lives before their children.* The best way to explain what a Christian is, is to be one. What kind of example do you give to your children? Once I heard about a drunken father who returned home one cold winter evening. Snow covered the ground. The father staggered up the walk, went into the house, and went to bed. The next morning he looked out the window and saw his young son. The boy played in the snow, but he staggered. The father asked, "What are you doing, son?" The boy replied, "I'm trying to walk in your footsteps."

Conclusion

Parenting is one of life's great responsibilities. What do you give a child who has nothing? You give instruction, personhood, discipline, and a godly example.

Sunday Evening, May 26

Title: A Knock at the Door

Text: "Here I am! I stand at the door and knock. If anyone hears my voice and opens the door, I will come in and eat with that person, and they with me" **(Rev. 3:20 NIV).**

Scripture Reading: Revelation 3:20–22

Introduction

A knock at the door is one of life's most interesting episodes. Guess who it is standing there—the paper boy who has come to collect? A Jehovah's witness? Someone collecting for a fund-raiser? "Avon calling"? A long-lost friend? In Revelation, John has a vision of Jesus standing at the door. He says, "Behold, I stand at the door and knock." This in itself is a glorious truth, for it points out that the Lord takes the initiative in reaching out to lost people. "While we were yet sinners, Christ died for us" (Rom. 5:8). Our text speaks to our hearts this evening on the various transactions taking place in the act of a soul's coming to accept Christ as Savior. Some of these transactions are:

I. The approach by Christ to the sinner.

"Behold, I stand at the door and knock."

A. *Jesus is knocking with concern.* He is concerned about total persons—their character, mentality, and physical well-being. Especially, however, Christ is concerned about their spirituality, about their souls' need. Jesus, while on earth, showed great concern over the spirituality and morality of humankind, for he was willing to be found in the company of publicans and sinners who were the admitted spiritual dross of his day. He was concerned about the Gadarene demoniac, and he was concerned about the greedy Zacchaeus. His concern spelled transformed lives for them.

B. *Jesus is knocking in a spirit of love and compassion.* "Love is blind," someone has said. Indeed, it is not blind, for it sees more of people's needs, not less. Because it sees more needs, it is willing to see fewer imperfections. The woman taken in adultery was worthy of death according to the laws of the day, but Jesus treated her with compassion and rescued her from her would-be executors. Jesus looks today with compassion and tender love upon every lost sinner, desiring to come into their hearts to abide with them.

C. *Jesus knocks in various ways:*

1. Through our failures. Sometimes we feel that everything we touch goes sour. At times we feel without a doubt that we are failure prone, that we cannot win for losing. However, in retrospect, we are made to realize that we have learned one of life's greatest lessons—that Jesus is trying to get our attention, that he is trying to tell us something.

2. Through our vision of a better self. Young Abe Lincoln, poring over his meager supply of books by the flickering light of the fire, had a vision of

173

being a better, more enlightened person. Only through faith in Christ Jesus can life truly be what one would desire it to be. Our Lord gives us visions of what life can be if we make conditions right. Every person's dream of a better life in the future can be realized only in Christ Jesus.

3. Through a glimpse of ourselves as compared with his righteousness, seeing the sin stains that are so heavy on us. Once a young street urchin was invited into a nice home among clean people. Suddenly he saw for the first time what it was like to be clean, and thus for the first time he realized how dirty he was. He began rubbing the dirt off his cheeks with his grimy hands. So it is with the sinner when through the convicting power of God's Holy Spirit he meets Christ Jesus face-to-face in a personal experience.

II. The response: hearing and opening: "If anyone hears my voice and opens the door...."

A. *Anyone hearing the knock may respond.* No one is excluded. It is not intended solely for those:
   1. Of a certain cultural group. Rich and poor, cultured and unsophisticated, meet together at Jesus' feet.
   2. Of a certain creedal background. Though Jesus came to present the way of life first to the lost sheep of the house of Israel, he came to present the way of salvation to all people. He came to touch the lives of all people everywhere and to meet their spiritual needs.
   3. Of a certain racial background. Christianity is equally effective for Asians, Scandinavians, Africans, Italians, and North Americans. "If *anyone* hears my voice and opens the door" applies to all people of all nations.
   4. Of a certain degree of sinfulness. Jesus came to seek and to save those who are lost, be they prostitutes, thieves, hypocrites, murderers, or the hardest of all sinners to reach—the self-righteous.

B. *The difficulty of hearing the knock of our Lord at our heart's door.* Once when making a call, a pastor stood on the front porch of a home and knocked for some time. Finally, he remembered that the elderly man who lived alone there was hard of hearing and that he played his television rather loudly. Naturally he could not hear the knock over the din in his living room. So it is with the noises of the world: they prevent our hearing the Master's knock at our heart's door. Some of these noises are:
   1. Clamor of the material world. A faithful Christian said, "The reason that the members of this rising generation have a standard of values based on material wealth is that we have taught them to be like that through our example before them. We have been constantly reaching out for this and that new material possession—small wonder they are like they are!"
   2. The sound wave interference of Satan. Once I read of a person who was taken prisoner during World War II. He salvaged enough equipment to send out a radio message calling for help. The enemy immediately

detected his faint message and jammed the airways, preventing the prisoner's fellow Americans from hearing his call for help. So it is with Satan's technique; he attempts to prevent our hearing the loving call of God.

3. Sinful habits that sinners know could not be permitted by Christ for a member of his family. Some people love their sins so much that they are not willing to turn away from them in true repentance. Thus their love of sins prevents them from hearing the knock of Jesus at their heart's door.

C. *Opening the door.* The door of one's heart must be opened from within before Jesus will come in and abide. "Today when you hear his voice, do not harden your hearts as in the rebellion" (Heb. 3:15 RSV).

III. What the Guest has to offer.

Jesus has said that if we open our hearts to him:

A. *He enters our hearts with all his cleansing power, taking the old heart and so remaking it that it is a new heart indeed.* He puts a new heart and mind into the old body, and we become a new person in Christ Jesus.

B. *He offers fellowship and peace.* "I will come in and eat with that person." The Lord humbles himself to stoop to fellowship with humans. He will be closer to us than a brother. This is the peace that passes understanding, a heavenly peace. Such fellowship with the Master reveals to us that we have indeed passed from death to life.

C. *We will rise to the occasion and enjoy this heavenly fellowship: " . . . and they with me."* That is, believers will enjoy fellowship with the Master. Believers who have acted in faith and have invited the Master into their hearts and lives will know the supreme happiness of daily fellowship with Christ. When you are at work, at school, or at home, you will have a song in your heart and a prayer of communion and fellowship on your lips. Christianity is a happy experience that reveals itself on the faces of believers.

Conclusion

Today Jesus is knocking at the door of the hearts of unbelievers. He is seeking to gain admission. Do you believe this enough to *act* and *open* the door of your heart and allow the Master to come in?

WEDNESDAY EVENING, MAY 29

Title: Show Me the Way to Go Home

Text: "We wept, when we remembered Zion" (**Ps. 137:1**).

Scripture Reading: Psalm 137:1 – 6

Introduction

The word *home* is associated with our deepest needs: to be somebody, to belong to someone in a relationship of love, and to know the security of permanence. God has made provision for us in the earthly and heavenly meanings of home.

I. The first home.

  A. *There is no place like home.*

    1. The Jewish exiles remembered Zion. The Jews in exile expressed their homesickness: "We wept when we remembered Zion" (Ps. 137:1). They had a natural love for the sacred soil of the Promised Land. No other place could be home. They would never be guilty of the disloyalty of forgetting (v. 5).

    2. Our memories of home are important to us. One never knows a person until he knows what he remembers about his childhood home.

      Our childhood home is more than the house where we lived with our families; it is a special place where we developed relationships with people who were a part of our lives. We remember the pride or shame we attached to our family name, the guilt of youthful transgressions, and our sense of worth as a person. "Home" represents the values, the accepted standards of conduct, and the traditions and customs that will live on within us always. *"Home" is who we are.*

  B. *Millions today have no home.* They are the uprooted. Countless numbers of Americans are homeless, living on the streets. Millions more American families will move this year. Families from farms and small towns will lose themselves in large cities. Others will be uprooted by large corporations. Before they take root, they will be moved again.

II. Looking for a home.

  A. *Spiritual life may wither away from home.*

    1. Not all of the Jews longed to return to Zion. They found wealth and power in Babylon. They were glad to be free of the external controls of their religious homes and communities.

    2. Families may never feel they belong in their strange or temporary homes. Thus they never belong to a church or Christian community.

    3. Young people, away from the expectations and controls of home and church, drift into ways of life that are destructive as they try to live without God.

  B. *Some experience new life when away from home.*

    1. The Jews discovered that God was in Babylon. "The whole earth is full of his glory." They built places of worship and established their faith in a strange land, and the "songs of Zion" were heard by the people there.

    2. God is not confined to any place or nation, for "God is Spirit."

III. Christ may call us to break the ties of our first home.

  A. *The widening circle of family and home.*

    1. Christ demands loyalty above our first home. He rejected his family's special claim on him. Nazareth was no longer his home. His mothers and brothers and sisters were those who did the will of God (Mark 3:31–35).

2. Christ promises a hundredfold in families and homes to those who must forsake all in obedience to him (Mark 10:29–30). He also said, "He that loveth father or mother more than me is not worthy of me" (Matt. 10:37).

3. Our first home's purpose is fulfilled. The time comes when we are independent of home. Parents should love their children enough to prepare them to leave home and find their place and service in the will of God.

B. *The church as the fellowship of God's people becomes our new home.*

1. A home that means "household of God." Its people are the people of God, called by a "new name" to live together in a community of love, forgiveness, and mutual burden bearing.

2. As God's family, we share a common mission on earth. Home is anywhere there are human needs and lost souls to be saved. The uprooted and homeless are the object of the Lord's compassion. "They were like sheep without a shepherd" (Mark 6:34 NIV). They need a place to call home, to be loved, and to belong.

Conclusion

"Come unto me," Christ calls to the homeless (Matt. 11:28). Christ shows us the way to go home. The ultimate meaning, the longing for permanence, is found in our eternal home. It is a special place prepared for us in the Father's house. Christ gave us the answer to our anxious question "How can we know the way?" "I am the way," he said; "I will take you there" (John 14:3–6). Blessed are the homesick, for they shall come home.

JUNE

■ Sunday Mornings

The Sunday morning messages continue to focus on the needs, problems, and potential of the modern family. "Christ's Concern for the Family" is the theme. On the Sunday preceding Independence Day, a sermon titled "The Christian and the State" is provided.

■ Sunday Evenings

All of us are guilty at times of passing the buck and blaming others when things go wrong. On one occasion, the Lord said through the prophet Jeremiah, "I have listened attentively, but [the people of Judah] do not say what is right. None of them repent of their wickedness, saying, 'What have I done?'" (Jer. 8:6 NIV). It is time for each of us to ask, "What have I done?" This question provides the theme for the Sunday evening messages beginning on the second Sunday in June.

■ Wednesday Evenings

Continue with the theme "The Needs of the Family."

SUNDAY MORNING, JUNE 2

Title: The Family Trust Fund

Text: "Now these three remain: faith, hope and love. But the greatest of these is love" (**1 Cor. 13:13 NIV**).

Scripture Reading: Hosea 3:1–5

Hymns: "Wonderful Story of Love," Driver

"Something for Thee," Phelps

"Somebody Needs Your Love," McKinney

Offertory Prayer: Holy Father, you have given us the gift of eternal life through faith in Jesus Christ. You have given us your Holy Spirit to dwell within our body and to make of it a holy temple. You have given us the privilege and the power to work and to get wealth. We come now bringing the results of our work, the fruits of our labors, in the form of a monetary offering for the use of your kingdom's work. Accept these tithes and offerings and bless them in ministries to those who are in need. Through Jesus Christ our Lord, we pray. Amen.

Introduction

Every family has a "trust fund." The size of that trust fund does not depend on the amount of money the family has. However, without a trust fund, there can be no family. When a family has spent its trust fund, the marriage is over.

We make our investments in this trust fund gradually. We are often unaware of how much we have invested in it. Developing trust is automatic for some families, but other families must work at it. A Christian family is known by the trust it possesses.

The book of Hosea in the Old Testament is a tragic parable of a bankrupt family trust fund. In the sad story of Hosea's marital misfortunes, God was demonstrating Israel's adulterous way of life. Hosea's wife was a woman he could not trust, just as Israel was a nation God could not trust. Yet God ordered Hosea to build a trust and a relationship of trust where there was very little to build on. We read about it in Hosea 3:1–5. Hosea was told to invest in a person who was a very unlikely prospect for marriage and motherhood. Hosea asked her to become the kind of person he could trust.

Jesus' definition of adultery in the New Testament is broader than sexual infidelity. He uses the term in such a way as to mean any breaking of the relationship of trust between a man and a woman in marriage. For him, adultery was synonymous with unfaithfulness of any kind. An adulterous person is a person who is unworthy of trust. Jesus indicated that trust is imperative for any meaningful relationship of life, just as Hosea had demonstrated.

I. Family life is impossible without a trust fund.

Suspicion destroys persons and destroys family life. No one can stand suspicion over a long period of time without being destroyed by it. A man was once accused of mishandling public funds. An audit was held, and it was proven beyond any doubt that he was entirely innocent. However, people continued to talk suspiciously and to cast doubt on his character. Finally, one day, in the desperation of being under the cloud of suspicion, he took his own life. In his suicide note, he asserted his innocence again, but he said it was impossible to live with the suspicion that people had created about him.

Some people can trust no one. They are suspicious of everyone and everything and cannot believe anyone has their interest at heart. They believe everyone is out to "get something for himself," even when that person is trying to help them. This kind of person may carry the attitude, "You have to look after yourself because everyone is out to get you." The agony of such a suspicious person is that he feels threatened all the time. He probably has never known any solid relationships in his life. People who live under suspicion become suspicious.

A woman came one day to accuse her pastor of bad motives for something the church was doing. He accepted her feelings of suspicion and got her to talk some more about how suspicion felt. Soon she began to talk about her parents and related that her father had always been a very suspicious person also. She told how suspicious he was of all his neighbors and that she never wanted to be that way. She could not realize that the very reason she was suspicious about her church was that she had lived with suspicion in her life.

Hosea knew he could not have a family if his family had to live in suspicion. He told his wife that he must be able to trust her. Family life is destroyed when the acid of suspicion is thrown on it.

Another symptom of mistrust is lying. We sometimes assume that people lie because they just want to be mean, and undoubtedly there are people who lie maliciously. However, others lie because they are afraid and because they have been taught to manipulate life by being less than direct. People who lie have never learned to face up to life. Such people live in a prison of their own making.

A young woman who had lied all of her life lost a marriage because of her lying. She admitted, as she prepared to marry for the second time, that she had learned to lie when it would be better to tell the truth. As she faced herself for the first time, she made a decision to give up lying. Two years later, she said she had not realized that life could be so meaningful as it had been since she had quit lying. At last she had learned to face life, and now she could build a healthy marriage.

In some families, deceit becomes a way of life. Mothers deceive fathers about what the children are doing. Fathers deceive mothers about what they are doing. And children deceive parents about what they are doing. Such patterns of deceit can only lead the family to get lost in the desert of suspicion and mistrust.

II. Family life is where we invest our best treasures.

Hosea knew that he was investing more than his money in Gomer; he was also investing himself in their relationship. For the trust fund to grow in a family, we must invest ourselves.

There is no better place to invest ourselves than in Christian family life. The things we invest in our families are more than we sometimes realize. Family is the place where love is risked.

It is really a risky business to give yourself to another person. Yet that is exactly what must happen to have marriage or a family. Hosea was risking himself for Gomer as God risked himself for the good of Israel. When that investing and that risking are done, you can only trust that the other person will take care of the investment.

A wife who had been deeply hurt by the unfaithfulness of her husband asked a counselor, "How can I be sure it won't happen again?" The counselor wisely replied, "You cannot know that, but you must be willing to trust if the relationship is to grow."

More than love is invested in the family trust fund. All of our other feelings, as well as our weaknesses and hurts, are risked in the family. The fact that we risk our weaknesses and hurts means that it is easy to betray another person in family life. Where the risk is high, the trust must also be high.

Hosea invested something else in his marriage and family. He was investing his hope in this relationship. He was hoping, in trust, that his wife would be a trustworthy person.

Family life is the place for sharing fortunes. Investing the fruits of our labor in life, family life grows. This labor and life are shared in hope for others in the family. Part of investing hope in a family is sharing goals we have for ourselves and for others in the family. A wholesome family is one in which the members sit down together and talk about where they hope they are going as individuals and as a family.

To be able to share this deeply means being able to share a deep faith. The whole foundation of marriage and family trust must be formed out of a solid relationship to Christ. Only persons who have trusted their lives to Christ can understand what it is to trust their lives to others in the family and have other persons trust their lives to them.

III. Family life has a goal of making persons trustworthy.

Hosea believed that if he invested enough love and trust in Gomer, he could make her a better person. He was willing for her to grow toward trustworthiness and integrity.

One of the worthy goals of family life is the development of trustworthiness and integrity for each person. Integrity and trustworthiness must be developed, but for some people they do not come easily. A Christian family is one in which the members grow in integrity and honesty with each other.

Trustworthiness as a goal of family life is enhanced when family members realize what others are investing. If Gomer could realize how much Hosea was investing in the marriage, she would be called to be a better person herself. Many family members are so conscious of what they are investing and so unconscious of what others are investing that they begin to protect themselves.

Growing in trustworthiness depends on being able to believe in the goodwill and the good intentions of other members of the family. A little girl cut out a jagged, not-very-pretty picture to give to her mother for her birthday. The mother was wise enough to thank and praise her daughter for what she had done for her for her birthday. She told her daughter, "You've made this the happiest birthday I could have." The mother was not looking at the picture; she was able to see the love and the good intentions of her daughter behind the picture.

It is in the Christian family that we learn to treat the investment of others with care. Whether we are handling love, trust, anger, hurt feelings, weaknesses, or even despair, Christians know how to take care of what others are risking. A Christian family is one in which trust is possible. If we have learned to trust Christ, we should learn to be more trustworthy because "He first loved us."

SUNDAY EVENING, JUNE 2

Title: Dealing with Difficulties in the Home

Text: "Finally, be ye all of one mind, having compassion one of another" (**1 Peter 3:8**).

Scripture Reading: 1 Peter 3:1–12

Introduction

A couple had been happily married for sixty years. When interviewed and asked for the key to their success, they said, "Do unto one another as you would a month before marriage." Someone else has said that the ABCs of success in marriage are Always Be Christian. Both of these bits of advice can be applied as we deal with difficulties in the home.

I. A great variety of problems plague the home.

  A. *Some problems grow out of the inevitable crises of life.*
   1. Financial difficulties.
   2. Relocation to a new community.
   3. Separation from loved ones.
   4. Illness.
   5. Death.
  B. *Marriages suffer because of character failure.*
   1. Dishonesty.
   2. Cheating.
   3. Infidelity.
   4. Gambling.
   5. Drinking and drug abuse.
   6. Pornography.
  C. *Marriages often collapse because there has been no growth of love, causing the relationship to deteriorate into nothingness.*
  D. *Another problem that often leads to unhappiness and suffering is incompatibility.*
   1. This could be discovered before marriage by those who have ears to hear and eyes to see.
   2. If either spouse has an unwillingness to adjust, compromise, and work, the couple will face much unhappiness.

II. Some scriptural suggestions that involve work (1 Peter 3:1–12).

  A. *Conduct yourself so as to win the unsaved companion to the Christian way of life (vv. 1–6).*
  B. *"Be ye all of one mind." Seek to unite in one great common way of thinking (v. 8).*
  C. *"Having compassion one of another." Have compassion toward each other (v. 8).*
  D. *"Love as brethren." Practice a persistent spirit of goodwill toward one another (v. 8).*
  E. *"Be pitiful." Be tenderhearted toward one another (v. 8).*
  F. *"Be courteous." Give attention to the little courtesies of life (v. 8).*
  G. *Return good for evil (v. 9).*
  H. *Watch your tongue (v. 10).*
  I. *Hate evil and love good (v. 11).*
  J. *Pursue peace (v. 11).*
  K. *Always pray (v. 12).*

Conclusion

All marriages face difficulties. Some marriages fail. Other marriages succeed. The difference between success and failure is not to be found in the absence of difficulties, but rather in the dedication of both husband and wife to work together continuously to achieve success and to fulfill God's plan for their lives. May God help you to deal with the difficulties in your home in a Christian manner. Christ the Lord will guide you and assist you if you will permit him to do so.

WEDNESDAY EVENING, JUNE 5

Title: " ... A Child Is Born"

Text: "And Jesus grew" (**Luke 2:52 NIV**).

Scripture Reading: Luke 2:39–52

Introduction

The term *silent years* refers to the silence of the Scriptures on the life of Christ from the events of his birth to the beginning of his public ministry. This silence was most significantly broken when Jesus was twelve years old. The statement in Luke 2:52 describes the purpose of the silent years: growth.

In this sermon we consider the meaning of parenthood in terms of the growth of the child through three stages of life lived under the direct guidance of parents.

I. "Unto us a child is born" (Isa. 9:6).
   A. *"A heritage of the LORD" (Ps. 127:3).*
      1. A child is born. Mary and Joseph were prepared by God in terms of a deep readiness for, and a deep acceptance of, the child when he came into the world. Such preparedness should be a characteristic of every Christian home as the miracle of birth is awaited. Expectant parents should recognize their coming child as a "gift of God" in order that the child may look upon life itself as a gift.
      2. Unto us. The child is born unto "us"—not into a vacuum but into a world of living people. How vital to the beginning of life is the adequacy of parents to respond to the needs of a child.
   B. *The foundations of life.*
      1. The parent image. From us come our children's first impressions of life. The first and deepest need of life is *basic trust*. Trust is the seed whose fruit will one day be faith. Trust is born of trustworthy parents.
      2. In God's image. The spiritual habits of Jesus were begun early and lived in him in his manhood. "He went into the synagogue, as was his custom" (Luke 4:16 NIV). In every crisis of life a truth from God's Word was his

183

answer to temptation or personal need. Prayer was as natural to Jesus as breathing. His disciples said, "Lord, teach us to pray" (Luke 11:1).

Every child builds on others' experiences. The secret of success is in the teacher. How often we as fathers neglect our responsibility as spiritual leaders in the family. How often are our children building without a solid foundation?

II. "My Father's business" (Luke 2:49).

A. *Becoming "inner-directed."*

1. Leaving childhood. The time comes when every person must yield to the inner need to stand on his own feet, have his own thoughts, and become independent and inner-directed. This stage is depicted in the life of Jesus, and its meaning is most clear for parents of adolescents. Upon being scolded by Mary for the concern and inconvenience caused the family, he answered, "Wist ye not that I must be about my Father's business?" (Luke 2:49). Even so, he went home and "was obedient to them" (v. 51 NIV).

2. Straining relationships. Youth is often a period of storm and stress. Young people's new attitudes and actions bring them into conflict with those they most need at this time. The chosen lines of battle are seemingly trivial and are often silly to adults. Clothing and hair styles, hypercritical attitudes, laziness, curfew, companions, etc., are the issues. Behind the boisterous and provoking attitudes is a very uncertain, insecure, and sensitive young boy or girl who is no longer a child but is not yet an adult.

B. *The help of the family.* The joy of the family and its overall purpose is the growth of the individuals in it.

1. Understanding. The climate of understanding supports growth. To be understood is one of life's exquisite joys. Being misunderstood can lead to isolation and illness. To feel understood is to feel loved.

2. Respect. Add to understanding, respect. Respect encourages growth.

III. "He was tempted" (Luke 4:2).

A. *The wilderness of decision.* Professor Wayne Oates sees the youth of our day as needing and seeking a sense of direction. Earlier we noted the call to inner-directedness. Next comes the time for "other-directedness."

1. The resources. Availability is key for parents. Parents underestimate the value young people place on them as listeners; otherwise they would make themselves more available.

   A father's diary entry may read, "An afternoon wasted—took my son fishing," while his son's diary reads, "The most important day of my life—went fishing with my dad today."

2. The choices. We should not be surprised that there are starts and stops and changes in direction. Few of us live our lives on the basis of first

choices, or second, or even third. Whom shall I marry? What vocational choice is best for me (God's will for me)? To whom or to what shall I give my loyalty? These are decisions that must be lived with, and we have only one life.

B. *Keeping in touch.*

1. "The far country." Sometimes foolish decisions are made. Parents must eventually yield to reality that each child is responsible for his or her own life. To make wrong choices is better than to make no choices. To return in shame is better than the fear of failure that keeps one from leaving at all.

   Just to know that someone somewhere continues to care and that one will always find welcome and temporary refuge strengthens and gives courage for life.

   What is learned in the "far country" could not always be learned at home. It is often in our self-made hells and predicaments that we "come to ourselves" (see Luke 15:17).

2. Son and heir. The prodigal learned what we all must learn about true friends. "No one gave him anything" (Luke 15:16). Instead of "the radar of public opinion," our young people need the testing and concerned fellowship of those who seek to "have this mind ... which was also in Christ Jesus" (Phil. 2:5).

Conclusion

The goal of parenthood is to help our children in the direction of the ultimate goal of life: "We shall be like him" (1 John 3:2). In this materialistic age with its philosophies of success, how much more we need to teach, through precept and example, that "what I become" matters infinitely more than "what I have." God willing, this training will be carried to our children's children and their children's children until Christ comes again.

SUNDAY MORNING, JUNE 9

Title: To Talk or Not to Talk

Text: "But let your communication be, Yea, yea; Nay, nay: for whatsoever is more than these cometh of evil" **(Matt. 5:37).**

Scripture Reading: Matthew 18:15

Hymns: "Come, Thou Almighty King," Anonymous

"Jesus Is All the World to Me," Thompson

"Let Jesus Come into Your Heart," Morris

Offertory Prayer: Father, we thank you for the gift of life. We thank you for the blessings that have come to us during the past week. We praise you for the blessings that you will bestow on us during this hour of worship. Help each of us to recognize our basic need to be a giver, a contributor to your kingdom's work, and to the hearts and lives of others. Help us to believe that it is more blessed to give than to receive. Help us to give to the extent that we can experience the joy of giving. Use these tithes and offerings for your glory and for the good of others, through Jesus Christ. Amen.

Introduction

"Don't just stand there, say something!" is the demand of being human. Human life must have expression. We find ways of saying things even when we don't realize it. Even alcoholism or mental illness is sometimes a way of saying something a person cannot say in words.

Our problem today concerns the wrong kind of communication. Some families that communicate a lot still destroy each other. Reuel Howe defined communication as "the attempt on the part of selves to find and call each other out of the loneliness of independent selfhood into a relationship of mutual interest and purpose" (Dwight Small, *After You've Said I Do* [Old Tappan, N.J.: Revell, 1968], 47). That is a refined way of saying that communication is sharing yourself with another person.

Jesus was an expert in communication. People understood him so well that they wanted to kill him. He encouraged directness in communication: "All you need to say is simply 'Yes' or 'No'; anything beyond this comes from the evil one" (Matt. 5:37). Very simply, he was saying, "Mean what you say, and say what you mean." If families could learn to do this, communication would be greatly helped.

Jesus also encouraged directness in expressing forgiveness. In Matthew 18:15, he said, "If your brother sins against you, go and tell him his fault, between you and him alone. If he listens to you, you have gained your brother." Then Jesus went on to describe what to do in case this fails. My point is that he used a very direct approach to handling conflicts and difficulties with people. The health of our own lives and the health of our families depends on learning the art of communication. Taking Jesus' cue of direct communication, let us look at the importance of communication for families.

I. The wrong kind of communication destroys families and persons.

Without knowing it, families fall into patterns of attacking one another. It is very difficult for us to hear ourselves the way others hear us. Some who attack others would deny it if it were called to their attention. This is contrary to the directness that Jesus was talking about.

Families use several different patterns of attack. One is the negative response. Some family members respond negatively to almost everything other members of the family do or say. For these persons, everything is bad. Without realizing it, they meet every suggestion and every comment with a "that's not right" attitude.

Another kind of attack that destroys communication is the constant use of sarcasm and cynicism. A sarcastic response can be a devastating experience for

186

the person who receives it. It is like a snowball with a rock in it. It has the covering of humor but the hard core of anger.

Family members also attack each other by their unspoken demonstrations. Persons who go through the house banging everything they touch may be communicating more devastatingly than if they were using words. Others use cold quietness to freeze out other family members. All of us learn to use charades in life. Our charades can attack just as much as if we used our fists.

Still another kind of family attack is the "Who's to blame?" approach. This is a very popular human game. It began with Adam and Eve. When Adam was caught up short in his disobedience, he blamed his wife. In turn, she blamed the serpent. The buck is still being passed today. Some families play the game with zest.

The wrong kind of communication makes people defend themselves, especially in their families. When we spend so much time caring for our own feelings, it is impossible to care for the feelings of others. We can even claim to be caring for others when we are actually defending or attacking. The way we communicate tells much about how we feel about ourselves. The wrong kind of communication usually comes from persons who are unhappy with themselves, but it lands on the people with whom they try to communicate.

II. Both acting and talking are necessary to communicate.

Jesus emphasized both acting and talking in his teaching and communication. He said our words should have direct meaning, and he is known as the one "who went about doing good." Christian communication is clear communication.

Some things have to be acted out in marriages and families. In fact, our words have meaning only if they are validated by our actions.

One of the acts of communication is listening. As Dwight Small says, "To listen is to be really present to another person, actually to give one's full presence" (*After You've Said I Do*, 89). A husband said to his wife, "I hear you; you don't have to shout." She replied, "Yes, but you're still not listening."

Other demonstrations of care also are as important as our words. Jesus said it very nicely: "If you love me, keep my commandments." If family members love each other, they will want to do the things that please one another.

However, we cannot depend on acting alone. Talking is not only helpful; it is necessary. Obviously, some people talk very easily, and their talking has little meaning. A wife was once asked, "Why don't you think before you speak?" She replied, "How can I know what I think until I've heard what I've got to say?"

Talking can be just talking, or it can be communication. Jesus was talking about talking as communication. Certain "rules" must be followed if talking is to be communication.

First, we must be able to ask questions. One of the most important questions family members and marriage partners must learn to ask is, "What do you mean?" In other words, we must be interested in the meaning the other person intends, not the meaning we give to what we hear. This is called "checking back." It is part of the art of good communication.

Second, we must state feeling as feeling and fact as fact. "Let your yes be yes; and your no, no." Some people state all their feelings as if they were proven facts. These persons cannot distinguish between what is their opinion and what is objective reality. This ruins communication.

Third, talking can be helpful communication if we try to be accurate about our feelings. Some people are extreme about everything they do. If someone disagrees with this kind of person, the person will go to the extreme of saying, "Then you think I'm no good at all." Such extremes are sometimes expressed when a husband or wife says the other person "always" does something. Throwing all of our feelings at another person at one time does not help communication. It may help us to get our feelings out, but it usually inundates the person we are trying to communicate with. Feelings and thoughts need to be stated as accurately as they can be.

Fourth, if talk is to be helpful, we must express appreciation as well as hurt. Isn't it interesting that we often remember for many months the things people have said to hurt us? We often forget the things they have said to express appreciation to us. For talking to be helpful in marriage, it must be used to carry gratitude as often as possible. People who really try to appreciate one another and express that appreciation will discover many more things they can be grateful for in each other. It is surprising how gratitude causes another person to grow both in a sense of his own self-worth and in an appreciation of the worth of the person expressing the gratitude.

Finally, if we are going to talk, we need to talk to God. Talking to God is the Christian's advantage. We can confess our family failures to him. When we have confessed our failures to God, it is easier to confess them to other people. John's words hold a life-changing promise: "If we confess our sins, he is faithful and just to forgive us our sins, and to cleanse us from all unrighteousness" (1 John 1:9).

The Christian also has the advantage of being able to pray about differences with other people. Praying about differences does not mean using prayer to manipulate other persons to get them to do what we want them to do. Praying about our differences is praying to accept other persons even if they have thoughts that differ from our own. When we pray about our differences, it gives us a perspective that few experiences can give.

In prayer we can also ask for grace to accept each other's humanness. Jesus said in Matthew 18:15 that direct communication is necessary in forgiveness. We must go to the person who has wronged us. When we have done that, we can also go to God who has loved us when we were wrong and accepted us even in our wrongness.

God is the Great Communicator. He communicated his love toward us in that while we were still sinning, Christ died for our sins. God has acted out his love, and he has also spoken his love in the person of Jesus Christ. That message of love changes our lives because it is communication with God. As the Great Communicator, he can help us to become communicators in our families.

Some say talk is cheap. But in many families it is very expensive. Talk can cost us the happiness of our families or it can create the happiness of our families. If Christ is in our hearts, then his care can be on our lips when we decide to talk.

Conclusion

"Let your conversation be always full of grace, seasoned with salt, so that you may know how to answer everyone" (Col. 4:6 NIV).

SUNDAY EVENING, JUNE 9

Title: What Have I Done with God's Word?

Text: "This book of the law shall not depart out of thy mouth; but thou shalt meditate therein day and night, that thou mayest observe to do according to all that is written therein: for then thou shalt make thy way prosperous, and then thou shalt have good success" (**Josh. 1:8**).

Scripture Reading: 2 Kings 22:11–20

Introduction

What place do you personally give to the Word of God in your life? The question is not "How important was the Bible to your parents?" The question is not "What has the church done with the Word of God?" The question is not "What have others done with the Word of God?" The important question each of us should face is "What have I individually done with the Word of God?"

When God commissioned Joshua to take over the responsibility for leadership of the twelve tribes of Israel, he commanded and advised him to give God's Word a very prominent place in his thoughts and actions. God commanded him to look upon it as a guidebook for successful living. Joshua was encouraged to meditate on it day and night. He heard the divine insistence that his conduct should be regulated by its teachings. He was assured of both prosperity and success if he made the proper response to the revealed will of God.

Is the Bible a lost book as far as you are concerned? Second Kings 22 records the finding of the lost Book of the Law by the high priest Hilkiah as workmen repaired the temple following the wicked, idolatrous reign of King Manasseh. The rediscovery of the Book of the Law and a positive response to it produced a powerful spiritual impact on the nation as the new King Josiah tried to recall the people to the truth of God's Word.

I. The Bible is God's Book.

The Holy Bible is uniquely the Book of God. One denomination has formulated the following statement concerning the nature of the Holy Bible:

We believe that the Holy Bible was written by men divinely inspired, and is a perfect treasure of heavenly instruction; that it has God for its author, salvation for its end, and truth, without any mixture of error, for its matter; that it reveals the principles by which God will judge us; and there is, and will remain to the end of the world, the true center of Christian union, and the supreme standard by which all human conduct, creeds and religious opinions should be tried.

A. *The divine source of the Scriptures (2 Tim. 3:16).* The Holy Scripture owes its very existence to the direct creative activity of God himself. Although humans wrote it, it was God who brought it into being. Its content and character were divinely determined. It was breathed into existence by God.

   The apostle Peter declared that the Holy Scriptures are the product of the activity of the Spirit of God (2 Peter 1:20–21).

B. *The Scriptures are unique in their nature (Heb. 4:12).* The Word of God is described as being alive and active. It penetrates, detects, judges, and exposes the secret thoughts, motives, and meditations of the mind and heart.

C. *The function of the Scriptures.* It is in the Word of God that we find a revelation of the nature of God and the way of salvation.

D. *The Scriptures provide us with authoritative guidance for conduct that is pleasing to God (2 Tim. 3:16).* They equip believers with insights necessary for fruitful service.

II. Making a personal response to the Word of God.

A. *The psalmist described the happy person as one who delights in the law of the Lord and meditates on its teachings both day and night (Ps. 1:2).*

B. *The psalmist described the Word of God as a cleansing agent for those who would live a life of purity (Ps. 119:9).*

C. *The psalmist described the Word of God as being able to help a person avoid falling into sin (Ps. 119:11).*

D. *Our Lord encouraged his disciples both to hear and to heed the words he taught them (Matt. 7:24–29).*

   We must study the Bible in its historical context if we are to interpret it correctly. We need to try to understand the words of the Bible and relate them to present-day living. We need to study the Bible logically in the sense that it is a perfect unity. There is no conflict or contradiction in the Bible when we properly understand what it is trying to communicate. We need to study the Bible as a spiritual book, for it is a record of a divine revelation. We need the guidance of the Holy Spirit to study it effectively.

Conclusion

The psalmist praised the Word of God in the following way: "Thy word is a lamp unto my feet, and a light unto my path" (Ps. 119:105).

What have you done with the Word of God? Have you neglected it? Have you ignored it? Have you forgotten it?

It would be wise to recognize it as uniquely the divine Word of God. You

190

would be wise to trust it implicitly. You are wise if you let it lead you to the Savior and to Christlike conduct.

The Word of God can encourage you when you are depressed. The Word of God can comfort you in your time of grief. The Word of God can strengthen you in your time of weakness. The Word of God can guide you in your time of uncertainty. Do not forget it. Do not neglect it. Do not ignore it. Give it a great place in your heart and life.

WEDNESDAY EVENING, JUNE 12

Title: Love, the Last Word for the Christian Home

Text: "The greatest of these is love" (**1 Cor. 13:13**).

Scripture Reading: 1 Corinthians 13

Introduction

Love is the "last word" in family relationships. We use the phrase "last word" figuratively to emphasize love as the greatest of "great words" for the Christian home. Without love, the other words are "as sounding brass or a tinkling cymbal" (1 Cor. 13:1). They are vibrations in the ear, stopping in the head and not reaching the heart.

I. The true test of love in the home.

A. *Love in action.* The New Testament does not give a definition of love; it describes love in action. Here love is described in the arena of family living.

1. Paraphrase of 1 Corinthians 13 (author unknown):

Though in the glamour of the public eye I sway the emotions of man by oratory, or by my silver singing, or by my skillful playing, and then go home and gripe because supper is late, or because my clothes weren't made to suit me, I am become as sounding brass or a tinkling cymbal.

And though I am able to impress others with my vast knowledge of the deep things of the Word of God, and though I am able to accomplish mighty things through faith so that I become famous among men as a remover of mountains, and have not the love that reads the deep longings of the hearts around the family circle and removes the barriers that grow up in shy and tender hearts, I am nothing.

And though in the glamour of public praise I bestow all my goods to feed the poor, and though I win the name and fame of a martyr by giving my body to be burned, and yet close up like a clam at home, or behave like a snapping turtle, knowing nothing of the glory of giving myself in unstinted, self-denying service to those nearest and dearest, it profiteth me nothing.

Love is never impatient, but kind; love knows no jealousy; love makes no parade; gives itself no airs.

Love is never rude, seeks not her own, nor fights for her own rights, is never resentful, never imagines that others are plotting evil against her.

[Love] never broods over wrongs, never exults over the mistakes of others, but is truly gladdened by goodness.

Love is the acid test of the truly yielded life, for in all other phases of Christian service there is a certain amount of glamour; but in the home one is confronted with the bare facts of life, stripped of all glamour. The home is given to help every Christian "not to think more highly of himself than he ought to think." And it is in the home that we have the privilege of demonstrating that the Christian life is "faith which worketh by love."

2. Love puts it all together: the inspired apostle shows how all of the "great words" are put together to give meaning and momentum to the Christian life. A common and popular comparison could be the modern football team. The coach knows that he has the ingredients for a winning formula—personnel, size, speed, ability, experience, etc.—but the team loses. Gradually or suddenly they put it all together. Some additions, some shift in emphasis, and he has an unbeatable combination.
B. *Love out of action.* The church, its pastor, and its people can offer the missing "Word" where it is lacking in the home.

II. The demonstration of love in the home.

A. *The "voices" of love.* The first sounds we need to hear from birth are the "voices of love." More than we know, deeper than we are able to understand, the infant listens and responds to the sounds of love. Love is essential to life. Modern research has revealed a much higher mortality rate among infants who don't receive personal loving care. Love gives the will to live. Little love weakens the desire for life.
B. *The faces of love.*
   1. Glory in a face. "The light of the knowledge of the glory of God [was] in the face of Jesus Christ" (2 Cor. 4:6). "The LORD make his face shine upon thee" (Num. 6:25). In the Bible, looking into the face of God is to see the reality of God—that is, of love. The psalmist prayed, "Hide not thy face from me" (Ps. 143:7).
   2. The look of love. Jacob saw God in the face of Esau when Jacob experienced his brother's forgiveness (Gen. 33:10). We read the faces of significant persons, hoping to see the "look of love." The look has many meanings. Some examples are the look of appreciation, of affection, of understanding, of trust, of assurance, of encouragement, and of respect. In endless ways and in every circumstance, those who most need our love search our faces for the "look of love" they need most.

Conclusion

Love is eternal. Love is the "last word" in family relationships. That which is highest in God speaks to that which is deepest in us. On the level of human relationships, "deep calleth unto deep" (Ps. 42:7). The first sounds that call us to life are voices of love. Our self-image—that is, who and what we are—is what we see reflected in the faces of those important to us.

Faith in love can be restored through experiences with those who love because God loved them first. When we are loved, it is not because we are lovable but because love himself is in those who love us.

"Down in the human heart, crushed by the tempter, feelings lie buried that grace can restore. Touched by a loving heart; wakened by kindness; chords that are broken will vibrate once more" (Fanny Crosby, "Rescue the Perishing").

SUNDAY MORNING, JUNE 16

Title: What Are You Feeding Your Family?

Text: "If a son shall ask bread of any of you that is a father, will he give him a stone? or if he ask a fish, will he for a fish give him a serpent?" **(Luke 11:11)**

Scripture Reading: Luke 11:11–13

Hymns: "God, Our Father, We Adore Thee," Frazer

"Great Is Thy Faithfulness," Chisholm

"Faith of Our Fathers," Faber

Offertory Prayer: Eternal Father of our Lord Jesus Christ, you are the giver of every good and perfect gift. Today we come to give ourselves to you. Accept our tithes and offerings as an indication of our desire to give ourselves completely to you. We rejoice in the gift of good health. We rejoice in the privilege of work. We thank you for the degree of prosperity that we enjoy. Accept these tokens of our love, and bless them to the enrichment of the lives of others, for in the name of Christ we pray. Amen.

Introduction

A Florida woman was convicted several years ago of poisoning her family by mixing poison in the family's food. Many of us are guilty of poisoning our families with what we feed them. If we do not feed them poison, we often allow them to be fed poison by others.

Jesus, like our heavenly Father, recognized that good parents want to give their children good things. He assumed we would not intentionally give our children the wrong things. This he said well in Luke 11:11–13. Yet there are parents who give their children stones when they ask for bread and serpents when they ask for fish. Just as seriously, we often allow our families to be fed the wrong things by sitting back and doing nothing about what they are fed. If you want your family to have the right things, you cannot be passive about their spiritual and intellectual diet.

I. Who is feeding your family?

It is possible that there are people feeding your family whom you do not know about. Interestingly enough, there are plenty of people who will feed our families with or without our permission.

Society feeds your family—that is, society feeds your family ideas, values, and concepts. Society teaches all who will listen, "Get what you can where you can in any way you can." Our families are given lessons and examples in becoming efficiently selfish.

Society also teaches our families that all other values are more important than spiritual values. Society feeds your family on the idea that spiritual values add little if anything to a person's life, telling them in a hundred ways that the church is unimportant. When your family asks for the bread of truth from society, it is given a stone of selfishness.

Society also teaches that the family itself is unimportant. Related to this idea is today's attitude toward sex. All of us are getting sex education. I'm not talking about courses that are officially set up for this purpose. I'm talking about the sex education that society gives you and your family every day you live.

If anyone wants to fight pornography and filth, there is a place to fight it: on the newsstands and in the movies. More than 75 percent of all movie offerings any day of the week in any city of the country are not for general audiences. Our children are being misinformed about God's purposes for sex by television sitcoms, soap operas, and movies.

Your friends also feed your family. Small groups within society that form their own circles of thought and value become more important to us as we become more isolated as individuals. The groups we associate with influence our values and our lifestyles, for we tend to adopt the values and lifestyles to which we are most often exposed. We must be aware that our families are being fed and know how they are being fed. Children and young people pick up from their friends and associates values and ideas we need to know about. They also need to be able to tell us about them.

Schools are another place where our families are fed. Too many families have made the school the only source of authority and information for their children. Christian parents have a responsibility to know what their children are learning and to be as involved as they can be in the education of their children. The writer of Proverbs recognized the importance of what we feed our minds: "As he thinketh in his heart, so is he" (23:7).

With so many others feeding our families, how do we go about feeding them too? The key is not to isolate our families, but to help them evaluate what they are receiving. We cannot shut them off from the flow of worldly ideas and anti-Christian concepts. However, we can help them find standards for evaluating what they are fed from any source. For example, if our children are going to see television programs that have pagan concepts of family in them, we need to evaluate the programs and develop some standards for ourselves.

Many Christian parents a generation ago felt that the answer was to isolate young people from bad influences. If that was ever the answer, it is not the answer today. The answer is to give young people an ability to evaluate and judge for themselves the things they see and hear. This means that we must give them a

Christian frame of reference that becomes theirs and that they can use. This leads to my second point.

II. You can feed your family.

Jesus assumed that we would feed our families. He also assumed that we would want to feed them good things. The standards we have been talking about can be developed in a number of ways.

First, we can give our families a Christian lifestyle. Christian habits in family life are indispensable for the growth of strong Christians. The science of family therapy has developed far enough now for us to know that good and wholesome families produce morally stable children.

Family members learn far more by observation of each other than they do by instruction. However, both the observation and the instruction must be Christian if we expect our homes to be Christian.

For thoroughly Christian homes, parents must allow the church to feed their families. There are a great deal of so-called Christian families that refuse in many ways to eat anything the church offers. In fact, families are often told that they won't like what the church has to offer. The habits we make a part of our family routine are important to our overall diet.

A second item on the menu for your family is the giving of Christian values. Most families teach that material, social, recreational, and educational values are most important. If our families learn that spiritual values are important, it will be because we feed them something different than they are fed any other place. The basic value Jesus talked about is that "man shall not live by bread alone" (Matt. 4:4).

The organizations and activities in which a family invests teach a family its values. If all other organizations and activities are important except the church, those priorities teach families something no lecture or sermon can ever undo.

Two young people were discussing religion one day. One of them was talking about how outmoded the church was and how his church was never doing anything for him or his family. He continued to tell how little they participated in the life of the church because everything about the church was bad.

The other young person said his experience had been quite different. He enthusiastically described the youth activities and how much his parents thought of the church. He spoke warmly of the friendships he had in the church, and he was grateful for the opportunities given him there to serve and to discover his talents.

As they continued to discuss the church, they discovered, to their amazement, that they belonged to the same church. Obviously the difference was not in the church; it was in the homes. If your son asks for bread, will you give him a stone?

The third way in which you can feed your family is to introduce them to the Bread of Life. Jesus repeatedly offered himself as the Bread of Life for all who know they should be hungry. Yet, sadly, families that would not take a passive attitude toward anything else will take such an attitude toward a relationship with Christ.

Families who talk *about* Christ in the home and who talk *with* him in the home can expect his presence and help. He should be made as familiar and as easy to talk with as any other person we know well. If we know him well, we will feel no stranger about talking with him and to him than we do with any member of the family. Our embarrassment and awkwardness in talking about Christ is an admission of our lack of acquaintance with him. We demonstrate that we do not feel at home with Christ.

An atmosphere in which we feel at home with Christ is one of the richest heritages we can give our children. This does not mean we force our faith on them and demand that they accept every iota of our belief. It simply means that we will share with them meaningfully and genuinely our experience with Christ. We will allow them the freedom to see and to decide for themselves whether they want to follow this Friend who has meant so much to us. I wonder if Christ has meant enough to you that you want to share his friendship with your family?

Conclusion

Others are feeding your family. They may be feeding them what you want, but none of us can escape the responsibility of feeding our own families. If we are Christians, we have a Friend to whom we ought to introduce our families so that he can always be the Bread of Life to them. If your son asks you for bread, will you give him a stone?

SUNDAY EVENING, JUNE 16

Title: What Have I Done with Prayer?

Text: "But thou, when thou prayest, enter into thy closet, and when thou hast shut thy door, pray to thy Father which is in secret; and thy Father which seeth in secret shall reward thee openly" **(Matt. 6:6)**.

Scripture Reading: Matthew 6:5–15

Introduction

The question in our title is not "What place did prayer have in the life of our Savior?" The question is not "What place did prayer have in the lives of the early Christians?" The question is not "What place is given to prayer in the contemporary church?" The question is not "What place did prayer have in the habits of our parents?" Let us make the question personal: "What have *I* done with the privilege of prayer?"

I. Have I misunderstood the nature of prayer?

Some people neglect to pray because they have misunderstood the nature of this most wonderful privilege that God has granted us. Prayer should not be considered as a mechanical, magical means whereby we can secure the favor of Deity. Nor is it a begging proposition in which we persuade God to give us something against his will. Prayer is not a reminder to the eternal God of something he has been neglecting to do.

Prayer must not be considered as a carte blanche in which God has promised to grant us anything we wish. And prayer must not be utilized as one would utilize a parachute to escape from difficult situations in life.

Prayer is an experience of communion and fellowship with the loving heavenly Father. It is a conference with our Creator, a conversation between the Father God and his needy children. It is an experience in which we lay claim to our heritage as the children of God.

II. Have I recognized the real value of prayer?

A. *A genuine experience of prayer brings one into harmony with God's gracious will.* It is a process in which we eliminate the discord and noises of life and get in tune with God.

B. *A true experience of prayer brings one an awareness of God's abiding presence.* For the sinner who is in rebellion or who labors under a burden of guilt, this could be terrifying. On the other hand, it could be most comforting to know that God is present to assist us in our time of need. It could bring great encouragement and motivate us to render the service that would be pleasing to God and helpful to others.

C. *In the prayer experience, God lets his power flow into our lives.* It has been said that there are three ways by which people can cooperate with God. They can work, think, and pray. There are times when we need the power from God to be able to say no to some of the great alternatives of life. There are other times when we need the courage and the fortitude to say yes. At other times we need the power of God to face the future with steady eyes. This power comes to those who have the habit of praying.

D. *A genuine experience of prayer brings peace of mind and relieves us of the agony of anxiety (Phil. 4:6–7).* When we draw near to God in prayer, he draws near to us in love and power (James 4:8).

III. Developing a victorious prayer life.

How does one go about developing a deeper prayer life? How can one enter into a deeper acquaintance with the eternal God? How can we experience the "sweet hour of prayer"?

A. *We can study the prayer life of our Lord.* The Gospels describe Jesus' prayer life. We can profit greatly by following his example.

B. *We can study our Lord's instructions concerning prayer.* Actually, that which we call the Lord's Prayer is really not the Lord's prayer. It is a model prayer that our Lord gave to his disciples. It is a blueprint for us to follow. It is a guideline that should give direction to our personal and public prayer life.

C. *We can study the prayers that our Lord heard but did not answer affirmatively.*

197

D. *We can study the prayers that were offered to our Lord that received an affirmative answer.*

E. *We can profit by an examination of the prayer habits of the early Christians.*

F. *We can learn much from studying the prayer life of outstanding Christians of the past and the present.*

Conclusion

Have you ever studied the Bible in an attitude of prayer, letting the words of Scripture be the divine side of the dialogue we call prayer? Have you listened as you read the Scriptures? It is more important that we hear what God has to say than it is that he hears our requests.

Begin the habit of praying early in the morning. Talk to the Lord concerning the problems, opportunities, and responsibilities you will confront throughout the day.

Develop the habit of praying in the evening. Thank God for his presence with you. Praise him for his blessings upon you. Commit yourself to him afresh as you face the rest of the night and the future.

WEDNESDAY EVENING, JUNE 19

Title: Overcoming Discouragement

Text: "Why art thou cast down, O my soul? and why art thou disquieted in me? hope thou in God: for I shall yet praise him for the help of his countenance" (**Ps. 42:5**).

Scripture Reading: Psalm 42

Introduction

Discouragement seems to be the common lot of most of us. Why do we mortals become depressed to the extent that we often quit before we reach our objective? Why is it that because of discouragement we deprive ourselves of the joy that we are capable of experiencing? There are probably a number of different explanations for our discouragement. Let us consider the following.

I. Our work for the Lord is a work of faith (2 Cor. 5:7).

A. *Perhaps it is a part of our human frailty that we lean on the arm of flesh.* We want to be guided by good, common sense. We want a rational explanation of all of the various alternatives of life. We would prefer to walk in a clear path with our objective in sight than to walk by faith.

B. *We must walk by faith if we are to face the future with courage.* We must live by the principle of faith if we are to move beyond the ordinary.

II. Our work is a work involving great difficulties.

A. *There are weaknesses within ourselves as individuals that make it difficult for us to work creatively and cooperatively with others.*

B. *There are weaknesses within others that make a cooperative work difficult.* The combination of our weaknesses with those of others has a tendency to bring discouragement to all at times.

III. Our work is a work above our capacity.

A. *To do the work of the Lord, people must depend on something other than their own talents.* If we take seriously the claims of the Great Commission, the task is so tremendous that it is overwhelming.

B. *The work that God has called us to is a work above our training and experience.* Often this can be very discouraging if we depend on our own resources rather than on God's. When we study the Scriptures, we discover that in every instance when God called a person to a particular task, he promised adequate resources for the performance of that task.

IV. Our work is much opposed by Satan.

Someone has speculated that discouragement is the tool that Satan uses most often to accomplish his evil purposes.

A. *He attacks us at our weakest point.* His name literally means "the accuser." There is a possibility that when we yield to temptation, Satan, rather than our Father God, is responsible for many of our negative feelings concerning ourselves. God's response to us is one of compassion rather than condemnation. It is the work of Satan to condemn and to criticize. By doing so, he discourages us to the extent that we are ready to drop out and quit.

B. *Satan will tempt us at our weakest point.*

C. *Satan will use our failures and our lack of perfect obedience to God to cause us to think negatively concerning ourselves.* He will do everything possible to nullify our witness for Christ.

Conclusion

The psalmist was distressed over his personal depression. He was unhappy. He was eliminated from the ranks of those who could sing the Lord's song with joy and effectiveness. So he gave himself a lecture. He said, "Hope thou in God." He recognized that he must put his confidence in God rather than depend solely on himself. He must not depend on others. Instead, he must put his hope and his confidence in the loving God. Let each of us keep our eyes on our loving Lord, and this will help us to eliminate distressing, depressing discouragement.

SUNDAY MORNING, JUNE 23

Title: What Do We Owe Our Children?

Text: "These words, which I command thee this day, shall be in thine heart: And thou shalt teach them diligently unto thy children, and shalt talk of them when thou sittest in thine house, and when thou walkest by the way, and when thou liest down, and when thou risest up" **(Deut. 6:6–7)**.

Scripture Reading: Colossians 3:16–21

Hymns: "This Is My Father's World," Babcock

          "Fairest Lord Jesus," Author Unknown

          "Happy the Home When God Is There," Ware

Offertory Prayer: Holy Father, in the beauty of summer we thank you for the sunlight of your love, which shines into our hearts through Jesus Christ. We offer to you the love of our hearts and the praise of our lips. We bring to you the strength of our hands. Accept these tithes and offerings as a portion of our very life, and bless them to the spreading of the gospel, to the healing of the sick, to the relief of the poor, and to the glory of your holy name. Amen.

Introduction

The title "What Do We Owe Our Children?" may provoke a negative reaction from parents and at the same time arouse the curiosity of the young. It is normal for children to feel that their parents and, for that matter, the whole world, owe them something. The immature are always self-centered. They think in terms of what others can and should do for them. Wise parents will guide their children away from selfishness yet will realize that they really do owe a number of things to their children. There are certain obligations, responsibilities, or debts that are involved in the parent-child relationship.

I. Children deserve to be desired.

It is a tragedy for a child to be born into a home where he is not wanted and where he is not fully accepted. A child will be much better able to withstand the shocks and deprivations of life if he has the inward assurance that he was desired and that he is fully accepted by his parents. It is tragic for a child to feel unwanted because he or she has overheard parents say that they wanted a child of the opposite sex.

II. Children need the devotion of their parents.

"As sunshine is to the plant, so love is to children." Affection and devotion are as necessary for the emotional well-being of a child as food is essential for physical growth.

III. Parents should disciple their children.

In the Great Commission, Jesus commanded his disciples to so conduct themselves that in their traveling about they would make disciples. In no place do we have a greater obligation to be obedient than within the home. By both profession and practice, parents should conduct themselves and instruct their children so that at the earliest possible time their children can make a personal response to Jesus Christ as their Lord and Savior. This is a responsibility that must not be repudiated or shifted to someone else.

IV. Children must have moral discipline.

The word *discipline* is related to the word *disciple*, which means a learner. Discipline refers to control, educating. With reference to the family, it means the control and directing of the members of that group, especially the children.

A. *The big problem is parental discipline.*

B. *The disciplining of children must be a partnership.*

C. *Discipline must be consistent.*

D. *Discipline must be firm, but it need not be harsh.*

V. Parents should dedicate their children.

A. *Hannah dedicated Samuel unto the Lord (1 Sam. 1:28).*

B. *Parents brought their little children to Jesus for his blessings (Matt. 19:13–15).*

C. *While parents cannot make spiritual decisions for their children, they can release their parental claims on those children by recognizing that God's claims come first.*

VI. Parents should develop their children.

"Train up a child in the way he should go: and when he is old, he will not depart from it" (Prov. 22:6).

A. *Mentally.*

B. *Socially.*

C. *Economically.*

D. *Spiritually.*

VII. Parents should defend their children.

A. *The world, the flesh, and the devil will devour and destroy our children unless there are some built-in defenses that will make this impossible.* Parents can build in these defenses against destruction.

B. *First, we need to be somebody for God.* By virtue of our parenthood, we are appointed as the stewards and custodians of the spiritual welfare and destiny of our children. If we respond to God's love and grace and power, we can be proper parents and meet our obligations to our children.

C. *We must do something for God.* Life is made up of being and doing. We must be somebody if we want to do something significant.

The best defense that we can provide for our children is inward rather than external.

Conclusion

We can meet our obligations and opportunities as parents through faith and faithfulness. We should put our faith in our Lord, and then we should follow him faithfully.

SUNDAY EVENING, JUNE 23

Title: What Have I Done with the Holy Spirit?

Text: "And because ye are sons, God hath sent forth the Spirit of his Son into your hearts, crying, Abba, Father" (**Gal. 4:6**).

Scripture Reading: Romans 8:1–17

Introduction

In the power of the Holy Spirit, our Lord overcame temptation, cast out demons, and did other wonderful works of God.

In the power of the Holy Spirit the early church continued the work of Jesus Christ. The book of Acts contains one success story after another of how an insignificant group of people turned the world right side up. They were able to do so because they made a proper response to the promise and the presence of the Holy Spirit.

What response have you made to the Holy Spirit? The question is not "How did Jesus relate himself to the Holy Spirit?" or "How did the early church treat the Holy Spirit?" or "How do other contemporary disciples of Christ relate to the Holy Spirit?" The real question is "What have I done with the Holy Spirit?" Because of a lack of understanding of what the Scriptures teach concerning the Holy Spirit and because of the fanaticism of others who have made an overly emotional response to the Spirit, many have avoided making any response at all.

I. Some are unaware of the presence of the Holy Spirit (I Cor. 6:19).

Because the Holy Spirit is spirit and consequently invisible and intangible, some have not detected or recognized his presence in their own hearts or in the hearts and lives of others. Evidently this was the case with some of the believers in the city of Corinth. They were making no positive response to the presence of the Holy Spirit who came to dwell within their hearts at the time of their conversion. The apostle Paul informed them that the body of each individual believer has become the temple in which the Holy Spirit dwells (1 Cor. 3:16).

If one does not recognize the presence of the Holy Spirit, it goes without saying that a positive and proper response is practically nil.

II. Some have quenched the Spirit (I Thess. 5:19).

The Holy Spirit comes into the heart of each believer to provide assurance of salvation (Rom. 8:15–16) and to reproduce within each believer the spirit and the character of Jesus Christ (Gal. 5:22–25).

When we fail to recognize his presence and thus make a negative response to the deep inward impulses that he creates within us, we pour water on the divine fire that God is seeking to build within us. We choke the life out of these heavenly impulses. We prevent the Holy Spirit from accomplishing the divine purpose within us. This is a tragedy for the individual involved, and it deprives others of the blessings God could give them through the believer.

III. Some of us are grieving the Holy Spirit of God (Eph. 4:30).

If we live by the mind of the flesh, and if we refuse to let the Holy Spirit bring cleansing, purity, and power into our lives, we can assume that we bring grief to the sweet Spirit of God who has come to dwell within us.

The Scriptures tell us that when our Lord looked down upon the city of Jerusalem, he shed tears of disappointment and grief for its people. Is it possible that the Holy Spirit, who dwells within each believer, is grieving today because of our lack of faith and faithfulness? Does he grieve because we have been silent when he wanted to use our tongue to communicate the truth about God's love and mercy? Is he grieved because we have contaminated the temple in which he dwells by a life that compromises with evil? Is he grieved because our hands are not yielded to the divine purpose for ministries of mercy to the suffering of the unfortunate?

IV. Some have responded by a walk of faith in and faithfulness to the leadership of the Holy Spirit (Gal. 5:16–23).

These individuals have made progress in their journey from the mind of the flesh to the mind of Jesus Christ. They have ceased living on the level in which their highest desire was to satisfy the lust of the flesh. They now live on a higher level in which they are seeking to bear the fruit of the Spirit. They recognize that eternity is involved in time. They have caught the vision of what they can be like by cooperating with the Holy Spirit as he seeks to reproduce within them the mind of Christ. They rejoice in his power as they do the work of Christ in the world today.

V. Some rejoice in the privilege of being filled with the Spirit (Eph. 5:18).

The apostle is illustrating what it means to be divinely intoxicated by the presence and power of the Holy Spirit. Evidently he is saying that being filled with the Spirit has some parallels to being under the influence of an alcoholic beverage. Let us consider a few of these parallels without considering a scientific explanation for these traits.

A. *The Spirit-filled believer is often brave and courageous.* Such was true of the early Christians. We need more of this in the present.

B. *The Spirit-filled believer is friendly and open.* As alcohol often releases inhibitions and contributes to a spirit of hilarity, even so, the Spirit of God produces a friendliness that is winsome and attractive.

C. *The Spirit-filled believer is generous.* Like a man who is under the influence of alcohol, there are times when genuine concern and a spirit of generosity will cause the Spirit-filled believer to share with the unfortunate beyond his real giving ability.

D. *The Spirit-filled believer is talkative.* He is an eager witness to the saving power of Jesus Christ. He is eager to share the good news of what God has done in and through him.

Conclusion

How have you treated the Holy Spirit? Are you afraid to recognize his presence within your heart? Are you afraid to trust yourself to his purposes? If so, your life will be barren and unfruitful as far as spiritual productivity is concerned.

Recognize the Holy Spirit's presence within your heart as one of God's best gifts. Respond to his leadership positively and completely. You will be surprised at what God will do in you and through you if you make a proper response to the Holy Spirit.

WEDNESDAY EVENING, JUNE 26

Title: Controlling Your Anger

Text: "He that is slow to anger is better than the mighty; and he that ruleth his spirit than he that taketh a city" **(Prov. 16:32).**

Scripture Reading: Psalm 37:1–8

Introduction

Personality is made up of intellect, emotions, and will. Exercising some degree of control over these three aspects of personality is our privilege and responsibility. Every human being is "emotional" and possesses feelings that can be motivated, disturbed, or agitated. We need to be on guard against destructive emotions. Particularly we need to exercise control over the emotion of anger. Unresolved anger is destructive to all concerned. The wise men of the past considered the man who was in control of his spirit as being a greater man than he who could rule a city. "He that hath no rule over his own spirit is like a city that is broken down, and without walls" (Prov. 25:28).

Are there some practical steps that one can take to gain control over his own spirit? Four are suggested.

I. Get acquainted with yourself.

A. *Socrates said, "Know thyself."*

B. *We could be wrong about some of our ways of thinking and acting (Prov. 12:15).*

C. *Find out what makes you tick.* Where do you get your satisfaction in life? What does it take to make you happy? What does it take to make you angry?

D. *Recognize your own human frailty and the limitations that are associated with such.*

E. *Go to work on yourself. Perhaps you need to be strict with yourself.* Or perhaps you need to be kind to yourself so that you can be kind to others.

F. *Recognize that some of the criticisms that are directed your way may come from a friend rather than from an enemy (Prov. 27:6).* There may be some truth in the comments of others that cause you to be angry and hostile. It might be very profitable for you to stop and look and listen to some of the things that are said concerning you that have made you so angry in the past (15:32).

II. Be generous with the one who criticizes you.

A. *Study the other person rather than concentrating on punishing him.*

B. *Walk in his moccasins for a month.* Find out what is bugging him. Maybe it is an unfortunate childhood, a painful home life, a crippling debt, or illness.

C. *Listen between the lines of what the other person is saying.* Try to see his side of the issue.

D. *Remember that just because someone says something about you, this does not make it true.*

E. *Recognize the wisdom of the wise in responding to others.* "A soft answer turneth away wrath: but grievous words stir up anger" (Prov. 15:1).

F. *It is always wise to have an attitude of forgiveness toward others.* This is more profitable to the person who does the forgiving than it is to the person who experiences forgiveness.

III. Evaluate properly the high cost of losing your cool.

Have you ever stopped to think about what it actually costs you to give way to fits and moods of anger and hostility?

A. *Consider what it costs you physically to live in an attitude of anger.* This can contribute to the development of ulcers, high blood pressure, and even a heart attack.

B. *Consider the high costs of anger to your family.* There is no way by which a member of the family can give way to anger and hostility without it hurting all of the interpersonal relationships within the home.

C. *Consider the high costs professionally or in your business.* No one likes to live close to or work with a person who has a short fuse and who is always blowing his stack about something. One of the most expensive liabilities to a business is for one to live in an attitude of anger.

D. *Count the high costs of anger, hostility, and grudge-carrying to one's spiritual life.* To mistreat your fellow human is to disrupt your fellowship with God.

IV. Practice the presence of God if you want to conquer anger.

A. *The advice of the wise man is, "Hear counsel, and receive instruction, that thou mayest be wise in thy latter end" (Prov. 19:20).*

B. *Turn prayer into an experience of listening to God.* The Holy Spirit will give you instructions concerning how to deal with the difficult and painful circumstances of life.

C. *Avoid thoughts that pour fuel onto the fire of anger.* Do not nourish and feed your memory of the mistreatment that you have received at the hands of others. Instead, try to put these thoughts from your mind.

D. *Give heed to what you read as you study the Word of God.* Let God speak to you and help you.

E. *Invite God to be a part of every contact and conference with those who might provoke you to anger or hostility.* Let God become very real to you.

Conclusion

The psalmist said, "I will lift up mine eyes unto the hills, from whence cometh my help. My help cometh from the LORD, which made heaven and earth" (Ps. 121:1–2). Perhaps the best source of help at the point of conquering our hostile instincts and emotions is to trust God for the help that we need that we might live by the principle of love rather than by the principle of hate. All of us need help at this point. With God's help we can break the hate habit and begin the love habit; we can conquer anger and hostility.

SUNDAY MORNING, JUNE 30

Title: The Christian and the State

Text: "I exhort therefore, that, first of all, supplications, prayers, intercessions, and giving of thanks, be made for all men; for kings, and for all that are in authority; that we may lead a quiet and peaceable life in all godliness and honesty" **(1 Tim. 2:1–2).**

Scripture Reading: 1 Peter 2:11–17

Hymns: "God of Our Fathers, Whose Almighty Hand," Roberts

"My Country, 'Tis of Thee," Smith

"America the Beautiful," Bates

Offertory Prayer: Holy heavenly Father, we thank you for your great blessings upon our country. Help us to appreciate the bounty of your provisions for us. Help us not to waste the natural resources of our country. We thank you for those who have been willing to live and labor, suffer and die, that we may enjoy the privileges of liberty and freedom. Today we bring our offerings to you, praying that they may be used to bring honor and glory to your name, and to make of our nation a godly people. Through Jesus Christ, help us to cooperate with you in delivering people from the tyranny of sin into the liberty of sonship. Amen.

Introduction

Does the Bible have any specific guidelines for Christians to follow as they relate themselves to the state in which they hold citizenship? What are the Christian's responsibilities toward a state that is something less than ideal?

Our nation is in peril by a constantly rising crime rate. How are Christians to respond to this threat? How can they be a part of the solution and avoid being a part of the problem?

Our nation is threatened by the breakup of home life. Loose attitudes toward marriage and the family and the increase in alcoholism threaten the very foundations of the most basic institution of our society. What can Christians do about this?

Our nation is threatened by a secular materialism that would eliminate God and Christian principles from our consideration. What is the Christian to do in the face of this?

How shall we react? Shall we retreat into isolation and solitude? Would it be wise for us to enter some monastic order where we could spend our time in meditation and prayer?

Shall we surrender in bleak despair, feeling that nothing can possibly be done?

Shall we dissent to the extent that we start a revolution?

Shall we identify the cause of the state with the cause of God and equate Christianity with democracy? Some people are forsaking the church in a desire to go "where the action is." They believe that if the kingdom of God is going to come, it will come through changes in government.

We believe that Scripture teaches that Christians should participate in a very responsible manner as citizens of the community and state to which they belong. We will look to the Scriptures for some guidance.

I. Christians are to recognize government as a divine institution.

A. *Government, as an institution, is of God (Rom. 13:1).*

B. *Resistance to constituted authority is disobedience to God and will be punished (Rom. 13:2).*

C. *Ideally, government officials are God's ministers appointed to encourage what is right and to punish what is evil (Rom. 13:3–4).*

D. *Only evildoers have anything to fear from properly constituted governmental authority (Rom. 13:4).*

E. *Christians should be law-abiding citizens for conscience' sake rather than from a fear of the consequences (Rom. 13:5).*

F. *Taxation is legitimate, and the payment of taxes is a Christian duty (Rom. 13:6).*

G. *Christians should fulfill their many obligations to the state (Rom. 13:7).*

II. Christians are to remember governmental officials in prayer (I Tim. 2:1–4).

Good government is conducive to the growth of spiritual life. It makes possible an enlightened culture, growth of the church, and development of good home life.

Christians should pray that the Spirit of God will guide and be with all of those who are in positions of responsibility where decisions are made and where the destiny of the nation is determined.

III. Christians are to live as citizens of the kingdom of heaven on earth (I Peter 2:11–17).

The testimony of our lips is to be verified and dramatized by the testimony of our lives. To be a poor citizen is to be a poor witness for Jesus Christ.

The apostle Peter was writing to the followers of Christ who lived in a very hostile atmosphere and environment. They were threatened with violent persecution. The apostle encouraged them to live in a manner that would refute the false accusations that were brought against them by those who wanted to destroy Christianity.

IV. Christians are to seek first the kingdom of God and his righteousness (Matt. 6:33).

Our highest loyalty, as the followers of Christ, belongs to God rather than to Caesar. If the demands of the state should ever conflict with or contradict the commandments of our God, then we are faced with a clear mandate as to what our decision is to be (Acts 5:29).

Dr. O. T. Binkley has made three suggestions concerning what responsible Christians can do to be good citizens. First, he suggests that "we can develop a kind of personal character that will stand the strain of responsible living in a dynamic society." Second, he says that "we can participate in the advancement of the Christian gospel in this generation." And third, he says that we should stand "on the front line of Christian conscience in the community in which we live." Dr. Henlee Barnette, in *Introducing Christian Ethics*, offered some excellent suggestions concerning how we can implement the responsibilities that are involved in good citizenship. If we are to make decisions in harmony with the Christian imperative of love and justice, he says, there are a number of things that we should do:

A. *We should strive to understand the nature and the processes of government.*
B. *We should participate in the selection of public officials and the formation of public policy.*
C. *We should work for the extension of justice, freedom, and equality for all citizens, regardless of race, creed, or color.*
D. *We should serve in places of political leadership for which we are qualified, regardless of the cost and the criticism that may be forthcoming.*
E. *We should challenge and criticize any force in society that denies basic human rights or runs counter to the claims of God.*
F. *We should align ourselves with a church and other constructive forces that seek to strengthen the spiritual and moral fiber of individuals and the nation.*

Conclusion

It is not an easy thing to be completely Christian in every area of life. With the highest part of our intellect, and with the deepest emotion of our hearts, and with a full commitment to Jesus Christ, let each of us seek to be a worthy citizen of our community and a good citizen of our country—for the glory of God and for the good of others.

SUNDAY EVENING, JUNE 30

Title: What Have I Done with the Church?

Text: "Husbands, love your wives, even as Christ also loved the church, and gave himself for it; that he might sanctify and cleanse it with the washing of water by the word, that he might present it to himself a glorious church, not having spot, or wrinkle, or any such thing; but that it should be holy and without blemish" **(Eph. 5:25–27).**

Scripture Reading: Ephesians 5:20–33

Introduction

Paul, speaking to husbands and wives concerning their responsibilities to each other, uses the relationship of Christ to the church to illustrate how they should relate to each other in love and faithfulness. He talks about how Christ loved the church and gave himself for it.

In spite of all the faults and flaws of the institutional church, we cannot help but be persuaded that the church is still the object of our Lord's continuing love. What have you done with the church? The question is not "What did your parents do with the church?" or "What have the majority of the citizens of our country done with the church?" or "What have my neighbors done with the church?" The real question is "What have I done with the church?"

I. The church is very important to our Father God.

We must not think of the church as merely an institution among institutions. We do great violence to scriptural teaching if we think of the church in terms of its being a building with a street address and a zip code. We need to recognize it as something even more than just a body of believers banded together for worship and for mutual assistance.

A. *The church is the people of God (1 Peter 2:9).* What Israel was before the days of Christ, the church is today in the purpose of God.

B. *The church is the body of Christ (1 Cor. 12:27).* Christ is the Head of the church. The church is the body through which he functions and through which he continues his ministry of proclamation and service in the world.

C. *The church is the dwelling place of the Holy Spirit (1 Cor. 3:16; Eph. 4:4–7, 11–16).* The Holy Spirit dwells within the heart of each believer and bestows on the church through these believers the gifts that are needed for carrying forward the work of God in the world today.

D. *The church has been given a divine commission to evangelize the world (Matt. 28:18–20).* All of us who claim Christ as Savior need to realize that we are

209

a part of the people of God, the body of Christ, the dwelling place of the Holy Spirit, and that we have been commissioned to spread the glad tidings of God's love to the ends of the earth.

II. How important is the church to you?

A. *Have you related yourself to the church as a vital part with love and gratitude to the Lord of the church?*

B. *Have you conducted yourself in a manner that would leave the impression that you despised the church and had no love at all for it (see 1 Cor. 11:22)?*

C. *Have you neglected the church and forsaken its services of worship and opportunities for study (Heb. 10:24–25)?*

Conclusion

Because the church has been given a divine commission and because of the world's desperate need for the message and the ministry of the church, there are a number of positive responses that each of us can make to the church.

1. We can renew or deepen our conviction of the importance of the church to the work of God and to the good of people. God is depending on his church. The community would indeed be a desolate and demoralized place if it were not for the influence of the church.
2. Each of us can renew our consecration to the work of the Lord in and through the church.
3. Perhaps each of us needs to reexamine the expenditure of our energy in the church and concentrate more on the work our Lord designated for the church.
4. All of us can reaffirm our determination to be cooperative and contributing members of the congregation in which we hold membership.

There is much that is right with the church. The Head of the church is right. The message, the life, and the mission of the church are right. Because it is the right thing to do, each of us can let the church mean more to us, and we can mean more to the church for which our Lord gave himself.

JULY

■ Sunday Mornings

The Sunday morning messages for July and August feature a series of sermons titled "Symbols for the Spirit."

■ Sunday Evenings

"The Greatness and Goodness of God" is the theme. We need to be honest with God and trust him implicitly. Our response to him should be one of love.

■ Wednesday Evenings

"Words of Encouragement from the Apostle Paul" is the suggested theme for a series of studies based on the epistle to the Philippians.

WEDNESDAY EVENING, JULY 3

Title: God's Good Work

Text: "Being confident of this very thing, that he which hath begun a good work in you will perform it until the day of Jesus Christ" **(Phil. 1:6)**.

Scripture Reading: Philippians 1:3–11

Introduction

It is interesting to note how our text is translated in some of the modern versions. Phillips translates this verse, "I feel sure that the one who has begun His good work in you will go on developing it until the day of Jesus Christ." The *New English Bible* translates it, "Of one thing I am certain: the One who started the good work in you will bring it to completion by the Day of Christ Jesus." *Today's English Version* says, "And so I am sure of this: that God, who began this good work in you, will carry it on until it is finished in the day of Christ Jesus." *The Living Bible* translates it, "And I am sure that God who began the good work within you will keep right on helping you grow in His grace until His task within you is finally finished on that day when Jesus Christ returns."

Our text contains the thought that salvation in its inception, in its continuation, and in its consummation is the work of God. "Salvation is of the Lord."

I. God's good work begins in conviction and conversion.

The apostle Paul is expressing his confidence that the great God and Father of our Lord Jesus Christ will continue the work he began in the conversion experience.

God always takes the initiative in confronting people with their need for the forgiveness of sin and the gift of a new life. The Holy Spirit brings about an awareness of this need for salvation. He convinces people in the deepest zone of their being that they are sinners in need of forgiveness and in need of a Savior who can deliver them from the tyranny of sin.

We become the children of God by a birth of the Spirit. The conversion experience is the beginning of God's good work rather than the full achievement of his purpose for us.

The apostle declares his confidence that God will continue to nourish and cultivate that which he began in the Philippians' initial experience with him, which brought about conversion.

II. God's good work calls for our cooperation (Phil. 2:12–13).

The hearts of believers become the dwelling place of the Holy Spirit in the conversion experience. The Holy Spirit comes in to reproduce within the minds and hearts of believers the very thoughts and emotions of Christ.

The heavenly Father is interested in something more than our being born into his family. He wants us to grow toward maturity and competence as his servants. This takes time and effort. It requires cooperation on the part of each one who puts faith in the Lord Jesus Christ as Savior.

God is not far off. He dwells within. He is present to assure us of our relationship with him. He is at work within us to manifest the superior quality of a life of faith and service in contrast to a life of no faith and selfishness.

If we would fully experience God's good work, we must cooperate with him as he works within us both to affect our choices and to direct the course of our conduct.

III. God's good work in us will reach a consummation (Phil. 3:20–21).

The salvation God begins in our conversion and continues throughout our total life span will reach its glorious consummation when the Lord Jesus Christ returns for both the living and the dead. At that time, we will be saved and delivered from the very presence of sin itself. We will be given glorious bodies like the resurrected body of the Lord Jesus Christ.

As followers of Christ, we can look back to our conversion experience as the beginning of God's good work in us. At that time, we were saved from the penalty of sin, which is death. We entered into a position of acceptance before God's throne of grace. God justified us on the basis of our faith in Jesus Christ, declaring that we were acceptable to him. This gives us a sense of security and a great inward peace of mind (Rom. 5:1).

From the moment of our conversion to the present and continuing on to the end, God will be at work within us to deliver us from the power and practice and habit of sin in our daily life. He is seeking to deliver us from this present evil world. He is seeking to develop us and to train us for ministries to others. During this time, we must cooperate with him by faith, obedience, and love. We must listen to the Spirit who dwells within. We must devotionally study his Holy Word. We must respond to the needs of those about us. We must give voice to the testimony of what Jesus Christ means to us. In the power of the Holy Spirit, we must overcome the evil that is within us and the evil that is about us. We can rejoice in the privilege of being in a process of being saved from the power and practice of sin.

With joy and gratitude, we can look forward to that glorious time when we shall no longer be afflicted with a sinful disposition and a sinful inclination. We can look forward to the time when sin will no longer allure us or torment us. We can look forward to the time when in perfect holiness we can serve God joyfully without the limitations that we know in the flesh.

Conclusion

God is good. All of God's works toward us are good. All of God's work within us is good. Let us respond to him with faith, love, and obedience.

SUNDAY MORNING, JULY 7

Title: Please Meet an Important Person

Text: "He shall glorify me: for he shall receive of mine, and shall show it unto you" **(John 16:14).**

Scripture Reading: John 16:7–16, 32–33

Hymns: "Come, Thou Almighty King," Anonymous

"The Holy Ghost Is Here," Spurgeon

"Pentecostal Power," Gabriel

Offertory Prayer: Our Father, we have been shaken awake by the assertion that Christianity is the most materialistic religion in the world. Teach us again that the word *secular* is from human vocabulary, that with you everything is sacred. With such conviction, we bring our gifts for your ministry to a needy world, in the name of your greatest gift to the world, Jesus, our Lord. Amen.

Introduction

It has been suggested that before Jesus was born, people lived in the dispensation of God the Father; that during the earthly life span of Jesus, people lived in the dispensation of God the Son; and that since Jesus ascended, people live in the dispensation of God the Spirit. This message is the first of eight Sunday morning messages in which our focus will be on the Holy Spirit. "Identity" and "personhood" are the drumbeats of our present-day march. In this introductory message, we meet the Holy Spirit in the emphases of these contemporary drumbeats but also in the light of Scripture. If, indeed, we can identify the Holy Spirit and our relationship with him, and if we can see his personhood, our moments will be a blessed threshold to further fellowship with him.

I. The Holy Spirit's presentation indicates that he is a person.

A. *"But if I depart, I will send* him *unto you" (John 16:7, emphasis mine).*

B. *"And when* he *is come,* he *will reprove the world of sin, and of righteousness, and of judgment" (John 16:8, emphasis mine).*

C. *"Howbeit when* he, *the Spirit of truth, is come,* he *will guide you into all truth: for* he *shall not speak of* himself; *but whatsoever* he *shall hear, that shall* he *speak: and* he *will show you things to come" (John 16:14, emphasis mine).*

D. *"He* shall glorify me: for he shall receive of mine . . ." *(John 16:15, emphasis mine).*

E. *Twelve times in this brief Scripture passage the Holy Spirit is represented by a personal pronoun.* The Holy Spirit is not an "it," but a person.

It is not hard to identify persons we have seen as persons. Yet we readily accept those we have never seen as persons. A person we have never met calls us on the telephone and identifies himself, and we do not think that an "it" has called: a person has called. A clear identification makes easy our classification.

II. The Holy Spirit's association indicates that he is a person.

A. *"All things that the Father hath are mine: therefore said I, that he shall take of mine, and shall show it unto you" (John 16:15).* Here the Holy Spirit—that is, "he"—is named with the persons of the Father and the Son. Where the Trinity is named, each is like in kind. It would be exceedingly awkward in the many such listings to have grouped two "persons" and a "thing."

B. *"Go ... baptizing them in the name of the Father and of the Son and of the Holy Spirit" (Matt. 28:19 NIV).* Our very commission illustrates this inseparable association.

C. *"The grace of our Lord Jesus Christ, and the love of God, and the communion of the Holy Ghost, be with you all. Amen" (2 Cor. 13:14).* This is but another of these beautiful divine associations.

III. The Holy Spirit's vocation indicates that he is a person (John 16:8–11, 13, 14).

A. *Principle.* What the Holy Spirit does is that which can be done by a person only. His performance is a key to his personality. Some tasks things can do, but the work ascribed to him can be done by a person only.

B. *Performance.*

1. He creates (Gen. 1:2).
2. He comforts (John 14:16).
3. He dwells (John 14:17).
4. He teaches (John 15:26).
5. He testifies (John 15:26).
6. He convicts (John 16:7–15).
7. He guides (John 16:13).
8. He hears (John 16:13).
9. He speaks (Acts 13:2).

10. He witnesses (Rom. 8:16).
11. He helps (Rom. 8:26).

IV. The Holy Spirit's characterization indicates that he is a person (John 16:7–16).

This is but another way of saying that his characteristics are those of a person, not of an impersonal force.

A. *He is aggressive (Rom. 8:27).* He is said to take the initiative in interceding for us.

B. *He has the capacity of being grieved (Eph. 4:30).* "Grieve not the holy Spirit" could refer to a person only.

C. *He is a friendly person (John 16:14–15).* He moves about speaking to people.

D. *He bridges the most important communication gap—between humanity and deity (John 16:13).*

E. *He engages constantly in unselfish activity (John 16:14).*

F. *He is truly rich in his possession and access (John 16:15).*

Conclusion

A. *Wouldn't you like to meet and associate with such a wonderful person?*

B. *If you know the Holy Spirit, wouldn't you like to get better acquainted with him?*

C. *You can! The way to know the Holy Spirit and to receive him is through Jesus.*

D. *It is in fulfillment of Jesus' promise that the Holy Spirit is in our world, and it is through appropriating Jesus' promises that we have the Holy Spirit.* What is more important, he can have us!

SUNDAY EVENING, JULY 7

Title: Being Honest with God

Text: "Thou hast not lied unto men, but unto God" **(Acts 5:4).**

Scripture Reading: Acts 4:32–5:11

Introduction

"All scripture is given by inspiration of God, and is profitable for doctrine, for reproof, for correction, for instruction in righteousness: that the man of God may be perfect, thoroughly furnished unto all good works" (2 Tim. 3:16–17).

Another passage of Scripture that is appropriate as we consider "being honest with God" is found in Paul's epistle to the Romans. "For whatsoever things were written aforetime were written for our learning, that we through patience and comfort of the scriptures might have hope" (15:4). Both of these passages of Scripture tell us that there is something we can learn that will be profitable in every portion of Holy Scripture.

Some passages we seemingly overlook, avoid, or even bypass. The account of the sin of Ananias and Sapphira is one of these. This passage reveals to us that dishonesty with God was the first and great sin that threatened the fellowship and ministry of the church as it sought to carry out the Great Commission.

The judgment of God fell in great severity upon Ananias and his wife, Sapphira. This judgment purified the church and increased the effectiveness of its witness. This judgment also revealed God's attitude toward dishonesty and hypocrisy.

Reading the account of the death of Ananias and Sapphira should cause some of us to tremble because of our pretense and phoniness. Someone has said, "Most of us would have had short lives if every half-truth or deception had been as severely dealt with."

What was the Holy Spirit seeking to communicate to the early church through this event? Why has this account been preserved for us as a part of the Holy Scriptures?

I. What was the sin of Ananias and Sapphira?

It can be discovered in the comments of Peter to both of them.

A. *It was a sin within the fellowship of the church that threatened the very nature of the church.*

B. *It was not a refusal to make a contribution to the needs of the church.*

C. *It was a sin of basic dishonesty.*

D. *It was a sin of deliberate deception and hypocrisy.*

E. *It was a sin of lying.*

F. *It was a sin of desiring the praise of people more than the praise of God.*

G. *It was a sin that threatened the purity and the power of the church in its witness to an unsaved world.*

H. *It was a sin in which Ananias and Sapphira submitted to and cooperated with the devil (Acts 5:3).*

II. The judgment of God upon this sin.

A. *The judgment of God was sudden.*

B. *The judgment of God was severe.*

C. *The judgment of God was supernatural.*

D. *The judgment of God was solemnizing.*

III. What does this judgment upon Ananias and Sapphira say to us?

A. *This event reveals the strategy of Satan and discloses that obedience to him is always dangerous.* It is never wise to listen to the devil's lies and suggestions.

1. Has Satan told you that you are too poor to tithe?
2. Has Satan told you that you are too busy to serve?
3. Has Satan told you that you are too inexperienced to assume a place of responsibility?
4. Has Satan told you that your testimony is so commonplace that it could not be used effectively?

B. *This account tells us to be cautious about whose applause we seek.*

It is only normal that we desire the acceptance and the applause of those who are important to us. Young people want the approval of the crowd. Employees desire the approval of their boss. All of us want the approval of the group whom we consider to be important. It is supremely important that in all of our relationships and activities we put the approval of God ahead of the approval of any other group.

C. *This account reveals the importance of being absolutely honest in all of our expressions of devotion to God.*
  1. We need to be honest with ourselves. "To thine own self be true."
  2. We must be honest with others.
  3. We must be honest with God. One can act a lie as well as tell a lie.
D. *This account warns us against the danger of imperiling the witness and the work of the church.*
  1. The church is God's chosen instrument for communicating the good news of his love to the world.
  2. The church, with its message of the love of God, is the only hope for the world.
E. *This event informs us that sin against and within the church may be dealt with drastically (1 Cor. 3:16).*

Conclusion

Have you been listening to the devil's lies? Are you cooperating with evil rather than with good? If so, you are walking in the footsteps of Ananias and Sapphira.

Each of us should be honest with God. We need his grace and mercy. We need his forgiveness and guidance.

We can depend on God to preserve us from starvation. We can depend on his promise to be with us in the future. Our response to him should always be characterized by sincerity and honesty.

WEDNESDAY EVENING, JULY 10

Title: A Prayer That Should Be Repeated

Text: "And this I pray ..." (**Phil. 1:9**).

Scripture Reading: Philippians 1:9–11

Introduction

Prayer must be sincere. Prayer must express the deep needs of the heart of the one praying. Prayer should be original and spontaneous. However, there are times when we need guidance in our prayer life. We can profit greatly by repeating from the heart some of the great prayers offered by our Savior. There are times when we can let the apostles give voice to our prayer. Our lives can be enriched by letting the psalmist voice the prayer that we do not have words to express.

In this prayer of Paul for the Philippians, we have a prayer that we should repeat from the heart for ourselves as well as for others.

I. Paul prayed that they might have an intelligent love that would increase more and more (Phil. 1:9).

Jesus lived by the principle of love and commanded his disciples to live by the principle of love (John 13:34). Most of us find it easier to hate than we do to love.

Paul was praying for the Philippians that they might have a greater love that would express itself in a discerning moral perception. The kind of love for which he prayed for them is the supreme gift of the Holy Spirit (1 Cor. 13:31).

II. Paul prayed for them a keen sense of moral and spiritual perception (Phil. 1:10).

The capacity to distinguish between good and evil and to form a judgment is one of the best gifts of God to man. It is not always easy to make these decisions.

There are times when we are faced with the alternative of choosing between that which is positively evil and that which is perfectly good. There are other times when we are faced with choosing the better of two goods or the lesser of two evils. Life is very complex. Things are not always simple and easy to determine.

Paul recognized that they would need divine wisdom to choose the good in order that they might be drawn to the highest and the best. This is a prayer that we should pray for ourselves and for others.

III. Paul prayed that they might reap an abundant harvest of spiritual fruit.

Paul was eager that the Philippians not experience a crop failure in the realm of the spirit. He was urging them to respond to God in a manner that would enable them to be fruitful.

Our Lord gave to his apostles some suggestions that, if followed, will ensure an abundant harvest of spiritual fruit (John 15:4–5, 8).

The psalmist describes the choices and the conduct that lead to an abundant harvest in the realm of the spirit (Ps. 1:2–3).

The wise man emphasizes that we must be diligent and apply ourselves if we want to reap an abundant harvest (Prov. 10:5). He describes this fruitfulness that is of eternal significance (11:30).

Conclusion

The purpose behind this prayer of Paul for the Philippians is something other than their own selfish satisfaction. He offered this prayer on their behalf to the end that God might receive glory and praise through Jesus Christ (Phil. 1:11). The chief end of man is to worship God and glorify him forever.

Paul's prayer for the Philippians is a prayer that we should pray for ourselves and for others.

SUNDAY MORNING, JULY 14

Title: The Holy Spirit as a Dove

Text: "And John bare record, saying, I saw the Spirit descending from heaven like a dove, and it abode upon him" **(John 1:32)**.

Scripture Reading: Matthew 3:13–17

Hymns: "Doxology," Ken

"Come, Holy Spirit, Heavenly Dove," Watts

"Seal Us, O Holy Spirit," Meredith

Offertory Prayer: Our Father, we gather all the gifts brought today, bind them together with the ribbons of our love, and place them at your altar. Remind us that the tithe is the Lord's. May our stewardship in giving reflect not only our love but our honesty. This is our payer, in the name of Jesus. Amen.

Introduction

Although we must avoid pressing too hard the types and symbols of the Bible, we must also avoid the opposite extreme of ignoring them. In the Bible, the Holy Spirit is repeatedly represented as a dove. We shall not use this figure as a tool to carve out our own truths; rather, we shall be sensitive to its meaning in revealing God's truth. We cannot grasp the full meaning of all divine truth. We can, through meaningful symbols, become the beneficiaries of spiritual wealth not otherwise available to us.

I. The priority of the Holy Spirit as a dove.

A. *The Holy Spirit is presented as a dove early in the Bible.* Present in the beginning, he is named near the beginning (Gen. 1:2).

B. *The Holy Spirit, as a dove, was primary in Creation.* "And the Spirit of God moved upon the face of the waters" (Gen. 1:2). The word "moved" means to brood, as a bird sits on a nest of eggs. The contents of an ordinary fertile egg are without form. Place it under the bird for a period of time, and the mystery of incubation occurs. The contents of the eggshell that are without form take living form. When "the earth was without form, and void" the Holy Spirit brooded upon the nest of the deep, and form and life came forth.

II. The picture of the Holy Spirit as a dove.

A. *"He saw the Spirit of God descending like a dove, and lighting upon him"* (Matt. *3:16).*

B. *"And straightway coming up out of the water, he saw the heavens opened, and the Spirit like a dove descending upon him" (Mark 1:10).*

C. *"And the Holy Ghost descended in a bodily shape like a dove upon him" (Luke 3:22).*

D. *"Upon whom thou shalt see the Spirit descending, and remaining on him, the same is he which baptizeth with the Holy Ghost.* And I saw, and bare record that this is the Son of God" (John 1:33–34).

It is not an accident that this beautiful and significant detail of our Lord's baptism is so vividly described by all of the gospel writers.

III. The parallel of the Holy Spirit as a dove.

A. *F. E. Marsh has suggested seven common qualities of the dove and the Spirit.*
   1. Clean in nature.
   2. Gentle in manner.
   3. Constant in love.
   4. Particular in food.
   5. Swift of wing.
   6. Beautiful.
   7. Social in habit.

B. *The parallel of the dove and the Spirit is emphasized in the performance of each.*
   1. Each is a great lover. The image of a dove is imprinted on some marriage licenses. By its nature, the dove is a love bird. Solomon said in his most picturesque poetry, "My love, my dove" (Song 5:2). Later he repeated the romantic figure, "My dove, my undefiled ... one" (6:9).
   2. Each is sacrificial. The dove was a bird of sacrifice (Mark 11:15). It surrendered itself in the ceremonial sacrifices of the people of God. The Holy Spirit does not "speak of himself" but sacrifices his position in favor of the Lord Jesus. He glorifies Christ.
   3. Each is the symbol of peace. It was the dove that brought back the olive leaf to Noah (Gen. 8:11). It brought a message of peace. Even today, in war jargon, we say people are "doves" and "hawks." "The fruit of the Spirit is love, joy, peace ..." (Gal. 5:22). Jesus sent his disciples forth, charging them to be "wise as serpents, and harmless as doves" (Matt. 10:16).

      I am told that the dove has no gall in its body. Could this say something to us of the Spirit without bitterness?
   4. Each mourns. Hezekiah said, "I did mourn as a dove" (Isa. 38:14). Isaiah said, "We roar all like bears, and mourn sore like doves" (59:11). The Holy Spirit mourns. "But the Spirit itself maketh intercession for us with groanings which cannot be uttered" (Rom. 8:26). He grieves (Eph. 4:30).
   5. Each is a messenger. As the dove bore the message to Noah, the Holy Spirit bears a message to the windowsills of our souls (Gen. 8:8–12). "He shall teach you all things" (John 14:26).
   6. Each loves a home. Isaiah asked, "Who are these that fly as a cloud, and as the doves to their windows?" (Isa. 60:8). Jesus discussed Father, Son, and Holy Spirit, and promised, "We will come unto him, and make our abode with him" (John 14:23). The Holy Spirit loves a home and wants to take up permanent residence in us.
   7. Each may depart finally. "He stayed yet seven other days; and sent forth the dove; which returned not again unto him any more" (Gen. 8:12).

In such a way, the Holy Spirit also sometimes departs finally: "My spirit shall not always strive with man" (6:3). It is of this fatal and final departure that Jesus speaks in Matthew 12:31–32.

Conclusion

A. *Let us review the symbolism of the Holy Spirit in the figure of the lovely bird, the dove.*
B. *Let us respond to his presence and work so that there will be no dreadful day of his departure.* The words of the English poet Joseph Addison sober us and should stir us to deeper Spirit-filled living:

> *There is a time, I know not when,*
> *A place, I know not where,*
> *Which marks the destiny of men,*
> *To heaven or despair.*
>
> *There is a line, by us not seen,*
> *Which crosses every path;*
> *The hidden boundary between*
> *God's patience and God's wrath.*
>
> *To cross that limit is to die,*
> *To die as if by stealth.*
> *It may not pale the beaming eye,*
> *Nor quench the glowing health.*
>
> *The conscience may be still at ease,*
> *The spirit light and gay.*
> *That which is pleasing still may please,*
> *And care be thrust away.*
>
> *But on that forehead God hath set*
> *Indelibly a mark,*
> *By man unseen, for man as yet*
> *Is blind and in the dark.*
>
> *And still the doomed man's path below*
> *May bloom as Eden bloomed.*
> *He did not, does not, will not know,*
> *Nor feel, that he is doomed.*
>
> *He feels, he says, that all is well,*
> *His every fear is calmed.*
> *He lives, he dies, he wakes in hell,*
> *Not only doomed, but damned.*
>
> *Oh, where is that mysterious bourne*
> *By which each path is crossed?*
> *Beyond which God Himself hath sworn*
> *That he who goes is lost?*

How long may man go on in sin,
How long will God forbear?
Where does hope end, and where begin
The confines of despair?

One answer from the skies is sent:
Ye who from God depart,
While it is yet today, repent,
And harden not your heart.

SUNDAY EVENING, JULY 14

Title: How God Works

Text: "And we know that all things work together for good to them that love God, to them who are the called according to his purpose" **(Rom. 8:28).**

Scripture Reading: Romans 8:26–39

Introduction

It is interesting to note how our text is translated in the modern versions of the New Testament.

The New Testament in Modern English: "Moreover we know that to those who love God, who are called according to his plan, everything that happens fits into a pattern for good."

Revised Standard Version: "We know that in everything God works for good with those who love him, who are called according to his purpose."

New English Bible: "In everything, as we know, he cooperates for good with those who love God and are called according to his purpose."

The Message: "That's why we can be so sure that every detail in our lives of love for God is worked into something good."

New International Version: "We know that in all things God works for the good of those who love him, who have been called according to his purpose."

I. The text deals with some problems.

A. *Does everything happen for the best?*
B. *Does everything work together for good?*
C. *Is God responsible for everything that happens?*
   1. Where does our personal freedom fit in?
   2. Where does the work of the devil enter the picture? (1 Peter 5:8).
   3. How does the "law of cause and effect" affect this text?

II. The text contains a great promise.

The truth of this great promise is illustrated often in the lives of God's people. Here are some example from Scripture.

A. *Joseph* was cruelly mistreated by his brothers. He was sold into slavery. Later he was falsely accused of a terrible crime (Gen. 39:9, 21). He was unjustly imprisoned. Sometime after his deliverance, insight dawned as to why this catastrophe had befallen him (Gen. 50:20). God was at work for good, not only for Joseph, but for his people.

B. *Moses*, although he was a prince in the empire of Egypt, was sympathetic to the oppressed Israelites. To help one of them, he killed an Egyptian. This brought about a loss of official favor, and Moses fled to the backside of the desert. For forty long years he was in training to become the deliverer of God's people from the bondage of Egypt. God was at work for good, not only for Moses, but for his people.

C. *Isaiah* was filled with grief in the year King Uzziah died. With thoughts of an empty throne, and with uncertainty concerning the future, he went into the temple for worship. His eyes were opened, and he saw the eternal throne of God, sovereign and supreme, majestic and holy (Isa. 6). He came forth to be the prophet of God's holiness and God's sovereignty.

D. *Ezekiel* was trained to be a priest in Jerusalem. His country was conquered by the Babylonians, and he was led as a captive into a foreign land. He found himself far from home in a strange and polluted land. He felt exiled not only from Israel, but particularly from the temple and its sacred precinct. While in an agony of soul by the river Chebar, Ezekiel was given a vision of God on a movable throne. God was coming out of the north. This was the route by which the captives had entered the land of Babylon. Ezekiel discovered that God was accessible to them in the land of exile. He was thus equipped to proclaim a new understanding of the nature and character of God.

E. *Saul*, a young Pharisee, stood by while a faithful follower of Jesus Christ was stoned to death (Acts 7:54–60). Possibly this experience equipped Saul—later Paul—to suffer as he did for the sake of Christ (Acts 9:13–16; cf. 2 Cor. 11:24–27).

III. The text speaks of a divine purpose.

A. *God is at work in the world today.*

B. *God has a wonderful plan for the lives of each of us (see Rom. 8:31–32).* God's wonderful plan includes:

1. Salvation from the penalty of sin.
2. Salvation from the power and practice of sin.
3. Salvation from the presence of sin ultimately.

It is the will of our God that we be fruitful and productive (John 15:2, 7–8). There are times when we cannot understand the experiences that befall us. With faith in God, we should move forward in the confidence that God will be at work to bring good in everything that happens to us.

Conclusion

Let us rejoice that God has a purpose for us. Let us face all of life in the confidence that God is at work in everything that happens to bring out all of the good that can be experienced. It may appear at times that God is working slowly. We can be certain that God is at work in terms of his love and power.

All that is in the past is preparatory for the present and the future.

The future is in the mind and heart of God. Not one thing can happen to us without the permission of the great God who never makes a mistake.

If we want to live confidently, we must trust and obey him. We must cooperate with him day by day as he works for good in our lives and in the lives of others.

WEDNESDAY EVENING, JULY 17

Title: Advancing the Gospel

Text: "But I would ye should understand, brethren, that the things which happened unto me have fallen out rather unto the furtherance of the gospel" **(Phil. 1:12).**

Scripture Reading: Philippians 1:12–18

Introduction

For a long time, Paul lived with the ambition of taking the good news of Christ to the capital city of the Roman Empire (Rom. 1:14–16). Paul arrived in Rome in chains as a prisoner, having appealed to the court of Caesar (cf. Acts 25:10; 28:16).

It is interesting and profitable for us to study the reaction of Paul to the circumstances in which he found himself. He could have loudly and vehemently proclaimed his innocence of any crime and made a plea for sympathy. He could have hung his head in shame because of the humiliation associated with being a prisoner and wearing a chain. He could have bowed his head in utter defeat and retreated into the isolation of self-pity. He could have reacted with an attitude of extreme hostility, leading to bitterness and despair. Instead, Paul met his circumstances with faith, hope, and determination (Phil. 1:20).

I. Paul experienced triumph instead of tragedy (Phil. 1:12).

Paul rejoiced exceedingly over the fact that the gospel was being advanced. Instead of experiencing defeat in the midst of adverse circumstances, he was experiencing victory. Instead of majoring on his misfortune, Paul rejoiced in the furtherance of the Good News into the hearts of people. He was seeing a demonstration of the fact that the gospel was the power of God unto salvation to the Gentiles (Rom. 1:16).

II. How can we advance the gospel today?

It is interesting to study Paul's epistle to the Philippians to discover the methods that were used in those days.

A. *The saints at Philippi were advancing the gospel by means of their contributions (Phil. 4:15–18).* These grateful people had sent offerings repeatedly to the apostle Paul that his physical needs might be met. By so doing, they released him from the responsibility of making tents so that he could give his time to proclaiming the gospel of Jesus Christ. He declared that their generosity would produce spiritual fruit as a dividend for their investment in missionary activity.

B. *They advanced the gospel by means of their prayers (Phil. 1:19).* He said, "I know that this shall turn to my salvation through your prayer." Paul's use of the word "salvation" at this time is interesting (note that the NIV has "deliverance"). Certainly Paul was not thinking about the salvation of his soul. Most likely he was referring to his desire to be saved from failing to be all that God wanted him to be when he faced the test of giving his testimony, whether it be by life or by death. The prayers of the people in Philippi would help him to escape this kind of failure.

How much sincere praying do we do for others who are seeking to communicate the gospel of Jesus Christ? While the missionaries around the world are dependent on our financial contributions, almost with one voice they say that their greatest need is for our prayers on their behalf.

C. *We can advance the gospel by living completely for Jesus Christ (Phil. 1:21).* There is no way by which we can effectively communicate the good news of God's love unless there are evidences of this work of God in our hearts and lives. The apostle Paul was utterly dedicated to letting Jesus Christ live within him and work through him. If we want to be effective advancers of the gospel today, we must let our life proclaim a more powerful message than we are able to proclaim with our lips.

D. *We can advance the gospel by means of our verbal testimony (Phil. 1:14).* It was not enough for Paul to live a genuine Christian life. It was not enough for the Philippian Christians to live an exemplary life. Those who do not know about God need to receive a verbal testimony. Paul rejoiced over the fact that the brethren in Rome were made bold to speak the good news of God's love without fear because of the manner in which he was wearing his chains as a prisoner for the gospel. We must be communicators of the good news if we want to advance the gospel.

E. *We can advance the gospel by being willing to suffer (Phil. 1:13, 27).* Being followers of Christ in the first century cost something. Paul had put his life on the line for the sake of the gospel. He had suffered greatly when he made his trip to Philippi, having been beaten with many stripes and thrown into prison. He was now suffering imprisonment because of his loyalty to Jesus Christ. He told his brethren in Philippi that suffering for the sake of Christ was a privilege. How much inconvenience have we endured for the sake of advancing the gospel? To what degree have we really sacrificed that the rest of the world might come to know the saving love of God? To what degree have we suffered criticism or persecution?

Conclusion

When life is over, will someone be able to say concerning you, "His [or her] life served to advance the gospel"? Will the kingdom of God be larger and richer because of your being a part of it? It is a sobering thought to recognize that only what we do for God and for our fellow humans can go through the strainer that we call death. Let each of us live in time with the issues and the values of eternity in mind.

SUNDAY MORNING, JULY 21

Title: The Holy Spirit as a Fire

Text: "There appeared unto them cloven tongues like as of fire, and it sat upon each of them. And they were all filled with the Holy Ghost, and began to speak with other tongues, as the Spirit gave them utterance" **(Acts 2:3–4)**.

Scripture Reading: Isaiah 4:2–4; Acts 2:1–4

Hymns: "Spirit of God, Descend," Croly

"Spirit Divine, Attend Our Prayer," Reed

"Holy Spirit, Faithful Guide," Wells

Offertory Prayer: Our Father, may thanksgiving be more of a mark of our character than it is a mark on our calendars. Let it be a daily habit and not just an annual holiday. With grateful hearts, we bring these tithes and offerings, remembering that they are yours. Let them reach around our world as channels of your grace, through Jesus Christ our Lord. Amen.

Introduction

Many of us love an open fireplace. There is a therapy in the flickering light, the crackle of fire, the smell of burning wood, the direct heat of a cheerful flame. Most of us do not have such fireplaces. But God has always had his fireplaces. The burning bush, the brazen altar of the tabernacle, Mount Carmel, and his Pentecost people — these are just a few of God's fireplaces. The only fireplaces he has today in all the world are the hearts of his people. The Holy Spirit appeared "like as of fire." Hebrews 12:29 declares, "Our God is a consuming fire." Isaiah spoke of "the spirit of burning" (Isa. 4:4). We are to be filled with the Spirit. The fire of the Holy Spirit is to burn in the fireplaces of our own hearts. He is all that fire is, and he does all that fire does.

I. Fire consumes.

The bonfire of Ephesus consumed the bad books (Acts 19:19). Fire consumed Sodom. Moses said to Israel, "Understand therefore this day, that the LORD thy God is he which goeth before thee; as a consuming fire he shall destroy them, and he shall bring them down before thy face" (Deut. 9:3). When the sin of Achan was discovered, the people stoned him and burned him with fire (Josh. 7:25). If we would but let the Fire fill us, all that is undesirable in us would be consumed. You see, one does not have to worry much about what to do with what has already been burned up.

II. Fire purifies.

Do you recall Isaiah's testimony? The house was filled with smoke, and where there was smoke there was fire (Isa. 6:4). After his confession, one of the seraphim came to him, "having a live coal in his hand, which he had taken with the tongs from off the altar: and he laid it upon [his] mouth, and said, Lo, this hath touched thy lips; and thine iniquity is taken away, and thy sin purged" (vv. 6–7).

The presence of so much that is impure about us is surely the result of the fact that the Fire does not burn within us. The way to get cleaned up is to get burned out. And the Holy Spirit is the divine conflagration without which we shall remain cluttered and polluted.

III. Fire prepares.

Following the resurrection, our Lord appeared to his disciples by the Sea of Galilee. One of the verses from the story states that "as soon then as they were come to land, they saw a fire of coals there, and fish laid thereon, and bread" (John 21:9). The food was made ready with fire. We push back a good many spiritual groceries and label them as inedible simply because we do not allow the Holy Spirit's fire to make them savory. The intolerable becomes delightful following the fire.

Could it be that we ourselves are raw and repulsive because we have not been made ready with the Fire?

IV. Fire cheers.

To see the burning lamp in the window brings cheer. To see the campfire in the night brings cheer. To come from the winter cold to an open fire brings cheer.

Without the Spirit we are caught in the cold grip of despair. With the Spirit, we are cheered on to victory.

In one of the unique word pictures of Jesus, there is a stroke that declares, "His eyes were as a flame of fire" (Rev. 1:14). The flame brought terror to the enemies, but it brought cheer to the friends.

The Holy Flame cheers us!

V. Fire softens.

The psalmist declared that "as wax melteth before the fire, so let the wicked perish at the presence of God" (Ps. 68:2). Isaiah prophesied, "As when the melting fire burneth ... the nations may tremble at thy presence" (Isa. 64:2).

The Holy Spirit softens the heart of the sinner. He makes people responsive. He prepares them to be remolded, remade, regenerated.

The people of God could spare themselves a lot of fatigue and failure by depending on and responding to the softening of the Spirit.

227

VI. Fire unites.

When the two disciples were on their way to Emmaus, a unity came to them after their hearts burned within them (Luke 24:32). The unity of metals comes only through applied fire. Much of the unity of ingredients in our food comes because of heat or fire. The unity of God's people comes only by the unifying power of God's fire. Fellowship is dependent on the Flame.

VII. Fire empowers.

We fail to get up much steam in many of our endeavors because we do not have enough fire under the boilers. In our do-it-yourself determinism, we insist on our spiritual programs of flameless cooking.

We are powerless because we are flameless. Our half-baked ideas come from our half-heated ovens.

Let us be reminded often of our Lord's clear words, "Ye shall receive power, after that the Holy Ghost is come upon you" (Acts 1:8).

Conclusion

A. *The fire for God's fireplaces is the Holy Spirit.*
B. *The consuming, purifying, preparing, cheering, softening, uniting, and empowering of the Holy Fire can be ours.*
C. *Let us prayerfully yield and say, "Set my soul afire, Lord; set my soul afire."*

SUNDAY EVENING, JULY 21

Title: Melody of Love

Text: "I love the LORD, because he hath heard my voice and my supplications" **(Ps. 116:1).**

Scripture Reading: Psalm 116

Introduction

There is something exceedingly personal about Psalm 116. A country boy of eleven had been attending the annual revival meeting in a small church. For several days and nights he had been under conviction for his own sin of unbelief in Christ. He had come to the "mourner's bench" but had received no relief from his burden of guilt. Then a loved one suggested that he go alone into a room, close the door, and read Psalm 116. In the afternoon he did just that. The psalm, more than any other Scripture, found the boy, described him, and pointed him to the Lord. That night he was saved. That boy, the writer of these sermon notes, will always have an understandably warm place in his heart for this portion of the Scriptures.

Real love is always a duet, a dialogue. Love is never isolated. There is action and response. There is the lover and the object of his love. So it is in this gracious passage. The overtures of God are answered by the responses of a loving heart. There are reasons for love and there are responses to love.

I. The reasons for love (Ps. 116:1–8).

A. *The Lord heard the psalmist (v. 1).* "He hath heard my voice and my supplications" (Ps. 116:1). God not only heard him in the sense of registering his call, but he heard him in the sense of answering his call and granting him the desires of his heart.

    The great God not only has ears that are open to our plea; he has hands that are open to our need.

B. *The Lord inclined to the psalmist (v. 2).* When the Lord "inclined his ear," he stooped down and leaned over to listen to what his child would say. It is one thing to hear one out. We may listen because there is no other alternative. Or we may suffer through whatever another has to say. But when a person listens to us gladly and eagerly, it is the nicest tribute he can pay us. In every congregation there are people who are eloquent listeners.

    The Lord was and is an eloquent and eager listener. He even stoops to our level so we may speak into his ear. He bends down to us to hear what we have to say to him. It ought not to be difficult to love a Lord like that.

C. *The Lord preserved the psalmist (v. 6).* The word *preserve* means to protect. God had not just stayed with the psalmist long enough for an audience and then gone on his way. God's presence was constant. Enemies from within and without might spring their trap at any moment. To the psalmist, and to all who put their trust in the Lord, God is the around-the-clock bodyguard of the soul. One can love a Lord like that.

D. *The Lord helped the psalmist (v. 6).* When death seemed certain, the Lord intervened and saved him. The psalmist stood at the edge of a precipice, ready to plunge to destruction, but God came and snatched him back. No wonder the rescued one could say, "I love the Lord."

E. *The Lord delivered the psalmist (v. 8).* This deliverance is threefold:

1. His soul was delivered from death. This is the beginning place. There really is no satisfactory deliverance until the soul is liberated. All other spiritual liberties spring from the liberation of the soul.

2. His eyes were delivered from tears. The Lord did not simply wipe away his tears one by one until he got through weeping. God does not merely do an exterior blotting job with his sanctified tissues. He does a job of interior correction so that the fountain of tears is transformed into a fountain of joy. Mrs. Charles E. Cowman said it like this:

> *He was better to me than all my hopes.*
> *He was better than all my fears.*
> *For he made a bridge of my broken dreams,*
> *And a rainbow of my tears.*

3. His feet were delivered from falling. Much is said in our day about the qualities of certain automobile and truck tires whose tread keeps vehicles from skidding or becoming stuck. Some are advertised as having an all-weather tread. Well, regardless of such claims, the Lord gives

us for our feet all-weather treads. He keeps us from stumbling when the path is rough. He keeps us from slipping when the way is treacherously slippery. He gives us traction for the unforeseen crises so that we may go through to victory. Praise the Lord!

II. Response to love.

In the beginning we said that love's road is for two-way traffic. There is human reaction to divine action. The psalmist declared himself in personal commitment.

A. *"I will walk before the Lord in the land of the living"* (Ps. 116:9). The psalmist had more than nebulous daydreaming about the sweet by and by. He had the assurance that he would walk before the Lord "in the land of the living." He would begin at that moment, where he was, with what he had. This is always the way for us. It is much easier to talk love than it is to walk love.

John had much to say about love's behavior. "If we say that we have fellowship with him, and walk in darkness, we lie, and do not the truth: But if we walk in the light, as he is in the light, we have fellowship one with another, and the blood of Jesus Christ his Son cleanseth us from all sin" (1 John 1:6–7). This is not just love talk; it is love walk.

B. *"I will take the cup of salvation"* (Ps. 116:13). The psalmist had two thoughts in mind. The first is that he would accept the cup of salvation. The prime response to love is to accept what love has to offer. The least we can do in recognition of God's great love is to accept what he offers us. The second idea is that he would bear the cup to others—he would be a cupbearer for the King. The lives of others need the refreshing draught. Here then is the evangelism of gratitude.

An enthusiastic old saint of the South tried to explain her constant praise of the Lord. She said, "I'm so happy he saved me. When I think of what I was and what he has done for me, he's never gonna hear the last of it!"

C. I will *"call upon the name of the Lord"* (Ps. 116:13). The attitude of gratitude takes the form of prayer. When the psalmist thought of what the Lord had done, he committed himself to ask the Lord to do even more and to thank him for what he had already done.

Prayer is the conversation of love. Prayer on our part is the echo of love on God's part.

D. *"I will offer to thee the sacrifice of thanksgiving"* (Ps. 116:17). This is but another way of saying that the psalmist is so grateful to God that he cannot but make a sacrifice to God.

Peter Marshall said that in all his life he had not seen among Christians any demonstration that would indicate real sacrifice on their part. Nothing short of our sacrifice can approach an adequate response to God's sacrifice for us.

It is not an annual feast of turkey and dressing but a daily cross that expresses the Christian's measure of thanksgiving.

E. *"I will pay my vows unto the LORD now in the presence of all his people.* In the courts of the LORD's house, in the midst of thee, O Jerusalem" (Ps. 116:18–19).

Gratitude always moves toward the balancing of the books. Looking up in gratitude must be accompanied by paying up in honesty.

1. The vows are *personally* made. They are "my vows." The Christian religion, with its joys and responsibilities, is personal.

2. The vows were to be *publicly* paid. They will be paid "in the presence of all his people." Billy Graham has made famous the assertion that the only profession our Lord recommended or recognized was a public one. Neither the nature of our personal faith nor the modesty of our culture must rob us of the blessing of declaring and dedicating some things publicly.

There is value in the public wedding, the public funeral, and public worship. The cause of Christian stewardship is always strengthened by public demonstrations on the part of God's people.

Conclusion

A. *Let us make our testimony attractive with a "melody of love" atmosphere in our living.*

B. *Let us make our own souls stronger with a "melody of love" climate in our public and private worship.*

C. *Let us make our God pleased with a "melody of love" accent in our dialogue with him.*

WEDNESDAY EVENING, JULY 24

Title: Living with a High Purpose

Text: "For to me to live is Christ" (**Phil. 1:21**).

Scripture Reading: Philippians 1:19–26

Introduction

Many people drift through life without purpose. Each of us should face the question, "Why am I living?" We might ask, "For what am I living?" Is it possible that some of us are just existing? That we are drifting hither and yon?

Others set their aim or their goal for something significant in life. This becomes the motive that moves them, the discipline that controls them.

Paul's aim in life was to magnify Jesus Christ. He was determined to do this both in his body and in his death (Phil. 1:20). Paul had a high controlling purpose in his life. His great accomplishments were due largely to his high purpose and the dedication with which he gave himself to that purpose.

I. The value of a high purpose.

   A. *It provides excitement to life.*

   B. *It eliminates pursuits of lesser importance.*

   C. *It helps us determine our priorities.*

   D. *It demands our very best efforts.*

   E. *It forces us to trust God if we really want to do our best.*

     1. It encourages our prayer life.

     2. It emphasizes the importance of obedience.

     3. It encourages us to follow the leadership of the Holy Spirit.

II. To magnify Jesus Christ is the highest purpose for life.

   A. *Let us recognize that Christ initiates good purposes for our lives (Phil. 1:6).*

   B. *Let us make Christ the model of our lives (Phil. 2:5–8).*

   C. *Let us permit Christ to be the golden aim of our lives (Phil. 3:13).* For some, to live means knowledge. For some, to live means athletics. For some, to live means wealth. For some, to live means power. For some, to live means pleasure. If we want to live life on its highest plane, we need to make Christ the goal and the aim of our lives.

   D. *Let us let Christ be the reward of our lives (Phil. 3:8).*

III. Magnifying Christ calls for positive attitudes and actions.

   A. *We must cultivate hope based on faith in God (Phil. 1:19–20).*

   B. *We must make much of the rich fellowship and the close partnership that united prayer provides (Phil. 1:19).* Paul had a great faith and a positive hope, and he was encouraged in them because of the prayers of the Philippian Christians on his behalf.

   C. *We must recognize and cooperate with the Holy Spirit of God (Phil. 1:19).*

   D. *We must dedicate ourselves to serving Christ and ministering to others (Phil. 1:23–26).*

Conclusion

You can discover the joy of a high purpose for your life if you will let Jesus Christ have the place that belongs to him in your heart and life. Do not just accept him as Savior, but respond to him as Lord, Teacher, Friend, and Guide.

SUNDAY MORNING, JULY 28

Title: The Holy Spirit as a Mighty Wind

Text: "And when the day of Pentecost was fully come, they were all with one accord in one place. And suddenly there came a sound from heaven as of a rushing mighty wind, and it filled all the house where they were sitting" (**Acts 2:1–2**).

Scripture Reading: John 3:1–8

Hymns: "God, Our Father, We Adore Thee," Frazer

"Breathe on Me, Breath of God," Hatch

Offertory Prayer: Our Father, we remember that "the earth is the Lord's and the fullness thereof; the world, and they that dwell therein" (Ps. 24:1). We would make this moment of appeal a moment of acknowledgment. We have nothing in the world we did not receive, and we have nothing we will not leave in this world. For your lordship in our stewardship we thank you. With this deep conviction we bring our gifts today. Amen.

Introduction

As a picture falls short of a person and as a biography falls short of a life, so any symbol or figure falls short of the Holy Spirit. Oswald Sanders said that there are eighteen different names given to the Holy Spirit in the Old Testament, and thirty-nine names ascribed to him in the New Testament. The New Testament has about two hundred fifty references to the Holy Spirit. No more significant word to describe him is used than the word *wind.* Jesus himself described the work of the Holy Spirit in terms of the wind. He spoke of the transformation that comes with the Spirit and said his presence is like the presence of the wind. This wind is the very breath of God. It was mighty because God is mighty.

I. The breath means the difference between an animal and a man.

"And the Lord God formed man of the dust of the ground...." So what? He formed everything out of unimpressive material. But wait! Read the rest of the verse: "and breathed into his nostrils the breath of life; and man became a living soul" (Gen. 2:7). It was the breath of God that made him become a soul. It is the Spirit, God's breath, who makes a man more than a man. As Adam was incomplete until the breathing of God, so is any person since Adam. As the breath of God made him to become, so the Breath enables any person to become.

II. The breath means the difference between life and death.

Read again the story of Ezekiel and the valley of dry bones (Ezek. 37:1–10). What an unpromising congregation: a valley of dry bones. What an unusual deputation: to preach to such a boneyard. What an unthinkable desolation came about: a valley full of bodies—worse than a valley full of bones. What an unprecedented transformation: they came alive! What is the explanation? "Prophesy unto the wind, prophesy, son of man, and say to the wind, Thus saith the Lord God: come from the four winds, O breath, and breathe upon these slain, that they may live ... and the breath came into them and they lived, and stood up upon their feet, an exceeding great army" (Ezek. 37:9–10). Let it be remembered that there was not life until there was breath. Nor is there life in our contemporary valleys. Let our prayer always be, "O breathe ... that these may live."

III. The breath means the difference between condemnation and salvation (John 3:5–8).

Our Lord insisted that Nicodemus—an educated, mature, religious, able man—be born again. Intellectual achievement does not always guarantee spiritual understanding. Nicodemus did not understand, so Jesus explained, "That which is born of the flesh is flesh; and that which is born of the Spirit is spirit" (John 3:6). Then Jesus described in one sentence what it is like to be converted, to be born again, in an experience that transforms one from condemnation to salvation: "The wind bloweth where it listeth, and thou hearest the sound thereof, but canst not tell whence it cometh, and whither it goeth: so is every one that is born of the Spirit" (John 3:8). The word for wind is *pneuma*, from which we get our words *pneumatic* and *pneumonia*. The breathless body is the lifeless body. Thus it is divine logic that "ye must be born again."

IV. The breath means the difference between defeat and victory.

"And when he had said this, he breathed on them, and saith unto them, Receive ye the Holy Ghost: Whose soever sins ye remit, they are remitted unto them; and whose soever sins ye retain, they are retained" (John 20:22–23). Sin is the difference in our defeat and victory, and our conquering of sin is a mark of our victory.

Our Christian enterprise is launched of the Spirit, is guided by the Spirit, and is sustained with the Spirit. With the Spirit we have power; without the Spirit we are powerless. With the Spirit we have life; without the Spirit we have death. In the Spirit we have victory; without the Spirit we are doomed to failure. Lord Byron put it like this:

> *I now have ashes where once I had fire.*
> *The soul in my body is dead.*
> *The things I once loved, I now merely admire.*
> *My heart is as gray as my head.*

V. The breath means the difference between mere people and a mighty Pentecost (Acts 2:2).

The disciples were ordinary people made extraordinary by the power of the Holy Spirit. Revivals do not have to have the dimension of Pentecost, but they do have to have the pattern of Pentecost. Review the pattern:

A. *There was unity (Acts 1:14).*
B. *There was prayer (Acts 1:14).*
C. *There was a return to the Scriptures (Acts 1:16, 20).*
D. *There was organization (Acts 1:26).*
E. *There was assembly (Acts 2:1).*
F. *There was the Holy Spirit (Acts 2:2).*
G. *There was preaching (Acts 2:14–36).*
H. *There was conviction (Acts 2:37).*

I. *There was repentance (Acts 2:38).*

J. *There was joyful obedience (Acts 2:41).*

K. *There was continuation (Acts 2:46–47).*

Here are eleven links in a chain, but note that there are five links on either side of the Holy Spirit's coming. It is he who connects all the other links, and it is he without whom all else fails. He is central.

A man once suffered a severe heart attack in church. It appeared he would die. But the visiting minister had received training in first aid and administered cardiopulmonary resuscitation, thus saving the victim's life. The man was rushed to the hospital, where the medical staff cared for him successfully.

Oh that in some comparable way we who occupy the pulpits could administer a heart-to-heart resuscitation that would sustain life in all who sit in our pews!

Conclusion

A. *Let us wait for the Breath of God, knowing he is indispensable.*

B. *Let us never seek to live on our own artificial life survival kits.*

C. *Let us remember that the Aeolean harp is made for the music that only the blowing of the wind across its strings can bring.* Our heartstrings are made for the blessed times when "the wind bloweth."

SUNDAY EVENING, JULY 28

Title: Our God Is Able

Text: "O Daniel, servant of the living God, is thy God, whom thou servest continually, able to deliver thee from the lions?" **(Dan. 6:20)**.

Scripture Reading: Daniel 6:1–23

Introduction

The Scripture lesson describes some political skulduggery on the part of some government officials in the kingdom of Darius, king of the Medes. Daniel, the Hebrew prophet of God and wise counselor, had been elevated to a position of prominence in the kingdom. The citizens of that country were jealous of him and plotted to bring about his downfall. They sought to do this in connection with his faithfulness to God (Dan. 6:5).

Daniel the prophet persisted in his practice of worshiping God even when his life was in danger. As a result of this total experience, he discovered that God was a very present help in a time of great trouble (cf. Ps. 46:1; Heb. 11:6). Daniel verified the hopeful wish of a pagan king who expressed rare confidence in the power of Daniel's God: "Daniel, Thy God whom thou servest continually, he will deliver thee" (Dan. 6:16). Daniel discovered the power of the living God because of the steadfastness of his faith in God.

Daniel is for us a dramatic example of one who lived in a dynamic relationship with God. We can assume that his life was one of joy and gratitude.

The New Testament portrays a group of people who lived lives of joy, victory, and gratitude. They demonstrated an amazing spirit of vitality and optimism.

These New Testament believers were energetic, optimistic, and positive. They were superbly adequate for the dangerous hour in which they lived. In reading the New Testament, we often find sudden lyrical outbursts of doxology. The inspired writers were characterized by an attitude of thanksgiving. Why was this so?

They discovered in Jesus Christ that God was alive and available with love and power to meet the deepest needs of human nature. They tested the promises of Jesus Christ and found them to be true.

These New Testament Christians had entered into an understanding of what really happened on the cross. They were overwhelmed with the victory that was achieved by the conquest of Christ over death and the grave. They were gripped by a new presence and power because of the coming of the Holy Spirit on Pentecost.

I. Our God is able to supply sufficiently the material needs of life (2 Cor. 9:6–8, 10).

Modern people worry unnecessarily about the material necessities of life.

A. *Material blessings are the lesser blessings of God.*

B. *Paul was encouraging the Corinthian Christians to be generous in their contributions to others.* God would bless them with a generous harvest.

C. *Paul was encouraging purposeful and proportionate giving on the part of these people to meet the needs of those who were suffering material difficulty.* Paul was encouraging them to be generous on the basis of thoughtful commitment rather than waiting for a mood or an impulse. He was encouraging them by reminding them of God's ability to meet their needs. "And God is able to provide you with every blessing in abundance, so that you may always have enough of everything and may provide in abundance for every good work.... He who supplies seed to the sower and bread for food will supply and multiply your resources and increase the harvest of your righteousness" (2 Cor. 9:8, 10 RSV).

II. Our God is able to save to the uttermost (Heb. 7:25).

The early followers of our Lord rejoiced in a full and complete salvation.

A. *They were confident that Christ had saved them from the penalty of sin, which is the death of separation from God.*

B. *They were confident that Christ was saving them from the power and practice of sin.* They experienced his strength in the time of temptation. They believed that he was able to assist them because he had overcome temptation (Heb. 2:18; cf. James 4:4).

C. *They were confident that Christ would eventually deliver them from the very presence of evil (Phil. 3:2–12; 1 Thess. 4:16–18).*

III. Our God is able to surpass our highest dreams (Eph. 3:16–20).

A. *God has a wonderful plan for our lives in the here and now.*

B. *God has made wonderful provisions for his children in the hereafter (John 14:1–3).*

Those who trust and obey Jesus Christ discover a joy, a fulfillment, and a happiness that they never dreamed possible before they came to have faith in him.

IV. Our God is able to provide perfect security for eternity (2 Tim. 1:12).

Paul faced the future in the confidence that he had entrusted his all into the hands of one who was adequate and capable to provide for him that which he needed as he faced the issues of eternity.

A. *It is good to have life insurance.*

B. *It is good to have fire insurance.*

C. *It is very wise to have liability insurance.*

Conclusion

Only in the grace and goodness of God can we find the security we will need when the storms of life beat down upon us. This security must be secured personally through faith in Jesus Christ. This security must be secured while one has opportunity and when God draws near and issues his call to repentance and faith. This security can be secured today through faith in Jesus Christ. Commit your past, present, and future to him in faith and faithfulness.

WEDNESDAY EVENING, JULY 31

Title: The Gain of Death

Text: "To die is gain" (**Phil. 1:21**).

Scripture Reading: Philippians 3:20–21

Introduction

Paul was a prisoner facing the possibility of being put to death following his trial before Caesar. As he contemplated such a possibility, he came to the conclusion that for him death would be a blessing. For him dying would be gaining rather than losing. We can find hints in the Scriptures that might help us to understand why Paul thought that for the Christian death would bring gain. A number of suggestions can be made at this point.

I. The Christian gains the presence of Christ at death (2 Cor. 5:8).

Although we are always in the presence of God, in a new and unique way we enter into his presence through the doorway of death. Jesus spoke to the repentant sinner while on the cross and said to him, "Today shalt thou be with me in paradise" (Luke 23:43).

II. At death the Christian will gain heaven, and this will be wonderful (John 14:1–3).

Heaven is a prepared place for a prepared people. Heaven will be a place of fellowship, not only with God, but with the family of God. We are separated from our loved ones only for a while. Through death we go to join those who have died in the Lord.

III. For the Christian, to die will be gain because he will be done with sin.

Sin is to blame for the suffering, sorrow, and tragedy of this life. We are troubled by the presence of sin in our own hearts, in the hearts of others, and in the world about us. Our only hope of escaping the contaminating effects of sin is through the Lord Jesus Christ. We will cease to be tormented by sin when either the Lord returns for us or we go to meet him in death.

It will be wonderful to be with our Lord without the limitations and hindrances that sin has put on us. It will be wonderful to have complete victory over the sin that has threatened to enslave us and to degrade us.

IV. For the Christian, to die will be gain because suffering will be a thing of the past (Rev. 21:4).

There will be no more suffering, pain, tears, or death. These things will have passed away once we enter into the presence of our living Lord.

V. For the Christian, to die is to gain rest (Rev. 14:13).

The rest of which Scripture speaks does not refer to a state of stagnation and idleness. Instead it refers to a release and relief from that which was painful and burdensome in life. We shall not "rest and rust" in heaven. The Bible tells us, "His servants shall serve him" (Rev. 22:3).

Conclusion

Life is wonderful. It is a precious thing to be in the land of the living. We have an opportunity here that we will not have in heaven: we can give our verbal testimony to the unsaved now. We will not be able to do that after we have entered heaven.

God has left us on earth for a redemptive purpose. He is not ready for us in heaven yet. There are services to be rendered. There are ministries to be given. There is work to be done. Let us do God's work in the world today while we are alive and while we have opportunity. Let us be comforted by the faith that for the Christian to die is to experience gain rather than loss.

AUGUST

- ## Sunday Mornings

    Continue the series "Symbols for the Spirit."

- ## Sunday Evenings

    "The Manner of Our Ministry" is the theme of these messages that deal with the ministries that we are to render to others in the name of the Lord.

- ## Wednesday Evenings

    Continue the studies based on Paul's epistle to the Philippians with the theme "Words of Encouragement from the Apostle Paul."

SUNDAY MORNING, AUGUST 4

Title: The Holy Spirit as Oil

Text: "Then he answered and spake unto me, saying, This is the word of the LORD unto Zerubbabel, saying, Not by might, nor by power, but by my spirit, saith the LORD of hosts" **(Zech. 4:6)**.

Scripture Reading: Zechariah 4:1–6

Hymns: "Holy Spirit, Faithful Guide," Wells

              "Come, Thou Almighty King," Anonymous

              "Pentecostal Power," Gabriel

Offertory Prayer: Our Father, let us not forget that you are the one who gives us the power to get wealth. May it dawn upon us increasingly that it is for you and your glory that we are entrusted with it. We honor the Lord with our substance and with the firstfruits of our increase. As we grow in our stewardship, help us to know the meaning of the greater blessedness "to give than to receive" (Acts 20:35). Grant us your grace to know this new blessing as from week to week we bring our tithes to this storehouse. In the name of Jesus we lift our prayer. Amen.

Introduction

Since oil is a major industry in our country, the figure of the Holy Spirit as oil ought to have special significance for many of us. Wherever we live, oil is a richly endowed symbol. We are reminded that we have sought to know the Holy Spirit better through four previous sermons in which we have considered the Holy Spirit in the biblical symbols of person, dove, fire, and wind. No more fruitful figure is found than that of oil.

Before we come to some of the practical suggestions, let us seek to recapture Zechariah's vision. An angel appeared to him and asked, "What do you see?" The prophet answered, "I see a solid gold lampstand with a bowl at the top and seven lamps on it, with seven channels to the lamps. Also there are two olive trees by it, one on the right of the bowl and the other on its left." When Zechariah asked what these were, the angel replied, "Do you not know what these are?" When Zerubbabel answered that he did not know, the angel interpreted the vision: "This is the word of the Lord to Zerubbabel: 'Not my might nor by power, but by my Spirit,' says the Lord Almighty" (Zech. 4:2–6 NIV).

I. The Holy Spirit provides the energy for light.

The bowl atop the golden lampstand was for the storage of the oil. The pipes carried the oil to each of the seven lamps. The burning oil provided light. Likewise, when the oil of the Spirit is in the "bowl of the soul" there is substantive energy for light. Where the oil is absent, a person's lamp is dark.

Someone has paraphrased the oft-quoted verse 6: "It is not by organization, nor by manipulation, but by my Spirit, saith the Lord of hosts." Organization may march around Jericho by companies for seven days, manipulation may blow the trumpets and break the pitchers, but only God can make the walls come tumbling down. Organization may seat the men by fifties on the grass, manipulation may distribute the loaves and fishes, but only the Spirit can provide the divine multiplication that makes possible the feeding of the multitude. Organization can put a man at each corner of a sick man's pallet, manipulation can tear a hole in the roof and let him down before the Lord, but only the Spirit of God can make his healed body stand and shout for joy.

In Matthew 25 Jesus told the story of the ten young women who went out to meet the bridegroom. They were very nearly alike. All were young. All were on a proper mission. All were present, dressed, and on time. The only difference was that "they that were foolish took their lamps, and took no oil with them" (v. 3). The wise took their lamps filled with oil. When the lamps of the foolish began to fail, they said to the five wise maidens, "Give us of your oil; for our lamps are gone out" (v. 8). It was that simple: no oil, no light. Their lament may well describe the plight of many today: "Our lamps are going out." We are in respectable places, following commendable schedules, and doing proper things, but "our lamps are going out." We fret and fuss, we blame others, we push panic buttons, but "our lamps are going out."

Must the lamp of any Christian go out for lack of oil? No. Do not forget Zechariah 4:3: "There are two olive trees by it, one on the right of the bowl and the other on its left" (NIV). The living olive trees provided perpetual olives from which the oil came. There is no need for the bowl to run dry as long as the olive trees live and bear fruit.

And there is no need for Christians in whom the Holy Spirit dwells ever to cry, "Our lamps are going out." Our Lord reminded us, "Let your light so shine before men." Only by the oil of the Spirit can our lamps keep burning.

II. The Holy Spirit prepares for service.

"And thou shalt anoint Aaron and his sons, and consecrate them, that they may minister unto me in the priest's office" (Ex. 30:30).

More than 150 times the Bible speaks of anointing. Priests were anointed for service, and kings were anointed for leadership. The psalmist spoke of God's goodness: "Thou anointest my head with oil" (Ps. 23:5). It was a symbol of initiation, of readiness to serve.

The anointing oil of the Spirit is the signature of God himself. When the sons of Aaron offered unauthorized fire before the Lord, the fire of God's judgment went out, and they died before the Lord. Moses then gave instructions and said to his sons, "The anointing oil of the LORD is upon you" (Lev. 10:7). Their action was determined by their being anointed with oil. It is so with all the priests of God, all Christians. We are to obey because of the oil; we are to act in the light of our anointing.

All through the Bible anointing with oil means a license to practice, readiness for ministry, God's validation of his commissions to people. We wait for the anointing of the Holy Spirit before we go into action. The oil upon us precedes obedience within us. We are never ready to serve until we are anointed with the oil of the Spirit, but we can always serve when the Spirit has set us apart for service. To undertake an assignment from God without the anointing of God is an anomaly before God.

III. The Holy Spirit produces healing.

"Is any sick among you? let him call for the elders of the church; and let them pray over him, anointing him with oil in the name of the Lord" (James 5:14).

Throughout the New Testament, oil was used as an agent of healing. It was not to be the gimmick of the fake healers. It had a practical medicinal value. It was a common practice to massage with oil. Oil was also used for cleaning and sealing out foreign substances. The Good Samaritan poured oil and wine on the wounds of the beaten man on the Jericho road (Luke 10:34).

This does not mean that if we are filled with the Spirit we will be healed of all our ailments (2 Cor. 7:9). F. E. Marsh has reminded us, "The Lord can heal, He has healed, He may heal, He does heal, and He may not heal." We must not insist that God heal in the ways and by the means that we prescribe. We must not affirm God's power to heal and at the same time deny his right to use whatever means he chooses for that healing.

Our spirits are sometimes wounded and bruised. We may bear open sores of distrust, prejudice, or hate. We may burn with the fever of faithlessness. Thus we greatly need the healing anointing of the oil of the Spirit on our troubled bodies and souls!

Conclusion

A. *Let us be grateful to God for his constant supply of oil for our lamps.* Therefore, "let your light so shine before men" (Matt. 5:16).

B. *Let us be mindful that we have been anointed for the priesthood of the believers.* Therefore, let us be faithful as "priests unto God" (Rev. 1:6).

C. *Let us be sensitive to the healing oil of the Spirit in a world of multiple ailments.* Therefore, let us maintain a close relationship with the Holy Spirit, for "the Spirit also helpeth our infirmities" (Rom. 8:26).

SUNDAY EVENING, AUGUST 4

Title: Applying Our Answer

Text: "Then Peter said, Silver and gold have I none; but such as I have give I thee: In the name of Jesus Christ of Nazareth rise up and walk. And he took him by the right hand, and lifted him up: and immediately his feet and ankle bones received strength" **(Acts 3:6–7)**.

Scripture Reading: Acts 3:1–10

Introduction

We have heard of a credibility gap and of a generation gap, but there is another gap: the application gap. The application gap refers to the length of time between a scientific discovery and its application. This gap has shrunk amazingly. It is estimated that from the discovery of the telegraph to its commercial application took fifty-six years; for the radio, thirty-four years; for radar, fifteen years; for television, twelve years; for atomic power, six years; and for transistors, five years. Now in this age of computers, the Internet, and digital technology, there is hardly a gap at all. By the time we inhale and exhale, it seems as if a discovery has already made its application.

Christians also suffer from an application gap. It takes us a long time to apply what we have learned from Christ. Christ came to relieve human needs — both physical and spiritual. In Christ, we have the answer for all our needs. We need to apply the answer and apply it more quickly.

Peter and John did just that. The lame man asked for gifts; they gave him grace. There were some things they could not give him — silver and gold, for instance. But there was one thing they could give him: the application of the answer that Jesus Christ gave to his need.

Ministry is the application of our answer in Jesus Christ to human needs.

I. The request to apply our answer.

A. *A common cry.* To Peter and John the beggar made a common cry. It was a request that he made to others all day every day. He wanted gifts.

There are some cries that are heard every day. Every day we hear cries of hunger and loneliness and cries born of the need for love, the search for meaning, and fear of the future.

B. *A complete answer.* Christ is the answer to all these problems.

"Look on us," Peter said. Peter was asking the beggar to really look at them, to *see* them, rather than just to be aware of them as passing figures.

Could the church dare to say to the world, "Look at me! I have the answer to your painful problems"?

But it was not a complete answer until it was applied. The precious gift of life in Christ cannot be kept; it must be given away.

II. The resources for applying our answer.

A. *The words about resources.*

1. A negative word: "Silver and gold have I none...." Peter first told the beggar what he did *not* have to give him. Many of us major on the negative resources. All we can consider when ministry is mentioned is what we do not have.

2. A positive word: "... but such as I have give I thee." Peter could not give him gifts of money. But he had something far greater to give. And what could Peter, the poor fisherman, give? He could give concern, willingness, and the power of Christ.

B. *The worth of resources.* The greatest resources the Christian church has are people and power.

1. People. People who care and are willing to serve Christ form a reservoir for ministry.

2. Power. The power with which ministry is performed is not personal power; it is the power of the risen Christ applied to the lives of individuals. It was "in the name of Jesus Christ of Nazareth" that the man was to rise and walk. And he did.

III. The results of applying our answer.

A. *Action.* Something happened when Peter and John applied the answer of Christ to the life of this lame man. The man was healed.

Consider all that could happen in our churches if we began to apply the answer that we have in Christ. Think of the healing, the helping, the comforting, the guiding, the relieving of acute human needs that would occur when we applied this answer.

A small boy was once asked why he walked three miles every week to D. L. Moody's church in Chicago. The boy replied, "They love a fellow over there" (John C. Pollock, *Moody* [Grand Rapids: Zondervan, 1967], 54).

B. *Amazement.* The world is looking for something to amaze it. People troop in masses to circuses, museums, amusement parks, sports stadiums, and national parks to see something that will amaze them.

A demonstration of the power of God at work in human lives is an amazing thing. It will happen when we apply our answer.

Conclusion

The greatest discovery of all time will not help persons until it is given practical application. We have this discovery in Jesus Christ. Now let us apply our answer.

WEDNESDAY EVENING, AUGUST 7

Title: Living Worthy of the Glad Tidings

Text: "Whatever happens, conduct yourselves in a manner worthy of the gospel of Christ" **(Phil. 1:27 NIV)**.

Scripture Reading: 2 Corinthians 3:1–3

Introduction

The apostle Paul was torn between two desires. He wanted to step through the veil and enter into the very presence of the living Christ. He considered this to be the best option for himself. When he considered the needs of his friends in Philippi, he came to the conclusion that it was better that he remain so that he might assist them in their progress toward spiritual maturity and in their efforts to tell the glad tidings of the living Christ who had conquered sin, death, and the grave.

In the words of our text, Paul challenged the Philippians to make certain that their lives corresponded with their message. He was encouraging them to do effective preaching by means of their practice. Paul used the same word translated "conduct" in Philippians 3:20 to refer to believers' "citizenship." Paul was saying that believers are citizens of Christ's kingdom—that is, their citizenship is in heaven. So Paul's challenge to them was that they live as citizens of the kingdom of heaven while dwelling in the city of Philippi, a province of the Roman Empire.

I. Desirable characteristics.

A. *We must stand steady and faithful (Phil. 1:27; Eph. 4:1; 6:13–14).*

B. *We must create and maintain a spirit of unity within the fellowship of believers (Phil. 1:27).*

C. *We must not permit ourselves to be terrified by opposition (Phil. 1:28).* Knox translates this phrase: "Show a bold front at all points to your adversaries."

D. *We must be willing to suffer for the sake of Christ and his cause when necessary (Phil. 1:29).*

II. Necessary attitudes of mind and heart.

A. *Humility and gratitude for salvation from the penalty of sin.* The glad tidings of how Christ was willing to suffer and die for our salvation should encourage both humility and gratitude.

B. *Confidence and trust as we struggle with the presence of sin in the present.* We live in a sinful world that is antagonistic to Christ and his disciples. Even though we are redeemed, sin is ever with us. Life will be a struggle to the end.

C. *Hope and joy as we face the future.* Our salvation is from God. He grants us salvation from the penalty of sin through faith in Christ. He works within to deliver us from the power of sin. He holds before us the promise of deliverance even from the presence of sin in the consummation of the ages when Christ returns.

244

Conclusion

Paul speaks of some great privileges that we have (Phil. 1:29). We have the privilege of believing in Christ and of suffering for his sake. We also have the privilege of serving him.

Perhaps our highest privilege is communicating the glad tidings of salvation through Christ to a needy world. We must live worthy of the glad tidings if we would be effective in ministering to others.

SUNDAY MORNING, AUGUST 11

Title: The Holy Spirit as Chief Counsel

Text: "Nevertheless I tell you the truth: It is expedient for you that I go away: for if I go not away, the Comforter will not come unto you; but if I depart, I will send him unto you" **(John 16:7)**.

Scripture Reading: John 16:7–14; 1 John 2:1

Hymns: "Holy Ghost, with Light Divine," Reed

"Holy Spirit, from on High," Bathurst

"Holy Spirit, Faithful Guide," Wells

Offertory Prayer: Our Father, teach us daily how to be *in* the world but not *of* the world. We do not want the luxury of isolation or insulation from the needs of our world. And so, as an act of helping to meet these needs, and for your glory, we bring our tithes and offerings today, in the name of Jesus. Amen.

Introduction

Billy Sunday is credited with the line that Jesus put the jam on the lower shelves of the pantry so that the little folk could reach it. This is another way of saying that Jesus talked in terms people understood. He put his message within the reach of all of us "little folk."

I. The name of counsel.

In his promise of the Holy Spirit, Jesus used the word *paraklētos*. It means "one called alongside." The same word is used in 1 John 2:1 with reference to Jesus and is translated "advocate." Webster defines an advocate as "one who pleads the cause of another, as before a tribunal or judicial court; a counselor, one who defends or espouses any cause by argument, a pleader … an intercessor." So in today's language, perhaps the best personification of this idea of the Holy Spirit is an attorney, a lawyer, a chief counsel who stands alongside us and argues our case and pleads our cause. This helps to put this unique fact of the Holy Spirit's ministry down where we can reach it. Jesus is our Advocate at the right hand of the Father, pleading our case. The Holy Spirit is the Father's Advocate in our world, representing him and pleading his case.

245

II. The need of counsel.

A. *We need counsel because the natural person is in trouble.* This is an understatement in the perspective of one brief look at our world: "Something went wrong." People were created in the likeness of God. Thus it was necessary for people to have a will. This asset became a liability when people used it to choose evil. The sins of people are deliberate: "We have turned every one to his own way" (Isa. 53:6). "For there is not a just man upon earth, that doeth good, and sinneth not" (Eccl. 7:20). "For all have sinned, and come short of the glory of God" (Rom. 3:23). The result is tragic: "For the wages of sin is death" (6:23).

B. *We need counsel because we do not have a perfect knowledge of the laws of God.* Who can understand his ways? "There is none that understandeth, there is none that seeketh after God" (Rom. 3:11). "For my thoughts are not your thoughts, neither are your ways my ways, saith the LORD. For as the heavens are higher than the earth, so are my ways higher than your ways, and my thoughts than your thoughts" (Isa. 55:8–9).

C. *We need counsel because our "do-it-yourself" method has failed.* This is a do-it-yourself generation. Look at the shade-tree mechanics or the Saturday builders or the Sunday yard men. Look at the kits for sale that you put together yourself. This syndrome of doing it yourself has crept increasingly into the area of the spiritual and especially into the central matter of salvation. I have a small model of an antique car that is partially assembled. I cannot get it together; the pieces do not fit. People are like that. We simply have not been able to put ourselves together successfully in our wisdom and strength. The leopard still cannot change its spots. People cannot save themselves. Salvation is not the achievement of people; it is the gift of God.

III. The nature of counsel.

It would be impossible, of course, to list all the adjectives that describe the Holy Spirit. He is holy, eternal, omnipotent, active, sensitive, friendly, constant, and incomparable.

To bring the "jam down to the lower shelves where the little folk can reach it," Hicks Epton—at the time the president of the American College of Trial Lawyers—offered to share what he considered the ten top qualifications for a trial lawyer. We consider our heavenly Advocate in terms of his contemporary scale of virtues.

A. *Diligence.* There is no substitute for the constancy of pursuit. Our Advocate is diligent. "But the Comforter, which is the Holy Ghost, whom the Father will send in my name, he shall teach you all things, and bring all things to your remembrance, whatsoever I have said unto you" (John 14:26). "And I will pray the Father, and he shall give you another Comforter, that he may abide with you for ever" (v. 16).

B. *Courage.* Legal counsel must be courageous. Our larger text indicates that our Advocate does three things that, were he human, would require supreme courage.

    1. He convicts the world of sin. This is because unbelief in Christ is the taproot of all sin.

    2. He convicts of righteousness. This is because Jesus, the embodiment of righteousness, would no longer be with people in the flesh as a visible pattern of the righteousness of God.

    3. He convicts of judgment. This is because the prince of the world, Satan, has been judged on Calvary; his defeat and our victory are already settled.

C. *Loyalty.* The earthly attorney must manifest complete loyalty. What about our heavenly Advocate? "Likewise the Spirit also helpeth our infirmities: for we know not what we should pray for as we ought: but the Spirit itself maketh intercession for us with groanings which cannot be uttered. And he that searcheth the hearts knoweth what is the mind of the Spirit, because he maketh intercession for the saints according to the will of God" (Rom. 8:26–27).

D. *Humility.* If this be a mark of a good attorney, how much more is it a becoming characteristic of our Advocate! True humility is not thinking of oneself as a worm; it is not thinking of oneself at all. "For he shall not speak of himself; but whatsoever he shall hear, that shall he speak: and he shall show you things to come. He shall glorify me" (John 16:13–14).

E. *Right perspective.* The good attorney keeps his perspective of the total picture. He does not fail because of one fragment. "Howbeit when he, the Spirit of truth, is come, he will guide you into *all* truth" (John 16:13). Three times in these three verses (vv. 13–15) Jesus promised that the Holy Spirit would show them things from the Father, things from the Son, and things of the future. He can show us all because he sees all.

F. *Sincerity.* The practicing attorney must be sincere, a true advocate rather than an affected actor. The sober credentials of our Advocate are promised by our Lord, and the Spirit has never negated the promise: "But when the Comforter is come, whom I will send unto you from the Father, even the Spirit of truth, which proceedeth from the Father, he shall testify of me" (John 15:26).

G. *Self-subordination.* The good attorney subordinates his own ego to the cause. Particularly graphic is this translation: "When the Holy Spirit, who is truth, comes ... He will not be presenting his own ideas, but will be passing on to you what He has heard" (John 16:13 TLB).

H. *Person awareness.* The good attorney always remembers that he is dealing with human beings. The ultimate importance is not legal papers but living people. The prophet spoke of the Holy Spirit in relation to, and awareness of, people. "I will pour out my spirit upon all flesh; and your sons and your daughters ... your old men ... your young men ... the servants ... the handmaids" (Joel 2:28–29). He works through people, with people, and for people.

I. *Leadership.* The good attorney is captain of the trial ship. He is on top of things. Our Chief Counsel is in control, and the victorious verdict comes with the assurance that "it is not by organization, nor by manipulation, but by my Spirit, saith the LORD of hosts" (Zech. 4:6, my paraphrase).

J. *Representation.* The profession is measured by the practitioner. Our divine Advocate bears in mind not only the majesty and name of the Trinity but judgment and justice for those whom our Lord said "shall believe on [him] through their word" (John 17:20).

Conclusion

A. *We are in trouble.*

B. *We are not equipped to represent ourselves in the supreme court of the soul.*

C. *We have adequate counsel—available, competent, and ready—in the Holy Spirit, heaven's court-appointed Advocate.*

SUNDAY EVENING, AUGUST 11

Title: A Pattern for Ministry

Text: "And, behold, men brought in a bed a man which was taken with a palsy: and they sought means to bring him in, and to lay him before him" **(Luke 5:18)**.

Scripture Reading: Luke 5:18–26

Introduction

In its simplest form, ministry is caring for others and sharing Christ and concern with them in meeting both their physical and spiritual needs. C. W. Brister wrote, "The servant motif of ministry was established ... as the Bible's most characteristic way of viewing the people of God. The church, like her Lord, is to be in the world as one who serves" (C. W. Brister, *Pastoral Care in the Church* [New York: Harper & Row, 1964], 83). We have a great need for a pattern for ministry. In the incident in which four men brought a paralyzed man to Jesus, we have such a pattern.

I. The purpose for ministry.

The purpose for ministry is to bring people to Jesus Christ and to help them mature in Christ. We are not the ones who heal, who forgive, who save, and who give meaning, purpose, and direction in life. Christ does that. These men were willing to go to a great deal of trouble to bring their friend to Christ.

II. The possibilities of ministry.

The possibilities of ministry are all around us. They are limited only by our concern, compassion, and ingenuity. The four men were interested in the possibility of ministry. By their concern they were able to find the possibility.

Carlyle Marney wrote about a man who once had served as pastor of a Christian congregation. But there were elements of freedom and inspiration in his personality that meant that no code or creed or rule or set of dogmas could quite confine him, and he left his official position. In a visit with him, Marney asked, "What do you do now to exercise your calling since you have no congregation and no pulpit?" He answered, "Who says I have no congregation? There is a lot of grief and pain that I can sit by" (Carlyle Marney, *Beggars in Velvet* [Nashville: Abingdon, 1960], 106).

In every neighborhood there is a lot of grief and pain that a Christian can sit by. The possibilities of ministry are all around us. We just have to be alert enough and sensitive enough to see them.

III. The performance of ministry.

A. *Priority.* Ministry must be a priority item for churches and Christians. It is not optional. It strikes at the very heart of the meaning of the Christian faith. Ministry was such a priority for these four friends that they were willing to do some unusual things to accomplish it.

B. *Patience.* Ministry takes patience. The amount of patience it took for these friends is obvious: they had to be patient enough to find another way of access to Christ. They had to be patient enough to remove the roof in order to let their friend into the presence of Christ. In ministry the results may not occur as quickly as we would like. The people may not respond just the way we would want them to respond. But patience in ministering in Christ's name is demanded.

C. *Persistence.* Persistence paid off for these ministering friends. Because of persistence, they were able to achieve their goal of getting their friend into Jesus' presence.

IV. The promise of ministry.

Christ promised healing and comfort to all who would come to him. But in coming to Christ, this man received an even greater gift: the forgiveness of sin.

Jesus had to prove the spiritual by the physical. The Jews did not think that he had the power to forgive sin. Only God could do that. When Jesus forgave the man's sin, he was assuming the prerogative of God. Perhaps, too, they had connected sin and suffering, thinking that the man could not be healed until he was forgiven. Jesus, to show that he had the power of forgiving, which they could not see, gave the man healing, which they could see.

Jesus always delivers what he promises. Jess Moody has observed that many people will go to the corner bar when they will not go to the church because the bar delivers what it promises (Jess Moody, *A Drink at Joel's Place* [Waco: Word, 1967], 17–22). Through Jesus Christ the church declares that whole persons are important, that all the needs of people are significant, and that Jesus can meet all those needs.

The promise of ministry is that we can show spiritual power by physical acts and that Christ can deliver what has been promised to others through his power.

Conclusion

We have a pattern for ministry. Now we need to follow that pattern in order to follow Christ's example as a minister.

WEDNESDAY EVENING, AUGUST 14

Title: A Plea for Unity

Text: "Make my joy complete by being like-minded, having the same love, being one in spirit and of one mind" **(Phil. 2:2 NIV).**

Scripture Reading: Philippians 2:1–11

Introduction

The churches of the apostolic period were plagued with diversity and division, even as is the case with present-day congregations. This lack of a warm unifying love that expresses itself in a unity of action was a hindrance then, even as it is a hindrance now.

God's family is a human family. It is no small achievement when we experience a unity of heart, of mind, and of effort that makes it possible for the Spirit of God to do his greatest work through us. The church at Philippi was threatened with disunity. Among the many things that were disturbing the fellowship of this dynamic congregation was a breach of fellowship between two of the leading women of the congregation (Phil. 4:2–3). The names of these two women are significant. Euodia means "prosperous journey" or "sweet fragrance," and Syntyche means "good luck." We can only speculate concerning the cause for this breach of fellowship between these two leading women. Their disagreement was hurtful to the church. Naturally, Paul was concerned. We can assume that this was not the only thing that disrupted the fellowship of the church at Philippi.

Paul makes a personal appeal to Euodia and Syntyche to settle all of their differences. He declares that if they will do so, this will make him happy and cause his cup of joy to overflow.

It is interesting to notice the basis for his real appeal for unity. The basis for such is found in verse 1 of the chapter.

I. He appeals to their relationship with Jesus Christ.

Each genuine believer had had a personal experience with Jesus Christ. They had recognized him as the promised Savior. They had trusted and received him as the Lord of their lives. He had entered their hearts. He was the one appointed to be their Lord. Paul appeals to their common experience with and relationship to Jesus Christ as a basis for unifying their thoughts and emotions and energy in the Lord's work.

250

II. He appeals to their new understanding and experience of love.

Because of God's love for them, they have experienced the gift of forgiveness and the bestowal of spiritual life. The Holy Spirit has brought the love of God into their hearts. This love was undeserved. It cannot be merited. It is free and wonderful.

Our Lord's new commandment to his followers was to the effect that they should love each other as he had loved them (John 13:34–35). Paul appeals to the Philippians for an expression of this divine love that they might function in unity as a congregation and as a work force for the Lord in the pagan city of Philippi.

III. He appeals to their experience of the Holy Spirit.

The Holy Spirit opened their eyes to the lostness of their condition without Christ. He magnified and exalted Jesus Christ as the one who could forgive their sins and give them new life. He gave them assurance of salvation and dwelled within them to accomplish God's work.

The apostle appeals to them to respond to the presence and power of the Holy Spirit who was seeking to lead them into spiritual unity where they could function effectively as the servants of Jesus Christ.

IV. His final appeal is on the basis of compassion within the heart.

Paul challenges them on the basis of their love for God and for him personally. He is saying to them, "If you have compassion for me or for the work of God, then you should work for a unity of mind and heart and soul in the Lord's work."

Conclusion

Are you out of harmony with members of your family? Are you out of harmony with members in the congregation where you worship? A lack of harmony and fellowship will hurt your own spiritual testimony and will deprive you of joy.

Because of your relationship to Christ, your experience of love, your fellowship in the Spirit, and your compassion, it is possible for you to love some who are unlovely and to at least be agreeable with some who may be difficult at times.

Division, strife, and hostility reflect on the cause of Christ. These must be avoided if we want to be pleasing to our Savior and be effective in our witness to an unsaved world.

SUNDAY MORNING, AUGUST 18

Title: The Holy Spirit as a Seal

Text: "Do not grieve the Holy Spirit of God, with whom you were sealed for the day of redemption" **(Eph. 4:30 NIV)**.

Scripture Reading: Ephesians 1:1–14

Hymns: "Since I Have Been Redeemed," Excell

"One Day," Chapman

"Seal Us, O Holy Spirit," Meredith

Offertory Prayer: Our Father, teach us that our well-being is not a product of our well-doing. We hear your word as it speaks to us: "Know ye that the LORD he is God: it is he that hath made us, and not we ourselves; we are his people, and the sheep of his pasture" (Ps. 100:3). You have not only made us, but you have made both the provisions and the capacity for us to enjoy all the good things we have. So, now, we gladly bring our tithes and offerings to our Maker, through our dear Lord. Amen.

Introduction

Words are vehicles that carry cargoes of wealth. Words are coined treasures that provide a medium of exchange for the riches of God. The symbol of the Holy Spirit as a "seal" comes to us loaded and impregnated with the wealth of the soul. In these Ephesian passages, there are four arresting ideas.

I. A prohibition (Eph. 4:30).

"Do not grieve the Holy Spirit of God" (NIV). He who helps us with our burdens must not be hurt with our adding other burdens deliberately. Because the Holy Spirit is a person, he has the capacity of being grieved. He can be hurt, offended, slighted. The word *lupeo*, which is used for "grieve," carries with it the idea of affliction. Before (4:25–29) and after (vv. 31–32) the text there is a list of human vices and virtues. The tense of the word "grieve" adds force to the prohibition. We are not to continue in a pattern of conduct that grieves the Holy Spirit. Every child has grieved his parents. Every child of God has at times grieved his heavenly Father. But to grieve him as a singular happening is not the same as to grieve him as a habit of life. Our conduct is to be such that it will bring joy to our heavenly Father.

The searching words of Oswald J. Smith may be pressed close to the heart of every Christian:

> *Have I grieved Thy Holy Spirit?*
> *Have I quenched His pow'r within?*
> *If I have, O Lord, forgive me,*
> *Cleanse my heart from every sin.*

II. A performance (Eph. 1:1–14).

A seal is always a silent testimony of a transaction. Something goes before the sealing and something is anticipated afterward. God does something to and for his children. See what God has done now!

A. *He has blessed us (v. 3).*
B. *He has chosen us (v. 4).*
C. *He has predestinated us (v. 5).*

D. *He has adopted us (v. 5).*

E. *He has accepted us (v. 6).*

F. *He has redeemed us (v. 7).*

G. *He has forgiven us (v. 7).*

H. *He has shared the mystery with us (v. 9).*

I. *He has remembered us in his will (v. 11).*

J. *Following all of these, he has sealed us "with that holy Spirit of promise" (v. 13).*

Where there is evidence of the seal of the Holy Spirit, it indicates that God has not been idle. "The Lord hath done great things for us; whereof we are glad" (Ps. 126:3).

III. A picture (Eph. 4:30).

A. *The seal meant sovereignty.* Sometimes precious documents or other parcels were enclosed securely and hot wax dropped on the seams. While the wax was still warm, the king would use his ring to stamp his royal insignia into the warm wax, leaving the seal of sovereignty when the wax hardened. But only a person with authority could affix his seal.

The Holy Spirit on the Christian is God's sovereign mark. As the notary public has the sovereign and exclusive right to use her seal in the light of her commission and covenant, so the divine seal of the Holy Spirit speaks of the sovereign right and covenant relationship of God. He never takes his Seal lightly or uses him carelessly.

B. *The seal meant signature.* As suggested before, the seal was a sort of notarized signature. When we are born again, we are born of the Spirit. We receive the Holy Spirit when we are saved. The Holy Spirit is the signature of God upon Christians—his new creations. The artist completes a beautiful painting and places his signature on it. We write a bank check and put our signature on it. The potter produces a lovely piece of art and places his mark or signature on it. The writer reveals his heartbeat on paper and puts his signature below what he has written.

It is so with God. How can we tell if the Christian product is real? "Hereby know we that we dwell in him, and he in us, because he hath given us of his Spirit" (1 John 4:13). The seal is the signature of God.

C. *The seal meant secrecy.* Frequently a secret was shared with an addressee far away by means of a sealed message. The message was not for publication but was reserved for those for whom the message was intended.

There is a sense in which the gospel of Jesus Christ is news—news to be published everywhere. Heralding it, we "publish glad tidings." In a sense, "it is no secret what God can do." But there is another side. Christians know something others do not know because they know Someone others do not know. The world's greatest mystery story is condensed into one verse: "And without controversy great is the mystery of godliness: God was manifest in the flesh, justified in the Spirit, seen of angels, preached unto the Gentiles, believed on in the world, received up into glory" (1 Tim. 3:16). The real secrets of salvation—of victorious living here and of life with God hereafter—are all under the seal of the Spirit.

D. *The seal meant security.* It was a lock to make that which was within secure. As long as the seal remained, the contents were secure.

It is true in the realm of the Spirit. When we are saved, the seal of the Spirit that accompanies our salvation makes us secure. Freedom from any condemnation is acclaimed by the seal of the Holy Spirit. "There is therefore now no condemnation to them which are in Christ Jesus, who walk not after the flesh, but after the Spirit. For the law of the Spirit of life in Christ Jesus hath made me free from the law of sin and death" (Rom. 8:1–2).

E. *The seal meant sincerity.* It was not a plaything. Because our church is incorporated within the laws of our state, the church has an official seal. But it is not kept in the nursery. It is not handled carelessly or used lightly. The church seal is used by our authorized trustees to validate and make binding certain contracts that involve present property and future promises. It is so with the Holy Spirit of God: "Ye were sealed with that holy Spirit of promise, which is the earnest of our inheritance until the redemption of the purchased possession, unto the praise of his glory" (Eph. 1:13–14). The Holy Spirit as a seal reflects the sincerity of God in a pledge in which God puts up earnest, the escrow if you please, as a guarantee that he will carry out his commitment to the contract.

Praise God, there is more to come, and the Holy Spirit with us now is heaven's guarantee that it shall be so then!

IV. A promise (Eph. 4:30).

" ... the Holy Spirit of God, with whom you were sealed for the day of redemption" (Eph. 4:30 NIV). Does this verse mean we are not yet redeemed? From spiritual death and the penalty of sin, yes. From the shackles of these physical bodies, from the spiritual environment of a corrupt society, from our own tendency to sin, from the limitations of human life, no. But someday our redemption will be complete. Praise God for the prophecy and the promise in the seal of the Holy Spirit!

Conclusion

In light of the Holy Spirit's seal on us, we will do the following:

A. *We will heed the prohibition not to grieve the Spirit.*

B. *We will appreciate God's performance.*

C. *We will contemplate the symbolic picture of the seal.*

D. *We will appropriate God's promise.*

SUNDAY EVENING, AUGUST 18

Title: Some Personal Questions about Ministry

Text: "And there came a leper to him, beseeching him, and kneeling down to him, and saying unto him, If thou wilt, thou canst make me clean. And Jesus, moved with compassion, put forth his hand, and touched him, and saith unto him, I will; be thou clean" (**Mark 1:40–41**).

Scripture Reading: Mark 1:40–45

254

Introduction

In the seventeenth century, Thomas Hobson rented out horses at Cambridge, England. He had a rule that any person who rented a horse must take the one standing nearest the stable door. No matter what station in life the customer held nor how the customer might wheedle and argue, Hobson stuck to his rule. It did not take long for "Hobson's choice," which really was no choice at all, to become a rather familiar phrase and pass into colloquial usage.

For Christians, ministry is a "Hobson's choice." They do not really have a choice about whether they will be ministers. Their only choice is about what kind of ministers they will be. Since this is true, there are some personal questions that every Christian should ask about his or her ministry.

For a background, consider the time that Jesus healed a leper who called to him as he passed by.

I. Some irrelevant questions.

A. *Does he deserve it?* There is no indication that Jesus ever asked that question of anyone. The presence of human need and suffering was reason enough for ministry in Jesus' eyes.

This man was diseased. He broke the law in approaching Jesus. But from Jesus came no word of reproach. We often ask, "Does he deserve it?" Jesus did not ask that question. To him it was irrelevant.

B. *Will he appreciate it?* Jesus did not ask if the man would appreciate what he could do for him. The man may not have appreciated it. But this did not deter Jesus. It is never any excuse not to minister to others just because they may not appreciate it. If we follow the pattern of Christ, we will not even ask that question.

II. Some relevant questions.

A. *Do I have compassionate concern?* When Jesus saw the leper, he was moved with pity. In all probability, this man was convinced that no one was concerned about him. He had been put outside the city. Others ministered to him only when they could not help it. But Jesus was compassionately concerned. He was so concerned that he did something about it: he healed the man.

There are many ways that we could minister if only we were concerned enough to do it. The problem many Christians face in ministry is not lack of opportunity but lack of compassion.

B. *What about the power to minister?* Jesus obviously had the power to minister. Somehow this man knew that Jesus had the power to do something for him.

The power to minister usually does not mean that we are able to do the spectacular things. The most effective ministry is sometimes in the simple, incidental things we do to help others.

Decades ago, a minister from Leeds, England, was fulfilling an engagement in Plymouth, England. Late in the evening he telephoned his wife. While waiting for the operator to put through the call, he murmured to himself a verse of a favorite hymn by Richard Baxter:

> *My knowledge of that life is small,*
> *The eye of faith is dim;*
> *But 'tis enough that Christ knows all*
> *And I shall be with Him.*

Suddenly a voice tinged with sadness came through the line, startling him by saying, "Say it again! Say it again!" The minister held the telephone more firmly and repeated the verse with intense eagerness. As he finished, the same piteous voice called back, "Thank you. Thank you" (Leonard Griffith, *Encounters with Christ* [New York: Harper & Row, 1965], 21–22). Even a simple and incidental act can minister to others' needs.

C. *Am I willing to minister?* Our own will is the turning point. The leper was convinced that Jesus had the power to help him, but he was not sure that Jesus had the desire. As it turned out, Jesus had both the power and the desire to minister to his need. Jesus touched him. He was willing to do the unusual in order to minister to another.

Conclusion

These questions are personal and must be applied to our own ministry.

WEDNESDAY EVENING, AUGUST 21

Title: The Mind of Christ

Text: "Let this mind be in you, which was also in Christ Jesus" (**Phil. 2:5**).

Scripture Reading: 1 Corinthians 2:12–16

Introduction

Paul's challenge to the Philippian Christians in our text contains one of the most exciting invitations in all of the Word of God. Paul is telling his readers that it is possible for redeemed human beings to rise to the level where they think with the mind of Jesus Christ. This should be our continual quest, the object of our prayers day by day, that we might have the mind of Christ as we face the issues and alternatives of life.

We do not naturally think with the mind of Christ. Consequently, we do not live and serve as Christ lived and served. We will never become Christlike in our conduct until we become Christlike in our thought life. Isaiah the prophet said, "Let the wicked forsake his way, and the unrighteous man his thoughts: and let him return unto the LORD, and he will have mercy upon him; and to our God, for he will abundantly pardon. For my thoughts are not your thoughts, neither are your ways my ways saith the LORD" (Isa. 55:7–8). The unrighteous man must forsake his unrighteous thoughts if he wants to escape from his wicked way. Repentance is not only an act; it is an attitude. Repentance not only takes place in a moment; it should be continuous. Repentance has been described as a pilgrimage from the mind of the flesh to the mind of the Spirit. The call to repent is in reality a call to accept the mind of Jesus Christ.

The apostle Paul tells us that with the help of the Holy Spirit it is possible for us to have the mind of Jesus Christ. To the degree that we do so, we will be Christlike in our conduct.

I. The mind of Christ calls for humility and surrender to the will of God (John 5:30).

Our Lord expressed his humility and his commitment to his Father's will by being willing to clothe himself in human flesh. He further expressed his humility and commitment to doing God's will to the point that he became a servant and yielded himself in service to the point of a shameful death on a cross. This is the example that Paul holds up before us as a challenge for us to seek after. By the pathway of the cross, the Christ was to find his throne and his crown.

II. The mind of Christ defines one's purpose for being in terms of service.

A. *Our Lord was a worker (John 9:4).*

B. *Our Lord believed with all his heart that the greatest joy possible in life came as a result of giving rather than getting.* Scripture describes our Lord as one who went about doing good. Paul tells the Ephesian Christians that God has created us in order that we might give ourselves to a life of good works (Eph. 2:10).

III. The mind of Christ calls for compassion (Matt. 9:26).

When our Lord saw the multitude, he was moved with compassion rather than by an attitude of critical condemnation. He came into the world not to condemn the world, but that through him the world might be saved (John 3:17).

If we would be true followers of Jesus Christ, we must let the love of God within us express itself both in concern and in help to the needy. We should demonstrate compassion toward those in our immediate surroundings. Compassion should flood our hearts as we think of those who suffer in countries ravaged by war and pestilence. Compassion must express itself in action to be genuine. Our Lord suffered with those about him and gave himself unreservedly in meeting the needs of others.

Conclusion

To have the mind of Christ will be costly. It will involve inconvenience. It will change the total course of your life. It should and will produce a profound change within you.

Only as we face the problems and potentials of life with the mind of Christ can we begin to be Christlike in our conduct.

SUNDAY MORNING, AUGUST 25

Title: The Holy Spirit as a Tree

Text: "But the fruit of the Spirit is love, joy, peace, longsuffering, gentleness, goodness, faith, meekness, temperance: against such there is no law" **(Gal. 5:22–23).**

Scripture Reading: Galatians 5:1, 13–25

Hymns: "Come, Thou Almighty King," Anonymous

        "Holy Spirit, Lead Us," Claire B. Kelly and Richard A. Kelly

        "Send a Great Revival," McKinney

Offertory Prayer: Our Father, as a well-known hymn says, "Safely through another week, Thou hast brought us on our way." We thank you for your accompanying presence. We search our hearts and ask what we can give a God who already has everything. We give our all as you have given us all. In this spirit we give you our hearts, our devotion, our service, and now this portion of our labor in the form of tithes and offerings. In the name of Jesus. Amen.

Introduction

Recently a dear friend sent me a beautiful book entitled *Famous Trees of Texas.* Full-page photographs carry captions with brief descriptions and histories of each tree. Readers are charmed and impressed with this book on trees.

There is another book that tells about trees—the Bible. The Bible's beginning and ending is punctuated with trees. And in between, the Bible speaks of the following trees: almond, apple, bay, box, cedar, chestnut, fig, fir, juniper, mulberry, myrtle, olive, palm, pine, pomegranate, shittah, and willow trees. In our Scripture passage for today, we consider another tree.

I. The figure.

The Holy Spirit is represented as a fruit tree in today's text. The psalmist said that a man is like a tree (Ps. 1). Jesus said good men and bad men are like good trees and bad trees (Matt. 7:16–20). Paul was led of the Spirit to present the Spirit in the symbolism of a fruit tree. The figure helps us to understand the nature and function of the Holy Spirit.

Sometimes, to decorate our homes, we place artificial plants that resemble real ones here and there for the best total effect. In the same way, people survey their spiritual houses and discover something is lacking and use artificial "trees" to fill the gaps. They put out their artificial trees of emotionalism, cultism, or extremism, hoping to improve their appearance and gratify their own longing for completion. But there is "nothing but leaves." What a pity that even Christians try to substitute their own dry arrangements for the living fruit tree of the Holy Spirit! Just now we have a cornucopia and wax fruit decoration on our dining table. It is lovely and impressive, but the fruit is not real. One would starve to death eating it. And in some comparable way, just for look's sake, we put out our own wax fruit, as religious status symbols, to try to convince others and perhaps even ourselves.

The Christian does not have to play such a game of make-believe. When the tree of the Spirit thrives within him, he can point to both the tree and its fruit and say, "It's the real thing."

II. The fruit.

Dr. A. T. Robertson said of this text, "It is a beautiful tree of fruit that Paul pictures here with nine luscious fruits on it."

Archbishop Harrison Lee has beautifully named these fruits nine flowers:

> Honeysuckle of love
> Daisy of goodness
> Rose of joy
> Forget-me-not of faithfulness
> Lily of peace
> Violet of meekness
> Snowdrop of longsuffering
> Wallflower of self-control
> Mignonette of kindness

Dr. J. C. Rolls suggests that in reality these fruits are but the characteristics of love:

> *Joy is love's cheerfulness;*
> *Goodness is love's character;*
> *Peace is love's confidence;*
> *Faithfulness is love's constancy;*
> *Longsuffering is love's composure;*
> *Meekness is love's comeliness;*
> *Kindness is love's consideration;*
> *Self-control is love's conquest.*

A. *Love.* The fruit of the Spirit is not the *eros* or *philia* love but the superior God-given *agape* love; it is the real thing.

B. *Joy.* When will people learn that there is no real joy *in* the world without the gospel of "joy *to* the world"? Real joy is not a temporary sensation of happiness; it is an abiding sense of the Holy Spirit's presence that remains steady in all circumstances.

C. *Peace.* There is a lovely rose called the peace rose. But there is also a lovely tree, the Holy Spirit, who may be called the Peace Tree. It is reported that during the War between the States, President Lincoln was found at his desk weeping softly. When asked the reason, he replied that men are like children in a nursery trying to spell "P-e-a-c-e" with the wrong blocks.

D. *Longsuffering.* The eternal Spirit enables us to endure the temporal problems. Our Paraclete gives us patience.

E. *Kindness.* Only the Holy Spirit can enable us to practice kindness in a world where we are surrounded by unkindness. He enables us to "be … kind one to another, tenderhearted, forgiving one another, even as God for Christ's sake hath forgiven [us]" (Eph. 4:32).

F. *Goodness.* The goodness the Holy Spirit builds in us is not negative and sterile. It is deposited in us to be checked out to others. It is not merely goodness possessed; it is goodness expressed.

G. *Faithfulness.* Awkwardly but accurately put, this faithfulness is "faith-ness." It is not an exterior resolve of conduct; it is an offshoot from the taproot of faith itself.

H. *Meekness.* "Blessed are the meek: for they shall inherit the earth" (Matt. 5:5). Meekness is not weakness; it is humility, pliability, and emptiness of vain ego. And how does one become meek? We recognize and accept this fruit of the Spirit.

I. *Temperance.* Perhaps a more meaningful translation would be "one holding control, or holding in." The surest formula for self-control is Spirit-control. We lose control and wreck ourselves when we do not have power brakes activated by the power of the Holy Spirit.

III. The fulfillment.

Now all of this is lovely: the flower garden of the Spirit, the characteristics of love. These are to be desired by every born-again person. But how can Christians cultivate this fruit?

A. *Make sure the right tree is planted.* The shrub of emotionalism is not the tree of the Spirit. Neither is the seedling of religious ambition nor the sprout of zeal. Yet sometimes these are planted, and the result is disappointment when harvesttime comes. How can we be sure if the right tree is planted?

1. Receive by faith the Father's Word. "For he that cometh to God must believe that he is, and that he is a rewarder of them that diligently seek him" (Heb. 11:6).

2. Receive by faith the Son's person. "Behold, I stand at the door, and knock: if any man hear my voice, and open the door, I will come in to him, and will sup with him, and he with me" (Rev. 3:20).

3. Receive by faith the Spirit's filling. "And be not drunk with wine, wherein is excess; but be filled with the Spirit" (Eph. 5:18).

B. *Give proper attention to the tree daily.* This requires an understanding of its nature. It requires cultivation. It requires a willingness to wait for the harvest. It requires the appropriation of the fruit.

We have a beautifully symmetrical apricot tree in our backyard. It is missing only one thing—life. It is dead. It will never bear fruit again. Because we did not give daily attention to it, borers got to the trunk of the tree, and as a result, the tree died. This is not to suggest that the life of the eternal Spirit is in danger. It is to remind us that the tree of the Spirit has enemies. So far as the Christian is concerned, the little borers, such as jealousy, unforgiveness, indifference, worldliness, and a score of other sins, can so make their attack that the result is the same: the tree is not permitted to flourish and bear fruit. Lord, keep us alert!

IV. The freedom.

It is no accident that Galatians 5 begins, "Stand fast therefore in the liberty wherewith Christ hath made us free, and be not entangled again with the yoke of bondage" (Gal. 5:1).

"Now the Lord is that Spirit: and where the Spirit of the Lord is, there is liberty" (2 Cor. 3:17). The fruit of the Spirit is liberating. Love begets freedom from hate. Joy brings freedom from gloom. Peace displaces conflict. Longsuffering makes free from impatience. Goodness liberates from evil. Faith brings freedom from confusion. Meekness delivers from arrogance. Temperance brings freedom from excesses.

Conclusion

A. *Every life bears some sort of fruit, good or bad.*

B. *To harvest the right fruits, there must be the right roots.* Let us make sure, therefore, that the right tree is planted.

C. *To ensure spiritual health, let us make sure that we give daily attention and response to the tree of the Spirit.*

D. *To live the abundant life, let us do right by the tree of the Spirit.*

E. *Remember the words of our Lord: "Herein is my Father glorified, that ye bear much fruit; so shall ye be my disciples" (John 15:8).* We will gladly let the tree of the Holy Spirit bear fruit through us.

SUNDAY EVENING, AUGUST 25

Title: Think Small

Text: "And the King shall answer and say unto them, Verily I say unto you, Inasmuch as ye have done it unto one of the least of these my brethren, ye have done it unto me" (**Matt. 25:40**).

Scripture Reading: Matthew 25:31–40

Introduction

One day I took my Volkswagen to the dealer for its periodic maintenance. While there, I picked up a unique book of matches. It is a very small matchbook: only about three-quarters of an inch wide, and the matches themselves are smaller than usual. On the front it has a picture of a VW "bug" and the words *Think Small.*

That is good advice for a Christian involved in ministry. Perhaps the biggest problem faced by Christians in ministry is knowing where to begin. Poverty seems so widespread, suffering is so universal, and ignorance is so pervasive. We have been simply overwhelmed by the statistics.

We are accustomed to thinking big thoughts. We dream big dreams and plan grandiose projects. And we are sometimes frightened by the magnitude of our own proposals. But Christian ministry demands that we think small. Think in terms of helping one person, of launching one project, of righting one wrong.

In the judgment scene in Matthew 25, Jesus portrays one standard of judgment: love as reflected in ministry. As a Palestinian shepherd would separate the sheep from the goats at night, the Lord is pictured as separating the righteous from the unrighteous. And the division is made on the basis of their ministering love. It is not based on their great projects; it is based on what they have done for individuals.

I. By thinking small we know where to start.

A. *Start where you are.* The place to begin ministry is right where you are. Those persons who are judged righteous in Jesus' story are persons who helped the people in need around them. Your own community has people who are hungry, lonely, sick, improperly clothed, and imprisoned. They are your starting place for ministry.

B. *Serve where you are.* As churches or individual Christians begin to minister where they are, new possibilities for ministry will present themselves. Each community will have different needs. Each church will have different possibilities. But there are needs and possibilities for each.

II. By thinking small we know how to start.

A. *Start with the simple.* Did you notice that the acts praised by the Savior in our Scripture reading are not big, spectacular projects? They are simple acts of human love and ministry.

It does not take a great deal of effort to feed, clothe, and visit those with particular needs. But it does take willingness.

In the summer of 1971 a disastrous rock festival was convened at McCrea, Louisiana. It never did get off the ground. Thousands of young people were marooned in a rural area. They were choked by dust, scorched by sun, and ridiculed by neighbors. As it was breaking up, a local pastor mentioned to his congregation that thousands of young people had been gathered in an area within easy driving distance of the church yet the church had done nothing to help them. That afternoon several of the men of the church drove to the area. They took cold water and sandwiches. They provided a bus and offered a way out for those who wished to leave. Then they carried them to Pineville where they were given food, a place to bathe and clean up, and travel connections. It was a simple act of ministry.

B. *Start with sympathy.* In Jesus' story, the persons singled out by the divine Judge for blessedness are surprised at the recognition. As far as they are concerned, their acts were the normal responses of Christian love. Love is the basis for all Christian ministry. Christian love provides the kind of sympathetic response to human need that will cause a person to minister without self-consciousness.

C. *Start with the Savior.* Jesus had identified himself with those in need. With this kind of identification, the Christian will minister. Bringing people to an understanding of Christ and an acceptance of him as Savior is a goal in ministry.

Conclusion

Think small. This gives you a place to begin in Christian ministry. If we think small, we can know where and how to start in our ministry to persons.

WEDNESDAY EVENING, AUGUST 28

Title: Let Jesus Christ Be Lord

Text: "Wherefore God also hath highly exalted him, and given him a name which is above every name: That at the name of Jesus every knee should bow, of things in heaven, and things in earth, and things under the earth; And that every tongue should confess that Jesus Christ is Lord, to the glory of God the Father" **(Phil. 2:9–11).**

Introduction

The words of our text are a shout of praise. They are a triumphant proclamation of what the Father God has done for Christ the Son as a result of the humiliation involved in his incarnation and shameful death on the cross. The apostle declares that because of this faithfulness of God's unique and only begotten Son, he has been highly exalted to a position of sovereignty over all created things both in heaven and in earth. He declares that every tongue should proclaim that Jesus Christ is Lord to the glory of God the Father.

Jesus Christ is Lord. What does that mean? Is that merely a complimentary title that has been bestowed on him? What are the implications of his being exalted to a position of lordship?

The title *lord* is not as well known in contemporary life today as it was in biblical times. We are more familiar with terms that have a similar meaning, such as *king, emperor, dictator, president,* and *commander in chief.*

The term *lord* is basically a title that carries with it the idea of ownership, authority, sovereignty, and power. The inspired apostle is informing us that Jesus Christ has been invested with this divine authority from God and that every heart should recognize this, every tongue confess it, and every knee bow in acknowledgment of his lordship.

I. Jesus Christ has been exalted to lordship because of who he is.

Jesus, the Christ, is the unique, sinless Son of God. He is the eternal Son who came and clothed himself in the garment of human flesh. He lived on earth with the limitations of humanity as the eternal God with a human body. He was tempted in all points like as we are yet did not yield to sin.

II. Jesus Christ is Lord because of what he did.

A. *The eternal Son of God did not greedily hold on to his being equal with God.* He humbled himself and clothed himself in human flesh, accepting the limitations associated with such.

B. *He became a servant of people.*

C. *He endured as a substitute the indignity, shame, and horror of death by crucifixion.*

D. *He lived and died in the faith that God would give him victory over death and the grave.* God did raise him from the cold chambers of death to live again.

III. Jesus Christ is Lord because of what he can do.

A. *Because he died for our sins, he can offer to us the gift of forgiveness.*

B. *Because he conquered death and the grave and came forth alive, he can offer to us the gift of eternal life.*

C. *He came, lived, labored, died, conquered death, and lives forever to lead us to God.* He lives and so is able to lead us into the world as servants of God. We should recognize his authority over our time and his right to command our talents. He has absolute claim upon all of our resources.

Conclusion

Make Jesus the Lord of your life. The more completely you yield yourself in submission to his loving will, the more you will discover the liberty of a life of freedom in the Spirit.

SEPTEMBER

■ **Sunday Mornings**

"The Ministries of the Church" is this month's theme. The living Lord is depending on the church to continue his ministry in the world in the power of the Holy Spirit.

■ **Sunday Evenings**

A series of biographical messages titled "Heroes of the Faith" is suggested. Hebrews 11 provides the biblical text for this series.

■ **Wednesday Evenings**

Continue the studies based on Paul's epistle to the Philippians with the theme "Words of Encouragement from the Apostle Paul."

SUNDAY MORNING, SEPTEMBER 1

Title: Can a Church Die?

Text: "To the angel of the church in Sardis write: These are the words of him who holds the seven spirits of God and the seven stars. I know your deeds; you have a reputation of being alive, but you are dead" **(Rev. 3:1 NIV)**.

Scripture Reading: Revelation 3:1–6

Hymns: "Come, Thou Almighty King," Anonymous

"Glorious Is Thy Name," McKinney

"Breathe on Me," McKinney

Offertory Prayer: Gracious Father, thank you for your eternal purpose, never ending, eternally victorious. Thank you for the gifts of life and the privilege of sharing them with others in need right here in our own community and throughout the world. In the name of Jesus Christ we dedicate these gifts to you.

Introduction

Something has happened to church life in England. Only 3 percent of the population attend worship on any given Sunday. William Barclay has said that as you look out upon the English church life, you see massive buildings, and you know that at one time church life in England was a great institution, having great importance. But the churches of England have come upon evil days and decay. Many of the buildings are now in ruins or disrepair or are converted for other purposes.

An American pastor and his family visited Charles Spurgeon's church in London in 1968 as a dream come true. The caretaker showed them the auditorium that seats about two thousand people. They asked him how many people attend services now. He replied, "It is a good Sunday when we have one hundred people in attendance!" I am aware that you do not equate life with size or bigness; however, when you compare a span of time and see what happens to a church's life—from large to small—then you cannot help but conclude that something has happened to that church.

"Can a church die?" is an appropriate question for today.

Something happened to the church at Sardis. It was located in a wealthy commercial center noted for its dissipated living. However, the church had a fine beginning. At one time it was a thriving, vigorous, pulsating church—full of life. Now Jesus says, "You only have a name that you are alive, when in reality you are dead."

Three questions may be asked in order to answer our primary question, "Can a church die?"

I. "When is a church dying?"

A. *G. Campbell Morgan says that a church is dying . . .*
   1. When it is not growing in Christlikeness and in souls.
   2. When it does not have the power to give birth to souls.
   3. When it is selfish; when the springs of compassion are dried up; when love, as the fruit of the Spirit, is missing.
   4. When there is disunity, disintegration, and divisions in the fellowship.
   5. When its emotions are cold; when it loses the capacity to become excited about the power of the gospel of Jesus Christ to change lives.
   Death is on its way when these factors are at work.

B. *William Barclay says that a church is dying . . .*
   1. When its members have interest without commitment.
   2. When it is substituting good things for truly central things in the faith.
   3. When it has lost its missionary dynamic.

C. *In addition to these descriptions, it may be suggested that a church is dying also. . .*
   1. When it forgets its unique nature. The church is the body of Jesus Christ himself! The local church is a manifestation of that body.
   2. When its unique mission goes unfulfilled. The church is the only body in the world that has the unique task of proclaiming God's love and forgiveness.
   3. When it is no longer uniquely Christian. Jesus suggests this in Revelation 3:4: "You have a few people in Sardis who have not soiled their clothes" (NIV). The church there was conforming to contemporary life rather than changing it.
   4. When it substitutes form for force. Jesus said, "You have a reputation of being alive" (Rev. 3:1 NIV). The image of this church was that it was an active, living church, but Jesus knew better! It lacked real life, and that

real life always comes from Jesus Christ himself. Jesus is the Vine, and we are the branches (John 15). Life flows from him.

5. When it does not change lives through the gospel of Jesus Christ. The tremendous truth is that when the gospel is proclaimed in love and faith there is power and life!

II. "How does a church die?"

Simply expressed, the church dies in the hearts of its members. We are the church, and whenever death comes, it always comes to us as individuals. I do not mean that it is a death to a program; it is a death to a personal relationship, a relationship to Jesus Christ.

The Christian's relationship to Christ becomes so strained that his or her Christian life is meaningless and powerless. Jesus Christ is not actively involved in that person's daily life. Life is not focused on Jesus Christ; consequently we do not become like him.

This way of life not only affects the individual Christian; it spreads to others' lives and damages their spiritual tone as well.

How is your relationship to Jesus Christ? Is he honestly your Savior and Lord? Is he guiding your life daily? Are you available to him?

III. "Can a church live in an age like ours?"

Jesus Christ, in speaking to Sardis, confidently states that a church *can* live. In fact, it *will not* die when it is truly related to Jesus Christ. Three observations are important.

First, a church can live if it responds to Christ properly. He uses three imperatives. In verse 2 he says, "Wake up!" (NIV). He calls his people to an awakening of spiritual conditions. In verse 3, "Remember," in present continuous action, means "never forget."

We Christians are always to be living in the atmosphere of Christ's mighty effect on our lives. Again, in verse 3, Jesus calls for repentance in the life of the Sardis church. We must constantly deal with the sins of our lives. It is sinful for a church to be spiritually lifeless when Christ will give it spiritual power.

A second observation is that a church can live even if only a few are concerned. Jesus refers to "a few people" who are faithful. These were truly committed believers devoted to him and his changeless challenge.

Third, a church can live when we come to Christ one by one. He has been speaking to the church as a whole, but now in verse 5 he says, "The one who is victorious...." (NIV). He singles us out one by one. The truth is, a church is never more than what we are as individuals in our personal relationship to Jesus Christ. And it is Christ who gives us that living triumph.

Conclusion

The same living Christ says to us today, "He that hath an ear, let him hear what the Spirit saith unto the churches" (v. 6). The Holy Spirit appeals to our lives to be fully responsive to Jesus Christ. That personal response results in spiritual power that fulfills the purpose of Christ for his church.

SUNDAY EVENING, SEPTEMBER 1

Title: A Man Who Pleased God

Text: "By faith Enoch was translated that he should not see death; and was not found, because God had translated him: for before his translation he had this testimony, that he pleased God" **(Heb. 11:5)**.

Scripture Reading: Genesis 5:21–31

Introduction

Towering above the men of his generation and impressing multitudes in the centuries that followed, is Enoch, that remarkable man whose eloquent, fascinating, and impressive biography is contained in Genesis 5:21–24; Hebrews 11:5; and Jude 14–15.

Enoch did not become great because of his profound scholarship, successful statesmanship, military renown, or philanthropic achievements, but because he "walked with God" and thereby "pleased God." That is the highest praise that can be bestowed on any person. A life that pleases God is a higher type than is exemplified by many Christians today. If, for three hundred years, Enoch could walk with God in a sinful world, it should not be considered impossible for us to walk with him today.

I. Requisites for walking with God.

A. *Genuine reconciliation with God.* Walking with God presupposes a personal faith in him. Having been reconciled to God through Christ, our walking with him implies trust; friendship; congeniality; fellowship; companionship; and unity of thought, will, and affection.

B. *Complete yieldedness to God.* Enoch yielded his mind and will to God. He knew that it was God's prerogative to choose the path, so he cheerfully went God's way instead of his own. Likewise, if we are wise, we as God's children will yield ourselves to him and walk with him in the path he chooses. Enoch also knew that it was the privilege of God to set the pace for their walk, so he neither ran ahead of God nor lagged behind.

C. *Supreme love for God.* Enoch loved God supremely. His love for God restrained him from indulging in the popular sins of his day and constrained him to walk closely with God.

D. *Unbroken fellowship with God.* Aware of God's abiding presence with him and of his own dependence on God, Enoch daily walked with him. In that fellowship, there was an intimacy that became increasingly delightful, beautiful, and alluring. When we as God's children walk with him, the Father directs our steps, protects us from danger, and comforts us in our sorrows.

II. Reasons for walking with God.

A. *It is proper.* Walking with God is a part of his plan for us. "What doth the LORD require of thee, but to do justly, and to love mercy, and to walk humbly with thy God?" (Mic. 6:8). Only when we walk with God can we perform our duties to him, to others, and to ourselves. Only thus can we render our best service.

B. *It is pleasant.* Enoch rejoiced in his relationship with God even though his walking with God alienated him from multitudes who were participating in the popular sins of those dark days. Unlike most people in his day, Enoch walked with God, worshiped him, worked for him, and derived great joy from so doing.

C. *It is profitable.* Enoch found it quite profitable to walk with God. As he walked with God, Enoch grew more like him. Walking with God was profitable to Enoch's family also.

As we walk with God in the path of Christian obedience and service, we shall be the recipients of his peace, purity, protection, power, and provision. What more can we ask than the guarantee of these invaluable blessings? To each of his obedient children who walks with him, God says, "Fear thou not; for I am with thee: be not dismayed; for I am thy God: I will strengthen thee; yea, I will help thee; yea, I will uphold thee with the right hand of my righteousness" (Isa. 41:10).

D. *It is pleasing to God.* I cannot think of any higher tribute being paid to a person than the one received by Enoch in Hebrews 11:5: "Before his translation he had this testimony, that he pleased God." By trusting him fully, walking with him faithfully, and serving him obediently, Enoch pleased God.

Isn't it thrilling to know that you, too, can please God and cause him to rejoice? To please him is the greatest purpose you can have. There is no satisfaction or joy in life comparable to the knowledge that you have been able to please God.

III. Results of walking with God.

A. *A blessed companionship.* A life of intimate fellowship with God is the sweetest and best that one can live. God always takes care of those who walk with him. Walking with God involves a realization of his abiding presence and a complete dependence on him. It produces an increasing likeness to him.

B. *An intense satisfaction.* There is no satisfaction in life comparable to that of knowing, as Enoch did, that one has been able to please God. What a joy to know we can do that! I am thrilled in knowing that it is possible to please and to glorify God by heartily praising him, by implicitly believing his Word, by daily walking with him, by faithfully working for him, and by persistently witnessing for him.

C. *A future blessedness.* After Enoch had walked in compliance with God's will and had found great delight in God's way, God removed him from this world of sin, sickness, suffering, and sorrow and took him to live with him in heaven. Enoch was missed greatly by those who had known him and appreciated his wholesome influence.

Conclusion

Any true child of God can do just what Enoch did—walk with God and please him. Let us walk with him, cost what it may, for there is no greater satisfaction than knowing we have pleased God.

WEDNESDAY EVENING, SEPTEMBER 4

Title: Working with God

Text: "Wherefore, my beloved, as ye have always obeyed, not as in my presence only, but now much more in my absence, work out your own salvation with fear and trembling. For it is God which worketh in you both to will and to do of his good pleasure" **(Phil. 2:12–13)**.

Scripture Reading: Romans 12

Introduction

Paul encouraged those whom he loved to cooperate with the Father God completely as he continued his good work within them. Paul had expressed his confidence that the God who had begun a good work in them would persist to the finish in bringing it to completion (Phil. 1:6). Paul was not expressing a fear that he might lose the salvation that he had through faith in Jesus Christ. He was confident of the eternal nature of the love of Christ and of the security each believer enjoys within that love (Rom. 8:31–39).

In our text, Paul is expressing a concern that the Philippian Christians will not cooperate with God in his continuing work of developing within them the Christian character and competence that the Father God desired.

I. The salvation experience has a commencement.

By commencement we refer to a beginning rather than an end. The conversion experience is the beginning of a new life with God as Father. This new life begins at the moment of the new birth. The new birth is a miracle wrought by God in the heart of a convicted guilty sinner who recognizes his need for forgiveness and comes to God in confession of sin and profession of faith in Jesus Christ as Lord and Savior. Conversion, or the new birth, marks the commencement of God's great salvation.

II. There is a continuation of salvation.

The beginning of the salvation experience is not all there is to it. The Father God is eager to do something more for us than merely forgive our sins. He is eager for his children to grow toward spiritual maturity and to develop a competence that will equip them as effective servants that they might be his ministers in the world. In order for God to succeed in this divine objective, there must be a human cooperation that is conscientious and continuous. The call to cooperative endeavor is the point at which the apostle Paul is challenging the disciples at Philippi.

Paul is not challenging the Philippians to work out some kind of salvation that will entitle them to go to heaven. He is not telling them that they must work if they want to go to heaven. The salvation that makes it possible for us to go to heaven is not his concern at this point. He is thinking in terms of their growth and progress. He is insisting that they must recognize the work of God's Spirit within them and make a positive and continuous response to that great work of God.

In the conversion experience, the Holy Spirit worked God's salvation into their hearts. They now face the responsibility of working out God's great program of salvation within their minds and hearts and lives.

The process of being saved from the practice and habit of sin begins at the moment of conversion and continues until either death overtakes us or the Lord Jesus Christ returns for his own.

Diligent Bible study, earnest prayer, loyalty to the church, obedience to the commands of Christ, a positive response to the leadership of the Holy Spirit, a generous expression of sacrificial giving—all of these go into the process of working out our salvation as God works within us.

III. There is a consummation of salvation.

We have been saved from the penalty of sin through faith in Christ Jesus. We are in a process of being saved from the practice of sin as we cooperate fully with the leadership of the indwelling Spirit. We will receive salvation from the very presence of sin when we die or when our Lord returns (Phil. 3:20–21).

Conclusion

We are past the point of the beginning of our salvation. There is not much we can do about the future prospect of being saved from the presence of sin. We are at that point where we can work with God to experience full salvation from the power, practice, and habit of sin in our daily lives. Let each of us eagerly and joyfully respond to the work of God's Spirit within our hearts.

SUNDAY MORNING, SEPTEMBER 8

Title: Excitement in the Church

Text: "These are the words of the Amen.... I know your deeds.... So be earnest and repent" **(Rev. 3:14–15, 19 NIV).**

Scripture Reading: Revelation 3:14–22

Hymns: "O Worship the King," Haydn

"He Lives," Ackley

"I Am Thine, O Lord," Doane

Offertory Prayer: Heavenly Father, you have said in your Word, "Bring ye all the tithes into the storehouse, that there may be meat in mine house, and prove me now herewith . . . if I will not open you the windows of heaven, and pour you out a blessing, that there shall not be room enough to receive it" (Mal. 3:10). Confirm your promise to our lives as we yield ourselves to you. In the name of Jesus Christ we commit these gifts to you.

Introduction

The church at Laodicea in Asia Minor could just as easily be some church at the crossroads of America, or in some county seat town, or in the countryside, or on some busy thoroughfare.

Laodicea was a well-located, wealthy commercial center. It was noted for both its medical influence and its industrial power. What the living Christ said to them, he says to us today; what he desired of them, he desires of us; and what he offered them, he offers us today. It is excitement in the church!

I. First, a *paradox* is described in these statements.

Here is the living Christ, the very embodiment of the absolute truth and faithfulness; the fulfillment of the purpose of God, the Creator, the all-powerful God.

Here also is a world of need: paganism, pessimism, and impurity—a world exploding in sin.

In this setting is a church composed of people whose relationship to Jesus Christ is personal and definite, people who claim eternal knowledge. As a church, it is a redemptive fellowship that possesses unusual power. It is a community of healing in the midst of sick influences. It is a church of potentially dynamic witnesses. It is a people from whom Jesus Christ is expecting positive power to flow to help a world in need.

But instead, here is a church that is "neither hot nor cold, but lukewarm." It has lost its capacity to care for the world around it. It has lost its glow for the wonderful will of God and its feeling for people. It no longer has the conviction to act. Its excitement quotient burns low. What a paradox!

The same paradox applies to us today. We have the living Christ, not only of the New Testament pages, but also of more than twenty centuries of history in seeing his power at work. The same living Christ speaks to us today. He is ready to pour fresh power through our lives now.

And we live in an exploding world of people and pollution, of lostness and lack of purpose, of emptiness and loneliness—a searching, spiritually hungry world.

What will churches do? Some are saying that the day of the church is over;

and others say, "When the church is gone, it will never be missed." But I say that these are the most spiritually exciting days I have ever known. Exciting things are happening all across America! Christian television programming carries the gospel into thousands of homes. And thousands more are exploring spiritual truths on the Internet. Countless believers are turning to Jesus Christ for abundant life and are experiencing and sharing the gospel daily with others. God still has great things for his people. We just need his spiritual excitement in our souls!

II. Second, these words to Laodicea express the *plan* of Christ for his church, then and now.

Christ knows the church (Rev. 3:15), commands it (v. 18), loves it, and offers himself to it (v. 20).

A. *It is not Christ's will for any church to be "lukewarm."* Such is a condition of lifelessness, apathy, and indifference. A lukewarm church is one that possesses no real excitement in its spiritual atmosphere. Enthusiasm and excitement are intangible evidences of life stirring in a church!

Laodicea evidently at one time had life. It was spiritually hot, involved, alive and serving, but something happened to it. See Colossians 2:1–2 for Paul's reference to this church.

Lukewarmness is a condition nauseating to Christ. He says, "I will spew you out." And what is more, the church at Laodicea is sickeningly proud. It says that it has no needs, yet Jesus knows that it is wretched, miserable, poor, blind, and naked. It is definitely not Christ's will for his church to be like this.

B. *It is Christ's will for the church to be alive, awake, alert, excited, and excitable.* The Holy Spirit is the one who creates life in the church. He indwells believers in the church (1 Cor. 3:16–17). He inhabits believers (Eph. 2:18–22) and makes the church live.

There is *power* in the church. The power of the Word of God and of the gospel of Christ can change lives. Romans 1:16 says that it is "the power of God unto salvation." Something happens when it is preached.

There is *love* in the church — God's love for us, our love responsive to him, and our love for others.

There is *fellowship* in the church. Fellowship is helping, sharing, and ministering to others. All of this is Christ's will and plan for his people. And this is exciting!

III. Third, the words of Christ point the *pathway* to excitement.

Jesus says four simple things will bring excitement to his church:

A. *Confession of need (Rev. 3:18).* He challenges the church to confess poverty and become rich, to confess nakedness and be clothed, and to confess spiritual blindness and receive sight. Confession is essential to experiencing the power of the Holy Spirit. Cleansing follows confession (1 John 1:9).

B. *Repentance (Rev. 3:19).* Repentance and zeal go together. Repentance is to recognize and acknowledge sin and to have sorrow for it and turn away from it. It is a change of mind resulting in a change of action and direction.

C. *Opening one's life to Christ (Rev. 3:20).* Jesus stands at the "door" of life awaiting our voluntary response. No one forces us, not even Christ. We must choose for ourselves. It is an individual act, one that each one of us must express when Christ begins to control our lives. And it is an act of faith, truly trusting him to do what he says he will do. Christ gives the excitement. The book of Acts is historical proof of this.

D. *Obedience to the Holy Spirit (Rev. 3:22).* When the Holy Spirit is obeyed and yielded to, life is exciting. We need to be filled with the Spirit according to God's command.

Conclusion

It is not the size of the church that counts; it is the spirit. Where the Spirit of the Lord is, there is excitement!

SUNDAY EVENING, SEPTEMBER 8

Title: A Witness for God

Text: "By faith Noah, being warned of God of things not seen as yet, moved with fear, prepared an ark to the saving of his house; by the which he condemned the world, and became heir of the righteousness which is by faith" **(Heb. 11:7).**

Scripture Reading: Genesis 6:11–22

Introduction

Noah, the descendant of godly ancestors, walked with God and became one of the most remarkable and outstanding personalities in the Old Testament.

I. The wickedness of man.

At the time of Noah's birth great wickedness abounded. It is interesting to note that man's wickedness is the only thing about him that God has ever called great. Of no era in history do we read of such aggravated vileness and inconceivable wickedness as that which prevailed in the days of Noah. Moral corruption and spiritual decline were accompanied by widespread violence.

This should be a reminder that the prevalent corruption and the terrible crimes of violence that shock and amaze us and contribute to making our national crime record worse than that of any other nation undoubtedly have a very close connection with the lack of faith in God and the practically total forgetfulness of him on the part of so many of our citizens.

Not only do people grieve God deeply by their sinful thoughts, words, and deeds, but they also injure themselves, deprive themselves of happiness and satisfaction, and impair or destroy their usefulness. This is as true today as it was in Noah's day.

The depth of the depravity of the human race in the time of Noah was revealed in these words: "And God saw that the wickedness of man was great in the earth" (Gen. 6:5) and "The earth also was corrupt before God, and the earth was filled with violence" (v. 11). That was the only time in history that humanity had sunk so low that the divine recorder had to say of humanity, "Every imagination of the thoughts of his heart was only evil continually" (v. 5). Unfortunately, the human race is rapidly sinking to that same low today.

In those days when it was becoming increasingly difficult to live a godly life, God observed Noah, who differed from all the rest, in that he was neither attracted to nor contaminated by wickedness. He was righteous, not merely in his own estimation or in the eyes of men, but in the sight of God. To Noah, God said, "For thee have I seen righteous before me in this generation" (Gen. 7:1). Thoroughly acquainted with God, fully aware of his abiding presence, and constantly relying on him for necessary strength, Noah walked daily in the peaceful and pleasant paths of righteousness. At no period since creation, except during the era of gross immorality and inconceivable wickedness in which Noah lived, has it ever been true that there was only one righteous man on the earth. How wonderful that in those dark days there was one man whose piety was distinguished for its sincerity and genuineness, and from whose household the light of God's truth continued to shine forth.

II. The building of the ark.

Observing the terrible wickedness that existed on the earth in those days, God honored Noah by revealing to him his purpose to destroy all of the wicked people. God said, "I will destroy man whom I have created from the face of the earth" (Gen. 6:7). By that statement, God meant that he was going to put out of existence that which he had brought into being. Noah accepted at face value God's warning of a forthcoming, devastating flood.

Accepting God's warning by faith, Noah promptly began the task of preparing an ark for the safety of himself and his family. When Noah communicated to others the information about the warning he had received, they treated it with scorn. Noah followed carefully the instructions God had given him. It is inspiring to observe Noah's meticulous obedience to every command of God concerning the construction of the ark.

While building the ark according to God's plan and directions, Noah fearlessly and faithfully preached the righteousness and judgment of God. The members of his immediate family were the only ones who responded favorably to Noah's preaching, but he refused to be discouraged. He was responsible for the delivery of God's message, but not for what the people did with it. He did what God directed him to do and left the results with him.

Eventually the ark was completed. At the appointed time, God said to Noah, "Come thou and all thy house into the ark" (Gen. 7:1). This invitation from God was personal and specific. In response to it Noah and his family entered the ark, and "the LORD shut him in" (Gen. 7:16). The divine fastening guaranteed their perfect safety.

III. The new beginning.

After God shut the door behind Noah, nobody else got into the ark. It then rained for forty days and nights. The mountains were not high enough to save the terrified people who fled to them for safety from the onrushing floods. Eventually the floodwaters subsided and the ark rested on the mountain. God commanded Noah to come forth from the ark, bringing with him his family and every living thing he had taken into the ark with him. Noah promptly obeyed God.

Noah's first act after placing his feet on the ground was to build an altar and to offer sacrifices to God, thereby expressing his gratitude for God's preservation of his life and the lives of the other members of his family. Following his acceptance of Noah's sacrifices, God made a covenant with his faithful servant and effective witness. The covenant contained an unconditional promise that never again would the earth be destroyed by a flood. God ratified his gracious promise by writing in the sky in the flaming colors of a rainbow. Every time Noah saw a rainbow in the sky, he was reminded that he owed everything to the grace of God, from whom comes every blessing that is received by any person.

WEDNESDAY EVENING, SEPTEMBER 11

Title: Do We Shine as Lights in the World?

Text: "That ye may be blameless and harmless, the sons of God, without rebuke, in the midst of a crooked and perverse nation, among whom ye shine as lights in the world" **(Phil. 2:15).**

Scripture Reading: John 9:1–15

Introduction

Paul described the church in Philippi as being a luminary that provided light for a dark world.

I. God would have his people to serve as light.

A. *Jesus said, "I am the light of the world" (John 8:12).* As the light of the world, our Lord provides illumination concerning the nature and purpose of God. He also comes to sensitize and seeks to immunize us against the evil nature of sin. He throws light on the meaning and purpose for life and points the way to happiness and fulfillment. Christ alone provides light for the darkness that we call death and gives us hope for eternity.

B. *Jesus said, "Ye are the light of the world" (Matt. 5:14).* On one occasion, our Lord said, "As long as I am in the world, I am the light of the world" (John 9:5). He implies that once his ministry has ended by means of crucifixion, resurrection, and ascension, his servants will become the luminaries that point people toward God.

II. God wants his people to serve as light in a dark world.

Paul was doing something more than complimenting the disciples of our Lord in Philippi. He was describing their divine function.

    A. *Light makes life possible.*

    B. *Light brings warmth.*

    C. *Light dispels darkness.*

       1. The darkness of ignorance.

       2. The darkness of impurity.

       3. The darkness of superstition.

       4. The darkness of unrelieved sorrow.

       5. The darkness of hopeless death.

    D. *Light awakens.* The sun rises in the morning to awaken the world from sleep.

    E. *Light reveals beauty.*

    F. *Light cheers and comforts and encourages.*

Conclusion

"Let your light shine before others" (Matt. 5:16). Light is self-manifesting. Light is silent yet very conspicuous. Light cannot be ignored except by those who close their eyes. Are you letting your light shine for the Lord? Do you illuminate the way to faith and faithfulness for others? Have you been able to help them find the way through the dark valleys of life?

We should not let our light shine dimly, uncertainly, or just occasionally. Instead, we should let our light shine for God naturally, willingly, openly, brightly, constantly, steadily.

SUNDAY MORNING, SEPTEMBER 15

Title: Spiritual Revolution Now!

Text: "These that have turned the world upside down are come hither also" (**Acts 17:6**).

Scripture Reading: Acts 17:1–9

Hymns: "Rise Up, O Men of God," Williams

         "Our Best," Tullar

         "Higher Ground," Gabriel

Offertory Prayer: Heavenly Father, thank you for the stewardship of life and the principles of wisdom in your Word by which we can live. Thank you for commanding us to give to the needs of others. Deliver us from the greed of the human heart and fill us with the generosity of the Spirit as we give our gifts to you. In Jesus' name we pray. Amen.

Introduction

These are the most revolutionary days in human history. There are revolutionary changes in almost every area of life. Ours is a time when all norms are broken and people are lost in frustration and futility. There is need for a revolution, not of force and fear, but of love and reason, a revolution such as the one the book of Acts describes.

Acts graphically describes the spiritual revolution Jesus Christ commandeered in a world of paganism and darkness. The word *revolution* means "to turn," or "to change." The people of Thessalonica were saying that Paul and Silas were turning the world upside down. It was a spiritual revolution! How can we experience the same?

There are five things that we must have if we are to have a spiritual revolution.

I. We must have a revolutionary leader.

We must have a leader so unique that no person in all history has ever been or ever will be like him. His personality must be so unique that he has power to accomplish great things. That person is Jesus Christ. The book of Acts says that it was the revolutionary Christ who was turning the world upside down.

Jesus Christ is unique in every sense of the word. He is unique in his claims, for no one else can say, "I am the way and the truth and the life. No one comes to the Father except through me" (John 14:6). He is the crucified, buried, and risen Savior and the Lord of life. We do not speak about him as living only in ages past; we speak of him as one who today is creating spiritual revolution in the hearts of thousands of people.

II. We must have a revolutionary message.

Do we have a message for this desperate and disillusioned generation? Is there a word of hope? This is exactly what the New Testament is—God's message of hope to humans.

We have a message of a personal relationship with Jesus Christ. It is a message of God's love and forgiveness. God *does* love you! This is a revolutionary truth. And we can be *free*! Forgiveness in Jesus Christ is made available to all. Jesus Christ changes lives wherever his witnesses go. This is the truth of the book of Acts. People believed and responded openly to the message of Jesus Christ. "The gospel of Christ . . . is the power of God unto salvation" (Rom. 1:16). Whether that gospel has been preached in America or Africa, multitudes have been transformed by its power.

III. We must have a revolutionary plan.

If there is to be a spiritual revolution in our world, we must have a plan so big that it is utterly impossible for us to accomplish it ourselves. It must be so big that it is humanly ridiculous to think it can be done.

The truth is, we have that plan. It is the plan Jesus Christ gave to a handful of people. He said to them, "Go ye therefore, and teach of all nations; baptizing them in the name of the Father, and of the Son, and of the Holy Ghost; teaching them to observe all things whatsoever I have commanded you" (Matt. 28:19–20). He gave this plan almost two thousand years ago, and it is still *his* plan today.

If we take this plan seriously, it means that we must have some priorities in our lives. Insignificant events and activities must be deleted from our schedules. And we must look at every person and every opportunity as a divine encounter. We must pour out our lives to reach for Jesus Christ every person we possibly can in our generation. Nothing short of this will be revolutionary!

IV. We must have a revolutionary power.

Jesus not only commanded us to fulfill his plan, but in almost the same breath, he promised to enable us to obey the command. He never gives us a command without enabling us to obey it. He did not expect his first followers to do this on their own. Neither does he expect us to do so.

Living the Christian life on our own is impossible. It is not just hard; it is impossible! When we realize that our power comes from Jesus Christ living in and through us day by day, we experience spiritual power.

The revolutionary power is promised in the words "You will receive power when the Holy Spirit comes on you" (Acts 1:18 NIV). This means that it is not political power, physical power, or even social power that revolutionizes the world; it is spiritual power that comes from the Holy Spirit in our lives. It is not our ability but our availability to his Spirit that fills our lives with fruitfulness.

V. We must have a revolutionary commitment.

Spiritual revolution requires people whose lives are thoroughly committed to Jesus Christ. What is your personal strategy in obeying the command of Jesus Christ? What do you plan to do with your life in relationship to his will? What is the priority in your life? What claims your attention? What motivates you? What thrills your life with excitement? What kind of commitment do you have to Jesus Christ to revolutionize the world? What can you do?

One thing all of us can do is to be sure that we are personally committed to Jesus Christ in our hearts. When we are, he fills us with his Spirit and makes our lives fruitful for his glory. We will experience the abundant life in Christ daily, and we will share our faith in Christ with others. Availability to the Holy Spirit means personal spiritual revolution in our lives.

It takes commitment. Three percent of the population in China changed the direction of the whole nation to communism. In 1903 communism began with seventeen persons, and until the collapse of the Soviet Union in 1991, almost half of the world was under its influence. Many communists are so committed to their cause that communism is the one priority in their lives. How about you, fellow Christian? Is Christ your master, your priority?

Conclusion

I urge you to pray this prayer: "Dear Father in heaven, I make myself available to you to do with me as you will. I want to be one of those through whom you bring your message of love and forgiveness to all people everywhere. I ask you to cleanse, empower, lead, inspire, and teach me, and to cause me to do that which will bring greatest honor and glory to your name. Enable me by your Holy Spirit to contribute my maximum to the fulfillment of the Great Commission in my time. Thank you for what you will do."

Pray this prayer sincerely, and revolution will begin in your life right now.

SUNDAY EVENING, SEPTEMBER 15

Title: A Friend of God

Text: "By faith Abraham, when he was called to go out into a place which he should after receive for an inheritance, obeyed; and he went out, not knowing whither he went" **(Heb. 11:8)**.

Scripture Reading: Hebrews 11:8–10, 17–19

Introduction

Of the many illustrious names that appear in the Old Testament, that of Abraham stands out as conspicuously as does the moon in a star-filled sky. It will certainly be good for us to study the life of this great man, whom God called "Abraham my friend" (Isa. 41:8), in order that we, too, may become such friends of God that he can and will make known his will to us.

I. His call.

While Abraham was living quietly under his father's roof in Ur of the Chaldees, supervising the servants who were attending his flocks and herds, in some mysterious way there came to him a call from God to leave his home, his relatives, and his country, and to go into a strange land. Abraham's call was to go from the idolatry of his nation, the fellowship of his kindred, and the pursuits in which he had been engaged to fellowship with God, purity of worship, and the accomplishment of the divine purpose for his life.

God's calls are not always accompanied by reasons, but they are always accompanied by promises, either expressed or understood. Along with the sovereign and gracious call of God to Abraham there came an invaluable sevenfold promise. According to Genesis 12:1–3, God promised to make of Abraham a great nation, to bless him, to make his name great, to make him a blessing to others, to bless those who would be a blessing to him, to curse any who might curse him, and through him to bless all the families of the earth. These glorious promises should serve as a reminder to all of us who are God's children that his protection, power, and provision are guaranteed to all who are engaged in doing his will.

280

II. His response.

It was not a small matter for Abraham to make a choice between the security he was enjoying and the uncertainty of the unknown future. It was not easy for him to leave those who had been united closely with him either by blood or by the ties of friendship, and to start toward the far-off land of Canaan, which he had never seen.

Without asking any questions or offering any objections to God's expressed will for him, Abraham promptly, cheerfully, and hopefully started on his pilgrimage without knowing where he was going or what the future held in store for him. Although Abraham did not know where he was going, he did know that God had called and commissioned him, and he firmly believed that God would guide him and provide for him on the way. It is certainly encouraging and strengthening to know and to remember that when God guides his children, he always provides for them.

God never puts one of his children to a test until that child is ready for it. Abraham had to pass through numerous trials before he was ready to gain the victory and to earn the names "the father of the faithful" and "the friend of God." When sixty years of preparation had elapsed and Abraham thought that his greatest trials were over, he was subjected to the supreme test. For the purpose of revealing the quality and maturity of his faith in him, God made this shocking request of Abraham: "Take now thy son, thine only son Isaac, whom thou lovest, and get thee into the land of Moriah; and offer him there for a burnt offering upon one of the mountains which I will tell thee of" (Gen. 22:2).

Without raising a question, offering an excuse, or voicing a protest, but in the fullness of a mature faith in God, Abraham unhesitatingly, resolutely, and promptly demonstrated his willingness and readiness to do a thing from which human nature shrinks, but which God had commanded him to do. When the patriarch lifted the knife to sacrifice his son, in whom his hopes were vested, reasoning that God was able to raise him up from the dead, his obedience had gone far enough to prove that he would give his very best to God, so the heavenly Father interposed by calling out and staying his hand. Accepting Abraham's intention for the actual deed, God prevented him from slaying Isaac and thereby set his seal upon the faith of his friend. Such an act of faith had never been seen before and has not been observed since. True faith always works itself out in obedience to God.

Conclusion

Abraham was truly a great man. He was great in the estimation of right-thinking people, and what is far more important, he was great in the sight of God. Because of his faith in God and his obedience to God, Abraham certainly merited the appellation "the friend of God." Through an implicit faith in God, all Christians can do what Abraham did—namely, go where God wants them to go and do what God wants them to do, and by so doing earn the superlative title "friend of God."

WEDNESDAY EVENING, SEPTEMBER 18

Title: Winning Heaven's Gold Medal

Text: "Brethren, I count not myself to have apprehended: but this one thing I do, forgetting those things which are behind, and reaching forth unto those things which are before, I press toward the mark for the prize of the high calling of God in Christ Jesus" **(Phil. 3:13–14)**.

Scripture Reading: Philippians 3:1–14

Introduction

Repeatedly the apostle Paul uses figures of speech from the athletic games of his day as a way of communicating the great truths of God.

The people were familiar with boxing, and Paul talks in terms of giving a knockout blow to the evil impulses that would destroy us from within (1 Cor. 9:27).

Wrestling was a great sport among the Greeks. Paul refers to our conflict with the evil one in terms of a wrestling match. He gives advice concerning how we must find our strength in the grace of God if we are to overcome the evil one who intends to pin our shoulders to the mat and destroy us (Eph. 6:12).

In our text, Paul uses terms that are familiar to those who participate in track tournaments in describing the forward thrust and the persistent effort of those who desire to win heaven's approval for outstanding achievement in the kingdom of God.

I. I count not myself to have apprehended.

Paul declares that the conversion experience is but the beginning of God's destiny rather than its climax and conclusion.

A. *Paul had many achievements for which he could be proud and grateful.*
  1. Missionary journeys made.
  2. Evangelistic success achieved.
  3. Churches established.
  4. Epistles written.

B. *Paul was not filled with an attitude of self-satisfaction.*
  1. He was still learning.
  2. He was still serving.
  3. He was still worshiping.
  4. He was still pressing on.

II. Forgetting the things which are behind.

Paul calls attention to the fact that a successful track man must forget the past and pay no attention to the things at the right or the left if he would press toward the mark for the prize in the race today.

A. *Some need to forget the successes of the past.*
B. *Some need to forget the failures of the past.*
C. *All need to forget the grievances of the past.*

282

D. *All need to forget the fears of the past.*

Many things must be forgotten if we want to reach forth to the things that are before.

III. I press toward the mark for the prize.

In ancient Greece, to be a victor in the games was to achieve great success. A city took great pride in the fact that one of its citizens was the victor in the great games. Statues were erected, banquets were held, and songs were sung in honor of these victors. To be the winner of an Olympic crown became the ultimate in human happiness.

A. *The heavenly prize to which Paul refers is not to be identified with eternal salvation.* To be converted and to receive the crown of God's approval and commendation are two entirely different things.

B. *The heavenly prize is not to be expected as the normal thing for every believer, but it must be something for which he earnestly strives (2 Tim. 4:8).*

C. *The heavenly prize will not be equal for each one; instead, it will be given according to our faithfulness to our opportunities.*

D. *The heavenly prize is not won by human ingenuity but by the power that grace makes available to faith.*

E. *The heavenly prize will not be given to the self-satisfied, but only to those who are striving to reach God's high and holy call for their lives as his children.*

Conclusion

Are you pressing toward the mark for the prize of God's high calling for your life? We are not in competition with others in our quest to do what God would have us to do.

If we would hear his commendation, and if we would achieve his goal for our lives, we must hasten with all diligence. We must concentrate on the doing of his will. We must not hesitate or pause. We must be careful lest we stumble.

Christ is our Savior, but he is also our Leader. We are to look to him for leadership, inward strength, and assistance. We are to trust him for his abiding presence with us at all times.

For the glory of God, for the good of others, and for the fulfillment of our own lives, each of us should continue to press toward the mark for the prize of the high calling of God in Christ Jesus.

SUNDAY MORNING, SEPTEMBER 22

Title: Commitment to Worldwide Involvement

Text: "He said unto them, 'Go ye into all the world, and preach the gospel to every creature'" (**Mark 16:15**).

Scripture Reading: Mark 16:9–15

Hymns: "Holy, Holy, Holy," Dykes

"I Love to Tell the Story," Fischer

"Hark, the Voice of Jesus Calling," Mozart

Offertory Prayer: Thank you, heavenly Father, for providing for our needs throughout this week. We acknowledge the Scripture passage that says, "My God shall supply all your need according to his riches in glory by Christ Jesus" (Phil. 4:19). We return to you through your church our offerings to be used to share Jesus Christ with all the people of the world. Bless them mightily to that end, for Jesus' sake. Amen.

Introduction

Two Scripture passages taken from Phillips's *New Testament in Modern English* will help us to see the importance of this morning's text. The first is Romans 1:28–32:

> Moreover, since they considered themselves too high and mighty to acknowledge God, he allowed them to become the slaves of their degenerate minds, and to perform unmentionable deeds. They became filled with wickedness, rottenness, greed and malice; their minds became steeped in envy, murder, quarrelsomeness, deceitfulness and spite. They became whisperers-behind-doors, stabbers-in-the-back, God-haters. They overflowed with insolent pride and boastfulness, and their minds teemed with diabolical invention. They scoffed at duty to parents; they mocked at learning, recognized no obligations of honor, lost all natural affection, and had no use for mercy. More than this—being well aware of God's pronouncement that all who do these things deserve to die, they not only continued their own practices, but did not hesitate to give their thorough approval to others who did the same.

That passage of Scripture describes the world of Jesus' day. And here is another, found in 2 Timothy 3:1–5:

> The times will be full of danger. Men will become utterly self-centered, greedy for money, full of big words. They will be proud and contemptuous, without any regard for what their parents taught them. They will be utterly lacking in gratitude, purity and normal human affections. They will be men of unscrupulous speech and have no control of themselves. They will be passionate and unprincipled, treacherous, self-willed and conceited, loving all the time what gives them pleasure instead of loving God. They will maintain a façade of "religion," but their conduct will deny its validity. You must keep clear of people like this.

This passage describes the God-defying society of Paul's day—a day that sounds much like our own.

What do you do with a world like that? Jesus gave the answer as recorded in

Mark 16:15: "Go ye into all the world, and preach the gospel to every creature." That is what you do with a world like the one the Bible describes. That kind of world is still in existence today, and the words of Jesus Christ are just as relevant today: "Go ye into *all* the world, and preach the gospel to *every* creature." This was our resurrected Lord's last command to his army of followers, and it is to be carried out until he comes again. These were his final words to his church before he was taken up from them to be seated at the right hand of the Father in heaven.

Christ's church must do nothing less than fulfill his command. And it is impossible for serious Christians to fail to commit themselves to Jesus Christ as Lord and to the great command to his church. If these words are that important, how do you go about fulfilling what Jesus said?

In verse 15, we find three principles on how to fulfill this command:

I. The principle of action.

"Go ye." To go means to set out, to depart, or to pursue a journey. It is to go with a purpose. There is no substitute in all of life for what Jesus says we are to be doing. We must not allow prayer or Bible study or giving to be a substitute in the Christian life for the principle of action in going to preach the gospel to every creature. Jesus used the word *go* numerous times in his ministry because this principle of action was so very important to him (see Matt. 10:1–5; Luke 14:21–24).

Here is the Lord of life, the Commander in Chief of the church, saying to every believer, "Go!" There is no *substitute* for it. We must be willing to accept by obedience the command of Jesus Christ in the fulfillment of his Word. There is no shortcut to it; there is no streamlined method to save the world. We must be willing to *go* in the fulfillment of his will.

II. The principle of saturation.

This is noted in the words "into all the world" and "to every creature." Saturation is preaching the gospel to every available person at every available time by every available means. Jesus Christ leaves out no possible place on the globe, and he leaves out no possible person.

This means that there are no geographical boundaries and no racial, cultural, or national limits. It means that God is no respecter of persons. The principle of saturation is Jesus' way. Mark 16:15 gives the general principle. Acts 1:8 states the specific plan for how to do it: "Ye shall be witnesses unto me both in Jerusalem and in all Judea, and in Samaria and unto the uttermost part of the earth." He tells us what not to exclude—Samaria (even though there were racial differences between the Jews and the Samaritans). This is the principle of saturation.

When this principle is applied to our own city and to our own church, it means that the goal of our church should be to share the message of Jesus Christ in a meaningful way with *every* household in this city and with every person within this geographical area. Jesus Christ's command is to begin sharing the gospel right where we are, reaching out and stretching as far as we can with the gospel to as many people as possible. Only then can we really begin to fufill his command. The principle of action is to go! The principle of saturation is to include all the world and every creature.

III. The principle of proclamation.

Jesus said, "Go ... and preach the gospel." It means to share Christ both publicly and personally. It means to share Christ with the thousands; it means to share Christ with individuals. Preach Christ! This is God's principle of wisdom.

This is the beginning point; this is what will bring about inner transformation that will in turn bring about society's transformation. You cannot transform a society without transforming the inner spirit of people, "for out of the heart come evil thoughts." Jesus Christ says it is the gospel that changes people's hearts.

Conclusion

Will God bless the proclamation of the gospel? Mark 16:20 says, "They went forth, and preached every where, the Lord working with them, and confirming the word with signs following." God is just waiting to demonstrate his power. As we yield ourselves to him, we too will experience the power of sharing the great gospel of Christ.

SUNDAY EVENING, SEPTEMBER 22

Title: A Man Who Was Faithful to the End

Text: "By faith Joseph, when he died, made mention of the departing of the children of Israel; and gave commandment concerning his bones" (**Heb. 11:22**).

Scripture Reading: Genesis 50:15–26

Introduction

Joseph, the eleventh of Jacob's twelve sons and the favorite of his father, had exceptional qualities that attracted the attention and elicited the admiration of others. But the father was unwise in giving Joseph a coat of many colors. This display of partiality aroused the jealousy and animosity of Joseph's brothers.

I. Joseph was hated and harassed.

One day Jacob sent Joseph to search for his ten brothers who were away from home, to inquire about their welfare and the safety of their flocks and to report his findings to him. When the brothers saw Joseph approaching, their jealousy came to a head. Not only did he live in a world of higher thoughts than they did, but he also had aims and ambitions they despised. Because Joseph set his affections on higher things and was fired by ambitions that they considered meaningless, his brothers branded him a dreamer. In derision they exclaimed, "Here comes that dreamer!" (Gen. 37:19 NIV). Joseph's brothers had been irritated greatly when they heard him talking about the great future that awaited him and informing them that in due time all of them would be kneeling at his feet and doing him homage.

To the brothers, Joseph was a pest to be gotten rid of swiftly and in the most convenient way. This they did by taking him by force, stripping him of his coat, casting him into a pit, and then selling him to a caravan of traders on their way to Egypt. Their excuse for this demonstration of their hostility toward their brother was the favoritism of their father, but their own wickedness was the reason for it.

Upon their arrival in Egypt, the traders sold Joseph to Potiphar, the captain of Pharaoh's guard. Determined that he would not brood over the wrongs he had suffered at their hands, Joseph courageously resolved that he would endure his injuries, forgive his brothers, and refuse to be discouraged. Soon after taking him into his palatial home, Potiphar observed Joseph's splendid conduct, recognized his ability and dependability, and gave him charge of his house. God blesses and honors those who honor him.

Before long, however, Potiphar's wife became infatuated with Joseph and attempted to seduce him, but he refused her amorous advances and solicitation rather than displeasing and dishonoring God by yielding. In his flight from temptation, Joseph lost his coat and his reputation but not his character. Potiphar's wife accused Joseph of the sin she had tried so artfully to induce him to commit. Because of her false accusation, Joseph was imprisoned. Doubtless this young idealist was shocked that he should be imprisoned, but he did not become embittered or yield to despair.

II. Joseph was exalted and esteemed.

A turn in the fortune of Joseph came when Pharaoh had a dream that no one could interpret. The butler informed Pharaoh of Joseph's ability to interpret dreams, whereupon Pharaoh ordered Joseph to be brought to him. Impressed by Joseph's modesty and ability and hearing that there would soon be a famine in the land, Pharaoh exalted him to the position of prime minister, an office second only to his own. People may be slow to recognize and reward faithfulness, but God never fails to do so. Once more God's promise "Them that honor me I will honor" (1 Sam. 2:30) had been fulfilled.

During the famine, people came from various places and asked Joseph for rations. Jacob sent his ten sons to Egypt to purchase supplies of grain. When they arrived, they bowed before Joseph, quite unaware that they were fulfilling Joseph's dreams. He recognized them, but they did not have the least idea that he was Joseph.

On another trip, they took Benjamin with them. Upon seeing him, Joseph announced that they would dine with him at noon. On that occasion, they "bowed themselves to him." Thus we see Joseph exalted and esteemed by his brethren who had wronged him so grievously.

III. Joseph was revealed and revered.

One day the ten men appeared before Joseph for the purpose of obtaining additional supplies of grain, and to them he said, "I am Joseph! Is my father still living?" (Gen. 45:3 NIV). Seeing how shocked and astonished they were when they recognized him, Joseph told them not to be afraid. They expected him to wreak vengeance on them, but as far as he was concerned, the past was forgiven. It takes a great man to forgive and to forget personal injuries, but it takes an even greater one to tell those who have wronged him that the injury has turned out to his advantage, and Joseph did just that. What they had done to him was cruel and wicked, but God had transformed it into good for Joseph, for his brothers, and for the whole nation. Joseph said, "You intended to harm me, but God intended it for good to accomplish what is now being done, the saving of many lives" (Gen. 50:20 NIV). As master of the situation, God had sent Joseph before them to preserve life. Aware of God's beneficent purpose in his adversities, Joseph refused to be resentful toward those who had abused him.

Believing that the time of his departure was drawing near, Joseph talked to his brothers. He predicted that in the future his relatives and descendants and other Israelites would be leaving Egypt and returning to their homeland. He asked them to do him the favor of carrying his bones with them when they marched homeward. Joseph exacted a promise from them that they would do so. Generations later their promise was fulfilled, and his bones were buried at Shechem (Josh. 24:32).

Conclusion

May God give us the faith that functions as Joseph's did in enabling him to overcome the world and to be faithful to the very end of life.

WEDNESDAY EVENING, SEPTEMBER 25

Title: Rejoice in the Lord

Text: "Finally, my brethren, rejoice in the Lord" **(Phil. 3:1)**.

Scripture Reading: Philippians 4:4–7

Introduction

Paul's epistle to the Philippians has been called his epistle of joy. Although he was a prisoner in Rome, his spirit was free and his cup overflowed with joy (Phil. 1:4, 18, 26; 2:16–18, 28–29; 3:1; 4:1, 4). Paul was filled with joy and wished that the Philippian Christians could experience the same. Jesus spoke to his disciples of his divine joy and desired for them that they might experience a fullness of joy (John 15:11; 16:24).

I. The command to rejoice.

The world needs a religion of joy. A sour-faced, pessimistic Christian is a very poor advertisement of what Jesus can do for a believer. To live a sad, melancholy, depressed life is to fail to take inventory of the blessings that are ours through faith in Christ Jesus.

II. Factors that contribute toward an unhappy frame of mind.

A. *The present world situation adds to the agony of anxiety.*

B. *Some are unhappy because of personal weaknesses that subject them to very strong temptations.*

C. *The competitive and materialistic spirit of our age contributes to our having a secular standard of success.* When people measure success in terms of gadgets and earthly goods, there are many who have reason to be sad.

D. *Some are disappointed by their own failures and live in despondency.*

E. *There are others who have let the failures of others, along with disappointment in others, deprive them of the joy and happiness that they would like to experience.*

III. The source of abiding joy.

A. *Some search for happiness in the wrong place or by the wrong method.* Paul did not say:

1. "Rejoice in material wealth."
2. "Rejoice in fame and power."
3. "Rejoice in the pleasures of the world."
4. "Rejoice in social prestige and prominence."

B. *Paul declared that Christ is the source of real joy.* Paul was once a self-righteous, egotistical persecutor of Christianity. He had a revolutionary experience with Jesus Christ on the road to Damascus. Jesus Christ, God's Son, became very real and personal and wonderful to him. Christ produced such a change that his life was transformed. He lived in the joy of many things through Christ.

1. We can have the joy of the glad consciousness of forgiven sin through faith in Christ (Acts 10:43).
2. Through Christ we can rejoice in the glad consciousness of being children of God (1 John 3:2).
3. Through Jesus Christ we have access to the power of God that will enable us to make any necessary adjustment to the circumstances of life (Phil. 4:13).
4. Through faith in Christ we can be assured that God will supply our basic needs for living according to his riches in grace through Jesus Christ (Phil. 4:13).
5. Through Jesus Christ we can rejoice in our citizenship in heaven and in our assurance that death will be a transformation rather than a tragedy (Phil. 3:20–21).

Conclusion

Is your life characterized by depression and defeat? If so, you are failing to enter into your heritage as a child of God and as a servant of the Lord Jesus Christ. You are missing the joy that is possible for you. You are depriving others of the testimony of a joy-filled life.

To rejoice in the Lord is a priceless privilege. To rejoice in the Lord is our daily duty. To rejoice in the Lord will add to our joy and will make life more beautiful for ourselves and for others. As Paul said, "Rejoice in the Lord always: and again I say, Rejoice" (Phil. 4:4).

SUNDAY MORNING, SEPTEMBER 29

Title: The Secret of Christian Influence

Text: "Now when they saw the boldness of Peter and John, and perceived that they were unlearned and ignorant men, they marvelled; and they took knowledge of them, that they had been with Jesus" **(Acts 4:13)**.

Scripture Reading: Acts 4:5–13

Hymns: "O Worship the King," Haydn

"One Day," Marsh

"Break Thou the Bread of Life," Sherwin

Offertory Prayer: Heavenly Father, we hallow your name as we think of life's blessings. You are the giver of every gift, and our hearts respond with love and thanks. We acknowledge that you give power to get wealth, and we desire to honor you with our substance. Accept these gifts from hearts that love you. In Jesus' name. Amen.

Introduction

The power of influence is unmistakable. It may be like light shining in the darkness. Whether a candle or a searchlight, it is penetrating. It may be like yeast that permeates the dough with its power as it does its work. Or it may be like a shadow, the shadow of a great life that falls across the path of another, causing the life to be blessed. Whatever it is like, Christian influence is undeniable; it is inescapable.

Not one of us lives a neutral life. We all influence others at all times in one way or another. We may be an influence for good or for bad. Our lives may lift people up, or they may drag them down. The fact is, in each one of us resides an influence that is undeniable and inescapable.

It is a marvelous thing to behold Christian influence at work. Let me point out from our text three things about the secret of Christian influence.

I. The scene involved.

The Sanhedrin was in session. This was the ruling body of the Jews, their supreme court. It was composed of leaders who represented the high-priestly class, the leading citizens of the nation, the lawyers, and the Pharisees. The air was electric with their authority. In the middle of this powerful body of men were two simple men, former fishermen, not long removed from the rough life they knew. The ruling body had already said contentiously, "These men are just unlearned and ignorant men."

290

Though they did not have a degree in the rabbinical school, these two men evidenced the fact that they had been to another kind of school, because there was a difference in their lives: they were bold. Scripture says, "They saw the boldness of Peter and John." There was something about these men that was inescapably frank. They were gladly fearless; they were courageous and confident. They could stand in the midst of this authoritative religious body and say what they wanted to say. They were free men with free speech. There was something different about them. They had a secret in their lives, and as they expressed themselves, it was their amazing Christian influence that carried their message across to the lives of those who were listening.

II. The secret involved.

If there was a secret to these men, what was it? The answer is found in this simple statement: "They had been with Jesus." Some say that this means that they were simply disciples of Jesus, but it evidently means more than that. It means that they were acting like Christ in what they said, in the manner in which they said it, in their very attitude toward life. They were demonstrating the influence of Christ in and through their lives.

The one great qualification for Christian influence is a personal experience with Jesus Christ. And there are at least three elements in a relationship with Christ that are expressed in a strong Christian influence.

A. *Christian influence begins with a conversion experience.* This is a spiritual experience whereby individuals turn from sin and self-will to Christ, who becomes their Lord, Leader, and Master. They have a new motivation—a new direction by which to live. Thus there is a new manifestation within them that something has happened and that they now have Jesus Christ in their hearts.

B. *A personal experience with Jesus means communion with him.* Jesus chose the Twelve that they might be with him. He chose them for at least one reason—companionship. The disciples' companionship with Jesus Christ created a change in their lives based on their personal experience of conversion. And this is an eternal principle—companionship in life always affects our influence.

C. *A personal experience with Jesus is related to a commitment of our lives to his life and teachings.* This means that he is to control our interests. What does Jesus Christ mean to your life? What if one day the door chime at your house sounded and, upon opening the door, you saw Jesus Christ standing there? What would you say? What would you say if Jesus said, "I want to come to live with you"? Or suppose one day, as a businessperson, you were sitting at your desk working on your papers and you looked up and there stood Jesus Christ asking to be your partner in business. Or youth, you were driving along with your date and Jesus came into your presence and said that he wanted to be with you on your date. Would he be welcome?

What would this kind of arrangement do to your home, your business, or your personal life? The fact is, Jesus *is* with us, and he is *in* us! And the person who has a tremendous influence is the one who is committed to Jesus Christ, his life, and his teachings. That is the secret of Peter and John, and that is the secret of all Christian influence. People notice whether we have a likeness to Jesus Christ.

III. The significance involved.

There are some eternal lessons to be learned.

A. *The first one is that any one of us can have a significant influence for Christ in our lives.* Peter and John were unlikely followers of Christ, and yet look at them after they were filled with the Holy Spirit! These were the very men who helped change the world, and the Christ who used them is the same Christ who is ready and willing to use *any* of us if we so make ourselves available to him.

In Abilene, Kansas, the hometown of Dwight D. Eisenhower, is a museum that holds the treasure that belonged to him. In the museum is a record of his Sunday school life. Could his teacher, whoever he or she was, ever have imagined that a restless boy with a ready smile could be someone whom kings and queens would honor? That teacher remains unnamed, but he or she had a lasting influence on the boy's life through the Word of God.

Into your hands are given potentialities and abilities. You have a mind to think, a heart to care, a voice to speak. You can share—silently or verbally—as an influence for Jesus Christ. Anyone can. That is the story of the book of Acts.

B. *A second lesson: Let us beware that we do not waste our Christian influence.* Let us not take it as a light and hide it under a bushel. Just what are you doing with your life? What does Jesus Christ have of yours that he can use? It is possible for us to waste our influence so that our lives do not really count for Christ. We miss *his* will for us, and thus we miss sharing life with others.

C. *A third lesson: The influence of Christ flows on and on in the lives of those who have found the secret.* It never stops. It flows like the mighty Mississippi through one's life, spilling itself out into an ocean of service and life. The influence of Jesus Christ flows on and on throughout eternity and will never cease.

A battle-hardened ex-marine, on a college campus, sat by a Christian girl in one of his classes. Day after day he observed her life, so that finally he said to her, "There is something different about your life. I would like to know what that difference is." She said, "I did not know there was anything different about me, but if there is, I am sure it is because of my relationship with Jesus Christ. I'm just trying to live the best Christian life possible."

Conclusion

Wouldn't you like to be that kind of person—known as one who has been with Jesus? The secret is your relationship with him. Have you made the wonderful discovery of knowing Jesus Christ personally? If you haven't, now is the time to do so. If you have, now is the time to intensify your commitment to him.

SUNDAY EVENING, SEPTEMBER 29

Title: A Giant for God

Text: "By faith Moses' parents hid him for three months after he was born, because they saw he was no ordinary child, and they were not afraid of the king's edict" **(Heb. 11:23 NIV)**.

Scripture Reading: Hebrews 11:23–27

Introduction

Moses was highly favored in being born into a home in which God was known, loved, honored, and obeyed. Pharaoh had decreed that all the male children of the Hebrews should be put to death. But Moses' parents displayed courageous faith in God when they defied Pharaoh's decree and attempted to conceal their young child. They placed him in an ark on the Nile River and committed him to God's keeping. Before long, he was discovered by the daughter of Pharaoh and was adopted into the royal family. His sister, Miriam, arranged for their mother to become Moses' nurse, and it seems that he remained in her care until he had placed his trust in God.

Reared as a prince, Moses was given the privilege of a royal education and all of the advantages of the Egyptian culture. He stood on the threshold of all that people desire most in this life. His worldly prospects were exceedingly bright. Position, prestige, possessions, pleasure, and power were within his grasp. Apparently there was not anything that wealth could give that Moses could not have had for the asking.

The real explanation of Moses' wonderful career, of his place in history, and of his unending influence on the world is that he believed in God and depended on him. Doubtless his faith in God was implanted in him first by his mother during his early life. That is how and when most heroic living begins. In original endowments, in the clarity of the divine call, in the grandeur of his mission, and in the permanence of his influence, Moses was certainly honored very highly. It was his genuine faith in God that influenced his thinking, determined his actions, and shaped his life.

I. His refusal.

"By faith Moses, when he had grown up, refused to be known as the son of Pharaoh's daughter" (Heb. 11:24 NIV). As a believer in God, Moses had developed a remarkable ability to distinguish between right and wrong. Moses' refusal "to be known as the son of Pharaoh's daughter" meant the forfeiture of the highest social position in Egypt. And social position is not something that people ordinarily despise. On the contrary, many are willing to pay almost any price to acquire and to retain a high social standing.

Moses' faith in God caused him to refuse to allow others to call him something that he was not. His faith implanted within him a longing for reality and a love for the truth. Moses wanted to be called what he was, and he wanted to be what he was called. Oh what some will do to be called something they are not! What one really is will determine the quality of one's service and the extent of one's usefulness.

II. His choice.

"He chose to be mistreated along with the people of God rather than to enjoy the fleeting pleasures of sin" (Heb. 11:25 NIV). Moses refused to allow personal interests to blind him or personal inclinations to cause him to choose the second best. Ample opportunities were afforded him to indulge in every type of sinful pleasure known to humankind. Knowing so well that the pleasures of sin were for a season only, and a very short one at that, Moses let it be known that pleasure was not his objective in life.

Moses was convinced that the time had arrived for him to decide whether he would identify himself with the suffering Israelites, whose cause was that of righteousness and mercy, or continue with their cruel oppressors with whom he had been associated. Aware that they were grievously oppressed by their Egyptian masters, Moses' heart ached for them. He could not bear to live at ease while they were suffering. He yearned to see them delivered from their bondage. He decided to forsake royalty and cast his lot with a brokenhearted, poverty-stricken, and despised people. He knew that he was assuming tremendous responsibilities in doing so.

Believing that the investment of his life in the liberation of the enslaved Israelites would bear dividends throughout eternity, Moses chose to sacrifice himself upon the altar of service rather than live in the realm of pleasure. His choice, which was contrary to the desires many have cherished, was costly to Moses but pleasing to God and profitable to his people. The thing that influenced Moses' thinking, determined his choice, controlled his actions, and shaped his life was his implicit faith in God. He certainly demonstrated great faith and remarkable wisdom in making his choice.

III. His evaluation.

"He regarded disgrace for the sake of Christ as of greater value than the treasures of Egypt, because he was looking ahead to his reward" (Heb. 11:26 NIV). The vision of faith Moses had was far superior to what his natural eye saw of worldly pleasures and temporal treasures. Moses weighed the results of giving himself to the interests of Egypt over against the rewards of acceding to the claims of God upon his life, and he was thoroughly convinced that reproach for Christ was far better than riches in Egypt.

As Moses went forth to emancipate an enslaved people, he was encouraged greatly by the assurance that God's wisdom and power were at his disposal. What more could he ask? It was God's work, to be performed by God's power, but Moses was the human instrument for doing the work, and the one through whom God's power would flow. Having made a correct evaluation, and having made a full commitment of himself to the doing of God's will, Moses went forth by faith, in complete dependence on God for the wisdom and strength necessary for the accomplishment of his mission. Because Moses proceeded in the pathway of obedience and counted the reward of God to be of utmost value, God was with him all the way, and at the end placed his stamp of approval on Moses' life and work.

OCTOBER

■ Sunday Mornings

The theme for Sunday mornings this month is "Christ Meeting Our Deepest Needs." Humanity's deepest need is for a right relationship with God. This need can be met only through the Christ who came to save, use, and transform our lives.

■ Sunday Evenings

We are to be missionaries in today's world, communicating the good news of God's love. "The Message of Missions" is the theme for these messages that emphasize our responsibility for communicating the gospel to the world.

■ Wednesday Evenings

We will begin a series of expository studies of Revelation 1–3 on Wednesday evenings. The theme is "Christ Speaks to His Churches."

WEDNESDAY EVENING, OCTOBER 2

Title: Christ Speaks to His Churches

Text: "The seven stars are the angels of the seven churches: and the seven candlesticks which thou sawest are the seven churches" **(Rev. 1:20)**.

Scripture Reading: Revelation 1

Introduction

Many Christians avoid the book of Revelation because they think it is incomprehensible. In this book we step into a strange and unfamiliar world. There are angels and demons, lambs and lions, horses and dragons. Seals are broken, trumpets are blown, and bowls are poured out. There is thunder and lightning, hail and fire, blood and smoke. The book contains many weird and mysterious visions. Everywhere in its pages there is bizarre imagery. The result is that some consider the book too enigmatic for serious study. This should not be, for the book of Revelation is a part of the divine Scriptures. The book claims a special blessing for both readers and hearers: "Blessed is the one who reads aloud the words of this prophecy, and blessed are those who hear it and take to heart what is written in it, because the time is near" (Rev. 1:3 NIV). Our purpose is to find some of these blessings in our Wednesday evening studies of the first three chapters.

I. The revelation.

A. *Whose is it?* In the King James Version the title of this book is "The Revelation of Saint John the Divine." But whose revelation is it really? The first verse gives us the answer: "The Revelation of Jesus Christ." This book, then, is the culmination of the Gospels. It is the story of Christ all the way through. The New Testament word for "revelation" is *apokalupsis.* It means "to uncover," "to take away the veil," or "to bring from hiding." The book does not try to cover up or hide the message of God but rather to reveal it, to uncover it. One need not identify every figure or symbol or detail to get the main message of hope. I do not need to identify each part of each flower in the garden to enjoy the beauty and fragrance.

B. *What is it?* The message of this book is a revelation of those "things which must shortly come to pass" (1:1). It is a message for our day—the church age. It is therefore important to us. Much is being written today about the churches. Some of it is complimentary, and more of it is not. But what does Christ say about the churches? He is the Founder, the Head, the Chief Cornerstone. Jesus said, "I will build my church" (Matt. 16:18). His last words to the church were, "Go ye therefore, and teach all nations" (Matt. 28:19). There is no further word from Christ to the church until the last book—Revelation, which is "the revelation from Jesus Christ, which God gave him to show his servants what must soon take place" (1:1 NIV). In the three chapters following is a clear, concise, and comprehensive message to the churches. In these verses, by praise and censure, by warning and exhortation, the risen Christ makes plain his word to the churches of this age. Here is a message for us today.

II. The churches.

This is a message "to [Christ's] servants" (Rev. 1:1). Christ speaks to his churches.

A. *The churches at that time.* The churches in the first Christian century were greatly oppressed. The persecution that began under Caesar Nero had grown steadily worse until the whole Christian movement was threatened with extermination. Could the church survive? Nothing before had been able to defy the might of the Roman Empire. But this was not the only peril. The churches were also hampered by the threat of doctrinal error and worldly living. Many believers were being deceived by false teachers.

B. *The churches today.* The churches today face many of these same perils. In scattered places of our world there is open hostility to Christian missions and persecution of believers. Everywhere we wrestle with a materialistic philosophy. The gospel seed is being choked out by the thorns of worldly care or plucked up by teachers of false doctrine.

III. The Christ.

A. *In glory.* The apostle John was "in the Spirit on the Lord's day" (1:10). While in this attitude of worship, John saw a vision of the risen Lord.

Think of what the apostle would have missed if he had not been in worship on the Lord's Day! What John saw of the Lord in glory is described in verses 12–16. The description is a compilation of the prophets' descriptions of the Son of Man in his glory. Daniel says that his hair is as white as wool and snow; Ezekiel says that his voice is like many waters; Job speaks of the stars in his right hand; and Isaiah says that out of his mouth comes a two-edged sword. Such a vision of our Lord in glory was too much for John. He fell down at Jesus' feet as though dead. Then, looking up again, he saw one of the most amazing parts of the vision.

B. *Among the churches.* Verse 20 says, "The seven stars are the angels of the seven churches, and the seven lampstands are the seven churches" (1:20 NIV). What the apostle John saw was Christ among the churches. In Ephesus he saw a church that had left its first love, a backslidden church. In Smyrna he saw a church in the midst of tribulation. In Pergamum he saw a church that was faithful to his name. In Thyatira he noticed a worldly church; in Sardis, a dead church; in Philadelphia, a church that had a great opportunity for missionary outreach; and at Laodicea, a lukewarm church.

I wonder what the risen Christ sees as he walks in our church? I'm sure he notices the empty seats. He sees the lack of commitment in Christian service and stewardship. He sees the compromising and worldly living of our members. He notices our lack of prayer. Throughout these chapters we are studying are the words, "I know your deeds" (NIV). Christ knows our church—what we do and what we neglect to do. He has something to say to us. It will behoove us to listen to what the living Lord has to say to his churches.

SUNDAY MORNING, OCTOBER 6

Title: The Determination of Jesus to Save

Text: "For the Son of man is not come to destroy men's lives, but to save them" **(Luke 9:56).**

Scripture Reading: Luke 9:51–62

Hymns: "Holy, Holy, Holy," Heber

       "He Lifted Me," Homer

       "Jesus Saves," Owens

Offertory Prayer: Our Father in heaven, we rejoice that our Savior came into this world to rescue us from the waste and disappointment of sin. Today we give ourselves that others might come to know him as a personal Savior from sin and as a wonderful Friend for the road of life. Receive our tithes and offerings as an expression of our love. Bless them that others may hear the gospel and respond with faith in Jesus Christ. May your name be honored and glorified. In Jesus' name. Amen.

Introduction

In our Scripture reading we are brought face-to-face with some ugly racial and religious prejudice. We discover that the apostles of our Lord were men of passions like ours. They reacted to this prejudice with hostility and with a desire to inflict punishment. Our Lord rebuked them because of their destructive feelings toward others of a different race and different religion. He gave expression to his determination to be humanity's Savior rather than their destroyer.

Christ came to bless you, not to curse you. Christ came to build your life, not to destroy your happiness. Christ came to help you, not to hinder you. Christ came to enrich you, not to impoverish you. Christ came to set you free, not to imprison you. Christ is your Friend.

Christ had a consuming ambition to be humankind's Savior. This was his controlling purpose in all of his ambitions and actions. This was his persistent determination.

What Christ was, he continues to be. What Christ sought to do, he continues to seek to accomplish. What Christ sought to achieve, he will continue to seek to achieve through his church (John 3:17; 12:47; Mark 10:45).

The cross was no accident in the program of God. It was not a strategy implemented to meet an unforeseen emergency. When the time came for our Lord to accomplish his passion in Jerusalem, "He steadfastly set his face to go to Jerusalem."

I. Examples of Christ's determination to save us.

A. *Our Lord revealed his determination to be our Savior during his temptation in the wilderness (Matt. 4:1–11).*
  1. Satan encouraged Christ to satisfy his physical appetites rather than give attention to his divine mission.
  2. Satan encouraged Christ to turn on the glamour and to overwhelm the people with an extravagant display of power and glory. He was seeking to lead him to establish a superficial kingdom.
  3. Satan sought to dissuade Christ from going to the cross by promising him the whole world if he would but fall down and worship him. He was challenging Christ to let this world become his home.

B. *The earthly family of Christ sought to persuade him to forsake his redemptive mission (Mark 3:31–35).*

C. *Our Lord resisted and rejected the counsel of his dearest friends when they sought to persuade him to forsake his mission if it involved the suffering of death (Matt. 16:21–23).* His disciples did not understand—perhaps they *could not* understand—why it was necessary that he expose himself to the danger of going to Jerusalem (John 11:8).

D. *Our Lord did not let the selfishness and indifference of his followers dissuade him from his determination to be our Savior.*
    The disciples were so self-centered that on the very night before Christ's death they were quarreling about which one would be the greatest in the hoped-for coming kingdom (Luke 22:24).

Even the most faithful three let weariness put them to sleep when they should have been encouraging their Lord with their united prayers on his behalf as he faced the agony in the garden (Matt. 26:40, 43, 45).

E. *Christ was so determined to save that he refused to call for ten thousand angels to rescue him in his time of need (Matt. 26:53).*

F. *Christ refused to come down from the cross to impress those who had plotted his agonizing death on the cross (Matt. 27:39–43).*

G. *Christ was so determined to be our Savior and to offer us the gift of forgiveness and eternal life that he laid down his life for us on the cross (Luke 23:46).*

II. Christ lives today with this same plan and determination to be our Savior.

A. *Christ came not to destroy your life or your happiness.* He came that you might have life and that you might find happiness.

B. *Christ wants to save your life. . .*
1. From emptiness.
2. From unhappiness.
3. From waste.
4. From failure.
5. From self-destruction.
6. From eternal separation from God and his people.

C. *Christ offers the gift of forgiveness and new life to those who will receive him as Savior and trust him as Lord.*

D. *Christ ministers today through the Holy Spirit, through his church, by means of the Bible, and by providential events.*

III. Christ requires faith and determination from us.

Christ is eager to do something more than just give us a ticket to heaven. He wants to come into our lives and deliver us from self-trust, self-love, and self-will. He wants to deliver us from the tyranny of the material and from that which is temporary in value.

He invites us to accept the principle of the cross as being the pathway that leads to fullness of life in the here and now as well as the hereafter.

A. *If we would truly be saved to the life of fullest joy and greatest achievement, there must be a detachment from the material things that would prevent or hinder us on our journey to Jerusalem (Luke 9:57–58).*

B. *If we would truly follow him, we must give him top priority over all other relationships (Luke 9:59–60).*

C. *If we would truly follow Jesus Christ and experience the fullness of life he offers, we must make a break with the past and face the future with hope (Luke 9:61–62).*

Conclusion

The Samaritans did not receive Jesus Christ as a guest into their city or as Lord in their hearts at this time (Luke 9:53). They made a fatal mistake. Each of us who has not yet received Christ would be exceedingly wise to receive him as Savior and Lord of our lives. Receive him as your Teacher and Guide for the road of life. Let him become your Friend and Companion. Make him the very God of your existence today.

SUNDAY EVENING, OCTOBER 6

Title: Prayer to the Lord of the Harvest

Text: "Then saith he unto his disciples, The harvest truly is plenteous, but the labourers are few; pray ye therefore the Lord of the harvest, that he will send forth labourers into his harvest" (**Matt. 9:37–38**).

Scripture Reading: Matthew 9:32–38

Introduction

Most of the people of the world today have never heard the good news contained in the account of the life, death, and resurrection of Jesus Christ. Instead of making progress toward winning the world to faith in Christ, we are losing the human race more and more with the passing of each generation.

What is to be the individual Christian reaction to this continuing decline in both our numbers and our influence?

We could let a spirit of defeatism destroy us. We could retreat into an attitude of hopeless fatalism and blame God for everything. Or we can place ourselves under the searchlight of our Lord's example, his instructions, and his disciples' example to see if we have misinterpreted his instructions or disobeyed his orders. Could it be that we have overlooked something that has contributed to our failure to win more people to faith in Jesus Christ?

Why are we dropping behind instead of making progress toward winning more and more to faith in the Lord Jesus Christ? Is the devil more powerful today than previously? Is God less concerned about the unsaved today than he was in years gone by? Does humankind have less need today for God than in a previous generation? It would be difficult to believe that any of these possibilities is true.

Have we missed the boat somewhere at the point of listening to our Lord and doing what he would have us to do? Have we substituted some human strategy for the divine program?

Perhaps the simple answer to the question that we are considering is that instead of responding with joyful obedience to our Lord, we have responded with disobedience to the claims of the Great Commission. Our Lord cannot be pleased with us at this point. Our world goes on in darkness to death. We miss our highest destiny, and others spend their lives without faith and enter eternity without hope.

Could it be that we have been disobedient to our Lord because of a combination of spiritual blindness and spiritual deafness? Could it be that we have failed to hear the heart's cry of those about us and that at the same time we have failed to hear the voice of the Holy Spirit from within? Surely, if we see the need of others for Christ, we will be more willing to accept our place in God's great redemptive program. We will be more inclined to listen to the voice of our Lord and to be obedient to his command at the point of witnessing to the unsaved world.

I. Christlike compassion is necessary.

A. *Our Lord was moved with compassion by human pain.* He suffered with those who quivered with agony. He was moved with compassion for the sick (Matt. 14:14), the blind (20:34), and those in the grip of demons (Mark 9:22). Our Lord suffers with us in all of our physical and emotional illnesses (Isa. 63:9).

B. *Our Lord was moved with compassion by human sorrows.* When our Lord saw the widow of Nain in her grief, we are told that he had compassion on her (Luke 7:11–13). When Jesus visited in the home of Mary and Martha following the death of Lazarus, we are told that "Jesus wept" (John 11:35). The Christ who is the same yesterday, today, and forever is moved with compassion toward us in our sorrows.

C. *Our Lord was moved with compassion by human hunger (Matt. 15:32).*

D. *Our Lord was moved with compassion by human loneliness.* A leper who had been banished from home and family and friends because of his terrible illness moved our Lord with compassion to exercise his divine healing power (Mark 1:41).

E. *Our Lord was moved with compassion by human distress and bewilderment (Matt. 9:36).*

F. *Our Lord was moved with compassion because of the lostness of people (John 3:16).* Compassion for the lost brought the Savior from heaven to earth to live, labor, suffer, and die that he might rescue people from the awful tyranny of sin and to prevent them from perishing forever.

We will never take our Lord's commission to evangelize the world very seriously until we let his compassion take command of our total being. We will hesitate to be obedient until, with eyes of compassion, we look below the surface of the external and see the deep-hearted need of those about us. Compassion is the supreme gift of the Holy Spirit. We must recognize and respond to the Holy Spirit who dwells within individual hearts.

II. Our Lord invites our communication and our cooperation (Matt. 9:38).

A. *The harvest is plenteous.*

B. *The laborers are few.*

C. *Prayer is to be made to the Lord of the harvest.*

This imperative word is addressed to all of us. It is an all-inclusive exhortation.

1. Who is the Lord of the harvest? Is Jesus referring to himself? Is Jesus talking about God the Father? Is he referring to the Holy Spirit?

2. The Holy Spirit is our Leader, our Enabler, our Teacher, our Companion, and our Source of power.

The prayer to which our Lord refers is something more than just asking God to do something. The type of prayer here referred to should be thought of as a dialogue in which we not only communicate with God but also listen to what he has to say. Like taxi drivers who use two-way radio sets to get instructions from their dispatcher, we are to listen for instructions from divine headquarters concerning which portion of the field of the world we are to work in each day. We are to make ourselves available for God's good pleasure.

D. *"Pray . . . that he will send forth laborers into the harvest."* The word translated "send forth" is the Greek word *ekballo*; it means to "cast out" or to "thrust out."

Our experience of the love of God combined with a knowledge of the needs of people should give us an inner compulsion to be our Lord's witnesses. Our sense of duty combined with the opportunities that are offered should challenge us to be busy in the fields that are "white unto harvest."

Conclusion

The Holy Spirit entered our hearts in the moment of conversion. He is present to lead us and empower us as we work in the fields of great human need. We should listen to him, obey him, and trust him. The Holy Spirit wants to use us to offer forgiveness to the guilty, eternal life to those in spiritual death, and joy to those who are living in hopelessness.

WEDNESDAY EVENING, OCTOBER 9

Title: Message to a Backslidden Church

Text: "I hold this against you: You have forsaken the love you had at first" **(Rev. 2:4 NIV)**.

Scripture Reading: Revelation 2:1–7

Introduction

This text is a message from the risen Christ to one of his churches. In fact, the church at Ephesus was one of the best and one that Paul founded. As recorded in Acts 19, Paul had come from Corinth and had found some believers at Ephesus. He instructed them in the Lord for two years and "so mightily grew the word of God and prevailed" (Acts 19:20).

Ephesus was a city of great prominence. As one Roman writer put it, "Ephesus was the first and greatest metropolis in Asia." It had one of the best harbors and was a busy overland trade center. Ephesus also enjoyed some special Roman privileges. It was a "free" city—that is, the people were self-governed and were exempted from having Roman soldiers garrisoned there. It was an "assize" city, the "county seat" so to speak, and Roman governors held council there. Also, the temple to the goddess Diana was located there. This temple was one of the wonders of the ancient world. It was 425 feet long and 225 feet wide with 120 columns embracing it. Each column was 60 feet high and had been the gift of some king. Ephesus was a magnificent city indeed!

I. Christ's message to his church.

The message to the church at Ephesus begins with a description of the risen, glorified Christ (2:1). He walks in the midst of the seven golden candlesticks. These are his churches. He knows them. Christ can call his churches by name, and he knows them intimately. He knows our church, too, and in his message to the church at Ephesus, he speaks to us. What does he say?

A. *Commendation (2:1–3).*

  1. Their works. The first word Christ speaks to this church is one of commendation. He says, "I know your deeds" (NIV). The word translated "deeds" means "hard labor." It means the kind of toil that takes all the energy of mind and muscle. This was an active, busy church. Their weekly calendar was full. The members gave themselves to their church work with great energy.

  2. Their perseverance. This steadfast endurance is not a fatalism that bows to whatever ill might come; it is a courageous gallantry that turns hardship and suffering into grace and glory. Ephesus was the headquarters of a pagan religion. The Christians there never had it easy.

  3. Their orthodoxy. The third word of commendation is "You cannot tolerate wicked people" (2:2 NIV). Jesus warned his church that false teachers would attempt to lead the faithful astray. Judaizers wanted the believers to adhere to law and ritual. Others turned the liberty of grace into license to sin. Some were professional beggars who preyed on the charity of the congregation. The Bible insists that we try the spirits and not allow those who deny the faith to teach and preach. Ephesus did this. This was a good church—loyal, faithful, hardworking, and orthodox. But in spite of all this, something was missing!

B. *Condemnation (2:4–5).* The word against this church is "You have forsaken the love you had at first" (NIV). The Ephesians' zeal in the Lord had grown cold. They had become a backslidden church. Let us be on guard. We can become so concerned about programs and works that the Spirit is forgotten. We can be so busy heresy hunting that love dries up and dies out. A church that was once a band of brothers can become an assembly of suspicious men. The earnest toil is still there, as is the gallant endurance, unimpeachable orthodoxy, and busy schedule—but the love is gone.

We often flog the church when the whip needs to be laid to our own backs. What about me? Have I lost some of that first zeal and love I had in the Lord when I first believed? I remember my fist love. It magnified my sin; it kept me faithful in daily Bible reading and prayer; it made me fervent to win my friends to Christ.

What, now, is the way back?

C. *Command (2:5)*.

1. "Consider how far you have fallen" (NIV). This is not a command to the person who has never been to church, but to the faithful. Memory is often the first step back. It was so for the prodigal son. He remembered the abundance in his father's house.

2. Repent. When we are brought to realize our loss, we are commanded to repent. Repent means to turn around, to change direction. Real repentance does not cause one to blame others. Real repentance says, "I have sinned and done evil in your sight."

3. Return. Remembering and repenting is not of value unless we return to that first love that brings about those first works. The word *works* here is not the same as the word in verse 2. In verse 2 it is hard labor and grinding toil. Here the word means "occupation," the job you have to do. Christ is telling this church to return to their first business, their first responsibility, their first charge. For any church, that ought to be the work of evangelism—reaching and winning people to Christ. Nothing can take the place of evangelism for the church—not orthodoxy, not a full program, not anything.

Conclusion

It was written of the church at Ephesus that "all the Jews and Greeks who lived in the province of Asia heard the word of the Lord" (Acts 19:10 NIV). May such be said of our church!

SUNDAY MORNING, OCTOBER 13

Title: Christ Can Change Things

Text: "Jesus said unto him, This day is salvation come to this house" **(Luke 19:9)**.

Scripture Reading: Luke 19:1–10

Hymns: "Joyful, Joyful, We Adore Thee," Van Dyke

"Blessed Redeemer," Christiansen

'The Old Rugged Cross," Bennard

Offertory Prayer: Holy heavenly Father, we thank you for your great gift to us through Jesus Christ. We thank you that he was willing to bear the burden of our sin and die on the cross for us. We thank you for the gift of new life through him. We thank you for your Holy Spirit who dwells within our hearts today. We thank you for material blessings that make it possible for us to bring a tithe and offering to your altar today. Bless these tithes and offerings that the world may hear the good news of your love through Jesus Christ. Bless those everywhere who proclaim the Good News. In Jesus' name we pray. Amen.

Introduction

The Christ of whom we read in the New Testament lives today as the conqueror of death. That which he did during his earthly ministry, he continues to seek to do through his church and through his individual followers in the church. Christ came to change things for the better.

Jesus sought to change the heart and mind of individuals by giving them new insight concerning the nature and character of God. Our Lord sought to change the structures of society by bring about great changes within individuals.

Jesus came to Jericho when Calvary was only one week away. It is interesting to note that he demonstrated deep concern for a man who was hated and despised by the people of the city. Instead of seeking popular applause, our Lord sought out the most hated man in town and demonstrated concern for him in order that changes might be made in his heart and life that would bring about changes within the city of Jericho. The pattern of our Lord should be our pattern today.

I. Christ became a self-invited guest.

"Zacchaeus, make haste, and come down; for today I must abide at thy house."

There was something very personal and very pressing about this statement of our Lord. This would be Jesus' only opportunity to render a personal ministry to Zacchaeus. This would be Zacchaeus's only opportunity ever to have a personal interview with Jesus Christ. Jesus was on his way toward Jerusalem. This was his last visit in Jericho. Our Lord seized an opportunity, and it was necessary that Zacchaeus respond immediately and decisively to his opportunity.

A. *Christ came in love for Zacchaeus.* The source of love must be discovered in the heart of God rather than in the loveliness of those who are the objects of his affection. It would be helpful if we would personalize and individualize the truth of John 3:16. God deals with people on the basis of his own love rather than on their loveliness. Because of God's love, Christ came to Zacchaeus, who was hated and despised. He continues to love in that manner.

B. *Christ came to Zacchaeus because of his love for others.* God loved Zacchaeus's neighbors. He needed Zacchaeus as a channel of love that he might be a blessing to those neighbors.

God loved Zacchaeus's enemies. He wanted to change Zacchaeus so that these enemies would be transformed into friends.

C. *Christ continues to seek the Zacchaeuses of our day.* God does not avoid people whose lives are unlovely. God's redemptive activity is motivated by divine love rather than by something lovely in people.

God wants to use each of his children so that he may bring redemption and the joy of sonship into the hearts and lives of those who are the outcasts of society.

II. A seeking sinner was found by the seeking Savior (Luke 19:3–6).

A. *The sinner does not consciously and deliberately seek God.* Humans, instead of choosing to cooperate with God, rebel against God in self-trust, self-love, and self-assertion. The Bible describes humanity as being dead in sin. People are cut off from God and do not seek God consciously and deliberately (Rom. 3:10–12).

B. *Every sinner away from God needs what only God can give.* Deep within the heart of every person there is a "God-shaped vacuum" that only God himself can fill. Some people seek to fill this vacuum with the security that wealth brings or the popularity that success brings. Others seek to fill this void by trying to satisfy all of the appetites of their human nature.

1. Zacchaeus was rich, but he was not happy. He had put riches above patriotism. He had put riches above his religion. He had put the desire for riches above popular approval. Although his stomach was satisfied, his heart was hungry for acceptance by God and acceptance by his fellow man.

2. Zacchaeus was loved by Christ even though he was unlovable. He was unloved in his city. Perhaps he was unloved even in his own home, for all he had to offer were material things. Most likely he could not see anything within himself that was very lovable. Zacchaeus had been looking for life in the wrong way and in the wrong place. Fortunate indeed he was that Christ Jesus came his way.

III. Christ came to change things.

Christ did not come to pronounce a benediction on the status quo. He came to produce revolutionary changes that transform and enrich life.

A. *He wants to change the attitude of those who consider themselves to be very religious (Luke 19:7).* Our Lord exposed himself to the hostility of the people in the city of Jericho as well as that of his own disciples when he decided to express friendship toward the publican Zacchaeus. Because of his relationship with the army of occupation, Zacchaeus was an outcast. He was unwelcome in any of the religious and civic activities in his city, but he was not outside the concern of the heart of God.

Have we abandoned some segments of our society and considered them to be outside the circle of God's love? If so, we need to reexamine the pattern that our Lord followed and identify with his program.

B. *Christ helped Zacchaeus to make some changes in his way of life.* We can only speculate concerning the things that were discussed during Jesus' visit in Zacchaeus's home. It is interesting to notice some of the results of that visit.

1. Christ helped Zacchaeus to replace the greed that was in his heart with graciousness and generosity (Luke 19:8). Perhaps our Lord helped Zacchaeus to see that true happiness does not come as a result of greedily grasping after material things. Jesus succeeded in helping Zacchaeus to change his philosophy of life. Perhaps Jesus repeated the great truth found in Luke 6:38 and Acts 20:35 during that visit.

307

2. Christ helped Zacchaeus to replace selfishness with righteousness in his mind and in his conduct (Luke 19:8). Only a profound change in the mind and life could bring about such an important change in the conduct of this man. It is evident that Zacchaeus decided to put the kingdom of God and his righteousness first in his life (Matt. 6:33).

3. Christ gave to Zacchaeus, and Zacchaeus accepted, a new purpose for his life.

IV. Christ can change things today.

Christ will not come into your heart merely to occupy a space as a silent, uninvolved spectator.

A. *He will change your heart and mind.* Let him be something more than a Savior from the penalty of sin. He wants to be the master of your life. He wants to be your Teacher and give to you authentic truth about God for the living of life. He wants to be your Friend and Counselor.

B. *He will bring about changes within your home life.* Christ will help you to be a better husband or wife. He will help you to be better parents to your children. He will help you as a youth to relate yourself properly to your parents in a creative and stimulating way.

C. *He will seek to bring about changes within the city and country as individuals let him become the guiding, controlling factor in their lives.*

D. *He will bring about changes in the church (Rev. 3:20).* These words actually were addressed to a church. Christ wanted to abide within the church and to use the church as an instrument through which he could bless the community and the world.

Conclusion

When Christ walked down the street of Jericho and found Zacchaeus on the limb of the sycamore tree, some great things happened. Zacchaeus discovered, "He sees me! He knows me! He loves me! He wants me!" And he decided, "He can have me!"

You are wise today to receive him! Rejoice in him! Respond to him!

Christ will continue to bring about change in those and through those who will let him come to dwell within them as he came that day to visit in the home of Zacchaeus.

SUNDAY EVENING, OCTOBER 13

Title: Our Father's Business

Text: "'Why were you searching for me?' he asked. 'Didn't you know I had to be in my Father's house?'" **(Luke 2:49 NIV)**.

Scripture Reading: John 5:15–18; 9:1–5; Isa. 61:1–2

Introduction

In his great High Priestly Prayer, our Lord said to the Father, "I have brought you glory on earth by finishing the work you gave me to do" (John 17:4 NIV). Then, while dying on the cross, our Lord said, "It is finished" (John 19:30). So who is to carry on Christ's work? We are, for Jesus prayed for his followers, "As you sent me into the world, I have sent them into the world" (John 17:18 NIV).

The clearest and most complete statement concerning the business of the Father and the ministry of our Lord is to be found in a passage Jesus read in the synagogue in Nazareth. When he returned after beginning his public ministry, he returned in the power of the Holy Spirit (Luke 4:14). He went into the synagogue, where he was handed a scroll containing Holy Scripture, which he was to read. He selected an appropriate passage and then announced the significance of that passage. As he read from Isaiah 61:1–2, he revealed the meaning of his divine mission. The passage described the method of his work, announced the message he was to proclaim, and implied the movement of his ministry.

The presence of the church in the world today indicates that the Lord wants this ministry to continue. The church is his body—speaking, ministering, and serving. Christ's church is to be busy—evangelizing, teaching, and encouraging.

The sequence of the activities described in the book of Isaiah and read by our Lord is of great importance.

I. He has anointed me to preach the Good News to the poor.

A. *Jesus knew the pinch of poverty. He did not live in an affluent city or time.*
B. *The poverty to which our Lord referred is that spiritual bankruptcy of the soul that makes beggars of all of us.* We live in utter spiritual destitution until we receive the forgiveness of sin and the gift of new life (Rom. 3:23; 6:23).
C. *Christ came with good news for those who are paupers in the realm of the spirit.*

    Jesus' chief ministry was proclaiming the good news of God's love to those in spiritual bankruptcy. We are safe in assuming that this is the primary business of the church today. Every activity of the church should concentrate on proclaiming the Good News. It is not enough that we live good lives in silence. We must verbally articulate the good news of God's love. Our supreme business must always be that of announcing the good news of God's love for a lost world.

II. He hath sent me to heal the brokenhearted.

Today we are amazed by open-heart surgery. Surgeons are now able to repair wounded and damaged hearts. Our Lord has been specializing in healing broken hearts for a long time.

A. *Some have broken hearts because of errors in judgment.*
B. *Some hearts have been broken by the cruelty of others.*
C. *Some have broken hearts because of the tragedies of life.*
D. *Some have broken hearts because of the complexities of modern life.*
E. *Some have broken hearts because of the destructive power of evil.*

It must be our business as individual followers of Jesus Christ and as the church to cooperate with our Lord in a ministry of healing the brokenhearted.

III. He hath sent me to proclaim liberty to the captives.

Christ is the Great Liberator. He came to set people free from that which imprisons them.

    A. *A captive is one who is imprisoned, restricted, deprived of liberty, not free to do or be as he would like.*

    B. *Some are restricted and imprisoned by the sins of others.*

    C. *Most are restricted and imprisoned by the sins of self.*

    D. *Some are restricted and imprisoned by the customs of society.*

Christ came to set people free from the slavery and the bondage of sin. He came that people might become the sons of God and the servants of God.

It should be our business to always cooperate with our Lord in proclaiming liberty to the captives.

IV. He hath sent me to restore sight to the blind.

Our Lord was concerned that people might be able to see, not only with their physical eyes, but with spiritual insight.

    A. *Christ restored physical eyesight to the blind on many different occasions.*

    B. *Christ also opened the eyes of the people to spiritual realities:*

        1. The goodness of the Father God.

        2. The emptiness of a life of no faith.

        3. The joy of a life of faith and service.

        4. The way of salvation through faith in God's gracious way of salvation.

V. He hath sent me to proclaim the year of the Lord's favor.

Through God's grace we are to proclaim that the jubilee year has arrived — that God is eager to forgive all sin and to pour out his blessings in abundance on all people everywhere. God has taken the initiative to pour out his blessings on people in the person of Jesus Christ.

Jesus came to tell people about God's love and his offer of grace, pardon, and life. Now it is the church's business to proclaim that God is favorably inclined toward people. God is not our enemy. He is our Friend. He is for us and not against us. He wants to help us and not hinder us.

Conclusion

If we want to be about our Father's business, we must identify with our Lord's concept of God's purpose for him. We must let his purpose become our purpose. If we are to truly achieve our purpose in the world, we will do so as we follow him in a ministry of proclaiming the Good News, healing the brokenhearted, proclaiming liberty to the captives, restoring sight to the blind, and announcing the year of the Lord's favor.

WEDNESDAY EVENING, OCTOBER 16

Title: Message to a Persecuted Church

Text: "Do not be afraid of what you are about to suffer" **(Rev. 2:10 NIV)**.

Scripture Reading: Revelation 2:8–11

Introduction

Smyrna was one of the few planned cities of the ancient world. It was founded as a Greek colony about 1000 BC. In about 600 BC, the Lydians broke through the fortifications and destroyed the city. It remained a dead city for four hundred years. About 200 BC, Lysimachus had the city rebuilt according to a great plan. The streets were broad and straight and were paved with huge blocks of marble. The city contained the famous "street of gold," which began at the temple of Zeus and ended at the temple of Dionysius, the god of fertility and joy.

The city lay thirty-five miles north of Ephesus and was one of the loveliest in all Asia. Smyrna became wealthy as a commercial center for all the Hermus Valley. It had one of the safest and best harbors and could be well protected from enemy attack.

Smyrna is not mentioned elsewhere in Scripture, and we have no way of knowing who founded the church there. What is the message of Christ to this church?

I. Commendation (Rev. 2:8–9).

Of all the seven churches mentioned in these first three chapters in Revelation, only two are not condemned — Smyrna and Philadelphia. These are the churches of persecution and opportunity. It was not easy to be a Christian in Smyrna. There was a large Jewish colony there that was especially influential in business, social, and political life. These Jews were extremely hostile to Christianity. Throughout all the record of the New Testament, the Jews had done all they could to stop the progress of the gospel. They had demanded the death penalty for Christ, put Stephen to death, jailed many of the apostles, and dogged the footsteps of Paul on all his missionary journeys. It is no wonder, then, that in the Revelation these Jews, who were not the spiritual sons of Abraham, are called "the synagogue of Satan" (2:9).

II. Persecution (Rev. 2:9–10).

Four things were involved in the persecution suffered by the church at Smyrna.

A. *Affliction (v. 9).* The Lord says to his church, "I know thy ... tribulation." The word literally means "to be pressured." The world and the devil are always trying to afflict the Christian. "Be one of the crowd," they say; "go along with the gang." "Don't be different." This kind of pressure is one of the devil's subtlest temptations. Yet the Bible says, "Be not conformed to

311

this world." Don't let the world press you into its mold. There was great pressure put on the Christians at Smyrna to conform. This kind of persecution is still with us today.

B. *Slander (v. 9).* The Lord says, "I know the blasphemy of them which say they are Jews, and are not." When the Christian will not conform, the next step in persecution is slander. So the Christians were falsely accused of being disloyal to the state, of being revolutionaries. In Acts 6:14 the disciples were slandered because they changed the customs "Moses handed down" (NIV).

C. *Poverty (v. 9).* If affliction and slander do not work, the next step is poverty. Many Christians in the first-century church were forbidden employment. Their homes and property were confiscated. Their families suffered from economic boycott. However, the Bible mentions that their poverty was of the body and not of the soul.

D. *Imprisonment and death (v. 10).* The early Christians often saw the inside of the prison. The story of the spread of the gospel just begins when Peter and John are imprisoned (Acts 4). Later Stephen was martyred for his faith (Acts 7), the first of a long line of Christian martyrs. Even now in many places of the world believers are afflicted for their faith. The apostle Paul wrote to Timothy, "All that will live godly in Christ Jesus shall suffer persecution" (2 Tim. 3:12). The lack of persecution among Christians in America may be a rebuke for the kind of lives we live. The world sees in us little to hate. We no longer are a conscience to our community. We do not condemn worldliness and sin. We hold our tongues and no one is embarrassed. We are respectable, conventional, and inoffensive; and as a result, we are ineffective. If we raise the standards of Christian conduct; stop our compromises with sin and the world; and dare to write on our vestures, "Holiness to the Lord," perhaps we will begin to suffer persecution again.

III. Reward (Rev. 2:10).

Jesus said, "Be thou faithful unto death, and I will give thee a crown of life." He did not say, "Well done, good and busy servant" or "Well done, good and successful servant"; but he did say, "Well done, good and faithful servant." Too many of us are like the apostle Peter, who was ready to declare boldly to Jesus, "I will die with thee" and then before the next day dawned had denied Jesus three times. The promised reward for faithfulness is a crown of life. This crown is the *stephanos*—the victor's crown. According to Roman custom, he who had won a crown in life could wear that crown in death. Such is also true for Christian faithfulness.

SUNDAY MORNING, OCTOBER 20

Title: Christ and the Conquest of Fear

Text: "The LORD is my light and my salvation; whom shall I fear? The LORD is the strength of my life; of whom shall I be afraid?" **(Ps. 27:1).**

Scripture Reading: Psalm 27:1–5

Hymns: "Praise to God, Immortal Praise," Barbauld

"Christ Receiveth Sinful Men," Neumeister

"He Included Me," Oatman

Offertory Prayer: Gracious Father, you have given us the best that heaven has to offer. We thank you for the gift of your Son, Jesus Christ. We thank you for the courage and the confidence that comes as a result of the awareness of his abiding presence. Today help us to give ourselves as completely to you as it is possible for human beings to do. Accept our tithes and offerings as an expression of our love and as indications of our desire to worship in spirit and truth. Bless those who give these offerings. In Jesus' name we pray. Amen.

Introduction

Napoleon Hill, author of the book *Think and Grow Rich*, said there are six basic fears that torment the mind and heart of every human being at some time or another. People are fortunate if they do not suffer from all six at the same time. Hill listed these six fears in the order of their common appearance: (1) the fear of poverty, (2) the fear of criticism, (3) the fear of ill health, (4) the fear of the loss of the love of someone, (5) the fear of old age, and (6) the fear of death. All other fears are said to be of minor importance because they can be grouped under these six headings.

What can one do about these six great fears that would torment and make life a burden instead of a blessing? Does the Bible have anything to say to us concerning the problem of fear? Is there a way by which we can conquer fear and live a triumphant and victorious life?

I. The Bible deals extensively with the problem of fear.

At the risk of oversimplifying, one could say that "fear is the result of estrangement from God." In the account of the events that gook place in the garden of Eden, we read that Adam said, "I was afraid" (Gen. 3:10). When man faces life without a proper relationship with God and without a confidence in his love and fellowship, there are many things that will cause him to have fear.

  A. *God spoke to Abraham concerning fear.* "Fear not, Abram: I am thy shield, and thy exceeding great reward" (Gen. 15:1).

  B. *God encouraged Isaac to overcome fear.* "The LORD appeared unto him the same night, and said, I am the God of Abraham thy father: fear not, for I am with thee, and will bless thee, and multiply thy seed for my servant Abraham's sake" (Gen. 26:24).

  C. *God spoke through Moses to Israel concerning fear.* "Moses said unto the people, Fear ye not, stand still, and see the salvation of the LORD, which he will shew to you today: for the Egyptians whom ye have seen today, ye shall see them again no more for ever" (Ex. 14:13).

  D. *God spoke to Joshua concerning faith's conquest of fear.* "Be strong and of a good courage; be not afraid, neither be thou dismayed: for the LORD thy God is with thee withersoever thou goest" (Josh. 1:9).

313

E. *God sought to encourage the exiles to overcome fear with faith.* "Fear thou not; for I am with thee: be not dismayed; for I am thy God: I will strengthen thee; yea, I will bless thee; yea, I will uphold thee with the right hand of my righteousness" (Isa. 41:10).

The psalmist overcame fear through faith in the promise of the abiding presence of his God whom he thought of as the Good Shepherd: "Yea, though I walk through the valley of the shadow of death, I will fear no evil: for thou art with me; thy rod and thy staff they comfort me" (Ps. 23:4).

II. Jesus suggested that faith should dispel fear.

Humans have always been fearful beings. They fear poverty, ill health, the loss of God's providential care, and all of the other things that seemingly threaten life. In the Sermon on the Mount, our Lord deals with this matter of fear. He makes at least four positive suggestions that can help us to conquer fear with faith.

A. *Our Lord tells us to evaluate ourselves (Matt. 6:25–26).* He uses God's providential care for the birds of the air to illustrate the fact that if God cares for the sparrows, we can be absolutely certain that he will care for us. People are of more value than the sparrows. Jesus encourages us to believe that the Father God will prevent us from starving to death (Ps. 37:25).

B. *Our Lord tells us to accept ourselves (Matt. 6:27).* Some of us worry ourselves into an agony of anxiety because we are not as we think we ought to be. Jesus says there are some things that people must accept as they are. If a man is short of stature, there is no way by which he can increase his physical stature. If a man is tall, there is no way by which he can become short. Some things must be accepted, and we must adjust ourselves to these facts.

C. *Our Lord tells us to dedicate ourselves (Matt. 6:33).* When we dedicate ourselves to God's kingdom rather than seeking our own kingdom, our faith in God will increase, and many of our fears and anxieties will cease to be. It is when we take our eyes off God's providential care and begin to worry about our own efforts that fear takes possession of the citadel of our own soul.

D. *Our Lord tells us to live life one day at a time by faith (Matt. 6:34).* Most of the things that we worry about and the things that paralyze us with fear never really happen. Today is the tomorrow that we worried about yesterday.

Conclusion

Do you fear the past? Do you live in a mood of fear, anxiety, and depression? Are you afraid of the future?

There is no way by which you can pile up enough money to dissolve your fears and anxieties. There is no health policy that you can secure that can take away your fears as far as your physical well-being is concerned.

The only antidote for anxiety, the only way by which one can overcome fear, is through faith in the Christ who came, not only to be our Savior, but to be our Friend and Companion along the road of life. We need to put our hand into his hand and let him guide us. We need to entrust our past, present, and future into his custody and depend on him to be with us whatever the future may bring. The great God who has been so good to us in the past will continue to be the same in the future. The only real security that we can have is the security that we find in God and in his promises to us. Let each of us live each day by faith in him, and we will discover as the days go by that our fears will be replaced with the faith that will bring joy, confidence, and victory.

SUNDAY EVENING, OCTOBER 20

Title: This Is a Day of Glad Tidings

Text: "Then they said one to another, We do not well: this day is a day of good tidings, and we hold our peace" **(2 Kings 7:9)**.

Scripture Reading: 2 Kings 7:1–11

Introduction

The Bible was not written merely to provide us with a history of the events of the ancient past. It speaks to our needs and to our opportunities in the present.

The account of the four lepers outside the walls of ancient Samaria speaks to our condition today. Their experience and their response illustrate our Christian responsibilities, duties, and privileges in the present.

Leprosy is a terrible contagious and incurable disease. It produces invalids out of sufferers and leads to isolation and ostracism.

Civil War general William Tecumseh Sherman said, "War is hell." The ancient Samaritans would have agreed with him. The city of Samaria had been surrounded, and allies had not responded to their pleas for help. Food was rationed, and water was limited. The king was distressed, and the leaders were rebelling against God. It was in this desperate situation that the prophet Elisha spoke and sought to minister.

Outside the walls were four leprous men who could not enter the city because of their disease. To surrender to the enemy was to face the possibility of immediate death. They came to the conclusion that they must take a chance. Their only hope was to throw themselves on the mercy of the Syrians who surrounded the city.

I. The lepers made a delightful discovery (2 Kings 7:6–8).

The Syrians had forsaken their camp and left their resources. God had intervened in a miraculous way, and they had fled.

The parallel for the present is found in the fact that God has stepped down into history in the person of Jesus Christ. We have the gospel, the good tidings of God's love, mercy, and grace.

Christ has revealed the nature and character of a loving God. He has borne the penalty of our sin and suffered on the cross for us. Christ has defeated the grave and the wicked one, and he grants us assurance of a similar victory.

Christ yearns for each of us to enter into abundant life. He wants us to be companions with him in his way of life.

II. The lepers made a true confession.

"What we're doing is not right. This is a day of good news and we are keeping it to ourselves" (2 Kings 7:9 NIV). These words from the lepers would reprove modern-day Christians for their indifference and unconcern. The knowledge of good news places on the recipient of that news an obligation to share it.

A. *The lepers remembered the imprisoned and desperate people inside the city of Samaria.* They recognized that they must share this good news that they had discovered in the camp of the departed Syrians.

B. *Silence can be most significant.*
   1. Silence can be golden.
   2. Silence can be criminal (Ezek. 33:1–6).

C. *To be silent in a day of good tidings is unnatural.*

D. *To be silent in a day of good tidings is inhuman.*

E. *To be silent in a day of good tidings is to contradict the very nature of Christianity.*

III. The lepers speak of a certain retribution.

"If we tarry till the morning light, some mischief will come upon us" (2 Kings 7:9). The lepers were afraid that someone might discover the vacated camp and slay them immediately. They decided that their wisest policy was to announce the good news immediately.

A. *We will be held accountable to God if we remain silent in a day of good tidings.*

B. *We will miss the joy of being a reaper of souls for the glory of God.*

C. *Our spiritual life is impoverished when we remain silent.*

D. *Our eyes will see mischief befall others if we neglect to tell them of our wonderful Savior.*

E. *If we remain silent in a day of good tidings, our Savior will be displeased with our conduct.*

F. *For us to remain silent is to go to heaven as empty-handed paupers instead of going to heaven with many joys and rewards for having been fruitful in the service of our Lord.*

IV. The lepers made a wise decision.

"Now therefore come, that we may go and tell the king's household" (2 Kings 7:9). We can be certain that these lepers were greatly appreciated and kindly treated in the future as a result of the good news they brought to the gate of the city of Samaria.

We would be wise to decide to become communicators of the good news of God's love and God's provisions for people.

A. *Perhaps we need to inform ourselves of the woeful condition of those who live inside the city of sin.* They are in a more desperate condition than were the people in the ancient city of Samaria.

B. *Outside the walls of the city of Jerusalem, the Savior died on a cross to set people free from the guilt and the condemnation of sin.* If we have been to the cross and discovered the love of God and received the gift of eternal life, we have good news for those who dwell inside the city of sin.

Conclusion

We must cease to be occupied with things of no importance. We must recognize the weight of the responsibility that is on us to share the good news of that which happened on that first Christmas day. We need to draw near to the cross that we may discover how great is the love of God for people. We need to visit the empty tomb that we may discover the extravagance of the provisions that God has made for us. We need to repent of our laziness, our disobedience, and our indifference.

This is a day of good tidings. We must not hold our peace. This could be our only day. It could be our last day. It is our best day for telling the Good News.

WEDNESDAY EVENING, OCTOBER 23

Title: Pergamos — The Compromising Church

Text: "There are some among you who hold to the teaching of Balaam" (**Rev. 2:14 NIV**).

Scripture Reading: Revelation 2:12–17

Introduction

Like most other Greco-Roman cities, Pergamos was filled with many temples. Its acropolis was covered with altars to many deities. There was an immense altar to Zeus and a beautiful temple to Athena, but the patron god of Pergamos was Asklepios, the serpent. Of course, emperor worship was also commanded, and as early as 29 BC a temple was erected to Caesar Augustus. This was the first provincial temple dedicated to a living emperor. In the midst of this center of paganism a little band of Christians lived and witnessed.

I. Satan's seat (Rev. 2:13).

This significant letter begins, "I know ... where thou dwellest." Christ knows all about his churches. He knows what they are doing and where they are living. He knows the address of our church; he knows the pastor, the deacons, the teachers, and the members. He knows our works—our lack and our luster. Christ walks among the churches. The church of Pergamos lived next door to Satan's seat. Quite an address for a church! This church was located downtown beside theater row and the nightclubs. Jesus promised that his church would not be overcome by the gates of hell, and that is exactly where this church was. Here, in downtown Pergamos, a little band of believers was trying desperately to fight for truth in the midst of error.

II. Commendations (Rev. 2:13).

A. *"Thou holdest fast my name."* The church that lives where Satan's seat is ought to be true to Christ's name. Christianity is a religion of the *person* of Jesus Christ. It is not so much a truth as it is *the* Truth — that is, Christ. To be a Christian is to experience Christ; that is the irreducible minimum.

B. *"Thou ... hast not denied my faith."* The Pergamene Christians had been put to the test for their faith in Christ — some of then even to death. Faithful martyr Antipas is named in verse 13. Through all this terrible testing, the believers had remained true to the faith. But with this word of commendation there is also a word of caution.

III. Condemnation (Rev. 2:14).

The story of Balaam is a remarkable one. It is recorded in Numbers 22–24. Israel was ready to make war against the king of Moab. The Moabites had heard what Israel did to the Amorites, and they were afraid. So the king sent for the prophet Balaam. The king of Moab offered to pay Balaam well if he would curse Israel. Balaam refused to curse what God had blessed, but he said there was another way to defeat Israel. He suggested that the daughters of Moab entice the men of Israel to participate in idol worship. Balaam reasoned that God could not bless a sinning people. Balaam was right, and Numbers 25 tells the awful story of sin, compromise, and defeat. Twenty-four thousand Israelites died of the plague. The "doctrine of Balaam" is the way of compromise and sin. It says you can worship both Jehovah and Ashtaroth. It asks, "What harm is there to a little compromise?" These are the subtle whisperings of the devil.

The devil has two ways to defeat the Christian. One is with the frown. He attempts to destroy by affliction and persecution. This is what he tried against the church at Smyrna. The second method is the smile — a subtle yielding to worldliness and sin. He tried to cause defeat by compromise with the church at Pergamos.

Compromise is one of Satan's best weapons against the church today. God cannot bless the compromising church. One word used to describe the state of the believer is *hagios*. The word means "set apart," "dedicated," "holy." The difference is not one of physical separation from the world. We are to be in the world but not of it. What about our church; are we being defeated in the work of the Lord by compromise? Have we defiled our separation? Have the cares of the world choked out the fruit of the Spirit? The word of warning, then, is to us: "Repent; or else...."

IV. Command (Rev. 2:16).

Jesus' command is for the worldly, compromising church to repent. Repentance means to change, to turn about, to walk the other way. A church needs to hear and heed the command to repent just as much as does the sinner. A church must never compromise its message of the gospel of grace. This church at Pergamos was commended for its orthodoxy. This was a church that held fast Christ's name and did not deny the faith, but there was danger that worldly compromise in the membership would bring about the defeat of their testimony. The danger is ever present among the churches today.

Conclusion

There is evidence that this message of Christ to his church was received. Soon after the book of Revelation was written, Polycarp became pastor of the church at Pergamos. In AD 167 a cruel persecution broke out against the Christians in Asia. For several weeks, Polycarp hid in a cave and the members brought him food and water. At last the Romans seized a young Christian and by torture learned from him where the pastor was hiding. Polycarp was taken to the temple of Dionysius and was commanded to sacrifice to the statue of Caesar. His persecutors asked, "What harm will it do to make one small sacrifice to Caesar?" Polycarp answered, "Eighty and six years have I served Christ. How can I deny him now?" In a rage and fury. the people gathered wood and piled it up against the stake where Polycarp was tied. The magistrate made one more appeal for a small sacrifice to Caesar. When Polycarp again refused, the fire was lit, and a disciple from Pergamos died for the faith.

SUNDAY MORNING, OCTOBER 27

Title: Life on Both Sides of Death

Text: "Yet a little while, and the world seeth me no more; but ye see me: because I live, ye shall live also" (**John 14:19**).

Scripture Reading: John 14:15–23

Hymns: "Rejoice, the Lord Is King," Wesley

"I Know That My Redeemer Liveth," Pounds

"What a Wonderful Saviour!" Hoffman

Offertory Prayer: Holy Father, today we come into your presence in the name of our Savior who died for our sins and gave himself on the cross for us. We bring ourselves to your altar and give ourselves in worship and service to you. Bless our tithes and offerings toward the coming of your kingdom in the hearts of men and women, not only in this community, but to the ends of the earth. For in the name of our Lord we pray. Amen.

Introduction

In Phillips's translation of our text, we read, "In a very little while, the world will see me no more but you will see me, because I am really alive and you will be alive too."

Our Lord came into a world in which death was king. Everyone fell victim to the march of the grim specter that we call death. Men lived in horror of entering the abode of the dead. Jesus Christ came into the world to destroy the power of death and to give us assurance that death is not the end and that the grave is not the goal of this life.

Christ came that people might experience life on both sides of death.

I. Christ demonstrated life on both sides of death.

A. *During his ministry on earth, Christ was a living exhibition of life as God meant for it to be.* He lived a happy, joyous, exciting life. There was something attractive and magnetic about him that drew crowds to him. There was something about him that did not alienate sinners. They felt that he loved them. Women were attracted to him and brought their children that he might bless them.

Christ did not offer the promise of fame and fortune. He did offer the hope of grace and glory and fullness of life. It is interesting to note that he defined his purpose for being in terms of life: "I am come that they might have life, and that they might have it more abundantly" (John 10:10).

B. *Christ entered the realm of death.* Mystery and miracle surround the death of our Lord Jesus Christ. His death was the result of the sin and organized cruelty of men. His death also was a demonstration of the greatness of God's love for sinners. His death revealed the extent to which God was determined to rescue people from the tyranny of sin.

C. *Christ conquered death and demonstrated life on the other side of death.* Until Jesus came, people had asked the question articulated by Job through the centuries: "If a man die, shall he live again?" (Job 14:14). There was always a negative answer to that question until our Lord came to conquer the abode of the dead and to demonstrate his power and authority over death (Rev. 1:18).

1. Christ was identifiable by his disciples after his resurrection from the dead.
2. Christ was the same Christ after his resurrection that he had been before.
3. Christ was different after his resurrection. He was not limited by time and space as he had been before.

The resurrection of Jesus Christ revealed and demonstrated who he really was. He was God in human flesh. His resurrection revealed that he had accomplished his purpose in both life and death. His resurrection was a demonstration of the fact that life is a reality on both sides of death.

II. Christ offered the gift of life on both sides of death (John 3:16; 10:28).

A. *Christ alone can offer life on the other side of death.* Humanity's only hope of victory over death and the grave is based on the assurance that Christ himself has conquered death and the grave and that he offers the same victory to those who trust him as Lord and Savior (1 Cor. 15:12–23).

B. *Christ offers real life in the here and now (John 10:10).*

1. Mary Magdalene found this real life as Christ gave her freedom and cleansing from guilt.
2. Zacchaeus found this real life when he was set free from the god of greed and the self-condemnation that this brought. He began to live a life of kindness and generosity toward others.
3. Paul found this real life through Christ as he discovered that God deals with people on the basis of his divine grace rather than on the basis of man's legalistic performance. Paul discovered the freedom that comes to those who live by faith.

III. Living the life that is eternal now.

Eternal life is not something that comes at the end of one's earthly existence if that person has lived a life that meets the requirements of a holy God. Eternal life is the present gift of God through faith in Christ Jesus. Eternal life is the possession of each child of God. John, the beloved apostle, was overwhelmed with this assurance of divine sonship in the present (1 John 3:1–2).

A. *Faith in Jesus Christ and his precious promise makes it possible for one to live with an untroubled heart in the present (John 14:1).*
B. *The faith in Christ that brings eternal life to a believer in the here and now will produce a love within the heart that leads to obedience (John 14:15, 21).* Our Lord tells us that as we give ourselves to a life of loving obedience, he will make himself very real and personal to us.
C. *The life that is eternal now is a life of fellowship with God the Father and with his Son, Jesus Christ (John 14:23).*

Conclusion

Christ came that we might have life hereafter. Christ also came that we might have life in the here and now. He offers life on both sides of death. To experience it, we need to put faith in him and give ourselves in obedience to him. Life, the real thing, will then be ours.

SUNDAY EVENING, OCTOBER 27

Title: Working with Christ

Text: "As long as it is day, we must do the works of him who sent me. Night is coming, when no one can work" **(John 9:4 NIV)**.

Scripture Reading: John 9:1–11

Introduction

As we experience the birth pains of the end times, we are dramatically reminded of the passing of time and opportunity. Soon the day will come to an end and the night will begin. Believers will never again have the opportunity to worship, minister, teach, witness, or serve in their flesh-and-blood bodies on the earth.

The living Christ continues his work in the world today through us, his disciples. The church is his body through which he glorifies God and ministers to the needs of people. The Christ who brought sight to the blind man continues in his desire to bring light and love into eyes that are blind and hearts that are cold.

Once as Jesus passed by a crowd, he saw a blind man. Jesus' compassionate eyes could see beneath the surface. He recognized the blindness of the man. The apostles, however, were concerned with theological questions. They were eager to fix blame for the man's blindness. Jesus was concerned about restoring sight. He declared that the blind man's need provided an opportunity for God's love and power to be at work. Jesus gave instructions to the blind man, and the man obeyed the Lord and received the sight he so desperately desired.

I. Our Lord speaks of a partnership ("We must work").

Our Lord associates us with himself in the work of God. He needs our assistance and energy. Our highest privilege is the joy of working with Jesus Christ.

Jesus declared, "As long as I am in the world, I am the light of the world" (John 9:5). Later he said, "I am come a light into the world, that whosoever believeth on me should not abide in darkness" (12:46). He had already declared that those who follow him would not walk in darkness but would have the light of life (8:12).

If we would truly be Jesus' partners, we must be available to assist him in helping others to put their faith in him.

II. Our Lord speaks of a divine mission.

Jesus had a fixed purpose for life. He felt himself under a binding obligation to do the will of God. We are invited to be a part of that mission.

A. *Our Lord was aware of the divine mission even at the age of twelve (Luke 2:49).*
B. *While on the cross, he cried out, "It is finished" (John 19:30).*
C. *The work goes on today.* The followers of Christ constitute the body through which he works in the world today (Mark 10:45; Luke 19:10).
D. *Christ has a continuing ministry for us.*
   1. The church is to concentrate on presenting Christ as the Savior from sin.
   2. The church is to concentrate on nourishing and building up the family of God.

III. Our Lord speaks of a specific time for work ("While it is day").

As we come to the end of the year, we recognize the limited nature of time. We should also recognize and respond to the infinite value of time.

A. *The day is that period of time in which we have life and opportunity.*
B. *The day is that time in which others have life and opportunity.* The night comes for us, but the night also comes for others.

IV. Our Lord speaks of the passing of opportunity ("The night cometh, when no man can work").

The night means the end of the opportunity for living and doing. There is something absolute and final about the night. When the night comes, the day is irrecoverable.

    A. *Death will come to each of us.* No longer will we be able to sing, to teach, to witness, to give, to preach, and to minister.

    B. *Death will come to the unsaved. We are commissioned to witness to them.* We are encouraged to win them. The night can mean for them eternal banishment from God, which is eternal hopelessness, helplessness, and lostness.

The night comes, the day wanes, opportunity passes, and eternity hastens for us all.

Conclusion

Christ opens our eyes to the wonder of our partnership and to the significance of our mission. He emphasizes that we have a specific time in which to work and that all of us face the fact of the passing of opportunity.

To those who have not yet received Jesus Christ as Lord, Christ wants to open your eyes to the love of God the Father, to the way of forgiveness and eternal life, and to the way of self-giving service that is the way of joy and gladness.

Let us face the future trusting in him who is the Light of the World. Let us determine to cooperate with him fully in doing the good works of the Father God.

WEDNESDAY EVENING, OCTOBER 30

Title: Thyatira—The Worldly Church

Text: "I have this against you: You tolerate that woman Jezebel, who calls herself a prophet. By her teaching she misleads my servants into sexual immorality and the eating of food sacrificed to idols" (**Rev. 2:20 NIV**).

Scripture Reading: Revelation 2:18–29

Introduction

The city of Thyatira lay in the long and beautiful valley of the Lycus River. The city was situated in the flats and had no promontory, so there was no acropolis. The city was a trading and manufacturing center, and the Roman army had a garrison stationed there. Pliny called it "an unimportant town." But Thyatira was famous for its guilds (trade unions), and archaeologists have discovered evidence of guilds for bronze and metals, cloth, pottery, baking, and weaving. The local hero-god was Tyrimnus, a warrior on horseback carrying a battle ax and a club. The New Testament does not reveal when or by whom the gospel came to Thyatira. When Paul visited Philippi, he met a woman from Thyatira named

Lydia. She was a "seller of purple"—a businesswoman. She became the first convert in Europe.

I. The Christ (Rev. 2:18–19).

A. *Description (2:18).* This letter to the church at Thyatira is stern and harsh. The description of the reigning Christ bears out the fearful tone of the message. The picture is of one whose "eyes are a flame of fire and whose feet are like burnished brass." He is in truth the "Son of God." The picture emphasizes the sovereignty and deity of Christ. Christ rules over his church; but more, he is sovereign over the whole world. One day he will rule the nations of the earth. We sing, "Gentle Jesus, meek and mild," and so he is in the day of grace, but what of the day of judgment? Scripture says, "My Spirit will not always strive with man." After grace comes judgment. And this judgment begins at the house of God. The eyes of Jesus that one day wept over a lost and wayward Jerusalem will on another day be as flames of fire.

B. *Christ's message (2:19).* "I know your deeds, your love and faith, your service and perseverance, and that you are now doing more than you did at first" (NIV). This was a very busy church. They had more activities than love; more doing than dedication—a full calendar every week. But with all of their doing, Christ had a word against them.

II. That woman Jezebel (Rev. 2:20–23).

A. *Jezebel.* Who is Jezebel? There are many and varied answers. Some manuscripts read, "Thy wife Jezebel." If the "angel" to the church at Thyatira was the bishop, then the pastor's wife was the troublemaker! Such is not impossible. Others say the message refers to a fortune cult operating in the city. One of the few distinctions of Thyatira was the temple of Sambathe—a fortune-teller goddess. The Greeks put great faith in oracles and omens. Some say this sorcery cult was the Jezebel. But I believe it is best to identify this Jezebel with the one whose story is recorded in 1 Kings 18–21. In all Old Testament history, there is no more evil woman mentioned than Jezebel. She is a synonym for all that is profligate; she is adulteress, idolater, and murderer. Her evil influence extended throughout the land. What the first Jezebel was to Israel, this Jezebel was to the church at Thyatira.

B. *Church and state.* Just as Jezebel through King Ahab exerted a religious as well as political influence over Israel, so there came a time in the history of the church when the state and church ruled as one. By the third Christian century there were churches in most of the cities of the Roman world. These churches were autonomous under the leadership of their own pastors. In AD 312 the emperor Constantine was baptized, and Christianity became a state religion. Thirteen years later, at the Council of Nicea, the bishops of Alexandria, Antioch, Constantinople, and Rome were given authority over the churches and pastors in their area. By AD 800 Moham-medanism (Islam) had spread over Asia and Africa. This left only the bishops of Constantinople and Rome as leaders over the churches. On Christmas Day in AD 800, Bishop Leo III crowned Charlemagne as the "holy Roman emperor." This brought about the union of church and state. Now the emperor and bishop were one. The emperor presided at the church councils, he appointed the church bishops, he dispensed ecclesiastical favors, and he punished church offenders. It was now within the power of the state to make converts. Spirit of Jezebel! Some of the darkest pages of church history were written when the state ruled the church.

III. Promises (Rev. 2:25–29).

The tone of these verses gives promise of the Lord's return and the reign of Christ. Christ is coming again, and then he will have "power over the nations" (v. 26). He will rule them (v. 27), and the wicked will "be broken." Christ promises overcomers the "bright and morning star." Later in Revelation, Christ himself is called the "bright and morning star" (22:16). The promise to believers is the personal presence of Christ now and forever.

NOVEMBER

■ **Sunday Mornings**

"The Biblical Doctrine of Stewardship" is the suggested theme for the Sunday morning messages. Stewardship is more than tithing. Stewardship deals with the whole of life. How we make money, spend money, save money, and give money is merely a part of our stewardship.

■ **Sunday Evenings**

The theme for Sunday evenings is "The Romance of Christian Living." If the church is to fulfill its divine mission in the world, Christians must live radiantly winsome and magnetic lives.

■ **Wednesday Evenings**

Complete the series of expository studies on Revelation 1–3 with the theme "Christ Speaks to His Churches." On the last Wednesday evening of the month, begin the series "Personalities in the Nativity Scene." There are some little-known personalities involved in the events surrounding the birth of our Savior who have a message for our hearts.

SUNDAY MORNING, NOVEMBER 3

Title: Give Him All the Keys

Text: "At the name of Jesus every knee should bow, in heaven and on earth and under the earth, and every tongue acknowledge that Jesus Christ is Lord, to the glory of God the Father" **(Phil. 2:10–11 NIV)**.

Scripture Reading: Philippians 2:5–11

Hymns: "Glory to His Name," Hoffman

"A Child of the King," Buell

"Our Best," Kirk

Offertory Prayer: Father, we acknowledge you as the Giver of every good and perfect gift. We praise you for your generosity and kindness toward us. We rejoice in your grace as the basis of your dealings with us. Help us to recognize how blessed we are so that we might be moved by love to serve you, through Jesus Christ our Lord. Amen.

Introduction

By what name do you call Jesus? Do you call him "Friend"? He is a friend. He is a "friend who sticks closer than a brother" (Prov. 18:24 NIV). He is a friend in the hour of trial and tribulation, but he is more than a friend.

Do you call Jesus "Teacher"? He is a teacher—the Master Teacher. No person ever spoke as he did, but he is more than a teacher.

Do you call Jesus "Savior"? He is the Savior. The angelic host announced his coming by declaring, "You are to give him the name Jesus, because he will save his people from their sins" (Matt. 1:21 NIV). But he is more than a Savior.

In the New Testament, Jesus is primarily called "Lord." Four hundred and thirty times in the pages of the twenty-seven books of the New Testament Jesus is designated as "Lord." The angels announced it: "For unto you is born this day in the city of David a Saviour, which is Christ the Lord" (Luke 2:11). Thomas recognized it: "My Lord and my God!" he exclaimed (John 20:28 NIV). Peter proclaimed it on Pentecost: "God has made this Jesus, whom you crucified, both Lord and Messiah" (Acts 2:36 NIV). Paul pointed toward it: "At the name of Jesus every knee should bow, in heaven and on earth and under the earth, and every tongue acknowledge that Jesus Christ is Lord" (Phil. 2:10–11 NIV).

There could be no better way to begin a stewardship emphasis than by saying, "Jesus Christ is Lord." If this is settled, then all else is settled. If this is true, then every other issue will fall into proper perspective.

I. What does it mean to say, "Jesus Christ is Lord"?

It means that Christ is master of one's life—that he is sovereign.

A. *Those early Christians knew that the term equated Jesus with God. Lord* was a common name for God in the Septuagint and was familiar to those who used the Greek version of the Old Testament.

B. *It was the earliest creed of the New Testament Christians and was an affirmation of their loyalty.* They were familiar with such terms as "Lord Serapis," naming a cultic god. The Roman government also required that they make a demonstration of loyalty by declaring, "Caesar is Lord." If they refused, they suffered the consequences that meant death to many. Christians could only say, "Jesus is Lord."

II. What right does Jesus Christ have to be Lord?

A. *He has the right of lordship because he is God.* John declared, "In the beginning was the Word, and the Word was with God, and the Word was God" (John 1:1).

B. *He has the right of lordship because he is Creator.* Genesis 1:1 declares, "In the beginning God created the heavens and the earth" (NIV). Psalm 24:1–2 declares, "The earth is the LORD's, and the fulness thereof; the world, and they that dwell therein. For he hath founded it upon the seas, and established it upon the floods."

C. *He has the right of lordship because he is Redeemer.* Paul asked, "Do you not know that your bodies are temples of the Holy Sprit, who is in you, whom you have received from God? You are not your own" (1 Cor. 6:19 NIV). Peter said, "You know that it was not with perishable things such as silver or gold that you were redeemed from the empty way of life handed down to you from your ancestors, but with the precious blood of Christ, a lamb without blemish or defect" (1 Peter 1:18–19 NIV). He has bought us, and we are his.

D. *He has the right of lordship because of dedication.* When we come to Christ, we surrender all into his hands. We dedicate, by choice, all of our lives to him. Romans 12:1–2 is an expression of this: "I beseech you therefore, brethren, by the mercies of God, that ye present your bodies a living sacrifice, holy, acceptable unto God, which is your reasonable service. And be not conformed to this world: but be ye transformed by the renewing of your mind, that ye may prove what is that good, and acceptable, and perfect, will of God."

This is vividly brought out in Exodus 21 where regulations are laid down concerning the practice of slavery in Israel. Motivated by love, a slave might decide to become forever the absolute possession of his master. The salient feature in this passage is the slave's avowal, "I love my master.... I will not go out free." When a slave chose to say that, by voluntary self-surrender he became forever the absolute possession of his master. And that is what we Christians must do if we would have Jesus as our Lord experientially. Frances Ridley Havergal caught the spirit and meaning of this spiritual transaction in her oft-quoted lines:

I love, I love my Master,
I will not go out free;
For He is my Redeemer,
He paid the price for me.

My Master shed His life blood
My vassal life to win,
To save me from the bondage
Of tyrant self and sin.

Rejoicing and adoring,
Henceforth my song shall be,
I love, I love my Master,
I will not go out free.

III. What are the implications of saying, "Jesus Christ is Lord"?

A. *It means obedience.* Jesus asked, "Why do you call me, 'Lord, Lord,' and do not do what I say?" (Luke 6:46 NIV). To say that "Jesus is Lord" is to say one will obey his every command — to follow him where he leads.

B. *It means that our talents will be his.* Too many are simply playing at this matter of Christianity. If Jesus Christ is Lord, we all will be using our talents for his glory. It is not enough simply to mouth pious phrases. Jesus said, "Not everyone who says to me, 'Lord, Lord,' will enter the kingdom of heaven, but only the one who *does* the will of my Father who is in heaven" (Matt. 7:21 NIV, italics added).

C. *It means that our possessions will be his.* If Jesus Christ is Lord, then *all* of our possessions will be his. We will use all for his glory. We are as accountable to him as Lord for the use of the nine-tenths that are left after the tithe is given as we are for the tithe.

The Bible declares, "All the tithe of the land, whether of the seed of the land, or of the fruit of the tree, is the LORD's: it is holy unto the LORD" (Lev. 27:30).

A friend of mine tells of seeing a little boy standing at the candy case in a dollar store one day. The boy's eyes were as big as silver dollars and his mouth was watering. My friend stood there and watched him for a minute, and the little boy's eyes seemed to get bigger and bigger. "Finally," he said, "I could stand it no longer and I went over to the sales clerk and bought a bag of candy, and then I gave it to the little fellow. Those chubby hands immediately reached down into the bag, and he began to cram the candy into his mouth without a word. I stood there and watched him for a while and then said, 'Well, son, how about letting me have a piece?' Immediately the little boy closed the sack and drew it close to his chest and said, 'No, it's mine. It's mine.'"

We can understand how a child can do this, but isn't this what we are doing with God? He who gave us so much says very simply, "Now, give me a part." Immediately our voices become hard and our eyes become steel and we say, "It's mine! It's mine!"

One day we are going to stand before our Lord, and he is going to say very simply, "Why didn't you tithe? Why were you not a good steward of what I gave you? I gave you command after command. Why didn't you?" And many are going to say, "Well, Lord, we didn't think you meant it." The truth of the matter is that we know he means it. We know that he has spoken to us, and if he is Lord, then he is Lord of all of life. He is Lord of our talents. He is Lord of our time. He is Lord of our possessions. This is the heart of the Christian life.

Conclusion

John R. Sampey, at the close of the first sermon of a revival, reached into his pocket and brought out a set of keys. Holding up the first key, he said, "This is the key to my house. I have given God this key. Have you?" Then the next: "This is the key to my office. I have given God that key. Have you?" Holding up keys to his desk, his car, and his safe deposit box, he said, "I have given God all of these keys. Have you given him yours? It has taken me a lifetime to give God all the keys."

He had given God the key to every area of his life. This is what it means to say, "Jesus Christ is Lord." This is stewardship at its best.

SUNDAY EVENING, NOVEMBER 3

Title: The Christian Life—What Is It?

Text: "I am come that they might have life, and that they might have it more abundantly" **(John 10:10)**.

Scripture Reading: John 10:10

Introduction

In its most scriptural and simplest meaning, "the Christian life" is "the Christ life." It is simply Christ living in you. The moment you accepted Christ as your Savior, you invited him to come into your life so that he might control and own you. You gave him your life, personality, and total being in which he might live each day.

The Christian life is not what *you* do; it is what *Christ* does through and in you.

I. The Christian life is a new experience.

Long before you were born, God had a wonderful plan for you. He desired that you get the best and most out of life. To make this possible, God created a plan that would enable you to live your life on the highest plane. This life is the Christian life. You come into this new life through an experience that we call a "new birth." Your need of this new experience is a need common to all people, "for all have sinned, and come short of the glory of God" (Rom. 3:23). The result of your sin is eternal separation from the saving presence of God. The Bible asserts, "The wages [result] of sin is death" (Rom. 6:23). But God does not want you to receive what you have earned (your "wage"). He has a "gift" he wants to give you instead: "But the gift of God is eternal life through Jesus Christ our Lord" (Rom. 6:23). This is an unmerited gift that was purchased by Christ when he died in your place on the cross (Rom. 5:8).

Now the question naturally follows, "How do I accept this gift?" And the answer involves two words—"repentance" and "belief" (Luke 13:3; Acts 16:31). Through repentance you turn *from* sin in sorrow. Through faith you turn *to* Christ in joy.

When you really want Christ to enter your life as Master and Savior, there is something you must do and there is something God will do. You must *ask* him for salvation, and he will *grant* it (Rom. 10:13).

Christ describes this new experience as a new birth (John 3:7), which makes you a member of God's family (John 1:12).

II. The Christian life is a new person within—"Christ in you."

Now that you have had a new experience, there is a new person within you. This person is Christ, who literally now lives *in* you. This is a very important fact, since the Christian life is not imitating Christ, it is not striving to act like Christ, it is simply allowing Christ to live in *you*. When this new person entered your life through your new experience, your old life was put to death and you were made an entirely new person (Gal. 2:20).

The confidence you have that you will share in the glory of Christ is based on the fact that Christ is in you (Col. 1:27). Your body is the residence of the Holy Spirit (1 Cor. 6:19). You now know that Christ lives in you because he enables you to obey his will (1 John 3:24).

III. The Christian life is new life.

By letting Christ into your life, you have not only made a new start in life, you have received a new life with which to start.

Since you have trusted one who had the power to overcome death, a real difference is seen in the way you live. Paul calls this "newness of life" (Rom. 6:4). Now that you have this "new life," you should live in the thrilling and joyful "newness of spirit" (Rom. 7:6). Yours should be a happy and full life because God has promised, "A new heart also will I give you, and a new spirit will I put within you: and I will take away the stony heart out of your flesh, and I will give you an heart of flesh" (Ezek. 36:26).

Conclusion

The Christian life is the greatest and most meaningful life possible on earth. It is a new experience, a new person within, and a new life. It is yours to accept as a sinner. It is yours to enjoy as a Christian.

WEDNESDAY EVENING, NOVEMBER 6

Title: Sardis—The Dead Church

Text: "You have a reputation of being alive, but you are dead" (**Rev. 3:1 NIV**).

Scripture Reading: Revelation 3:1–6

Introduction

Seven centuries before the book of Revelation was written, Sardis was founded. It was one of the greatest cities of the Greek world. From Sardis the king of Lydia ruled an Asian empire of splendor, magnificence, and luxury. The city was located on the ridge of Mount Tmolus, 1,500 feet above the plain of Hermus. Its commanding position made the city almost impregnable from attack. The ridges were precipitous, and there was only one possible approach to the city. One regiment could hold off an army. The city stood like a giant watchtower guarding the Hermus Valley.

The wealth of Sardis was legendary. But when Revelation was written, only a little of its former glory was evident. Sardis lost much of its glory when Cyrus conquered the city. Cyrus had laid siege to the fortress city for two weeks. No way could be found to break its defenses. But while Cyrus and his men watched one evening, they saw the helmet of a soldier of Sardis fall inside the wall and, to their amazement, roll beneath the wall and down into the valley. Under cover of darkness, Cyrus discovered a small break in the foundation of the wall. Three Persian soldiers wiggled their way through and, once inside, opened the gates of the city to the enemy. How vivid, then, is the message to the church at Sardis: "Be watchful, and strengthen the things which remain."

I. Message to a dead church (Rev. 3:1–3).

A. *Alive in name only (3:1).* The church at Sardis had a good history, but it was now living on its former glory. At one time it was a powerhouse for God, but not anymore. Prosperity can do strange things to a church. It can make a church grow fat and lazy. The apostle Paul described such a future church when he wrote that they would have "a form of godliness ... denying the power thereof" (2 Tim. 3:5). Their routine of work and service seemed solid and worthy enough to the world, but God said they were dead. It was all an empty shell. The poet Longfellow wrote of such a church:

> *Outwardly splendid as of old,*
> *Inwardly sparkless, void and cold,*
> *Her force and fire all spent and gone,*
> *Like the dead moon she still shines on.*
> *It's not the walls of the church without*
> *That make her building small or great,*
> *But the Christ-light shining round about,*
> *And the love that stronger is than hate.*

Everyone speaks well of a dead man. "He was a good man; he was kind; he was a fine citizen," they say. Jesus warned, "Woe unto you, when all men shall speak well of you" (Luke 6:26). The church at Sardis had a great name, a glorious past—"Alive!" But now it was alive in name only.

B. *Watch and strengthen (3:2).* This command is in the present imperative and means "Keep on watching and strengthening." Wake up, and stay awake, Christ says. No commandment appears more often in the New Testament than that of watchfulness. Watchfulness needs to be the constant attitude of the church. Through failure to watch and be awake, the proud city of Sardis fell to the enemy.

C. *"Remember" (3:3).* The second command to this church is to remember. Specifically they were to remember how they heard and received the gospel. We are not told in the Bible how the gospel came to Sardis, but it must have been a dramatic story. Perhaps by Paul and Silas, or Mark and Barnabas, or Apollos, or Timothy. Whoever first brought the gospel to Sardis, its coming must have been in demonstration of faith and power. It came through someone's faithfulness, hard work, and sacrifice. One can suppose that

God blessed those first efforts, and the little band of faithful believers grew rapidly. Such is the story of the beginning and early years of many of our churches: a miraculous beginning, and then decline, decay, and death. "Remember your early days in the gospel" is good advice to any church.

D. *"Hold fast" (3:3).* Hold fast to what? The verb must have an object, but none is mentioned in this verse. One might say, "Hold fast to the gospel" or "Hold fast to sound doctrine." This is good, but sound doctrine alone will not bring a church back from the dead. Orthodoxy can be the deadest thing in the world! Paul said to the Corinthian church that he had come to them in the "demonstration of the Spirit and of power." This is what we need to get hold of and secure — the Spirit and power!

There is no more urgent message needed by our churches than this. Remember that these commands are in the present tense and mean continued action. Christ is saying, "Keep on watching, keep on strengthening, keep on remembering, keep on holding fast."

E. *Repent (3:3).* Now the verb construction changes from the present tense to the aorist, from a continual action to a once-for-all action. Christ is saying to this church, "Keep on being awake, and strengthening, and securing fast, and remembering; but once for all, repent!" Let your repentance be a definite, decisive thing. That is the only way you can repent. You cannot do it halfway. You cannot do it looking back. Repentance is a turning around, a forsaking.

II. Promise (3:4–6).

A. *"Walk . . . in white" (v. 4).* White is the predominant color of the book of Revelation. The promise here is that the faithful believer will walk in "white garments." How did the garments get white? Revelation 7:14 says, "They . . . have washed their robes, and made them white in the blood of the Lamb."

B. *Name in the Book of Life (v. 5).* God has a Book of Life. Is your name written in it? Your name can be on a church roll yet not be in the Book of Life. The double negative in the Greek text indicates the impossibility of the believer's name being blotted out of the Book of Life. Christ is saying, "I will not, no never, blot out his name." What blessed security this is!

C. *Confessed before the Father (v. 5).* In the Gospels, Jesus said, "Whosoever shall confess me before men, him shall the Son of man also confess before the angels of God" (Luke 12:8).

SUNDAY MORNING, NOVEMBER 10

Title: When Success Is Failure

Text: "So is he that layeth up treasure for himself, and is not rich toward God" **(Luke 12:21)**.

Scripture Reading: Luke 12:16–21

Hymns: "Guide Me, O Thou Great Jehovah," Williams

"I Love Thy Kingdom, Lord," Dwight

"Take My Life, and Let It Be," Havergal

Offertory Prayer: Father, we rejoice in this day you have made. We worship and praise you with all of our hearts, for out of your abundance you have blessed us. We bring our tithes and offerings that others might hear of your love, grace, and mercy. Accept these tithes and offerings and bless them for your purposes. In Christ's name. Amen.

Introduction

We worship at the feet of success. There is nothing worse in our society than failing.

The man in Jesus' parable was, by the world's standards, a success. He could point with pride to his great harvest. The community would admire his new buildings. The banks would seek his accounts and perhaps even elect him to the board of directors. Parents would use him as an example for their children.

The world called this man a "success," but Jesus called him a "fool." Why? Let's look closely at this man and find Christ's lessons in life.

I. The commendation of the man.

One's first impression is to cry out, "There's nothing wrong with this man. Why, he is one of the finest citizens of that community. Surely the Master must have been mistaken." And on the surface it does seem so. There is much about the man to commend him.

A. *First, he was rich.* He knew how to select the best seed and the richest soil. He knew how to take advantage of every shower and every ray of sunshine, and soon his barns were overflowing.

There is nothing in God's Word against riches per se. Nowhere is there a hint that it is a sin to be rich. Many of God's greatest people were men of great possessions. Abraham and Isaac, Jacob and Job, David and Solomon—all were men of great wealth and great spirituality.

Money is neither good nor bad. It is neither moral nor immoral. Its goodness or its badness is determined by the one who controls it. Money is simply the servant of humans. It can send missionaries around the world to proclaim the unsearchable riches of Christ Jesus, or it can be used to degrade and destroy.

B. *Second, this man had come by his money honestly.* There is no indication that he had acquired his wealth dishonestly. He had not broken the law or mistreated his employees. His business was not one that injured and damaged people.

It matters not how rich nor how liberal persons may be; if they did not come by their wealth in a godly way, they cannot honor God with it. A doctor who is guilty of malpractice, a lawyer who has a corrupt practice, a

334

salesperson who misrepresents and deceives to make a sale—these cannot honor God no matter how generous they may be.

II. The conversation of the man.

If you will listen, you can hear the man talking within himself: "What shall I do? I have no place to store my crops.... This is what I'll do. I will tear down my barns and build bigger ones, and there I will store my surplus grain. And I'll say to myself, 'You have plenty of grain laid up for many years. Take life easy; eat, drink and be merry'" (Luke 12:17–19 NIV).

This conversation of the man is revealing.

A. *It reveals an omission of God from his plans.* In the entire conversation of the man, there is not one mention of God.

1. He recognized no sovereignty of God. He failed to recognize the ownership of God. He had forgotten that "the earth is the LORD's and the fulness thereof, the world and they that dwell therein." All that we have and are comes from God.

2. He realized no partnership with God. The Scripture declares, "We are laborers together with God." This man failed to realize this. A pastor was talking to a wealthy man about his relationship to God. "Surely," he said, "you must realize how much God has blessed you." The man answered, "Yes, the Lord has blessed me, but *I* was there." What he meant was that in reality the Lord had little to do with it. His own efforts counted for more.

3. He forgot about accountability to God. This man was living his life as if there were no God. Is there any wonder that Jesus called him a fool? In the forty-six Greek words, the man referred to himself twelve times; "I," "me," "my," and "mine" are repeated again and again. His very language reveals him to be self-centered.

B. *It reveals a covetous heart.* This man had become the victim of his desire to possess. Covetousness had become a cancer eating away inside his heart.

A covetous heart is never satisfied. Someone says, "I'm going to be happy when I have larger barns filled with grain," but as he reaches out, happiness eludes him. "I'll be happy when I graduate from high school," "when I finish college," "when I get married," "when I have a new home," "when I get that promotion," "when I get that new car," etc. A college degree, a happy marriage, a lovely home, a good job—all these things may fit into the picture of true happiness, but real happiness is to be found only in Christ Jesus and his will and purpose for men and women.

R. C. Campbell tells of a legend that runs like this: A man who owned uncounted acres told a young man that he would give him all the land in the circumference measured by a radius that he could traverse on foot, going and returning in a half day. He must be back on a certain mark before the sun went down out of sight. The young man gladly accepted the invitation and went in a run. On and on he went, traversing mile after mile. Now he must turn back, for if he failed to get back before the sun went down, his efforts would be lost. Faster and faster he ran as he glanced westward and saw the sun nearly down. Finally, his friends, who were eagerly watching for him, saw him coming. They stood in anxiety, for the sun was sinking fast beyond the western horizon. Would he, could he, make it? He did make it! One cheer after another rang through the hills and echoed in the valleys as he threw himself across the goal. He lay there strangely still. They called him. They turned him over. They bathed his face, but he did not move. He was dead. He had won the prize he so much coveted, but in doing so, he had lost his life.

C. *It reveals a trust in things.* "You have plenty of grain laid up for many years. Take life easy; eat, drink and be merry" (v. 19 NIV). He thought that money could do everything. He thought that things could make life meaningful and secure.

We are guilty of this thinking sometimes. We think that all one needs to live is money. A Texas millionaire had one request when he died: "I want to be buried in my red Cadillac." Arrangements were made, and the whole town gathered. One man elbowed another and said, as the cranes lowered the car into the grave, "Boy, that's really living, isn't it?"

But Jesus said, "Watch out! Be on your guard against all kinds of greed; life does not consist in an abundance of possessions" (Luke 12:15 NIV).

Someone has well said, "Money can buy everything but happiness and take you everywhere except to heaven."

D. *It reveals a concern for time and not eternity.* Among the many stories told in connection with the search for gold in the Klondike, there is one that stands out. A prospecting party, penetrating far into the country, came upon a miner's hut. All was as quiet as a graveyard. Entering the cabin, they found skeletons of two men and a large quantity of gold. On a rough table was a letter telling of their successful search for the precious ore. In their eagerness to get it, they forget the early coming of winter in that northern land. Each day they found increasingly more gold. One morning they awoke to find a great snow storm upon them. For days the tempest raged, cutting off all hope of escape. Their little store of food was soon exhausted, and they lay down and died amid abounding gold. Their folly was not in finding and gathering the gold but in neglecting to provide against the inevitable winter. So also, a man is not a fool to prepare wisely for the material demands of life, but he is a fool if he forgets to prepare for the spiritual needs of life and eternity.

III. The condemnation of God.

After the man had decided what to do with his goods and his life, it was God's time to say something. And God said, "You fool! This very night your life will be demanded from you" (Luke 12:20 NIV). Here, in one stroke, God stripped the cloak of hypocrisy from him, and he stood as a naked soul in the presence of God. He had been weighed in the balance of God and found wanting.

Ultimately the time will come when all people must stand before God. It will be a sad day to realize that one has failed in stewardship and to hear the condemnation of God.

The conclusion Jesus drew from the parable is significant. "This is how it will be with whoever stores up things for themselves but is not rich toward God" (Luke 12:21 NIV).

SUNDAY EVENING, NOVEMBER 10

Title: Confidence in the Christian Life

Text: "These things have I written unto you that believe on the name of the Son of God; that ye may know that ye have eternal life, and that ye may believe on the name of the Son of God" **(1 John 5:13)**.

Scripture Reading: 1 John 5:11–15

Introduction

You should live with greater confidence than ever before now that you are a Christian. No other person has the certainty and confidence that a Christian has. This is not "self-confidence"; it is "Christ-confidence," and there is a difference. You share in that same confidence expressed by Paul when he said, "I can do all things in him who strengthens me" (Phil. 4:13 RSV).

John asserts that the purpose of his letter is to make clear the confidence in which Christians are to live their new lives (1 John 5:13). Faith in God's Word, not feelings, is the spring from which this confidence flows. Feelings are changeable and therefore unreliable. God's Word is changeless and therefore most reliable. Thus the basis for the confidence of your Christian life is the Word of God.

So that you may see even clearer the confidence of the Christian life, consider your salvation in three tenses — past, present, and future.

I. Salvation and your past life.

What is required of you in order for Christ to take care of the sins of your past life? Are we not told that if we "confess" and "believe," we shall be saved (Rom. 10:9–10)? Haven't you done this? If you have, there is no cause to doubt nor reason to lose confidence.

When Christ died on the cross, he took your sins, and you were forgiven and made spiritually whole (1 Peter 2:24). God has forgiven your sins (Ps. 86:5); he has made them "white as snow" (Isa. 1:18); he has blotted them out (Isa. 44:22); he has forgotten them (Jer. 31:34); he has pardoned you (Jer. 33:8); he has healed you, freely loved you, and turned his anger away from you (Hos. 14:4). How can you fear any longer? How can you doubt? How can you have anything but the greatest confidence as you read these many promises of God relating to your past sins?

II. Salvation and your present life.

A Christian said, "I am sure my sins have been forgiven. I am sure I'm going to heaven. But my hang-up isn't my past sins or my future destiny. My difficulty is the present—the here and now. Tell me, does salvation relate to my life *today*? How do I stand before God *now*?"

"There is therefore *now* no condemnation to them which are in Christ Jesus" (Rom. 8:1, italics added). "We *are* the children of God" (v. 16, italics added). That is how you stand before God *now*!

You are to live each day in step with Christ. If you do, you have the confidence of daily fellowship with Christ and a continual cleansing of sin (1 John 1:7).

Here are three reasons why you can face temptation every day with confidence. First, no temptation will come your way that has not been faced and conquered by someone else just like you. Second, because God faithfully stays with you, he will not allow a temptation to come your way that you will not be able to resist. Third, with every temptation God promises to provide "a way to escape" (1 Cor. 10:13).

III. Salvation and your future life.

You can be confident that the same Christ who forgave your past and keeps your present will guard your future.

All three tenses of your life are secure in the hands of God. Christ himself promises that you have already passed from death to life (your past), that you have everlasting life right now (your present), and that you will never be condemned (your future) (John 5:24).

Your future life is made secure, because Christ makes this promise to all who come to him: "I give unto them eternal life; and they shall never perish, neither shall any man pluck them out of my hand" (John 10:28).

Your confidence in the future does not rest in self but in Christ (1 Tim. 1:12). Nothing is capable of separating you from the saving and keeping power of God's love (Rom. 8:35–39). This does not mean that you won't have difficulties (John 16:33) or that you won't have any desire to sin, for you will (1 John 1:8).

Satan will remind you of recent sins and failures. He will constantly tell you how unworthy you are (and he is right). The memory of your failures can shake your confidence and rob you of joy. But how wonderful that you can claim the promise of 1 John 1:9: "If we confess our sins, he is faithful and just to forgive us our sins, and to cleanse us from all unrighteousness."

Conclusion

Confidence in the Christian life is yours for the taking. You have the right to possess it and enjoy it. God still says to you, with all your failures and past mistakes, "Never will I leave you; never will I forsake you" (Heb. 13:5 NIV).

WEDNESDAY EVENING, NOVEMBER 13

Title: Philadelphia—The Church of Opportunity
Text: "See, I have placed before you an open door" **(Rev. 3:8 NIV)**.
Scripture Reading: Revelation 3:7–13

Introduction

Philadelphia was the youngest and smallest of the seven churches mentioned in Revelation. The city was founded in 140 BC by Attalus and some Greek colonists from Pergamos. The word *philadelphos* means one who loves his brother. The city was named for the love Attalus had for Eumenes. Philadelphia was founded to spread the Greek language and culture in that part of Asia. It was never a Roman town. It was completely and thoroughly Grecian. By New Testament times, the Greek language and customs had spread throughout Asia. Philadelphia had done its work well.

But the city had its problems. It was situated on the edge of the great productive plain called Kata-ke-kaumene, "the burned-over land." The plain was a lava bed, so the soil was very fertile. Grain fields, vineyards, and fruit were abundant. However, there was the constant threat of earthquakes. In AD 17 the city was almost destroyed. Ground tremors were so frequent that Strabo wrote, "The city is full of earthquakes. Shocks are felt daily. Buildings are cracked and walls are down. Those who dare live there are reckoned mad. The remaining buildings are shored up with poles."

I. The living Lord (Rev. 3:7).

One can imagine the feeling of anticipation in the hearts of the little band of believers in Philadelphia when they learned that the Lord Jesus had a special message for them. What could the Lord have to say to them? What a pleasant surprise awaited them! This church was one of only two churches in Revelation that did not receive a rebuke from their Lord.

God does not reckon the worth of a church on its size or past history. The door of opportunity is open not just to the churches that are famous and strong. Jesus reminded this little group of believers that he knew them too.

II. The open door (Rev. 3:8).

A. *What is it?* Jesus had just said that he has the "key of David" (v. 7). By the nature of things, a key and a door go together. Christ holds the key, and he makes possible the opportunity for service. He can open and close the door according to his sovereign will.

Scripture needs to be interpreted by Scripture. What is the meaning of "door" in other writings of Scripture?

The apostle Paul spoke of the opportunity for witnessing and work at Ephesus as "a great and effectual door opened to me." He mentioned that when he came to Troas to preach the gospel "a door was opened" to

339

him by the Lord. To the Colossians he wrote, "Pray that God would open unto us a door of utterance." And when he reported on his first missionary journey, he said, "God had opened the door of faith to the Gentiles." What do all of these passages have in common? They all refer to a door of opportunity to witness, to spread the gospel. Now the living Lord says to this church at Philadelphia, "I have given you such an opportunity, a chance for real mission work, an opportunity for Christian missions."

B. *History of evangelism.* After the third Christian century, the churches forsook the command to evangelize the world and locked up the message of the gospel behind monastic walls. The Bible was denied the common people, and the liturgy of the church was spoken in a foreign language. History has called this time the Dark Ages. But all the while God was preparing the world for the missionary advance of the gospel. It was an age of world exploration, colonization, and trade. For two hundred years after Columbus discovered the new world, explorers opened the door of other continents to the Western world.

Finally, in 1793 William Carey took the gospel to India. Soon others followed to take the Christian message to the world: Morrison to China, Judson to Burma, and Livingstone to Africa. God had opened the door of the great continents of the world to the gospel. To the evangelical churches that emerged from the Reformation, God was saying, "I have placed before you an open door."

C. *Trends today.* Every national gathering of evangelical churches today hears a call to world missions. God has set before us today a door of opportunity. But what is happening? Mission boards are reporting losses in personnel and financial support. There are fewer Christians in proportion to the world population today than a generation ago. There seems to be an unconcern among us to reach the lost. We have become sidetracked from the mainline of evangelism. Other ministries and bigger buildings have demanded our energies. Something must be done to reverse this trend. We must call our people back to the primary task of the church: winning a world to Christ. Missions require personnel and money. Both are necessary if we are to take advantage of the open door God has set before us today.

III. The promises to the faithful (Rev. 3:9–12).

In quick succession there follow five promises to the faithful church. Each promise begins with an "I will."

A. *The promise of revival:* "I will make them come and fall down at your feet and acknowledge that I have loved you" (v. 9 NIV).

B. *The promise of God's keeping power:* "I will also keep you from the hour of trial that is going to come on the whole world to test the inhabitants of the earth" (v. 10 NIV).

C. *The promise of Christ's return and personal presence:* "I am coming soon" (v. 11 NIV), and "The one who is victorious I will make a pillar in the temple of my God. Never again will they leave it" (v. 12 NIV).

D. *The promise of a new relationship:* "I will write on them the name of my God and the name of the city of my God, the new Jerusalem" (v. 12 NIV).

E. *The promise of a new name:* "I will also write on them my new name" (v. 12 NIV).

Conclusion

The message to the church at Philadelphia closes with the promise of Christ's imminent return and the blessings of the kingdom of God. While we await these things, our task is to be faithful to the commission to share the saving message of the gospel with the whole world.

SUNDAY MORNING, NOVEMBER 17

Title: "My Cup Runneth Over"

Text: "Thou preparest a table before me in the presence of mine enemies: thou anointest my head with oil; my cup runneth over" **(Ps. 23:5)**.

Scripture Reading: Psalm 23

Hymns: "We Gather Together," Baker

"Count Your Blessings," Oatman

"Make Me a Channel of Blessing," Smyth

Offertory Prayer: Heavenly Father, we thank you for your bountiful blessings on our land and on its people. We offer you the gratitude of our hearts and the praise of our lips. We bring our offerings, which represent the bounty of the land and the fruits of our efforts. Accept them and bless them in advancing your kingdom. Help us to give ourselves to you. In Jesus' name. Amen.

Introduction

The late Dr. William Stidger tells in *Guideposts* of writing to his boyhood school teacher to thank her for giving him a love for poetry. Weeks later the lovely lady wrote him: "I want to let you know how much your letter meant to me. I am an old lady in my eighties, living alone in a small room. I taught for fifty years, yet in all that time, yours is the first letter of appreciation I have ever received."

Could this be a characteristic of our age? Never has a people received so much and given so little. Never has a nation been so blessed and yet been so proud and arrogant! Never has a land been so favored by God and then so completely unmindful of the one from whom all blessings flow!

Perhaps the time has come, in this Thanksgiving season, for us to pray the brief prayer of George Herbert, the English poet: "Thou hast given so much to me! Give one thing more — a grateful heart!"

The psalmist had no need of such a prayer. We can hardly read any of his hymns of praise without hearing him say, "Thanks be to God." Especially is this true in the Twenty-Third Psalm. David had come to his latter years and now looked back over his life. With thanksgiving, he exclaimed, "My cup runneth over."

Think with me of some ways in which this is true.

I. My cup runneth over with love.

Being a shepherd himself, David well knew the love of a shepherd for his sheep—a love that was willing to face storms and cold and even risk life to care for the sheep and provide for their needs. We cannot understand such love, but we know that such is God's love for us. Paul prayed that we might be able to comprehend what is the height and depth and breadth and length of the love of God for us. Although we cannot fathom its dimensions, we can see some of the varied facets of its beauty.

A. *It is a love that seeks.* The Good Shepherd himself told us of the shepherd who left the ninety-nine safe in the wilderness and then scoured the mountainside to find the one sheep that had gone astray. It is his way of saying that we are loved and sought out with an unchanging love.

Susan Webber, a college sophomore, wrote the following poem entitled "Lost" (*The Young Calvinist*, September 1967, 40).

> *O Lord, what happened to you after high school graduation?*
> *Did you go on to trade school when I went to college?*
> *I looked everywhere for you—in the corridors, in the library, in the biology lab.*
> *Once I thought I had found you in the Audio-Visual Department at school—record number 47, The Messiah;*
> *But no—I was mistaken. Again, I thought I had heard you on the radio—speaking through a man named Malcolm Boyd.*
> *I was mistaken again.*
> *I tried to find you in others—but they had lost track of you too.*
> *Some had never heard of you.*
> *I looked in nature. I searched the sky, the forests, and the valleys.*
> *I decided to halt my search for a while; I wasn't getting anywhere. But wait—I think I see something! I can feel someone in my presence.*
> *Is it you, Lord? I pray, and for the first time since graduation, you are here.*
> *Why couldn't I find you? Where were you hiding?*
> *"What do you mean where was I? I was looking for you...."*
> *Yes, Lord, you're right ... I should have searched my heart first....*
> *You were there all the time.*
> *It was I who was lost and didn't slow down to let you find me.*

B. *My cup runneth over with a love that secures.* Jesus said, "I am the good shepherd.... My sheep hear my voice, and I know them, and they follow me: And I give unto them eternal life; and they shall never perish, neither shall any man pluck them out of my hand" (John 10:11, 27–28).

Paul put it another way when he said, "I am persuaded that neither death, nor life, nor angels, nor principalities, nor powers, nor things present, nor things to come, nor height, nor depth, nor any other creature, shall be able to separate us from the love of God, which is in Christ Jesus our Lord" (Rom. 8:38–39).

How we need this word for the living of these days! In a world of wars and rumors of wars, a world of chaos and confusion, a world of strife and conflict, we need to know that there is a hand upon the helm—an omnipotent hand of love.

When we look at our world, we are likely to go to one of two extremes. We are tempted to say that God is a powerless love or that God is a loveless power.

The Bible says both of these are wrong, for "God is at work in all things for good" (Rom. 8:28). Let the armies march, the missiles soar, the satellites encompass the globe. Let the bombs be stored and all hell be loosed. God is at work, and victory is his. We are secure in his will and his purpose.

II. My cup runneth over with providential care.

"I shall not want," declares the psalmist. "Thou preparest a table before me in the presence of my enemies."

We so often are like the prodigal son in the far country. When we have wasted our substance in riotous living and have begun to be in want, we sit down in self-pity and cry and whine: "Why has God dealt thus with me?" Our greed and pride blind us to a thousand mercies that are ours for the asking. When he came to himself, the prodigal said, "My father has enough and some to spare. I will arise and go to him."

Recently the paper carried the account of a man who died in a one-room apartment. He had lived all his life in poverty. When his room was being cleaned, thousands of dollars were discovered hidden away in the dirt and debris. How like us—living in poverty and self-pity when so much is ours!

III. My cup runneth over with comfort.

Again the psalmist says, "Thy rod and thy staff they comfort me.... Yea though I walk through the valley of the shadow of death I will fear no evil for thou art with me."

Make no mistake about it—the valleys and shadows of life are ours. "Man is born unto trouble, as the sparks fly upward" (Job 5:7). We are not immune as Christians. We cannot claim "spiritual immunity" from the sorrows and heartaches of life. But we can find that in the midst of all of this, there is a presence to sustain. We are never alone: "Thou art with me."

Paul discovered this when he prayed about his "thorn in the flesh." God said, "I'll not remove it, but my grace is sufficient for thee."

A friend of mine told me recently of a young couple in his church—dynamic Christians—he was a deacon, and she was a soloist in the choir. At the prime of life, he died of cancer. The funeral was on Thursday. The next day she asked the pastor if she might sing the coming Sunday. "My dear," he said, "you do not realize what you are asking. You know how music tears at the soul." But she insisted, and on that Lord's Day she stood with a Christian radiance and sang:

> *What a friend we have in Jesus,*
> *All our sins and griefs to bear!*
> *What a privilege to carry,*
> *Everything to God in prayer!*
> *Oh, what peace we often forfeit,*
> *Oh, what needless pain we bear,*
> *All because we do not carry,*
> *Everything to God in prayer!*
>
> *Have we trials and temptations?*
> *Is there trouble anywhere?*
> *We should never be discouraged,*
> *Take it to the Lord in prayer:*
> *Can we find a friend so faithful,*
> *Who will all our sorrows share?*
> *Jesus knows our every weakness,*
> *Take it to the Lord in prayer.*

This is the difference Christ makes. Truly, "my cup runneth over" with comfort.

IV. My cup runneth over with assurance.

"I will dwell in the house of the LORD forever," the psalmist exclaims. This is what Jesus said in John 14: "Let not your heart be troubled: ye believe in God, believe also in me. In my Father's house are many mansions: if it were not so, I would have told you. I go to prepare a place for you. And if I go and prepare a place for you, I will come again, and receive you unto myself; that where I am there ye may be also" (vv. 1–3).

A great Christian who had lost her companion tells of her experience with death. "For years Ben would go off to work, and every day I would wait at the gate for his return. When I saw him coming in the evening, I would rush out to meet him, embrace him, and then, arm in arm we would go into the house together. Now he is in heaven and I am here. But things haven't changed much. I used to wait for him to come home—now he waits for me to come home."

Thanks be to God! "My cup runneth over."

V. What should be our response to all this?

In Psalm 116 the psalmist asks, "What shall I render unto the LORD for all his benefits toward me?" (v. 12). He mentions at least three things:

A. *"I will take the cup of salvation" (v. 13).*
B. *"I will walk before the LORD in the land of the living" (v. 9).*
C. *"I will pay my vows unto the LORD now in the presence of all his people" (v. 14).* "I will offer to thee the sacrifice of thanksgiving" (v. 17).

SUNDAY EVENING, NOVEMBER 17

Title: Daily Exercises for Spiritual Strength

Text: "This I pray, that your love may abound yet more and more in knowledge and in all judgment" **(Phil. 1:9).**

Scripture Reading: Philippians 1:9–11

Introduction

Becoming a Christian is described by the Bible as being "born again." Your new birth was a wonderful experience. In that moment of faith, you became a child of God. Yet it would be tragic if you failed to grow as God's child because of your neglect of daily spiritual exercise.

Your faithfully practicing of five daily spiritual exercises will result in growth and personal happiness. To help you remember these exercises, remember the acrostic DAILY.

Devote a definite time to the Word of God.

Always pray.

Introduce Christ to others.

Live in the fellowship of other Christians.

Yield your life to Christ's control.

I. Devote a definite time to the Word of God.

Developing the practice of having devotions at a set time each day is vital. Just as you need physical food each day, you need the spiritual food of God's Word.

And just as you cannot eat enough food in one day to last for the rest of the week, neither can you feed on God's Word one or two days a week and maintain a spiritually happy and healthy life. This is why you must read the Bible each day as a daily exercise.

As you prepare to read your Bible each day, ask the Holy Spirit to guide you in discovering those truths God would have you learn that day (John 16:13). Then you should ask God to open your eyes to the wonderful lessons contained in the particular passage you will study (Ps. 119:18).

God has given us his Word so that we may mature and do the good things that both please God and make us happy (2 Tim. 3:17). Regular Bible study and meditation will give your life stability, productivity, and spiritual prosperity (Ps. 1:2–3).

Memorization of Scripture is a strong deterrent against personal sin (Ps. 119:11). And it cannot be overemphasized that study and Scripture memorization should be a daily exercise (Acts 17:11).

II. Always pray.

Christ clearly taught this as a daily exercise when Luke summarized one of Christ's parables in these words: "Men ought always to pray, and not to faint" (Luke 18:1).

345

At the first part of each day, you should follow the example of Christ who arose early in the morning, went where he could be alone, and prayed (Mark 1:35).

Through prayer you will get to know God better. Your living a victorious life is dependent on your practice of daily prayer (Matt. 26:41). Should you have difficulty in prayer, be assured that the Holy Spirit understands and will help you (Rom. 8:26).

Three guidelines to effective prayer are (1) pray according to God's will (1 John 5:14), (2) ask in faith (James 1:6), and (3) ask in Christ's name (John 14:13–14).

Should you feel that there is some sin in your life that would keep your prayer from being answered, you should do two things: confess it and quit it (Prov. 28:13).

III. Introduce Christ to others.

This is the normal response of one who has just come to know Christ as Savior (John 1:40–46). As a "witness," you must speak. The term *witness* is borrowed from the courtroom, and a witness in a courtroom must speak. A good life will add strength to one's testimony, but even so, the witness must speak in order to be a witness.

John 1:40–42 is an excellent witnessing study. The witness was Andrew. The one to whom he witnessed was Peter. His testimony was that Jesus was the promised Savior (Messiah). And after witnessing to Peter, Andrew brought Peter to Christ.

Thus you are to share with others what you have "seen and heard" concerning Jesus.

IV. Live in the fellowship of other Christians (Phil. 1:3–6).

A glowing coal will soon lose its warmth when set apart from the mass of glowing coals. So a Christian will find it difficult to maintain warmth and spiritual glow when apart from the fellowship of other Christians. This is one reason Christ established the church. Acts 2:41–42 tells us that the new Christians were added to the church the very same day they trusted Christ. We are warned never to be guilty of forsaking regular group worship (Heb. 10:25). We should participate in worship with joy and gratitude.

V. Yield your life to Christ's control (Gal. 2:20).

This is not a once-in-a-lifetime experience. You must do this daily. Paul expressed this daily exercise beautifully: "I die daily" (1 Cor. 15:31).

Begin each day by praying, "Christ, here is my life, my body, my all for you to use. I do not ask that you 'help' me do anything. Rather, I ask that I die and that you come to do whatever you desire to do this day in and through me."

Because you, apart from God, cannot do good, it is necessary that you yield yourself every day to Christ's control (Rom. 7:18).

In England the queen gets the honor and praise, but the prime minister governs. Christ deserves more than your praise and respect. He has the right to govern your life.

Conclusion

Each day as you awake, let your hand be your reminder of your five daily exercises. Use your fingers as a checklist for your spiritual exercise. You will be stronger, happier, and securer as you practice these five daily exercises.

WEDNESDAY EVENING, NOVEMBER 20

Title: Laodicea—The Lukewarm Church

Text: "So, because you are lukewarm—neither hot nor cold—I am about to spit you out of my mouth" **(Rev. 3:16 NIV)**.

Scripture Reading: Revelation 3:14–19

Introduction

There were six cities in Asia called by the name Laodicea. The one in Revelation was distinguished from the rest by the full name "Laodicea on the Lycus." The city was founded in 250 BC by Antiochus of Syria and named for his wife Laodice. The name means "pleasing to the people." Laodicea was on the trade road to Ephesus, and this commerce assured the city of great wealth. Pliny called it a "city most distinguished."

The message of Christ to this church contains three things: a claim, a charge, and a counsel.

I. The claim of Christ (Rev. 3:14).

A. *The Amen.* Christ begins this letter by mentioning who he is and what he knows. He is the "Amen." This is a strange title. The word is usually used at the end of a prayer. But it literally means "truly" or "verily." Since the word here is capitalized, it is a proper name. Christ is the True One, the Veritable One.

B. *The witness.* The word *witness* is our word for "martyr," designating one who gives his life for a witness or cause. Here Christ is called the faithful and true Martyr. The martyrdom of Christ was real. The death of Christ accomplished all that God had planned. He "died according to the Scriptures."

C. *The ruler of God's creation.* Christ is the Creator. This is exactly what John meant when he declared, "All things were made by him; and without him was not any thing made that was made" (John 1:3). And Paul wrote, "In him all things were created: things in heaven and on earth, visible and invisible ... all things have been created through him and for him. He is before all things, and in him all things hold together" (Col. 1:16–17 NIV).

This is the claim of Christ as to who he is; now what does he claim to know? He says, "I know your deeds" (Rev. 3:15 NIV). Christ knows every one of his churches. He knows our works, our labors, our doings.

II. The charge of Christ (Rev. 3:15–17).

There is here no word of praise or commendation for the church in Laodicea. This is the only church of the seven about which the Lord has not had one good thing to say. Ephesus left its first love, but they did hate the Nicolaitans. Pergamos had a false prophet, but many remained faithful. Thyatira tolerated Jezebel, but others had not known the depths of Satan. Sardis's works were not perfect (mature), but some had not defiled their garments. Philadelphia had little strength but great opportunity. To Laodicea, however, there is not one word of commendation. No faithful few are mentioned. This church was not infected by any special sin or vice; no heretics are mentioned. What then is wrong? They are lukewarm.

A. *Neither cold nor hot.* The words the Lord chooses are important here. For "cold," he uses the word *psuchros*, which means "freezing cold"; and for "hot" he uses the word *dzestos*, which means "boiling hot." In between is this word *lukewarm*. The regular word for "warm" is *thermaino*; but this word is *chliaros*, which means "barely warm." They were like a cup of lukewarm coffee—something to be spit out.

This must be the attitude God dislikes most about his church: a feeling of indifference and unconcern. This attitude will grieve the heart of God—and the hearts of some pastors. This was a halfhearted church. How descriptive of our churches today! We are nominal, skin-deep, unemotional. Ours is an anemic Christianity.

How did the church at Laodicea come to lose its fire and zeal?

B. *Material possessions.*

1. Their wealth. The city of Laodicea was famous for its wealth. It was the great banking and financial center for the province. In AD 61 when an earthquake devastated a great part of the city, the citizens refused the aid of the Roman government. One citizen alone gave the city the equivalent of a million dollars! The Laodiceans felt they needed nothing. This attitude made its mark on the church. Because of their great wealth, they felt self-sufficient. Jesus had much to say about the dangers of wealth and the love of money.

2. Their clothes. Laodicea was the fashion center of Asia. The area was famous for its soft black wool. The wool was used not only for fine garments but also for the popular Persian rugs. This city was the "Paris" of the Roman world.

3. Ointments. There was a famous medical center at Laodicea. Two of her doctors, Zeuxis and Alexander, had won universal fame and appeared on some coins of the period. They specialized in eye and ear diseases. The Scripture mentions in verse 18 an "eyesalve." This was a Phrygian powder in tablet form that was especially recommended for "aches about the head." These things they boasted about: their wealth, their clothes, and their ointments. But how did Christ see them? "Thou art wretched, and miserable, and poor, and blind, and naked" (v. 17).

III. The counsel of Christ (Rev. 3:18–19).

The living Christ says to his church, "Buy of me gold, and raiment, and ointment" (v. 18). Christ is the only source of spiritual riches.

A. *Gold.* The gold of God is that tried in the fire. The apostle Peter reminds us that "the trial of [our] faith, being much more precious than of gold that perisheth, though it be tried with fire, might be found unto praise and honor and glory at the appearing of Jesus Christ" (1 Peter 1:7). Gold ore in its natural state is worth little until it is refined with fire and made into a useful instrument or ornament. So is the faith that stands the test.

B. *Raiment.* The Laodiceans boasted about their expensive clothes. But God requires a different kind of clothing: a robe made white in the blood of the Lamb.

C. *Eyesalve.* This anointing of the eyes must surely mean the illumination of the Holy Spirit. For any church to "see," there must be the presence and power of the Spirit in its pastor and people.

Conclusion

As in Revelation 3:19, "repent" is the oft-repeated word in these messages to the churches. To Ephesus Christ says, "Repent and do the first works." To Pergamos, Thyatira, and Sardis, Jesus says, "Repent." Now to Laodicea, Christ says, "Be zealous therefore, and repent." Repentance is a word commanded as much of the saint as the sinner. I like the way Phillips translates this verse: "Therefore, shake off your complacency and repent." No word is more needed in the church today than this.

SUNDAY MORNING, NOVEMBER 24

Title: Questions People Ask

Text: "In everything I did, I showed you that by this kind of hard work we must help the weak, remembering the words the Lord Jesus himself said: 'It is more blessed to give than to receive'" (**Acts 20:35 NIV**).

Scripture Reading: Acts 20:32–38

Hymns: "Love Divine, All Loves Excelling," Wesley
"Something for Thee," Phelps
"All Things Are Thine," Whittier

Offertory Prayer: Our Father, help us to see how richly and how abundantly you have bestowed your blessings on us. Help us to recognize the presence of your loving purpose in all of the events and gifts that you bring into our lives. Today we bring the fruit of our labor and place it on the altar as an act of worship and adoration. We express the gratitude of our hearts and at the same time share the good news of your love with a lost and needy world. Accept our tithes and offerings and bless them to the salvation of the unsaved in this community and in the uttermost part of the earth. In Jesus' name. Amen.

Introduction

Each year as the church budget takes shape and is reviewed by the congregation, we are asked to make a financial commitment to the work of the church of Jesus Christ. Whether or not we use pledge cards—some churches do—each of us is challenged to examine our giving in the light of the budget, but even more so in light of the counsel of the Bible.

The kind of commitment we make reveals a lot about us. It reveals our character, and it indicates our love for Christ and his church. It shows our concern and compassion for God's world. It marks our faith in God and his Word. And it reveals our faith in the future of our church and its program of work.

Before we make this commitment, before we indicate our degree of participation in the church's ministry, each of us should gather the family about, pray about it, and then ask ourselves the following questions.

I. Why should I give?

    A. *If you asked me why you should give, I would remind you of the love of Christ.* It was he who said, "It is more blessed to give than to receive"—he, whose face was smitten by evil men, whose back was beaten with many stripes, whose side was pierced by the Roman spear, whose hands and feet were nailed to the cruel cross. It was he who did this for sinful people—for you and me.

    B. *If you asked me why you should give, I would point out to you the need of the world.* I would show you people in our community. I would tell you of a ten-year-old girl who had never heard the story of Jesus Christ until last month when one of our Sunday school teachers led her to a knowledge of Christ. I would direct your attention to the darkness of South America and Africa. I would show you hospitals that need doctors, nurses, and medicine; schools that need teachers and equipment; villages crying for a missionary to show them the way to God.

    C. *If you asked me why you should give, I would point out to you the teachings of the Bible.*

        1. The Bible declares God's ownership of everything: "The earth is the Lord's, and the fulness thereof; the world, and they that dwell therein" (Ps. 24:1). "The silver is mine, and the gold is mine, saith the Lord of hosts" (Hag. 2:8). "What? know ye not that your body is the temple of the Holy Ghost which is in you, which ye have of God, and ye are not your own?" (1 Cor. 6:19).

        2. We are but stewards. This means we are accountable to God for administering our stewardship. We cannot choose whether we will be stewards. We can only choose whether we will be good stewards or bad stewards.

    D. *If you asked me why you should give, I would ask you to look within your heart and see the need to give.* God anticipated man's every need. He saw that man needed oxygen, so he provided air for him to breathe. He saw that he

350

needed food, so he provided a garden to grow. He saw that he needed a companion, so he brought forth woman. He saw that he needed forgiveness, so he provided a Savior. He also saw that man needed to give in order to break the power of a covetous life.

We need to give in recognition of the fact that God is Sovereign and Lord and that we are but stewards.

E. *If you asked me why you should give, I would show you the welfare of the home.*

We give our children everything with which to live without giving them a reason for living. In this respect, we have failed.

The greatest thing we can do for our children is to introduce them to Jesus Christ as Savior. This is basic. All else centers in this experience. The second greatest thing we can do for our children is to give them a proper understanding of stewardship. Unless your children learn in their early years that life is more than things, they will never be happy. Unless they learn that money is not an end in itself, they will never have useful and meaningful lives. If they learn this, they will be successful regardless of what their vocation may be.

F. *If you asked me why you should give, I would tell you that you cannot worship without giving.*

Every time worship is mentioned in Scripture, it is either explicitly stated or basically assumed that giving is involved. In Psalm 96—a psalm of worship—we find these words in the very center: "Bring an offering, and come into his courts." In fact, God has said, "You cannot come before me with empty hands" (Ex. 23:16; 34:20; Deut. 16:16).

It is not that God primarily wants your money. He wants you. And he does not have you unless he has your possessions. All worship must begin here. When God has the person, he will also have the person's money.

II. What are the returns if I give?

The returns are great. God has promised to bless the faithful steward. It pays to be a Christian. I believe, all things being equal, that God does bless financially one who is a good steward. Scripture says, "Bring ye all the tithes into the storehouse ... and prove me now herewith, saith the LORD of hosts, if I will not open you the windows of heaven, and pour you out a blessing, that there shall not be room enough to receive it" (Mal. 3:10).

But God's chief concern is not to make you wealthy; it is to make *you*. A young fruit farmer, greatly disturbed, came to his pastor and said, "Pastor, I've lost my faith. I tithe; I worship; I live a clean life—and yet God let my peaches freeze." His pastor replied, "Young man, God's chief task is not growing peaches. It's growing men."

A. *The first return is that we are laying up treasures in heaven.* One day we will hear the Lord say, "Well done, good and faithful servant! You have been faithful with a few things; I will put you in charge of many things. Come and share your master's happiness!" (Matt. 25:21 NIV).

B. *Second, there is our increased usefulness as partners with God.* We are able by means of our gifts to preach, teach, and heal throughout the world. This we could never do alone, but by the miracle of good stewardship, our gifts multiply our outreach.

C. *Third, we have a good conscience toward God and our fellow humans.* We can meet the Savior face-to-face in worship without shame and guilt when we have been faithful stewards. We can face our fellow church members knowing that we have done our part.

III. How much shall I give?

I can't answer this question for you in dollars and cents. But I can give you two principles from God's Word that can settle it for you.

A. *The minimum giving is the tithe.* This is the starting point in our giving. Scripture says, "Bring ye all the tithes into the storehouse" (Mal. 3:10).

B. *One's giving should be sacrificial.* When David sought to make an offering to his God and was given the opportunity to do so at no sacrifice on his part, he exclaimed, "I will not sacrifice to the Lord my God burnt offerings that cost me nothing" (2 Sam. 24:24 NIV). God did not ask the Israelites to sacrifice their sick or lame or dying animals: he demanded the best of the flock.

Conclusion

We have heard that we should give "until it hurts"; however, someone else has suggested that we should rather give until it feels good. "God loves a cheerful giver" (2 Cor. 9:7 NIV).

SUNDAY EVENING, NOVEMBER 24

Title: How to Recover from Defeat

Text: "For this my son was dead, and is alive again; he was lost, and is found. And they began to be merry" **(Luke 15:24)**.

Scripture Reading: Luke 15:11–24

Introduction

Defeat is not a stranger to the Christian life. In time you will experience the sorrow of defeat. You may be shocked and discouraged that defeat has cast a shadow over the joy of your life. When you are winning the victory and living above defeat, faith comes naturally and easily. But that unexpected moment of defeat puts your faith to a fiery test.

Realizing that we as Christians are still human and in time may well suffer defeat, I offer eight steps to recovery.

I. Recognize that your relationship to Christ has not changed.

Sure, you have fallen, you have suffered defeat, you have sinned. But will the Christ who died on the cross for you do any less for you now? Does he love you any less as his child than when you were not his own? Absolutely not! God is still your Father, and you are still his child. He will forgive you, restore you, love you, and put you back on the right path.

Yours was the same problem as the prodigal's. You were defeated because you were seeking to satisfy your will rather than the will of your heavenly Father (Luke 15:12). This has brought sorrow, not happiness, into your life (vv. 14–16).

When the prodigal returned home, he addressed the one who loved him as "father," and his father addressed him with the loving words "my son" (Luke 15:21, 24). Their relation was unbroken, and so is your relation to Christ unbroken. God is still your Father, and you are still his child.

II. Realize that God expects only failure from you.

God was not surprised that you failed. He knew the moment you started trying to live the Christian life alone that you would fail. Isaiah says, "Even the youths shall faint and be weary, and the young men shall utterly fall" (40:30).

Simon Peter suffered humiliating defeat for the same reason. He tried to live his life alone. He neglected prayer and discovered how weak each of us is in the face of temptation. Jesus warned him that "the spirit indeed is willing, but the flesh is weak" (Matt. 26:41).

III. Face up to your defeat and admit the sin involved.

There is nothing to gain by covering up our sins. The proper way to handle sin is to admit it and abandon it (Prov. 28:13).

God promises that he will deal kindly and mercifully with those who confess their sin (1 John 1:9).

IV. Admit the one real cause for your defeat.

You have again dethroned "self" in your life.

Simon Peter had this same problem. He said, "Even if all fall away on account of you, I never will" (Matt. 26:33 NIV). "Even if I have to die with you, I will never disown you" (v. 35 NIV). Shortly afterward he denied his Lord three times.

You must face this fact and ask Christ to crucify "self" and to put himself back on the throne of your life.

V. Remember that forgiveness is not a matter of worthiness.

Restoration and forgiveness are always matters of divine grace. Christ says, "You have trusted me for the eternally significant thing—salvation. Now you must trust me for forgiveness and victory."

When the prodigal came home to his father, he said, "I am no longer worthy to be called your son" (Luke 15:21 NIV). But even though he was not worthy, he nevertheless remained his father's son and was received, restored, and forgiven—not on the basis of "worth," but on the basis of his father's "grace."

VI. Trust in God's honesty that makes sure he will keep his promises of forgiveness and victory.

God has made more than seven thousand promises that relate to this life. He has even dared to put these in writing. When God says something, that both establishes and settles it!

You may have failed, for we all do. But you can rest assured that God does not break a single promise to you or to anyone else. You must learn to relax in the simple knowledge that God will see you through your dark hour.

The most difficult lesson you will learn will be to do nothing when you have suffered defeat. You have done enough already. Now you must "wait for the LORD; be strong and take heart and wait for the LORD" (Ps. 27:14 NIV).

VII. Really believe that God can bring good out of your experience of defeat.

"We know that all things work together for good to them that love God, to them who are the called according to his purpose" (Rom. 8:28). Please realize that this does not mean that your defeat is good—it is not. Rather, it asserts that your Lord can take your bad experience and bring good out of it. There is no reason in this world why your defeat should become a permanent defeat in your life. There is no logic in allowing it to destroy you. You are simply to take hands off and turn it completely over to Christ. He will then take that remorseful experience and bring good out of it. You dare not trust your own understanding to solve the problem (Prov. 3:5–6).

VIII. Begin a faithful practice of five daily spiritual exercises using the acronym DAILY.

> **D**evote a definite time to the Word of God.
> **A**lways pray.
> **I**ntroduce Christ to others.
> **L**ive in the fellowship of other Christians.
> **Y**ield your life to Christ's control.

Conclusion

The God who made the infinite universe and who keeps track of the trillions of stars also keeps track of you, your problems, and your defeats. Not even a sparrow falls to the ground without God's knowledge.

The very same God who cares for his stars and watches over his birds loves and cares for you. He asks only this: "Believe in me, trust me, and relax in my goodness and mercy." When you do these things, he will surely bring victory out of defeat and save you from despair!

WEDNESDAY EVENING, NOVEMBER 27

Title: Too Good to Be True

Text: "Do not be afraid, Zechariah, for your prayer is heard, and your wife Elizabeth will bear you a son" (**Luke 1:13 RSV**).

Scripture Reading: Luke 1:5–25

Introduction

Occasionally we hear someone exclaim, or we exclaim ourselves, "Why, it's just too good to be true!" Something happens that is beyond our fondest hope, and we can scarcely believe anything so delightful could come about.

In our Scripture reading, Zechariah received a report that his wife, Elizabeth, was to have a baby despite her advanced age. More than that, their baby was to grow into a remarkable individual who was to make ready the hearts of the Jewish people for the Messiah. Zechariah and Elizabeth had been childless for many years. Undoubtedly they had prayed many times for God to send them a child, for Jewish people considered it a reproach to be childless. Judging from the splendid character of Zechariah and Elizabeth, they had a natural desire to express their love to a child. These factors, almost certainly, gave intensity to their petitions for a little one.

An angel, God's special messenger, appeared to Zechariah and said that God had heard his prayers, and a child was to be born to him and Elizabeth.

We can draw several lessons from this unusual encounter that filled Zechariah with a "too good to be true" feeling.

I. God does not always answer prayers when we want him to.

Who has not occasionally believed he could improve on God's timetable? There are three answers God can give to our prayers: "Yes," "No," or "Wait a while." Obviously God felt it wise to wait a while before affirmatively answering the prayers of Zechariah and Elizabeth for a child. "When the fullness of the time was come, God sent forth his Son" (Gal. 4:4). This means that God waited until the wisest possible time, when all conditions indicated the stage was set for Christ to make his entry.

There are times when God is not ready to answer our prayers. Perhaps our hearts are not sufficiently mellowed. Perhaps the heart of the one for whom we pray is not ready. God knows "when the fullness of time" has come for your petition.

II. There are times when God gives us more than we expect or dream.

Any true father would want to give the very best he was capable of giving to his children. The same is true of God.

Zechariah and Elizabeth had prayed for a child, but until the angel's announcement, they did not realize how very special that child would be. The angel revealed that their child would be one of God's great men and that even from his birth he would be filled with the Holy Spirit. His would be a disciplined life so that his spiritual perception would be sharp and incisive. His persuasive preaching would turn many to righteousness, and disobedient minds would be changed into minds filled with the wisdom of God.

God has always wanted to give more than his children expected. The psalmist said, "He leadeth me in the paths of righteousness for his name's sake" (Ps. 23:3). This means that the reputation God has for integrity is at stake in the matter of providing for his children. Because of God's basic nature of love and kindness, he will supply our needs beyond our highest expectations.

III. Our praying should be persistent.

Zechariah, despite his intense desire for a child, evidently had given up hope that a little one would ever come into their home. This accounts for his incredulity at the angel's announcement. Persistence is not to be used in an attempt to wear God down so that he will grant the petition. Rather, it is to prepare our hearts for a greater blessing.

Praying with persistence helps us realize what we really want. If our desires are Christ-centered and will glorify God, then why give up easily? Here is a promise from Christ himself: "Ask and it will be given to you; seek and you will find; knock and the door will be opened to you. For everyone who asks receives; the one who seeks finds; and to the one who knocks, the door will be opened" (Matt. 7:7–8 NIV).

Conclusion

Unfortunately, most of us are like Zechariah. After long years of waiting, his faith had grown dim. God has always had this trouble with his children. A lack of faith caused Israel to wander in the wilderness for thirty-eight years. Except for a lack of faith, they could have been in the Promised Land.

Because his hopes had withered, Zechariah was punished by being unable to speak until the birth of John. Perhaps our mouths are silent as far as praise to God is concerned because our lack of faith has prevented God from blessing us.

If we keep our hope and faith alive, we will find our lives so richly blessed that we will say with deep emotion that the blessings of God are really "too good to be true."

DECEMBER

■ **Sunday Mornings**

With Christmas in the thoughts of everyone, it is highly important that we emphasize the spiritual nature of this event that is threatened with secularism and commercialism. The suggested theme is "Proclaiming the Real Meaning of Christmas."

■ **Sunday Evenings**

Continue the series "The Romance of Christian Living."

■ **Wednesday Evenings**

Continue with the theme "Personalities in the Nativity Scene."

SUNDAY MORNING, DECEMBER 1

Title: Sin and Salvation

Text: "So God created man in his own image, in the image of God ... he created them" **(Gen. 1:27 RSV)**.

Scripture Reading: Genesis 1:27–28; 2:15–17; 3:1–13

Hymns: "Come, We That Love the Lord," Watts

"Come, Thou Long-Expected Jesus," Wesley

"Come to the Savior Now," Wigner

Offertory Prayer: Eternal God, in whom our promises can be made certain, give strength to us that we may be true to our promise to live as your children. Our inward obedience yearns for outward expression. So today we give our money to the treasury of this church because we want to obey what we believe to be your wishes. Through Jesus Christ our Lord. Amen.

Introduction

We enter this Advent season, hopeful that through the disciplines of waiting in prayer and confessing our sins we will come to hear the angel's proclamation: "Glory to God in the highest, and on earth peace among men with whom he is pleased!" (Luke 2:14 RSV). We may travel any number of paths in our preparation for the celebration of that great event in which God came to us. I propose that today we go the way of self-examination. When we see ourselves as the sinners we are, our joy in knowing that God comes to us should be all the greater.

I. Humans, the sinners.

Something is wrong with human life. We are attracted by good and lovely things, but our attainment of the good life falls short. We wrestle with frustration and defeat. Powerful antagonism exerts its influence in a down-dragging fashion. In the biblical accounts, this is recognized as sin. "For all have sinned ..." (Rom. 3:23).

Some people possess a naive optimism about people as "sinners," and they do not take sin seriously. Let it be observed that history discloses no pattern of humanity's moral perfectibility and inevitable progress. The unredeemed 2013-model human under sufficient stress will do deeds of evil as cruel and terrible as anything in history. The self-sufficiency of a morally religious person is itself the full measure of sin.

Christian doctrine repudiates with equal decisiveness a cynical pessimism about humanity. Thorough-going despair is pagan.

II. The nature of sin.

From the book of Genesis, we learn that humans are God's last and highest earthly creatures. Humans' creatureliness is inescapable, but they are lifted above all other earthly creatures by being made in the "image of God" and being aware of it. What is meant by this "image of God"?

The image of a past president or other national hero on a coin is part of the coin and cannot be separated from it. Even though such a person may have died, the image remains on the coin. A different kind of image is that of the moon reflected in the still water of a lake on a clear night. This image can be distorted by wind that brings waves on the water, or it can be destroyed by clouds coming between the moon and the water. The image depends on a certain relation between the moon and the water. The image of God in humans is more like the latter analogy. It depends for its existence on the relation between God and humans, a relation of loving trust and obedience toward God and in God's love of humans.

In the garden of Eden the tempter very subtly suggested to Eve that God should have given people freedom to eat of every tree. He suggested that human limitation is due to some lack in God's love. That seed of distrust was the beginning of temptation. A new suggestion followed closely: "You shall be as God." When humans cease to trust God completely, they want to be god themselves in the sense of deciding what is good, satisfying, and so on. It means that individuals want to be the center of their own world and that they regard their own good as more important than anything else. Instead of loving God and honoring their distinctive endowments as God's creation, instead of loving God with all their heart and soul and mind and strength, they love themselves. The essence of sin is distrust of God, and this issues in unbelief, rebellion, and alienation (Lesslie Newbigin, *Sin and Salvation* [Philadelphia: Westminster, 1957], 16–24).

III. Disharmonies produced by sin.

Because humans violated the nature God gave them and transgressed the limit God placed for them, the unity and harmony of life is badly distorted, if not utterly destroyed. This is seen in four principal ways in the early chapters of Genesis: (1) There is disharmony within humans themselves; (2) there is disharmony between humans and nature; (3) there is disharmony between humans; and (4) above all, there is disharmony between humans and God.

Let us not miss the great impact of this truth by getting hung up with the hopeless task of fitting Adam's fall into some datable aboriginal calamity in humankind's historic past. Let us not fail to see in these chapters a dimension of human experience that is always present—that is, that we who have been created for fellowship with God repudiate it continually, and that the whole of humankind does this along with us (ibid.).

IV. Salvation offered.

God has provided a way of salvation for people who acknowledge their sin, confess it, and turn to God's Anointed One for healing. The word "salvation" means "wholeness." Disharmonies are dissolved; people are released from bondage. It means the healing of that which is wounded, the mending of that which is broken.

Conclusion

If we will use these four weeks of Advent to consider, among other things, ourselves as sinners who have fallen short of the glory of God, we will welcome all the more the angels' announcement to the shepherds: "Be not afraid; for behold I bring you good news of a great joy which shall come to all people; for to you is born this day in the city of David a Savior, who is Christ the Lord" (Luke 2:10–11 RSV).

SUNDAY EVENING, DECEMBER 1

Title: How to Live Victoriously

Text: "In all these things we are more than conquerors through him that loved us" (**Rom. 8:37**).

Scripture Reading: Romans 8:31–39

Introduction

Your living victoriously does not depend on what *you* do, but rather on what you permit Christ to do in you. Yours is not to discover a multiplicity of good things you can do in order to live victoriously. Yours is to decide to relax in the tender care of Christ—to die to self and to allow Christ to live your life for you.

I. Realize your relationship to Christ.

Jesus teaches that yours is a vital relationship with him. Your life and his life are intertwined (John 15:4–5).

Jesus is the main "vine" from which the victorious life comes. You are a branch of this vine through which this life from Christ flows. His life in you results in your being able to live a happy and victorious Christian life.

The prerequisite established by Christ if you are to "bring forth much fruit" is that you must "abide" in him (John 15:5). By this Christ is saying you must have a relation to him as a branch has to the main vine. That is, you must really belong to him through faith in him as your Savior. Then you must honestly try to maintain an unbroken relationship with him each day.

II. Admit your dependence on Christ.

Jesus said that you (the "branch") cannot live victoriously apart from him (the "vine") (John 15:4).

One of the most prevalent reasons many Christians are defeated is that they either fail to realize their dependence on Christ or refuse to admit it. An individual cannot live the victorious Christian life alone. God never meant for you to be able to do this, and he does not expect you to. He only asks for the right to enter your life, living in it each moment of each day.

III. Live each moment by faith.

John says that it is possible for you to live a victorious Christian life—by faith! "This is the victory that overcometh the world, even our faith" (1 John 5:4). The first part of 1 John 5:4 flatly states that a Christian ("whatsoever is born of God") can and should "overcome the world." It is simply a matter of our believing this, claiming the victory in Jesus' name, and having the faith to hold on until the victory comes.

It is not necessary for you to have been a Christian for many years, or to be strong, or to be free from recent defeats to win. If you believe that Jesus is the Son of God, then you can overcome any problem or frustration the world may thrust at you (1 John 5:5).

The strange thing about so many Christians is that they admit they are introduced into the Christian life by faith, but then they shift this thinking and begin to act as though they are to live this life by works. Paul says, "Just as you received Christ Jesus as Lord, continue to live your lives in him" (Col. 2:6 NIV). And how do you receive Christ? By faith! So then, live by faith. Quit worrying, quit trying, and start trusting. This is the way to the victorious life!

IV. Master your own body.

Claim Christ's help in getting in control of your body. By his grace, refuse to allow your body to participate in any activity that would keep you from winning the victory.

The Scripture is very practical here, for it says, "Do not offer any part of yourself to sin as an instrument of wickedness, but rather offer yourselves to God as those who have been brought from death to life; and offer every part of yourself to him as an instrument of righteousness" (Rom. 6:13 NIV).

V. Live a life of love.

Christ's love in us is a special kind of love that is directed away from things that defeat and turned toward things that bring victory (1 John 2:15–17).

A warm and responsive love for others has always been an ingredient in the victorious Christian life (1 John 3:11). Such love must have more than a verbal expression. It must express itself as naturally in deeds as an apple tree bears apples (1 John 3:18).

The incentive for our loving each other is the wonderful fact that God loves us (1 John 4:11).

VI. Be filled with the Spirit.

This is a direct command to every Christian. "And be not drunk with wine, wherein is excess; but be filled with the Spirit" (Eph. 5:18). This is the quiet claiming of Christ's promise of the fullness of the Holy Spirit and then allowing him to bear his fruit through us. A tree does not strive to bear fruit. Nor does it get all worked up about it. It just bears fruit naturally. So the Holy Spirit will bear fruit through us if we let him.

The fruit of the Spirit is "love, joy, peace, longsuffering, gentleness, goodness, faith, meekness, temperance" (Gal. 5:22–23).

Conclusion

You can live victoriously! Remember that the Holy Spirit lives in you. If you think of the Holy Spirit as living near you rather than in you, you will get into a vicious frustrating cycle of feverish efforts to "get closer to him." The fact is that the Holy Spirit lives in you. Believe it! Now allow Christ to win the victory through you.

WEDNESDAY EVENING, DECEMBER 4

Title: The One Whom God Can Use

Text: Luke 1:20, 31, 38

Scripture Reading: Luke 1:26–45

Introduction

God's children have a natural desire to be of service. No one likes to be useless. Even young children gain a sense of importance when they feel they are helping their mothers. It has been correctly said that if you want to endear people to you, do not try to do them a favor; instead, ask them to do a favor for you.

A committed Christian will have a natural desire to be of service to God. It is the very nature of God to give, and when this nature is allowed to be operative in our lives, we will want to give ourselves through service.

God does not always use all those who volunteer for service. Something could be missing in their lives that precludes God's using them. Others are used of God but not to their deep satisfaction. Resisting qualities are in their spiritual makeup, preventing their being of the fullest value to God.

Why was it that God was able to use the Virgin Mary to be the mother of the Messiah? There were sterling qualities in her spiritual makeup that permitted her to be of highest service to God. These same qualities, if found and developed in our lives, will allow us to be creatively used of God.

Mary's kinswoman, Elizabeth, provides for us one of the reasons as to why she was used of God. As she received Mary into her home, she said, "Oh, how happy is the woman who believes in God, for he does make his promises to her come true!" (Luke 1:45 PHILLIPS).

I. It is as simple as this: Mary believed the message God sent through the angel Gabriel, and consequently, God was able to use her.

Our usefulness to God is in direct ratio to our belief in him. The greater our belief, the greater our usefulness. The weaker our belief, the less will be our usefulness.

In the New Testament, belief always implies more than mere intellectual assent. It involves the emotions as well as the intellect, so that genuine belief means "to rely on," "to trust in," or "to cling to." The study of many biographies reveals that people with limited abilities can be, and have been, used in significant fashion, for the simple reason that they had a great belief. A great dream, a great hope, a confident assurance that a goal should, could, and would be reached has made many lives, of otherwise mediocre nature, to be of much more significance and worth.

But consider what Mary believed. She believed that a child would be born of her without benefit of an earthly father. It sounds so utterly impossible that many reject the biblical account. But may it be noted that pastors who fail to so believe are not deeply involved in significant evangelism and are preaching to empty pews, while those who do believe are being greatly used of God in his redemptive effort. The battle to believe has always been a great one. But those who in childlike faith accept the biblical account are greatly used of God.

In our scientific age, we have allowed skepticism to become rampant. Whatever does not fit into our theories, we regard as impossible. Consequently, our usefulness to God is curtailed. Without belief, life as we understand it would cease. The very basis of society is belief. Anarchy results when these beliefs are rejected. Human relations always break down in the pressure of unbelief. It started when Satan talked Eve into disbelieving the command of God. Individual breakdowns and the breakdown of societies always start with disbelief.

II. Another reason why Mary was used of God was that she was submissive to his will.

After the angel Gabriel made the announcement to Mary that she would be the mother of the Messiah, she replied, "I am the Lord's servant. May your word to me be fulfilled" (Luke 1:38 NIV).

She could have said, "Oh, no! No one will understand. Joseph, my betrothed, will think me immoral. The townspeople will be suspicious. Please use someone else." But her attitude of submission made it possible for her to be the mother most beloved of all ages.

Mary allowed no care or interest to get in the way of her submitting to God's will. Competitive interests always rob people of being significantly used of God. The chief reason for a sense of frustration and defeat in the lives of many Christians is simply that they have allowed Christ to live within them but not to reign within them.

If a person could but see the wisdom of allowing Christ to be in "the driver's seat" of their lives, how very productive their lives could be. "Remain in union with me, and I will remain in union with you. Unless you remain in union with me you cannot bear fruit, just as a branch cannot bear fruit, unless it remains on the vine" (John 15:4 GNB).

Conclusion

Has your life been joyless and lacking in vital service? Believe with all your heart that Christ can and will use you. Be submissive to his leadership, and your heart will exclaim with Mary, "My soul glorifies the Lord" (Luke 1:46 NIV).

SUNDAY MORNING, DECEMBER 8

Title: What Does It Mean?

Text: "The people that walked in darkness have seen a great light.... For unto us a child is born ... and his name shall be called Wonderful, Counsellor, The mighty God, The everlasting Father, The Prince of Peace" **(Isa. 9:2, 6)**.

Scripture Reading: Isaiah 60:1–2; 9:2, 6; Ephesians 5:15

Hymns: "O Worship the King," Grant

"Watchman, Tell Us of the Night," Bowring

"Take My Life, and Let It Be," Havergal

Offertory Prayer: In all of our giving during this season, Our Father, help us to give both from the heart and with the hand. May true love abound to such generous proportions within us that goodwill may flow out to others. Bless this offering, so motivated, to the end that the good news of your coming in Jesus may be proclaimed. Amen.

Introduction

Edwin Arlington Robinson expressed the sentiments of many when he asked:

> *What does it mean, this barren age of ours?*
> *Here are the men, the women and the flowers,*
> *The seasons of the sunset as before,*
> *What does it mean?*

The symbols and the legends, the music and the poetry, the colors and traditions, the gifts and the bills we associate with the season—are these all that Christmas means? People are searching for meaning.

In spite of the secularism in which our lives are embedded, most people feel at Christmastime some mellowing of heart, some meaning in Tiny Tim's "God bless us everyone." Yet powerful forces militate against the meaning of Christmas. To many children, Santa Claus, who comes where we are and brings what we want, is a more vivid reality than a baby born in a manger a long time ago. As for their elders, tiring shopping trips and the problem of thinking up something to give at permissible cost to somebody who already has everything keep them from pondering much on the real meaning of the festival.

The coming of God to humans to bring healing and salvation, an event we celebrate at Christmas, means so much that the whole great drama of Christian redemption takes its rise from it. Though all that it means is too much to be spoken, we articulate what we do know and believe.

I. Christmas means that light shines in the darkness.

God spoke through Isaiah concerning Israel that "the people that walked in darkness have seen a great light: they that dwell in the land of the shadow of death, upon them hath the light shined.... For unto us a child is born, unto us a son is given" (Isa. 9:2, 6). Light and darkness are important symbols in the Bible. Generally light symbolizes fellowship with a holy God and darkness represents life apart from him.

The exegesis of Isaiah 9 has occasioned much debate, and scholars today differ in their interpretation. Did Isaiah have a then-living person in mind when he said, "Unto us a child is born"? Or was he prophesying some far-off divine event? It could have been both. Prophecies sometimes had a double meaning—relating to a specific immediate situation in the mind of the prophet and also relating to a larger fulfillment down the corridors of history.

We read these words from Isaiah or hear them sung today, and as Christians, we exult in the gift of God's love in Jesus Christ. That hope that burned in yearning hearts through centuries of darkness flashed out at Bethlehem, and it continues to shine forth wherever his name is revered. How wonderfully the details of Isaiah's story fit the Bethlehem event!

Suddenly, out of the darkness that covers the last verse of Isaiah 8, the light comes, and in the course of time, it has been recognized by many as the light from God. Christmas comes as a reminder that light shines in the darkness.

II. Christmas means that the God whose coming we celebrate is available if we seek him.

There is still much darkness in our world and many things within our individual lives that are displeasing to God. Matthew tells us that in Jesus was born Emmanuel, which means "God with us." As the hymn "Hark! The Herald Angels Sing" says it,

Veiled in flesh the God-head see;
Hail th' Incarnate Deity,
Pleased as man with men to dwell,
Jesus, our Emmanuel.

We need someone who can bring order to our chaotic lives. History has enough illustrations to teach us that no mere human ruler can control or give proper guidance to the vast forces that surge through the human heart.

Jesus entered the arena of human conflict ("the Word became flesh and dwelt among us"). He came, not under sponsorship of men, but at the behest of the Father. Throughout his earthly days, he pointed the way for people to go—summoning them to the kingdom in a spirit of forgiving and redeeming love. "To as many as received him, to them he gave the right to become the sons of God."

Jesus' life was the demonstration of a God-oriented life, and he makes this life available to us. For all who look into his face and see there the face of God, life can never be the same again. We are redeemed from the burden of sins that would break us if they were not forgiven. We are saved from a meaningless existence, redeemed from bewilderment and lostness.

III. Christmas means that we must look up to a higher world before we can look out on a better one.

With the coming of Christ, we are given the promise of a continuing and sustaining power. In all of our haste and obsession to find the shortcuts, we have abbreviated the angels' song. We have left off the first part—"Glory to God in the highest"—but it has not worked. We have tried to solve the human problem, all the while ignoring humanity's relation to God. People are created to be children of God. If we will not live as children of a heavenly Father, we are not likely to live as brothers and sisters to each other. The old saying is true: we must put God at the center of life, or life will be off center. We must keep contact with the dynamo of God's love, or there will be no current of warmth and goodwill coursing through the tangled wires of human relationships. Christmas approaches slowly again to tell us, to urge upon us, the old, old truth that we must first look up to a higher world before we can look out on a better one.

Conclusion

Because of Christmas, Paul's exhortation to the Ephesians is timely: "Live life, then, with a due sense of responsibility, not as men who do not know the meaning and purpose of life, but as those who do" (5:15 PHILLIPS).

SUNDAY EVENING, DECEMBER 8

Title: Preparing for God's Blessings
Text: "He said, Thus saith the LORD, Make this valley full of ditches" (**2 Kings 3:16**).
Scripture Reading: 2 Kings 3:6–18

Introduction

The showers of God's blessings do not fall on God's people when they fail to get ready to receive them. God's Word teaches that he is eager to pour out his blessings on our spiritually thirsty land. But it also teaches that he will impart no more blessings than we have made provision to receive.

Revival is simply a period of receiving God's blessings, which are made possible by prior preparation of his people. But how do you get ready to receive God's blessings? How do you prepare the soil of your spiritual life so that God will pour abundant blessings on you and your church?

Woven into the story of three kings and the Moabite rebels is found the key to getting ready to receive God's blessings.

I. Unity among God's people.

The kings of Israel, Judah, and Edom were united by a common enemy—Mesha, king of Moab (2 Kings 3:4).

A. *Unity forgets petty differences and thus strengthens the forces of God (2 Kings 3:6–7).* Around 975 BC, after Solomon's reign, the kingdom was divided into the kingdoms of Judah and Israel. Hostilities existed between these two forces for many years. But all of these were now forgotten, and a spirit of unity prevailed between their kings.

The urgency of the hour demanded that petty differences be forgotten. If Moab was to be successful in rebelling against Israel's king, Moab would in time turn on Israel, Judah, and Edom and attempt to destroy them. What the kings had to do they had to do quickly.

And if we are to see revival in our time, it must be soon. It is our responsibility to unite and reach the unreached. The strife of Christians in the church is a danger that threatens the unity of our faith.

B. *Unity instills a common purpose.* Among the three kings, there was no conflict of interest—no arguing over the direction to be taken. Unity had instilled a common purpose (2 Kings 3:8). Unity brought about the clarification of one primary purpose: the suppression of the Moabite rebellion.

A church can be going in a thousand different directions and accomplish nothing. Where unity prevails, one dominant objective is seen by all.

Unity imparts power to accomplish the dominant purpose. No one power or combination of any two of these powers could conquer the Moabite forces. But all three, united, had power to gain the victory.

Wilbur Chapman tells of calling on an unsaved physician for whom several men had been praying. The physician refused to talk to him about Christ. Discouraged, Mr. Chapman went home. To his surprise, the next night the physician made a public profession of his faith in Christ. Mr. Chapman then learned that four other men in his prayer group (unknown to each other) had visited this same physician within two hours' time. Unity and prayer had instilled a common purpose.

II. Confidence in God's Word.

These kings realized that their need could be met only by God. When they learned that Elisha was near, they turned to him with complete confidence in God's Word (2 Kings 3:11–12).

Verses 9 and 10 tell us that the kings had done all in their power. For seven days they marched. They had the finest armies, the best equipment, and the most adequate provisions. But they needed water. They realized the futility of human effort in meeting this need.

Their solution couldn't be found in the digging of wells, the transportation of water, or the rechanneling of a river. What they really needed was a supernatural creation of water, and this was beyond them!

Our task is not accomplished by the power of persuasion or the logic of reason. Rather, it is the supernatural regeneration of lost souls, and this is beyond us!

Confidence in God's Word claims the promises of God (2 Kings 3:12). When the kings learned that Elisha was near, they rushed to him to claim whatever promises God's Word might offer.

We are in no condition to receive God's blessings until we claim the promises of God and believe they will come to pass. God has promised to forgive the wayward Christian (1 John 1:9), to empower the dedicated Christian (Acts 1:8), and to honor soul-winning efforts (Ps. 126:6).

III. Provision for God's blessings (2 Kings 3:16–18).

Had water come, it would have been wasted, for no provision had been made to receive it. God was saying, "Make provision for my blessings, and then you will receive them." How often we pray for blessings for which we have made no provisions.

A. *Provision for God's blessing determines the abundance of the blessing received (2 Kings 3:16).* As much water would be received as they had made provision for. In 2 Kings 4:6, the account of God's provision of oil for a widow to sell, we read, "Then the oil stopped flowing" (2 Kings 4:1–7 NIV). Why? The widow had made no more provision. Her blessing was in proportion to her provision for it.

B. *Provision calls for unusual action (v. 16).* These were soldiers, not ditch diggers! They were called on to do the unusual. To receive unusual blessings, God calls on you to take unusual action. It is not the usual thing to pray, to ask for another's forgiveness, to witness to others. But unusual action brings unusual results.

Conclusion

Many a Christian, like Jehoshaphat, finds himself in a waterless valley: but even there, if he gets ready for God's blessings, grace will fill the valley with refreshment and victory.

Two cities at one time obtained permission to secure water from the same nearby river. Each built its own reservoir, opened the water gates at the river, and filled its reservoir. One city immediately complained that the other was getting much more of the river's water than they. An investigation revealed that the complaining city, because of an unwillingness to vote a large bond issue, had built a small reservoir, which it felt it could afford. The other city, guided by a progressive spirit and faith in the future, constructed a large reservoir and had adequate water for its population.

We are like one of these two cities. We may halfheartedly prepare for God's blessings, receive but a few, and allow the rest to drift on down the river of life, at last to be swept into the ocean of a lost eternity. Or we may begin today preparing for the blessings to come and claim multitudes of souls for Christ.

WEDNESDAY EVENING, DECEMBER 11

Title: The Importance of Praise

Text: "And the shepherds returned, glorifying and praising God for all the things that they had heard and seen, as it was told unto them" **(Luke 2:20)**.

Scripture Reading: Luke 2:8–20

Introduction

The element of praise is evident in nearly every incident related to Christ's birth. The heavenly host praised God when the angel of the Lord gave the birth announcement to the shepherds. After the shepherds found the Christ child, they went back to their fields and flocks, giving glory and praise to God. There is an implied element of praise in the story of the wise men; and the same is true of Simeon and Anna, as the Christ child was presented at the temple eight days after his birth.

Praise is a dominant feature in many parts of the Bible. Refer to your concordance, and you will find literally hundreds of references in regard to the praise due to God. Despite this pronounced theme of praise, about the nearest most people come to praising God today is a mumbled and often inarticulate "thanks" for obvious benefits received. In four books of sermon illustrations, one containing five thousand illustrations, only three illustrations related to praise. In a recent edition of a set of books containing an anthology of the best preaching since the time of Christ, there was not one sermon on the subject of praise to God. Praise is vitally important, and I will suggest several reasons why I believe it to be so.

A definition of praise will be helpful as we consider our reasons for the importance of praise. To praise is "to ascribe honor, power, beauty, worthiness, or glory to someone or something."

I. Praise helps us evaluate our priorities.

If no praise to God flows from our hearts, then our relationship to him is shallow. If we cannot help but praise God, it means our hearts are deeply attached to him.

Is it not a valid conclusion that we ascribe honor to that which we admire? If we do not express our adoration to God and ascribe to him majesty, power, and glory, is it not a natural deduction that our relation to him is not a vital one? The word *worship* comes from the Old English word *worthship*. If we do not worship God, does it not mean that we do not consider him worthy of our praise and adoration? A vibrant relationship to God is impossible apart from the commitment of both intellect and emotion, which in turn calls forth the expression of deepest praise.

The psalmist, because of his deep rapport with God, cried out, "The heavens declare the glory of God; the skies proclaim the work of his hands. Day after day they pour forth speech; night after night they reveal knowledge" (Ps. 19:1–2 NIV). When one has such a relationship with God, rhapsodies fill the spirit and praise flows from the mouth.

II. Praise gives indication of a divine encounter.

After the shepherds had their rapturous encounter with the angel, the heavenly host, and the Christ child, "They made known abroad the saying which was told them concerning this child" (Luke 2:17).

The reaction on the part of those who heard the shepherd's report was wonder and amazement. Is this not the first step in encouraging divine encounters for other people? If there is no praise and joy in the lives of Christians, why would others want a Christian experience of conversion? Too many people have a borrowed creed, one handed to them from others. Such a belief is of the mind only and does not embrace the emotions. Such a belief emphasizes the principles that Christ taught rather than the person of Christ himself. Such a faith is superficial, having no roots to tap divine resources of strength and wisdom. We must all say with Job, "My ears had heard of you but now my eyes have seen you" (Job 42:5 NIV).

III. Praise develops our own faith.

It has become almost axiomatic that expressed emotion grows, whereas failure to express it causes it to wither. If you keep your joy to yourself, it withers. If you are depressed and turn your thoughts inward and do without human relationships or activity, your depression will deepen. If you are happy and express it, your happiness will grow.

In the light of this principle, we observe that an expression of praise causes more praise to fill the heart. As we express praise to God, more and more of his benefits are brought to mind. As our praise grows, our appreciation deepens. As our appreciation deepens, we discover how barren and unproductive our life is apart from God.

Conclusion

At this most delightful of seasons, as we consider God's priceless gift to his creation, let us find an expression of praise escaping our lips. If we do so, we will find it growing until our life will be changed. Truly praise is vitally important.

SUNDAY MORNING, DECEMBER 15

Title: Christ the Lord

Text: "For unto you is born this day in the city of David a Saviour, which is Christ the Lord" **(Luke 2:11)**.

Scripture Reading: Isaiah 9:6–7

Hymns: "Hark! The Herald Angels Sing," Wesley

   "Joy to the World! The Lord Is Come," Watts

   "Ye Servants of God," Wesley

Offertory Prayer: Gracious and loving Father, during this time of year we are reminded over and over of the lavishness of your gift to us in your Son, Jesus Christ. Today we bow with the wise men and present to him the gift of our love, the gift of reverent worship, the gift of grateful hearts, and the gift of dedicated lives in his service. Bless the bringing of these tithes and offerings that his name might be made known to the ends of the earth. Amen.

Introduction

The mysterious wise men came from the East in search of the one whose birth was to usher in a new era. They came saying, "Where is he that is born King of the Jews? for we have seen his star in the east, and are come to worship him" (Matt. 2:2). The mention of an unborn babe who was to be a king aroused the jealousy and fear of Herod. The possibility of a rival king stimulated his fear to the extent that he commanded that all male children in the city of Bethlehem below two years of age were to be slain to eliminate this suspected future rival for the throne.

The title *king* in those days had a significance that is almost forgotten in our day. A king exercised authority over a nation of individuals, and according to the king's wishes, people perished or prospered. Today we give little thought to the title *king* because there are very few kings who exercise any authority over their subjects.

During this Christmas season, it would be profitable if each of us would listen to the angelic announcement of the birth of the Christ and make a positive response to the title of King, or Lord, that was bestowed upon him at the time of his birth. In our sentimental consideration of the Babe who was born in Bethlehem to be our Savior, we might miss the title that provides us with a clue to understanding the means by which he is to be the Savior of humankind.

There are few words in our religious vocabulary that have suffered a greater loss of original meaning than the word *Lord*. In modern usage, this word has been robbed of its original content. We let this title glide across our tongues rather glibly, as if it were nothing more than a given name. In reality it is not a name; it is a title. To use it as a name is to misrepresent its significance.

We need to understand the meaning of *Lord* so that we might properly respond to the person whose birth we celebrate at this season of the year. To neglect or to refuse to respond to the implications of this title of the Savior is to deny ourselves of that which he came to accomplish in the lives of men.

The Greek word *kurios* is a word with a wide variety of meanings, each of which has significance for understanding the person and ministry of Jesus Christ.

I. *Kurios* (lord) was the normal address of respect in everyday Greek.

The corresponding modern term for the Greek word *kurios* is *sir* in English, *herr* in German, *monsieur* in French, and *señor* in Spanish.

II. *Kurios* was a title of authority.

A. *By this title a distinction was indicated between the master and a slave.* In the ancient world, slavery was a universal practice. The population was divided into free men and slaves. The slave's owner was a *kurios*—a master. As such he could command the energies and efforts of his slaves. He could buy a man as a slave, and he could sell a slave that he owned to someone else. The slave was at the disposal of his *kurios*—his master.

B. *Jesus used this word to distinguish the slave from his master.* "No one can serve two masters. Either you will hate the one and love the other, or you will be devoted to the one and despise the other. You cannot serve both God and money" (Luke 16:13 NIV).

C. *This title* Kurios, *which the angels ascribed to the babe born in Bethlehem, indicated that he was one who would have the right to command.* Many of us have failed to recognize and to respond to this fact.

   The captain of a ship has the right of command. He is the executive officer over all that transpires on the ship. At his command, the ship departs from port, and at his command, the ship follows a course to his chosen destiny. The captain is *kurios*.

   The commanding officer of a military base is a *kurios*. His authority is respected by both the officers and the enlisted men. He has the right of command. The men on the base pattern their lives according to his orders.

   The angel announced, "Unto you is born this day in the city of David, a Saviour, which is Christ the Lord." Are we guilty of anarchy and rebellion against him whom God ordained to be our Lord and Master?

III. *Kurios* was used to describe absolute possession or ownership.

He who owned a house, a field, an animal, or a slave was a lord. The word that Jesus used in describing the owner of a vineyard is this word *kurios* (Luke

20:13). This word is also used to describe the owner of the colt on which Jesus made his triumphal entry into Jerusalem (Luke 19:33).

In announcing that Jesus Christ is Lord, the angels were actually introducing him to us as the owner of all things.

In John's gospel we read, "He came unto his own, and his own received him not" (John 1:11). He came to his own people, and they refused to recognize him and respond to him. Israel's tragic response to him has been repeated over and over through the centuries. When the Lord is rejected and man is left to his own resources, he loses his proper perspective.

IV. *Kurios* **was used to denote one who served as a guardian.**

In the ancient world, legal rights were denied to women as individuals. To engage in business, enter into a contract, or possess property, a woman had to have a guardian. This guardian could be the woman's husband, brother, or possibly a more distant relative. By means of a guardian, the rights of the unfortunate were protected.

An entire sermon could be constructed on the idea of Jesus Christ serving as our Guardian, Savior, and Redeemer. He protects us not only from ourselves but also from satanic forces. He is a guardian who has promised to be with us throughout all of our days in all of our ways.

V. *Kurios* **was the standard title of the Roman emperors. To be lord implied sovereignty, power, and authority.**

A. *By means of this title the emperor issued orders and decrees.* Often when a pastor writes to his people, he will affix his signature over his title or office as pastor. When a Roman emperor issued an edict, proclamation, or order, he would sign it with his signature and the title *Kurios.*

B. *This title summed up the emperor's authority in the same way that a president serves by virtue of his office and a police officer serves by virtue of his oath and uniform.* The emperor exercised his authority in more instances and far more extensively than that of any present ruler.

The angelic announcement of the Christ child's birth contained the idea that Christ was to exercise this kind of authority over the souls of men. For us to recognize this may help us to understand why Herod was concerned to the extent that he eliminated the male children in the vicinity of Bethlehem.

VI. In the Greek translation of the Hebrew Bible, *Kurios* **was regularly used as the name of Israel's God.**

In the ascending scale of the various meanings of the word *kurios*, this is the highest. It is used of him whom the Hebrews considered to be their God. We are not reading too much into the angelic announcement when we declare that they were announcing that the eternal God had chosen to enter the realm of human activity through the womb of a virgin. God had chosen to clothe himself in human flesh and dwell among men to disclose the divine love, mercy, grace, power, and purpose for men.

Conclusion

From your heart are you able to say to Jesus, "You are my Master, and I will be obedient to you as a devoted slave"? Can you honestly say, "You are my Owner, and I will let you occupy every portion and position of my life"? Can you say, "You are my Guardian upon whom I depend for protection and guidance"? Are you willing to say to him, "You are my Emperor, and because you loved me enough to die for me, I want to be faithful to you in living a life dedicated to the growth of your kingdom"?

Can you with Thomas say to Jesus, "My Lord and my God!" (John 20:28 NIV)? When we make Jesus the Lord of our lives, he becomes our Savior and brings us an inward assurance of peace and helps us to relate to others in a manner that produces peace among them.

If we are to observe this Christmas in a proper manner, we must yield the sovereignty of our lives to him who alone is Lord.

SUNDAY EVENING, DECEMBER 15

Title: The Call to Christian Commitment

Text: " 'The least of you will become a thousand, the smallest a mighty nation. I am the LORD; in its time I will do this swiftly' " **(Isa. 60:22 NIV)**. "These that have turned the world upside down are come hither also" **(Acts 17:6)**.

Scripture Reading: Isaiah 60:22; Acts 17:6

Introduction

The prophet Isaiah speaks of a 100,000 percent increase. Applied to commerce or agriculture, this would turn the world upside down!

This is the reputation those Christians had who went to Thessalonica. For three days they shared their faith in Christ with others and were charged with "turning the world upside down."

Why had this little band of Christians made such a tremendous impact on their world? Because they were genuinely committed! The secret is the same today as it was then—genuinely committed Christians. Our world can be "turned upside down" again for Christ when Christians hear and respond to the call of Christ in commitment.

I. Christian commitment calls for "giving up."

Jesus made this clear: "Those of you who do not give up everything you have cannot be my disciples" (Luke 14:33 NIV).

The question naturally follows: "Giving up what?"

A. *A giving up of worldliness is required.* Paul asserts, "Teaching us that, denying ungodliness and worldly lusts, we should live soberly, righteously, and godly, in this present world" (Titus 2:12). You may be saying, "I may be a lot of things, but I am hardly 'ungodly.'"

Wait a minute. Just what does the word *ungodly* mean? It means exactly what it says — to be "unlike God." To the degree that you are not like God or as God wants you to be — in word, action, and thought — you are "ungodly."

1. Worldliness makes God's Word ineffective. "The worries of this life and the deceitfulness of wealth choke the word, making it unfruitful" (Matt. 13:22 NIV).
2. Worldliness hinders your own spiritual growth. "If I regard iniquity in my heart, the Lord will not hear me" (Ps. 66:18). Things "unlike God" have a way of turning the heavens to brass when we pray.

B. *A giving up of any possible means of retreat is required.* Jesus said, "No one who puts a hand to the plow and looks back is fit for service in the kingdom of God" (Luke 9:62 NIV).

1. Worldly associates may be a means of retreat. To no longer allow worldly people to be your closest friends is not self-righteousness; it is common sense. Even though Christ associated with sinners to help them, he made Christian men his closest associates.
2. Questionable habits may be a means of retreat. Paul urges us to "abstain from all appearance of evil" (1 Thess. 5:22).

II. Christian commitment calls for a devotion.

Jesus said, "Thou shalt love the Lord thy God with all thy heart, and with all thy soul, and with all thy mind" (Matt. 22:37).

A. *Such devotion is to be stable, unchanging.* James says that God cannot count on a person whose devotion is fickle (James 1:6–8). You must have a reliable devotion that refuses to be negatively influenced by others. Christ's parables of the yeast in the bread, the light in the darkness, and the salt all stress that we are to influence and be influenced for good.

B. *Such devotion is a giving of one's whole self to Christ (2 Cor. 8:5).* God cannot bless a divided loyalty. "No servant can serve two masters"(Luke 16:13). In 1872 Henry Varley said, "The world has yet to see what God can do with and for and through and in a man who is fully and wholly consecrated to him." Dwight L. Moody said, "With God's help I will be one of those men." And by God's grace, Moody did become such a man.

III. Christian commitment calls for a contention.

"I felt compelled to write and urge you to contend for the faith that was once for all entrusted to God's holy people" (Jude 3 NIV).

Prior to the battle of Iwo Jima, the landing craft loaded with our invasion forces circled out away from the shore, waiting for the signal to land. When the flag dropped, they were committed to the battle. That was no time to request furlough or discharge. The battle was on! And as far as we are concerned, the flag was dropped; we are called to be totally committed to the battle! We hear Jeremiah proclaim, "A sound of battle is in the land" (50:22).

A. *Some have never engaged in this battle (Ezek. 8:14).* A nation never poses a threat to another nation when it is torn with internal civil war. This may be your problem.

Your personal battle must be fought and won before you can give yourself entirely to God's battle. Get that matter settled before God so that you do not have to keep fighting the same battle again and again. Then take to the battlefield and conquer new ground for God!

B. *Great victories will be won in this battle (1 Cor. 15:57).* Lord Nelson, describing his victory over the French in the Battle of the Nile, said that *victory* was not big enough a word to describe what had happened. And Paul contends that the word *conqueror* is not adequate to describe the victory that comes through Christ. We are "more than conquerors"!

Conclusion

The call of Christian commitment comes to you and me. We cannot escape the pointed question, "Who then is willing to consecrate his service this day unto the Lord?" (1 Chron. 29:5). Are you?

WEDNESDAY EVENING, DECEMBER 18

Title: The Way to Go Home

Text: "And being warned of God in a dream that they should not return to Herod, they departed into their own country another way" **(Matt. 2:12)**.

Scripture Reading: Matthew 2:1–12

Introduction

After the wise men had visited the Christ child, they were warned in a dream that they were to return home by another route. King Herod wanted them to come back through Jerusalem and reveal to him where the Christ had been born. It was his evil desire to kill the baby Jesus, removing him as a threat to his throne.

The wise men went home a different way geographically, and they went home a different way spiritually. This change in the spiritual direction of their lives could have several applications.

I. The wise men went home with a higher spiritual elevation.

Generally, following an exciting, satisfying, or awe-inspiring experience, there is an emotional letdown. As the wise men journeyed to Bethlehem to see the one "born King of the Jews" (Matt. 2:2), they had a natural curiosity that added stimulus to their steps. Questions crowded their minds. What unusual qualities would this child have? What would his appearance be? Who were his parents? How could they identify him? Would the star continue to guide them?

Each Christmas untold millions journey to Bethlehem in a spiritual sense. This delightful event brings joy and excitement for the most part. Our worship of the baby Jesus can be intensely satisfying. But Christmas can also be an exhausting experience. Many go back to their normal routine with a sigh of relief that the whole thing is over.

What produces the difference between a new elevation of the spirit or a letdown feeling? Several things could make a difference, but principally it is whether Christmas is kept in honor of the Christ child or for our own selfish pleasure. Have you really worshiped him this Christmas? Is there a warm glow, an elevated sense of joy, or are you glad it is nearly over?

II. The wise men went home with a changed sense of values.

How amazed the wise men's minds must have been as they observed the simplicity of the humble home and as they learned of the Christ's lowly birthplace. A king born in a stable! Why not a palace? He had slept in a manger from which animals ate! Why not a cradle with damask coverings? This King of the Jews had worn only swaddling clothes! Why not more luxury? A carpenter as the child's foster father! Why not a prince? A peasant girl for a mother! Why not a princess? A small community for the place of his birth! Why not Jerusalem?

Was this not God driving home the truth that "the meek shall inherit the earth" (Matt. 5:5)? God is not, nor ever will be, impressed by the artificial standards of humans. In the final analysis, life has never honored status seekers.

How different is the usual observance of Christmas! So many exhaust themselves physically and financially trying to impress with more and more expensive gifts and elaborate decorations. So many forget to see with the eyes of the heart the first Christmas, in all its magnificent simplicity.

Phillips Brooks expressed this truth for us when he said in his hauntingly beautiful hymn, "O Little Town of Bethlehem":

> *How silently, how silently,*
> *   the wondrous gift is given!*
> *So God imparts to human hearts*
> *   the blessings of His heaven.*
> *No ear may hear His coming,*
> *   but in this world of sin,*
> *Where meek souls will receive Him still,*
> *   the dear Christ enters in.*

III. The wise men went home as better men because they had identified with a person truly worthy of worship.

We all feel nobler as we identify with great persons. We have a natural desire to relate to outstanding personalities. But this natural desire can be debased if we honor those not worthy of honor. This happens when unthinking people give adulation to tyrants, dictators, despots, and religious quacks.

The truly wise of the world feel elevated in heart and soul as they give themselves in worship to the divine Son of God, Jesus, our Lord. If we have truly worshiped him this Christmas, the return to our routine will be characterized with a new sense of identity with the Christ of the ages. No person ever has contact with Christ in true worship without being changed into a better person.

Conclusion

As you go back to your normal routine after the holiday season, you will not have an emotional letdown in the sense that you are relieved that the holidays are over—if you have met the Christ of the ages, allowed him to change your sense of values, and truly yielded yourself to him in worship. When you have done this, you will find that he is the way to your eternal home, for he has said, "I am the way, the truth, and the life; no man cometh unto the Father, but by me" (John 14:6).

SUNDAY MORNING, DECEMBER 22

Title: Christmas Wrappings

Text: "So the Word became flesh; he came to dwell among us, and we saw his glory, such glory as befits the Father's only Son, full of grace and truth" (**John 1:14 NEB**).

Scripture Reading: John 1:1–14

Hymns: "Joy to the World!" Watts

"O Little Town of Bethlehem," Brooks

"O Master, Let Me Walk with Thee," Gladden

Offertory Prayer: We bring these offerings, O God, with the prayer that you will help us to have a true sense of values. We bring them, cognizant of their earthly value, and put them into the treasury of this congregation for the doing of your work in the world. Bless the distribution of these gifts to the end that others may come into that experience that transcends all mere earthly values. Amen.

Introduction

Friendly pranks are sometimes played on others by taking an object of little value and putting it in a beautifully wrapped gift package, spending more on the packaging than the gift merits. Or sometimes a very small, expensive gift is wrapped in a large box in the hope of producing a surprise for the person who daily checks packages under the Christmas tree. Sometimes a gift is wrapped so beautifully—tied with pretty ribbons and artistically decorated with bows and things—that the recipient is hesitant to open it because of the attractiveness of the wrappings.

This may happen to Christmas. It comes packaged in such beautiful sounds and colors, excitements and associations, that we may become so absorbed in these that we miss what they signify. The cynic who has no stake in the Christmas commerce must regard the whole package—that is, the Christmas season—as a big prank insofar as any real religious significance is concerned.

I. Familiarity with the wrappings of Christmas is no guarantee that the gift will be opened.

"He came to his own home, but his own people did not receive him" (John 1:11 RSV). Even though we hear the nativity stories read and sung, even though we have the real joy of giving and receiving presents, we can leave God's great gift to the world unopened. Perhaps this is why the apostle John began his gospel by going straight to the heart of the matter. (It was the last of the Gospels to be written, near the end of the first century.) He did not wrap the gift or, at least, not in any way that would call attention to the wrappings.

In the introductory verses, John refers to the rejection of God's gift and alludes to the cross we associate with the rejection. "He was in the world ... yet the world knew him not." Though the Jews were looking for a leader to relieve them of Rome's power and oppression and to bring some social reforms, they did not see and hear in Jesus what they wanted. We are not told in these verses why the people did not receive him, but there is ample evidence in the fuller gospel accounts to leave us in no doubt.

II. Christmas is unwrapped when we become wrapped in what it is all about.

For centuries people had been seeking a fuller knowledge of the nature of God and his purpose for humankind. God revealed aspects of his character and purpose through the prophets, singers, and wise men of Israel, bit by bit, as they were able to understand. But at best people saw in a mirror darkly. Then in Jesus "the Word became flesh and dwelt among us, full of grace and truth; we have beheld his glory, glory as of the only Son of the Father" (John 1:14 RSV).

Knowledge of God's character and plans was not all that people needed and wanted. They felt helpless under the load of their sin as they struggled to live up to the demands of the law. The more earnest among them sought desperately to make themselves worthy of God's love. Even if they willed to, they did not have the power to do it. When Jesus came and people got to know him, they discovered available in him a power such as they had never known before. John put it succinctly: "To all who received him, who believed in his name, he gave power to become children of God" (v. 12 RSV).

Do not leave this gift unopened because of familiarity with or admiration for the beautifully wrapped package. This redemptive power of God is at work still, and streams of grace flow from the life and continuing Spirit of Jesus Christ.

An intellectual understanding of the theological implications of Jesus' birth, life, death, and resurrection is not enough if one is going to be absorbed in what the Christian Christmas celebration is all about. One must have a personal experience of trust in and commitment to the living God in Christ. "Christ in you, the hope of glory," Paul wrote (Col. 1:27).

> *Though Christ a thousand times*
> *In Bethlehem be born,*
> *If He's not born in thee,*
> *Thy soul is still forlorn.*
>
> > — "Though Christ a Thousand Times"
> > Lyricist unknown

Conclusion

We do not have to accept Christ. We can refuse him just as many people did during the days of his flesh. God has given people other gifts, too, such as the gift of freedom. He does not withdraw it. Alice Meynell said, "Given not lent, and not withdrawn, once sent." Yield yourself to Christ to receive his forgiveness and love. Unwrap the gift.

SUNDAY EVENING, DECEMBER 22

Title: The Life That Wins

Text: "Therefore we are buried with him by baptism into death: that like as Christ was raised up from the dead by the glory of the Father, even so we also should walk in newness of life" **(Rom. 6:4)**.

Scripture Reading: Romans 6:1–14

Introduction

For more than one hour, Theodore Milford, a British minister, pled with a young stenographer not to leap off a ledge some two hundred feet above the street. Her only answer to her problems, she was convinced, was suicide. Mr. Milford used all of his persuasiveness, but still she jumped.

What if you had been in Theodore Milford's place? What would you have said to try to persuade her not to take a fatal plunge two hundred feet to the ground?

Would you have been able to look at your own life and say, "This is a life that has victory and peace and purpose"?

Your ability to answer the question is important. You may be called on one day to persuade another to retreat from the ledge of self-destruction. The ledge may not be two hundred feet above the ground. It may be the ledge of an emotional, moral, or spiritual catastrophe. At that moment, your answer and the other person's salvation may depend on your certainty that you are living "the life that wins."

I. The life that wins begins by facing a probing question.

"What shall we say then? Shall we continue in sin, that grace may abound?" (Rom. 6:1). This is the question you must squarely face: "Are you going to continue to sin, or are you going to make a clean break with sin?" What are you going to do about it?

Only when you are courageous enough to face this question honestly and to answer it candidly will you ever attain "the life that wins."

A. *This question unmasks the sincerity of your faith (Rom. 6:1).* Paul asks the Christians at Rome if they are really earnest about their faith.

B. *This question reveals your concept of God's grace (Rom. 6:1).* This question is occasioned by what Paul had just said in Romans 5:20: "But where sin abounded, grace did much more abound." A wrong concept of this grace concludes, "Let us continue to sin in order that God's grace will have occasion to continue to abound."

II. The life that wins requires an understanding of the mechanics of the Christian life.

This is what the apostle is saying in Romans 6:2–10. You must understand what a Christian life is, how it came about, and how it operates before you can live it.

So many Christians are not experiencing consistent victory because they simply do not have an adequate understanding of the mechanics of the Christian life.

A. *The Christian life has experienced a separation (Rom. 6:2, 6–7).* "Dead to sin" does not mean "extinction"; it means "separation." Physical death is the separation of soul and body. Death to sin is separation of the believer from the dominating power of sin. The Christian life is a life emancipated from slavery to sin. You are free, so live like a free person! You have the right to live "the life that wins."

B. *The Christian life has an identification with Christ.* "For if we have been planted together in the likeness of his death, we shall be also in the likeness of his resurrection" (Rom. 6:5). "Likeness" speaks of your identification with Christ. You have an identification with both his death and his resurrection. You are identified with a winner. So live like a member of a winning team!

C. *The Christian life has received an implantation (Rom. 6:3–4, 8–10).* Implanted within you is a new nature since you are made a partaker of the divine nature of Jesus Christ.

1. A *new heart* has been implanted (Rom. 6:3). This is a spiritual "baptism" that took place the moment you placed faith in Christ. It resulted in the implantation of a new heart. There is no possibility of the old body's rejecting the new heart, for the new heart rejects the old body (Rom. 6:6).

2. A *new power* has been implanted (Rom. 6:4, 9). This new relation with Christ gives you both the desire and the power to do God's will. "For

it is God which worketh in you both to will and to do of his good pleasure" (Phil. 2:13).

3. A *new life* has been implanted (Rom. 6:4, 8). "Newness of life" does not refer to a new kind of life or to new deeds that you will do. Rather, it means the new life implanted, which is a motivating energy providing both the desire and the power to live "the life that wins."

III. The life that wins is experienced by following proper instructions.

The Christian who does not grasp the truth of Romans 6:11–13 is like the man who purchases a new car but does not read the operator's manual. He fails to follow proper instructions and gets something less than maximum performance from his car.

A. *Proper instructions require an accurate calculation.* "Reckon, count, calculate" on the fact that you are dead to sin (Rom. 6:11). Your attitude then will be, "Since the power of my evil nature is broken, I am under no obligation to obey its will."

B. *Proper instructions emphasize a forbidden continuation (Rom. 6:12).* God is not unreasonable in his demands. He says, "Don't allow sin to control you." He lives in you to make your keeping this command a possibility.

C. *Proper instructions offer a certain exhortation (Rom. 6:13).* The exhortation is negative as well as positive. It is negative when it says, "Stop habitually putting your members at the service of sin." It is positive when it says, "Yield yourself to God."

Conclusion

Romans 6:14 promises that if you will face and properly answer the probing question of verse 1, "What shall we say, then? Shall we go on sinning so that grace may increase?" (NIV), gain an understanding of the mechanics of the Christian life, and faithfully follow God's instructions, you will be free from the domination of sin and will joyfully live "the life that wins." "Sin shall no longer be your master, because you are not under the law, but under grace" (NIV). The life that wins is yours for the taking!

WEDNESDAY EVENING, DECEMBER 25

Title: Prayers for the Coming Year

Text: "Pray without ceasing" (**1 Thess. 5:17**).

Scripture Reading: Matthew 6:5–13

Introduction

In our text, the apostle Paul encourages the believers in Thessalonica to develop the habit of praying and then not to break that habit.

As we approach the beginning of a new year, we can most appropriately and profitably spend some time in earnest prayer. Let us allow some saints who were poets to lead us in this time of prayer. Many of the hymns and songs in our hymnal take the form of earnest, fervent prayers. Let us join together on this last Wednesday evening in the year in singing some prayers to our Lord.

I. Let our lives sing a prayer of adoration and consecration.

Fanny J. Crosby would lead us in praying:

> *I am Thine, O Lord, I have heard Thy voice,*
> *And it told Thy love to me;*
> *But I long to rise in the arms of faith,*
> *And be closer drawn to Thee.*
>
> *Consecrate me now to Thy service, Lord,*
> *By the pow'r of grace divine;*
> *Let my soul look up with a steadfast hope,*
> *And my will be lost in Thine.*
>
> *Draw me nearer, nearer, nearer, blessed Lord,*
> *To the cross where Thou hast died;*
> *Draw me nearer, nearer, nearer, blessed Lord,*
> *To Thy precious, bleeding side.*

II. Let our lives sing a prayer regarding Bible study for the coming year.

All of us need to spend some time with God's Word each day to grow spiritually (Josh. 1:8). Mary A. Lathbury voices for us a prayer that is appropriate when we open up God's Word and read.

> *Break Thou the bread of life, Dear Lord, to me,*
> *As Thou didst break the loaves beside the sea;*
> *Beyond the sacred page I seek Thee, Lord;*
> *My spirit pants for Thee, O Living Word.*
>
> *Bless Thou the truth, dear Lord, to me, to me,*
> *As Thou didst bless the bread by Galilee;*
> *Then shall all bondage cease, All fetters fall;*
> *And I shall find my peace, my all in all.*
>
> *O send Thy Spirit, Lord, now unto me,*
> *That He may touch my eyes, and make me see;*
> *Show me the truth concealed within Thy Word,*
> *And in Thy book revealed I see the Lord.*

III. Let our lives sing a prayer for spiritual illumination.

Only God can open our eyes and help us see spiritual reality. Clara H. Scott wrote a prayer to God for us at this point.

> *Open my eyes, that I may see,*
> *Glimpses of truth Thou hast for me;*
> *Place in my hands the wonderful key*
> *That shall unclasp, and set me free;*
> *Silently now I wait for Thee,*
> *Ready, my God, Thy will to see;*
> *Open my eyes, illumine me, Spirit divine!*
>
> *Open my ears, that I may hear*
> *Voices of truth Thou sendest clear;*
> *And while the wave-notes fall on my ear,*
> *Ev'ry-thing false will disappear;*
> *Silently now I wait for Thee,*
> *Ready, my God, Thy will to see;*
> *Open my ears, illumine me, Spirit divine!*

IV. Let our lives sing a prayer to the Master Teacher regarding prayer.

Our Lord's disciples requested not that he teach them how to preach or to teach, but to pray. He is the perfect Model and Master Teacher at this point. Albert Reitz voices our prayer for help.

> *Teach me to pray, Lord, teach me to pray;*
> *This is my heart-cry day unto day;*
> *I long to know Thy will and Thy way;*
> *Teach me to pray, Lord, teach me to pray.*
>
> *Power in prayer, Lord, power in prayer!*
> *Here 'mid earth's sin and sorrow and care,*
> *Men lost and dying, souls in despair;*
> *O give me power, power in prayer!*
>
> *My weakened will, Lord, Thou canst renew;*
> *My sinful nature Thou canst subdue;*
> *Fill me just now with power anew;*
> *Power to pray and power to do!*

V. Let our lives sing a prayer of commitment to personal witnessing.

Some unknown servant of our Lord prayed the first stanza of the prayer that we will pray, asking our Lord to lay upon us a new and deeper concern for the souls of the lost about us. With all sincerity let us join in this prayer.

> *Lord, lay some soul upon my heart,*
> *And love that soul through me;*
> *And may I bravely do my part*
> *To win that soul for Thee.*

Lord, lead me to some soul in sin,
And grant that I may be
Endued with power and love to win
That soul, dear Lord, for Thee.

To win that soul for Thee alone
Will be my constant prayer;
That when I've reached the great white throne
I'll meet that dear one there.

Some soul for Thee, some soul for Thee,
This is my earnest plea;
Help me each day, on life's highway,
To win some soul for Thee.

VI. Let our lives sing a prayer of personal commitment to our Savior as we face the coming year.

Take my life, and let it be
Consecrated, Lord, to Thee;
Take my hands, and let them move
At the impulse of Thy love,
At the impulse of Thy love.

Take my feet, and let them be
Swift and beautiful for Thee;
Take my voice, and let me sing
Always, only, for my King,
Always, only, for my King.

Take my silver and my gold,
Not a mite would I withhold;
Take my moments and my days,
Let them flow in ceaseless praise,
Let them flow in ceaseless praise.

Take my will, and make it Thine,
It shall be no longer mine;
Take my heart, it is Thine own,
It shall be Thy royal throne,
It shall be Thy royal throne.

—Frances R. Havergal

VII. Let our lives sing a song of faith for the new year.

Ours is not a dead Christ. He is alive from the dead to be our Leader and our King as we face the coming year. Let us rejoice as we respond to his living presence. Ernest W. Shurtleff wrote a prayer of triumphant faith.

Lead on, O King Eternal,
The day of march has come;
Henceforth in fields of conquest
Thy tents shall be our home:
Through days of preparation
Thy grace has made us strong.
And now, O King Eternal,
We lift our battle song.

Lead on, O King Eternal,
Till sin's fierce war shall cease,
And holiness shall whisper
The sweet amen of peace;
For not with swords' loud clashing
Nor roll of stirring drums;
With deeds of love and mercy,
The heav'nly kingdom comes.

Lead on, O King Eternal,
We follow, not with fears;
For gladness breaks like morning
Where-e'er Thy face appears;
Thy cross is lifted o'er us;
We journey in its light;
The crown awaits the conquest;
Lead on, O God of might.

Conclusion

When we pray, we let God come into our lives to help us. We also dedicate ourselves to helping him with his work in the world. Let us rejoice because of the year that is ahead of us.

SUNDAY MORNING, DECEMBER 29

Title: When the Past Is Not Dead

Text: "Remember how the LORD your God led you all the way in the wilderness these forty years, to humble and test you in order to know what was in your heart, whether or not you would keep his commands" **(Deut. 8:2 NIV)**.

Scripture Reading: Deuteronomy 8:1 – 3; Psalm 137:1 – 6

Hymns: "O God, Our Help in Ages Past," Watts

"Another Year Is Dawning," Havergal

"Great God, We Sing That Mighty Hand," Doddridge

385

Offertory Prayer: Teach us again, O Lord, that where our treasure is, there our heart will be also. We bring now some of our earthly treasures to the altar of this church for the work we do in your name. It is brought here for consecration and then for God-directed distribution. Bless the givers and receivers, through Christ Jesus, our Savior. Amen.

Introduction

Churches have been criticized for curriculum and sermons so concentrated on the past that they have left no time for today and tomorrow. It has been said that people will be interested if present-day problems are dealt with, but they are not interested in church history, theological discussions, or the Bible. "It has to be alive," one may hear — the inference being that the past is dead and the Bible antiquated. There is validity in the criticism if we dwell exclusively on past events and treat the Bible as a reference book.

Standing at the end of an old year and looking back over some of the mistakes of 2013, who among us does not wish that certain things of the past were dead, gone, and forgotten, forever beyond memory's recall? But we cannot escape the past or cut ourselves loose from it so easily.

Neither can we return to it. Elizabeth Akers Allen wrote in 1860:

> *Backward, turn backward, O Time in your flight,*
> *Make me a child again just for tonight.*
> *Backward, flow backward, O tide of the years!*
> *I am so weary of toil and of tears.*

It is good to recall a happy childhood, but it is not good to use one's memory of the past as an escape from present work and involvement.

I. The past is not dead when it has provided us with the opportunity to establish a relationship, the results of which continue to influence and bless our lives.

Moses urged the Hebrews to remember. In Deuteronomy, especially in chapter 8, God speaks through his servant to the people about remembering. Israel was at the parting of the ways when these words were uttered. A change was imminent, both of leaders and of circumstances. Moses knew that very soon he would lay down the burden he had borne for so long and that another would be commissioned to lead the people. He also knew that soon the Israelites would leave the wilderness and enter the land "flowing with milk and honey." Looking back over the years and then ahead into all that he envisioned before the Israelites, Moses spoke to them out of the fullness of his heart. In reading these closing messages, one is impressed by his concern that the people remember.

Moses recognized the influence of memory. Properly stored and used, memory can be a perpetual inspiration to present endeavor and one of the great forces that shape the future. But Moses was careful to charge his people with what they were to remember. (The word translated here "remember" means literally "to mark.") The pictorial suggestiveness is that of a chart or map on which certain facts were to be marked and thus riveted to the memory. He desired to direct the memory of the people to supreme matters, urging them to look back from the right standpoint and see things in proper perspective.

Moses urged the Israelites to remember that God was their Leader. God had delivered them from Egypt. The same theme runs through the New Testament, as applied to Christians. In many places in the Epistles we read that we are set free from our sins by the blood of Jesus Christ. Every appeal to Christian character and conduct relates to that emancipation, that experience of turning from sin's bondage to accept Christ's forgiving love. The past is not dead when it has provided us with the opportunity to establish a relationship, the results of which continue to influence and bless our lives.

II. The past is not dead when it becomes a reservoir from which we may draw lessons for current needs.

Moses wanted the people to learn a threefold lesson of the years of God's leadership.

A. *"That he might humble you."* Pride is the most ghastly of all failures. Proud people deny a very important truth about themselves and about God. God's character-producing purposes are frustrated to the extent that we are proud.

B. *"Testing you to know what was in your heart. . . ."* Through a varied range of experiences, God helps us to know what we really are.

C. *"Man does not live on bread alone."* Each of these lessons that God wanted the Hebrews to learn can be applied to our own day and needs.

Conclusion

Someone has said that "the memory is a treasurer to whom we must give funds if we would draw the assistance we need." If we make children happy now, we make them happy fifty years later by the memory of it. The size of our reservoir of memories and the nature of its contents are being determined by us each day that we live. But once it has been put into the reservoir, we must be careful to appropriate it for beneficial purposes. The past is not dead when it has produced the conviction that God in his loving-kindness in Jesus Christ will guide us.

SUNDAY EVENING, DECEMBER 29

Title: How to Get the Most Out of Life

Text: "Again, the kingdom of heaven is like unto a merchant man, seeking goodly pearls: who, when he had found one pearl of great price, went and sold all that he had, and bought it" **(Matt. 13:45–46)**.

Scripture Reading: Matthew 13:44–50

Introduction

Life at its fullest ends all too soon. As you pass across the stage of history, you have but one chance to get the most out of life, for there is no curtain call when the last act has been concluded. Either you will make your mark on the world during these fleeting years, or your mark will go unmade throughout the endless aeons of eternity.

The shame of so many souls is that they have lived a lifetime satisfied with something less than God intended for them. They have settled for something less than the best.

God's will for each of us is that we get the most out of this life. Christ's parable of the pearl of great price tells us how to get the most out of life.

I. You must have a definite purpose (Matt. 13:45).

The Greek word for "merchant man" does not refer to a local merchant; it refers to a man who travels to buy what he wants. This man knew precisely what his purpose was. He was searching for pearls—not simply anything of value but one definite thing of value.

A. *A definite purpose brings happiness that can never be found in aimlessness.* No person void of purpose is ever happy. Most of the restlessness and frustration of our world can be attributed to sheer purposelessness.

H. H. Farmer observes that too many people are guided by the joy-rider's attitude toward life. They care nothing about their direction or destination. Not only do they burn up their energies without getting anywhere, but they also miss the joy of the ride.

B. *A definite purpose produces power that comes by concentration of energy.* Enough energy exists in an acre of sunlight to turn rocks into liquid if the rays are focused on one point. And there is enough power in the weakest of us to achieve the highest tasks if only they are focused by a dominant and definite purpose.

C. *A definite purpose avoids pitfalls that would otherwise lure you.* Keeping your eye on a single purpose will not allow you to be distracted. When others would have prevented Nehemiah from achieving his heart's desire, he said, "Why should the work stop while I leave it and go down to you?" (Neh. 6:3 NIV).

II. You must have high standards (Matt. 13:45).

The traveling merchant was not simply searching for the good. He was searching for the very best—"goodly pearls." The pearl was the most cherished jewel, and he would settle for nothing less.

A. *High standards cannot be easily satisfied.* This man could not be satisfied with just anything with luster. His standards were high. It had to be pearl!

Your standards must be high if for no other reason than that you know a better way of life. The merchant had seen good pearls, and he would never settle for less.

B. *High standards must never be compromised.* This man was in search of "goodly" pearls. This was his single purpose. To compromise and settle for imitation pearls would have defeated his whole purpose.

Compromise prevents you from getting the most out of life. Be honest now! What is "compromise"? It is settling for something less than what you want. You want the most out of life! Compromise means that you are willing to settle for something less than the best.

C. *High standards always win the respect of others.* The pearl merchant had a good reputation because he handled only the best. Your high standards will win the respect of others because you are above the ordinary, and you are what others would like to be. You never win such respect by compromise — never!

III. You must have a proper sense of values (Matt. 13:46).

When the merchant found the pearl of great price he was not uncertain. He knew its worth. His good sense of values detected its worth immediately.

A. *A proper sense of values does not confuse value with popularity.* We often conclude that simply because so many are rushing after certain things they must be of great worth.

When I was a boy in Louisiana, my task was to feed scraps to the chickens. We always had plenty of scraps, but often one foolish chicken would greedily grab one scrawny scrap and take off running as though he had gotten the most prized scrap in the yard. Instead of ignoring this foolish chicken, six or seven others more foolish than she would run after her, leaving behind a whole heap of untouched scraps far better than the one she had. Many people have never outgrown the "chicken" philosophy of life.

B. *A proper sense of values chooses things that are worthy.*

IV. You must have a sacrificial spirit (Matt. 13:46).

The merchant's purpose, his high standards, and his proper sense of values all would have been futile had he not been willing to sell "all that he had" in order to purchase the pearl of great price.

It is precisely at this point that so many of us fail. We want the pearl, but we simply are not willing to sacrifice to receive it.

A. *A sacrificial spirit forsakes all that comes between oneself and God because of a genuine love as well as a genuine need for God.*

B. *A sacrificial spirit is incapable of giving more than it receives.* It is well to note that although the merchant gave all he had, the pearl was worth much more.

C. *A sacrificial spirit does not follow the crowds who are waiting for "dollar day" to be declared in God's kingdom.* The pearl will never cost less than your all.

Conclusion

Our Savior asks, "Suppose one of you wants to build a tower. Won't you first sit down and estimate the cost to see if you have enough money to complete it?" (Luke 14:28 NIV). And he asks you today to count the cost. But whatever it costs you to gain the pearl of great price, it will be worth it all. For only when you possess this pearl, Jesus Christ, will you get the most out of life.

MISCELLANEOUS HELPS

MESSAGES ON THE LORD'S SUPPER

Title: A Look at Calvary

Text: "And sitting down they watched him there" (**Matt. 27:36**).

Scripture Reading: Matthew 27:32–44

Introduction

It is almost impossible for us to imagine the cold cruelty of people who could idly sit down in the presence of such agony and torture as that experienced by those who were suffering crucifixion. Our text tells us that once the crucifiers had nailed Christ and the two thieves to their crosses, they sat down and watched them. This probably was a routine action for these executioners. They had been brutalized to the extent that they were almost inhuman. However, something happened during these hours while they tarried by Christ's cross that radically affected the thinking of the centurion who was in charge of the execution. Matthew records, "Now when the centurion, and they that were with him, watching Jesus, saw the earthquake, and those things that were done, they feared greatly, saying, Truly this was the Son of God" (Matt. 27:54).

Perhaps our Lord's willingness to forgive even his crucifiers touched the heart of these cruel men. Perhaps the compassion of the Christ for his mother and the provisions he made for her while he was on the cross reminded the centurion of his relationship to his own mother. Perhaps our Lord's concern for a fellow sufferer, demonstrated in his promise of paradise for the penitent thief, stirred the emotions of the centurion. Perhaps it was the absence of profanity and pleas for release that caused him to behold the Christ with wonder and speculation. Perhaps it was our Lord's confident trust and the calm commitment of his soul into the care of God that affected the centurion.

It could also have been the violent revolt of nature accompanying the death of Christ that produced such a radical change in the mind of the centurion. The sun refused to shine on this event, which seemingly was extinguishing the light of the world. The rocks revolted against the thought of men putting to death him who was the Rock of Ages. Tradition tells us that the centurion was converted to faith in Jesus Christ and became an ardent servant of the Lord Jesus.

As we partake of the elements of the Lord's Supper, let us by inspired imagination stand outside the walls of Old Jerusalem and behold the death of Jesus Christ our Savior.

I. The death of the Christ on the cross reminds us of the awfulness of human sin.

Christ Jesus came into this world to die for the sins of a guilty humanity. It was the guilt of our sin that necessitated his substitutionary death on the cross. He was dying under the penalty of our sin.

At the same time, the crucifixion of Christ reveals the depth of human depravity. The people of that day rejected divine love personified in Jesus Christ. Modern-day humanity continues to reject that love. Every rejecter of God's love is involved in the crucifixion of God's dear Son, the Lord Jesus Christ.

II. The death of Jesus Christ reminds us of the divine estimate of human worth.

It was in the death of Jesus Christ that God revealed his evaluation of the worth of the soul of a human. We live in a world in which human life is considered cheap. Humans are often depersonalized and degraded to the extent that they are considered only as objects. By giving his Son to die for us, God revealed that people are very precious in his sight.

If the biblical concept of the worth and dignity of humans is rejected, then humans descend to the level of educated animals. We learn the divine concept of the value of humans as we behold the divine willingness to suffer the agony of Calvary on our behalf.

III. The death of Christ reveals the divine determination to deliver us from the tyranny of evil.

It was not enough that God should provide a great lawgiver and teacher in the person of Moses. It was not enough that God should give guidance through the psalm writers and the prophets. It was not enough that the Christ should come as heaven's infallible, inerrant Teacher. Sin continued to hold sway over the minds and hearts of people. God was willing to give his Son to rescue and to deliver us from this present evil world (Gal. 1:3–4).

Conclusion

Our great and wonderful God is eager to deliver us from the guilt and stain of the past. Our Father is eager for us to experience abundant life here and now. This life is found through faith in Christ who so loved us that he was willing to die on the cross for us. He was divine, and therefore he arose triumphant over death and the grave.

As we partake of the Lord's Supper, we remember what Christ did for us on the cross. We feed our souls on spiritual nourishment that will add strength and vitality to our lives in the present. We proclaim Christ's future return to the earth for his own.

With humbleness of heart, with gratitude of soul, with confession of every known sin, and with a plea for assistance to forsake all evil, let us participate in the Lord's Supper, remembering the shedding of Christ's blood and the giving of his body for us.

Title: How Do You Remember Jesus?

Text: "And he took bread, gave thanks and broke it, and gave it to them, saying, 'This is my body given for you; do this in remembrance of me.' In the same way, after the supper he took the cup, saying, 'This cup is the new covenant in my blood, which is poured out for you'" **(Luke 22:19–20 NIV)**.

Scripture Reading: Luke 22:7–20

Introduction

Memory can be a most precious possession. Particularly is this so if our memories are pleasant. We erect monuments to preserve memory. We take photographs to preserve memory. Artists paint pictures to preserve memory. Authors write books to preserve memory.

Our Lord was eager that his disciples remember him in a proper manner. He knew that certain memories could serve as the motivating force for faith and faithfulness.

How do you remember Jesus? There are many beautiful memories that can bless the heart.

I. We should remember Jesus as a teacher.

One of the most beautiful memories that we can have of the Christ is that of him seated on a mountainside in the midst of his followers. He taught them heaven's infallible truth concerning life. He described the inward spiritual characteristics of the citizens of his kingdom and the inevitable influence of such people. He set before them illustrations of the superlative conduct of his true followers. He described their motives and their fruitfulness and the stability of their lives.

It is not enough that we have this memory; we should heed what Jesus had to say, and we should recognize his authority as a teacher.

II. We can remember Jesus as he dealt with sinners.

In John 4 we have the record of how our Lord crossed racial and religious barriers in order to minister to an outcast woman who no doubt was crushed in her own eyes and who was considered as nothing in the eyes of those who knew her. Our Lord was concerned for this sinful woman. He communicated with her the truth of God's great love. He transformed her from being a fallen woman into being a true servant of God. Through her testimony he blessed an entire village. This memory of our Lord can encourage us to recognize the worth of every individual in today's world.

III. We can remember our Lord asleep in the ship in the midst of the storm.

There are times when each of us feels threatened with the circumstances about us. There are times when it seems that the ship of our life will be destroyed on the rocks of adversity and failure. When this happens, we should remember

393

the Christ who commanded the winds to cease their blowing and the waves to cease their tossing. He will come to us in the midst of the storm of life to give us safety and poise and inward peace.

IV. We can remember our Lord as the Good Shepherd.

In John 10 our Lord describes himself as the Good Shepherd. He loves and leads and provides for his sheep. He protects them and calls them by name. He gives the eternal life and the security that can come only from the safety of dwelling in God's presence. This memory of our precious Lord can give us comfort and courage in our times of need.

V. We can remember Jesus in the presence of his death.

The shortest verse in the Bible is John 11:35. It preserves for us a photograph of the grief of the Son of God in the presence of those who were suffering because of the death of a loved one. This verse contains only two words, and yet there is a volume of truth contained in it. The eternal Son of God, clothed in human flesh, was weeping with Mary and Martha in their time of sorrow. Because he is the same yesterday, today, and forever, we can be assured that he weeps with us in our times of sorrow today.

VI. We should remember Christ on the cross.

Of all the memories our Lord desired that his disciples retain, the one that he specifically requested that they remember was that of his death on the cross. He instituted what we know as the Lord's Supper in order that his memory might be perpetuated. He took the elements that remained from the Passover supper and gave to them a new content and a new significance. He did this in order that the minds and hearts of his disciples might be reminded again and again of the primary purpose for his coming into the world. He came to die for the sins of a wayward, lost, helpless human race. He wanted this memory preserved, because this memory, more than any other, reveals the greatness of the compassionate heart of the Father God. Christ, the sinless, stainless, spotless Son of God, was dying on the cross to reveal the greatness of God's love for sinners. Evidently we need to be reminded of this over and over, or our Lord would not have specifically made plans to perpetuate this memory.

It is the memory of Christ's death on the cross that reveals to us in the most dramatic manner the worth of the individual human soul in the eyes of God. This great truth should not be neglected or rejected.

How do you remember Jesus? As we partake of the elements of the Lord's Supper, let us focus our minds and our emotions on that most significant event in all of history, Jesus Christ's giving his life for us. As we visit Calvary and contemplate his death, let us inform our intellect concerning God's great love. Let each of us allow this experience to stir our emotions and cause us to love him and trust him. Let us make decisions during this experience to change our ways and bring them into conformity with the will of our loving Lord.

MESSAGES FOR CHILDREN AND YOUNG PEOPLE

Title: "Bread!" It's for Real

Text: "Jesus replied, 'I am the Bread of Life. No one coming to me will ever be hungry again. Those believing in me will never thirst. But the trouble is, as I have told you before, you haven't believed even though you have seen me. But some will come to me—those the Father has given me—and I will never, never reject them. For I have come here from heaven to do the will of God who sent me, not to have my own way. And this is the will of God, that I should not lose even one of all those he has given me, but that I should raise them to eternal life at the Last Day. For it is my Father's will that everyone who sees his Son and believes on him should have eternal life—that I should raise him at the Last Day'" **(John 6:35–40 TLB)**.

I. What do you mean by "bread"?

    A. *Bread is necessary for living; without it you cannot continue to exist.*
    B. *What do you mean by "exist"?*
        1. It is more than physical.
        2. It is spiritual.
    C. *Existence here means to be alive in Christ.*
        1. An existence you can trust.
        2. An existence that is real.
        3. An existence you can obey.
        4. An existence you can fall in love with and be certain of the outcome.
    D. *This existence is made available by Jesus Christ.*
    E. *When we do not have Jesus, we do not have existence—life in the fullest sense.*
    F. *Jesus makes eternal existence a reality, therefore he may be described as the beautiful Bread of Life.*
        1. It is free.
        2. It satisfies the thirst and hunger of the heart.

II. Stages of the real life.

Jesus communicates to those who look for him.
    A. *How do we find Jesus?*
        1. Through reading the New Testament.
        2. Through the teaching of the church.
        3. Through the lives of his followers.
        4. Through a face-to-face encounter, an awareness of his presence.
    B. *Now that we have located Jesus, what next?*
        1. We turn to him.
        2. He is no longer just an idea or thought.
        3. He is no unconcerned hero.
        4. He is real, and we can come to him.
    C. *We submit ourselves to Jesus' will.*

D. *We gain eternal life and become brothers of Jesus and sons and daughters of God.*
E. *The Bread of Life is a free gift and is for everyone.* The Bread of Life is yours for the asking and receiving.
F. *Bread of Life can come only through Jesus Christ.* No amount of research or thirsting of the human heart can find the fullness of God without Christ.
G. *God is behind the whole scene.*
  1. It is God who set the goal.
  2. It is God who created the hunger in people.
  3. It is God who removes the rebellious spirit and the pride that prohibits us from following after his will.
  4. We would not seek God if he did not make us aware of him.
H. *Man is stubborn and refuses God's free offer.*

Conclusion

When we accept God's free gift, we have a peace and joy never before experienced. The longing is gone, and we are secure for all eternity. Christ paid the price and gives us life now and forever. Do not continue beating yourself out of this peace and joy. Submit to God's free gift now. Accept the Bread of Life.

Title: Superself or Superspiritual?

Text: "What is causing the quarrels and fights among you? Isn't it because there is a whole army of evil desires within you? You want what you don't have, so you kill to get it. You long for what others have, and can't afford it, so you start a fight to take it away from them. And, yet the reason you don't have what you want is that you don't ask God for it. And even when you do ask you don't get it because your whole aim is wrong—you only want what will give you pleasure" **(James 4:1–3 TLB)**.

Introduction

What is your goal in life? Is it to bring pleasure to self or to be tuned in to the will of God? James warns that if you tune in on pleasure only, then you can expect rough riding. Emphasis on selfish pleasures brings a multitude of hate and war, not love and peace. To be a superself dwarfs the superspiritual nature of youth.

Each of us must ask, Do I seek after selfish pleasures or God's pleasures? What is going to happen if I follow the superself?

I. Selfishness brings war with your friends.

A. *It may cause a person to be at war within oneself.*
B. *It may cause you to want the same thing your brother or sister wants: money, popularity, best grades, etc.*
C. *It may cause you to lie, cheat, and steal—anything to achieve your own selfish pleasure.*
D. *When you turn to Christ, you will be drawn to an attitude of peace and love for others.*

II. Self-pleasure pushes you to do things you are ashamed of later.

A. *It causes jealousy and can lead to killing.*

B. *People may control these compulsions, but as long as they let these superself desires have control, they are in constant danger of losing control. Every murder or bank robbery comes from a superself desire that began to grow and devoured the person.*

III. Selfish pleasure crowds out communication with God.

Selfishness causes a gap in your spiritual life.

A. *When your prayers are simply for things, your superself is dominating, and it is not possible for God to answer them.* If God were to give us everything we ask for selfishly, he would be equipping us with ways of sinning.

B. *The truest goal of prayer is not the superself way but the superspiritual.* "Thy will be done."

C. *It is difficult for the superself to communicate with God in a right way.* Superself must give the right of way to a keen awareness of God's way.

Conclusion

Life requires a choice from everyone. What is our ultimate purpose for living—to glorify self or to seek God's will? If we choose self-glorification, we create a gap between ourselves and our fellow students and separate ourselves from God. Let God help you to remove your superself and become totally involved in living out God's will. True happiness, love, and peace will result.

Title: Take a Trip with Jesus

Text: "Enoch walked with God: and he was not; for God took him" **(Gen. 5:24)**.

Scripture Reading: Genesis 5:21–24

Introduction

Ever been on a high emotional trip? It is exciting, is it not? Have you ever gone on a trip with a group of people your own age and wished it could go on forever? We can take a trip with Jesus that goes on forever.

I. We enter the scene.

A. *Physical birth.* We did not ask to be born, but someone cared for us and wanted us to grow, and so we began our trip.
1. Mother and Dad cared.
2. Relatives were interested.
3. Friends were concerned.

B. *Physical growth.*
1. We were given milk to start our trip.
2. As we grew and developed, we were put on solid foods.

C. *Physical death.*
1. We may have to be cared for again.
2. We may be childlike before physical death.

II. We begin our trip.

    A. *Learning to walk is more difficult for some children — so it is with the beautiful life in Jesus.*

    B. *Keeping your balance is a real accomplishment — spiritual balance requires a keen awareness of Christ.*

    C. *Planning a worthy goal for our trip.*

        1. We consider the opportunities: Do we choose Christ or Satan?

        2. We look at the hazards and risks. Our total life is at stake in time and eternity.

III. Off we go with Jesus.

    A. *Our course has been charted.* Eternity with him is our destination.

    B. *The way is not always smooth.* There will be many temptations, but he will see us through. He is the greatest guide!

Conclusion

We all are on a trip. Whom we choose as our guide is up to us. Enoch walked with God. Someone has said, "One day Enoch and God got so far away from Enoch's home that God took him on to his home to stay." The Scripture says, "And he was not." Who will lead your trip? Take a trip with Jesus in the present and for all eternity.

FUNERAL MEDITATIONS

Title: God's Provision for Soul and Body

Text: "... absent from the body ...present with the Lord" **(2 Cor. 5:8)**.

Scripture Reading: 2 Corinthians 5:1–8

Introduction

Everyone spends some time thinking about death, for the word *death* carries with it the ideas of mystery, a lonely separation, and a final going and no returning.

This statement of being absent from the body and being present with the Lord is one of the finest in the New Testament and can help clear up our thinking about death.

I. Absent from the body.

When a Christian leaves his body, it brings about a condition called death; but it is death for the body, never for the soul.

Death does not destroy the inhabitant of the body; it just takes down the house, the dwelling place in which the person lived.

God put soul and body together in the first place. Eventually he will do it again, and the Christian will then be the whole individual God desired and designed in the beginning.

II. Present with the Lord.

When Christians are absent from their bodies, they are with the Lord. The process called death has separated soul and body, and though the body remains with us, the soul returns immediately to the Lord. What a happy thought! Death is a release to the soul: it is removed from a tired, worn, and wrinkled body to be really free of all that which has been of the flesh. And to be present with the Lord promises far more than description allows.

III. This is the hope of the Christian.

How does one make certain of such a hope? Jesus said, "I am the way, the truth, and the life: no man cometh unto the Father, but by me" (John 14:6).

The greatest experience possible for a man is to become one with God. Jesus said, "I and my Father are one" (John 10:30). To become one with Jesus is to personally invite him into one's life to forgive sin and save the soul. When this happens, one becomes a Christian, and at separation of soul and body, the soul, already one with God, simply continues with him in another place. The body is tenderly placed in the ground to await the moment when God will again unite the soul and the body. We do not know what kind of person we will be, but we will be like Jesus, for we will see him as he is.

Conclusion

We do not sorrow as people with no hope. Let us give thanks for the promise and provision God has made, not only for this life, but for the next also.

Title: The Phasing Out of an Earthly Life

Text: "Neither death, nor life ... shall be able to separate us from the love of God, which is in Christ Jesus our Lord" **(Rom. 8:38–39)**.

Scripture Reading: Romans 8:37–39

Introduction

People go through three phases in the life cycle. The first two earthly phases are measured by months and years; the last phase will be without measure.

I. Prenatal phase.

From the moment of conception, people begin to live. The few months they spend developing in their mothers' wombs are critical ones that affect all the years of their lives on earth. At the close of this development they are born and begin phase two. This is a highly expectant moment as a person is welcomed into this span of time we call life on earth.

II. The earthly phase.

From the moment of physical birth, people begin adjusting to this world's environment. As they mature, they are offered many, many opportunities. They are invited to learn, to play, to marry, to be parents, to be responsible citizens, and most of all, to call on the Lord to forgive their sins and save their souls. When they do this, they become children of God (John 1:12). This is their greatest and most beneficial honor, for it allows God to prepare them for heaven and to prepare heaven for them.

III. The eternal phase.

When Christians have lived out their physical span, they begin their third and final phase of life. This phase begins with leaving the physical body and immediately going to be with the Lord (2 Cor. 5:8). There they will enjoy the presence of not only Jesus but also of all those believers who have preceded them in death.

Conclusion

When we all get to be with Jesus, it will be an eternity of rejoicing! Time will be no more, and all the problems that grieved us here will likewise be no more. Death is the first step toward that final, eternal, glorious phase of life. Paul's statement, "Thanks be to God, which giveth us the victory through our Lord Jesus Christ" (1 Cor. 15:57) can and should become our triumphant thought for this and all the other days of our lives.

Title: The Best of Two Worlds

Text: "For to me to live is Christ, and to die is gain" **(Phil. 1:21).**

Scripture Reading: Philippians 1:19–24

Introduction

The child of God can have the best of two separate worlds. Frequently we hear, "Do whatever you think best" and "I wish the best for you." The best, as people understand, does not always appear to be what we want or need. God is not bound by such limited sight, and seeing the entire scope of time, he can provide what is really best for us.

I. The best of this world (Phil. 1:21).

Paul insists that for him to live is Christ. The pursuit of that goal guarantees the best on earth.

To have the privilege of hearing and responding to the gospel; to be received by a warm church family; to serve the Lord; to become a good parent, neighbor, and citizen; to have the high honor of being indwelt by the Holy Spirit; to know sins are forgiven, that condemnation has been removed, and finally, that a home in heaven is waiting—this is the best earth has to offer.

II. The best of the next world (Phil. 1:21).

In heaven God will be able to show us the exceeding riches of his grace. What an experience to belong to his family here and then to be present with him personally! Death is his plan for removing us from this world and placing us in the next.

As God prepared our bodies to function in this earthly environment, he will prepare them to function in the heavenly environment, and we will be like Jesus. To die is gain!

Conclusion

Death will never be considered our friend, but it is God's plan to place us with himself that we may receive the best of both his worlds. Let us sound a note of praise in the midst of grief for God's thoughtfulness and planning that makes our hope a reality!

WEDDINGS

Title: Christ and Marriage

Text: "And the third day there was a marriage in Cana of Galilee; and the mother of Jesus was there: and both Jesus was called, and his disciples, to the marriage" **(John 2:1 – 2).**

Introduction

By our Lord's presence at the wedding in Cana, he placed his stamp of approval on the marriage contract. He was concerned about the happiness and well-being of the friends involved in the ceremony. While attending the wedding, he rendered a valuable service that prevented the family from experiencing embarrassment. At the same time, he manifested his glory and revealed the unique nature of his ministry.

Christ should be invited to every wedding. It has been truthfully said that it takes three to make a happy marriage: a bride, a groom, and God.

We are reminded that marriage is a divine institution born in the heart of God and was instituted for the welfare of the race. Marriage establishes the home, which is the most basic institution in our society.

It is altogether fitting that family, friends, and neighbors come together to witness and to participate in the pledging of marriage vows. Let us all join our hearts together in prayer for the couple involved.

The pastor prays.

Who gives this woman to this man in marriage? (*The father may answer, "I do" or "Her mother and I."*)

If you, then,_____(Groom) and_____(Bride), after careful consideration and in the fear of God, have deliberately chosen each other as partners in this holy estate and know of no just cause why you should not be so united, in token thereof, you will please join your right hands.

Groom's Vow

_____, wilt thou have this woman to be thy wedded wife, to live together after God's ordinance in the holy estate of matrimony? Wilt thou love her, comfort her, honor her, and keep her—in sickness and in health, and forsaking all others, keep thee only unto her so long as you both shall live?

Answer: *I will.*

Bride's Vow

_____, wilt thou have this man to be thy wedded husband, to live together after God's ordinance in the holy estate of matrimony? Wilt thou love him, comfort him, honor him, and keep him—in sickness and in health, and forsaking all others, keep thee only unto him so long as you both shall live?

Answer: *I will.*

Vows to Each Other

I,_____(Groom), take thee,_____(Bride), to be my wedded wife, to have and to hold from this day forward, in prosperity or adversity, in sickness or in health, in advances or reverses, to love and to cherish till death do us part, according to God's holy ordinance, and thereto I plight thee my troth.

I,_____(Bride), take thee,_____(Groom), to be my wedded husband, to have and to hold from this day forward, in prosperity or adversity, in sickness or in health, in advances or reverses, to love and to cherish till death do us part, according to God's holy ordinance, and thereto I plight thee my troth.

Then are you each given to the other for richer or poorer, for better or worse, in sickness and in health, till death alone shall part you.

From time immemorial the ring has been used to seal important covenants. The golden circlet, most prized of jewels, has come to its loftiest prestige in the symbolic significance that it vouches at the marriage altar. Its untarnishable material is of the purest gold. Even so may your love for each other be pure and may it grow brighter and brighter as time goes by. The ring is a circle, thus having no end. Even so may there be no end to the happiness and success that come to you as you unite your lives together.

Do you,_____(Groom), give this ring to your wedded wife as a token of your love for her?

Answer: *I do.*

Will you,_____(Bride), receive this ring as a token of your wedded husband's love for you, and will you wear it as a token of your love for him?

Answer: *I will.*

Do you,_____(Bride), give this ring to your wedded husband as a token of your love for him?

Answer: *I do.*

Will you,_____(Groom), receive this ring as a token of your wedded wife's love for you, and will you wear it as a token of your love for her?

Answer: *I will.*

Having pledged your faith in and love to each other in the sight of God and these assembled witnesses, and having sealed your solemn marital vows by giving and receiving the rings, acting in the authority vested in me as a minister of the gospel by this state, and looking to heaven for divine sanction, I pronounce you husband and wife.

Therefore, what God hath joined together, let no man put asunder.

Prayer.

Title: Love Is the Theme

Text: "For this cause shall a man leave his father and mother, and shall be joined unto his wife, and they two shall be one flesh" (**Eph. 5:31**).

Scripture Reading: Proverbs 31:11–28; Ephesians 5:22–33

Introduction

Marriage is God's ideal way of preserving the finest and most intimate relationship known. This voluntary relationship causes a man to leave his father and mother and the security of a home he has known all his life, to set up a similar unit of his own. It likewise causes a woman to sever strong ties and cast her future with the man of her choice. Their new home unit must receive their most careful attention. It is not a casual arrangement for convenience but a covenant—a binding contract for life.

The Ceremony

Into such a relationship_____and_____wait to be joined. Do I hear any reason why they should not be?

Question to the Father:

Who gives this woman to be married to this man?

Answer: "I do," or "Her mother and I."

Question to the Groom:

_____, do you take this woman to be your wife; do you promise to comfort her, to honor her, and to love her in sickness and in health, and forsaking all others, keep yourself only unto her so long as you both shall live?

Answer: "I do."

Question to the Bride:

_____, do you take this man to be your husband; do you promise to comfort him, to honor him, and to love him in sickness and in health, and forsaking all others, keep yourself only unto him so long as you both shall live?

Answer: "I do."

Join right hands and repeat after me:

Groom: I,_____, take thee,_____, to be my wife, to have and to hold from this day forward; for better, for worse; for richer, for poorer; in sickness, in health; to love and to cherish till death do us part, according to God's holy ordinance.

Bride: I,_____, take thee,_____, to be my husband, to have and to hold from this day forward; for better, for worse; for richer, for poorer; in sickness, in health; to love and to cherish till death do us part, according to God's holy ordinance.

As a token of these vows you will now give and receive the wedding rings.

Rings

Groom: This ring I give you as a token of my continuing love.

Bride: This ring I give you as a token of my continuing love.

Since_____and_____have pledged their love and purpose to each other before God and these witnesses, I am happy to pronounce them legally married, husband and wife.

Prayer: Our Father, we love you for this joyous and sacred moment. We thank you for love and convictions that accompany it. We thank you for the parents of this couple and for every effort made to prepare them for this new venture. Bless this couple's new relationship, and may they build their home unit on your Word and be directed by your Spirit. Through Jesus Christ, our Lord, and theirs. Amen.

Traditional kiss.

Introduction to audience.

Recessional.

Sentence Sermonettes

The Almighty gives the best to those who leave the choice to him.

Sin thrills and then it kills.

The heart of religion is the heart.

Today is the first day of the rest of your life.

Sin always carries with it a built-in deception about judgment.

If you are happy, tell your face about it.

Are you on a collision course with God?

Your soul will live forever, somewhere—where?

Love gives and forgives.

Good works are the fruit, not the root, of salvation.

God's will is not always easy, but it is always right.

Not to decide is to decide.

Sin is personal but not private.

Life without Christ is an empty existence.

Every problem is in reality an opportunity.

Prejudice is a lazy person's substitute for thinking.

Hell is a place of no hope.

People judge each other by rank; God judges all by service.

Happiness is a sweet perfume you cannot pour out on others without getting a few drops on yourself.

No joy is complete unless it is shared.

Not failure, but low aim, is the real crime in life.

A sharp tongue will cut your own throat.

Life is like a bicycle—stop pedaling, and you fall.

Worry is a mental tornado.

A problem honestly stated is half solved.

Blessed are those who can give without remembering and receive without forgetting.

You cannot prevent the birds of sorrow from flying over your head, but you can prevent them from building nests in your hair. — *Chinese proverb*

One may be better than one's reputation but never better than one's principles.

It is evil not to do good.

Is your heart on its knees?

Love is the only effective way to deal with a problem.

To poison a person's mind is a worse sin than to poison a person's food.

If you kicked the one responsible for most of your troubles, you wouldn't be able to sit down for six months.

Forgiveness: man's deepest need and highest achievement.

Two things are hard on the heart—running up stairs and running down people.

Most friction in life is caused by the tone of the voice.

Unfounded and unnecessary fears are deadly enemies that paralyze the will, poison the affections, and if allowed to continue, may destroy the soul.

If you want to be rich, give; if you want to be poor, grasp.

Cast all your care on God! That anchor holds. — *Alfred Tennyson*

It is natural to be religious; it is supernatural to be Christian.

God's wisdom is both timely and timeless.

Gratitude is the memory of the heart.

Subject Index

Home, spiritual, 175, 375
Home, the, 147, 153, 154, 160, 162, 170, 178, 181, 191, 193
Honesty, 215
Hope, 162, 166
Humility, 261
Invitation from God/Christ, 78, 173
Jesus, 54, 102, 110, 153, 173, 298, 305, 393; as Liberator, 11; as Lord, 263, 326; as risen Lord, 119; as Savior, 81; character of, 75, 393; childhood of, 183; death of, 44, 133, 319, 391; joy of, 145; leadership of, 263, 326; ministry of, 305, 308
Joseph, 286
Joshua, 113
Joy, 25, 145, 288
Judgment, 28
Judgment Day, 30
Leadership of Jesus, 263, 326
Lepers, 254, 315
Life: battle of, 129; changed, 305; purpose in, 231; ultimate questions of, 126, 387; way to, 49
Listening to God, 97
Lord's Supper, the, 391, 393
Loser in life, 129
Love, 160, 168, 191, 228; of God, 46
Lukewarmness, 347
Marriage. See Family, the
Metaphors, 219, 226, 233, 239, 245, 251, 258, 395
Mind of Christ, 256
Ministry, 224, 248, 254, 261, 265, 283
Missions, 283, 301
Moses, 293
Naboth, 122
New birth, 54
Noah, 274
Oil metaphor, 239
Opportunity, 339
Paul, 19
Persecution, 311
Pleasing God, 268
Poverty and prosperity, 25
Praise, 368

Prayer, 86, 196, 217, 301, 355, 381
Promises of God, 94
Provision, 235, 365
Purpose in life, 231
Reflection on the past, 385
Rejection by God, 89
Relationships, 185, 251
Restoration, 60, 352
Resurrection of Jesus, 110
Revolution, spiritual, 277
Reward, spiritual, 282
Salvation, 100, 117, 270, 298, 337, 357
Sanctification, 282
Saul, King, 136
Seal metaphor, 251
Security, 175
Self-control, 204
Self-pity, 142
Sentence sermonettes, 405
Service, 102, 138, 321, 361
Sin, consequences of, 33, 84, 89, 357
Sonship of Jesus, 54
Spiritual growth, 282, 345
Spirituality, 282, 346, 354, 396
State, the, 206
Stewardship, 349
Success, 333
Sufficiency of God, 235
Thankfulness, 132, 138
Tree metaphor, 258
Trust, 178
Truth, application of, 242
Unity in the church, 251, 365
Usefulness to God, 113, 361
Victorious living. See Christian life
Walking with God/Jesus, 25, 268, 397
Wind metaphor, 233
Wise men, the, 375
Witnessing, 274, 276, 283, 290, 301
Word of God, 94, 189
Work, 198, 321
Working with God/Christ, 270, 331
Worldliness, 323
Worship, 92
Young people, 395, 396, 397
Zacchaeus, 147, 305

Index of Scripture Texts

The Expositor's Bible Commentary Series

*Tremper Longman III
and David E. Garland: General Editors*

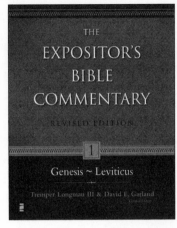

Continuing a Gold Medallion Award-winning legacy, the completely revised editions of *The Expositor's Bible Commentary* series puts world-class biblical scholarship in your hands. Based on the original twelve-volume set that has become a staple in college and seminary libraries and pastors' studies worldwide, this new thirteen-volume edition marshals the most current evangelical scholarship and resources.

Volumes include:

Available in stores and online!

ZONDERVAN®
.com

Folly, Grace, and Power
The Mysterious Act of Preaching

John Koessler

When you stand before your congregation, what do you hope to accomplish when you preach the Word? If people have Bibles and the freedom to read and pray on their own—why do they need you? In short, what do you bring to the table?

Author, pastor, and professor John Koessler answers those questions and many more.

Why does one sermon have a powerful effect on the audience while another falls flat? Why should listeners heed what the preacher says? Is human language adequate for facilitating an encounter with God? What is the point of preaching a sermon?

Folly, Grace, and Power is a must-read for pastors, seminarians, and lay leaders charged with the task of preaching God's word. It was named one of the 2011's "Best Books" of the year by *Preaching Magazine*, and also won a Preaching Today Book Award in 2012. This essential book is both a stern reminder of the sacredness of the awesome "job" of being a preacher, as well as a how-to that reveals the key to speaking powerfully on God's behalf.

The Hardest Sermons You'll Ever Have to Preach

Help from Trusted Preachers for Tragic Times

Bryan Chapell

Contributors: Dan Doriani, Tim Keller, George Robertson, John Piper, Wilson Benton, Robert S. Rayburn, Bob Flayhart, Jack Collins, Mike Khandjian, Michael Horton, and Jerram Barrs; Bryan Chapell, Editor

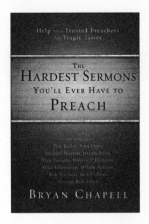

Cancer. Suicide. The death of a child. As much as we wish we could avoid tragedies like these, eventually they will strike your church community. When they do, pastors must be ready to offer help by communicating the life-changing message of the gospel in a way that offers hope, truth, and encouragement during these difficult circumstances. Those asked to preach in the midst of tragedy know the anxiety of trying to say appropriate things from God's Word that will comfort and strengthen God's people when emotions and faith are stretched thin.

The Hardest Sermons You'll Ever Have to Preach is an indispensable resource that helps pastors prepare sermons in the face of tragedies. It provides suggestions for how to approach different kinds of tragedy, as well as insight into how to handle the theological challenges of human suffering. For each type of tragedy a specific description of the context of that tragedy is provided, the key concerns that need to be addressed in the message are highlighted, and an outline of the approach taken in a sample sermon follows.

Topics addressed include abortion; abuse; responding to national and community tragedies; the death of a child; death due to cancer and prolonged sickness; death due to drunk driving; drug abuse; and suicide. In addition, further suggestions of biblical texts for addressing various subjects as well as guidance for conducting funerals are provided in appendices.

Bryan Chapell, author of *Christ-Centered Preaching*, has gathered together messages from some of today's most trusted Christian leaders, including John Piper, Tim Keller, Michael Horton, Jack Collins, Dan Doriani, Jerram Barrs, Mike Khandjian, Robert Rayburn, Wilson Benton, Bob Flayhart, and George Robertson.

Available in stores and online!

Share Your Thoughts

With the Author: Your comments will be forwarded to
the author when you send them to *zauthor@zondervan.com*.

With Zondervan: Submit your review of this book
by writing to *zreview@zondervan.com*.

Free Online Resources at

www.zondervan.com

Zondervan AuthorTracker: Be notified whenever your favorite
authors publish new books, go on tour, or post an update
about what's happening in their lives at www.zondervan.com/
authortracker.

Daily Bible Verses and Devotions: Enrich your life with daily
Bible verses or devotions that help you start every morning
focused on God. Visit www.zondervan.com/newsletters.

Free Email Publications: Sign up for newsletters on Christian
living, academic resources, church ministry, fiction, children's
resources, and more. Visit www.zondervan.com/newsletters.

Zondervan Bible Search: Find and compare Bible passages in
a variety of translations at www.zondervanbiblesearch.com.

Other Benefits: Register to receive online benefits like
coupons and special offers, or to participate in research.

ZONDERVAN®

ZONDERVAN.com/
AUTHORTRACKER
follow your favorite authors